THE EUROPEAN ECONOMY 1750–1914

edited by Derek H. Aldcroft and Simon P. Ville

The European economy
1750–1914

A thematic approach

Manchester University Press
Manchester and New York

distributed exclusively in the USA and Canada by St. Martin's Press

Published by Manchester University Press
Oxford Road, Manchester M13 9PL, UK
and Room 400, 175 Fifth Avenue,
New York, NY 10010, USA

Distributed exclusively in the USA and Canada
by St. Martin's Press, Inc.,
175 Fifth Avenue, New York, NY 10010, USA

> *British Library Cataloguing-in-Publication Data*
> A catalogue record for this book is available
> from the British Library

> *Library of Congress Cataloging-in-Publication Data*
> The European economy, 1750–1914: a thematic approach/edited by
> Derek H. Aldcroft and Simon P. Ville.
>   p.   cm.
> Includes bibliographical references and index.
> ISBN 0–7190–3598–8. — ISBN 0–7190–3599–6 (pbk.)
>   1. Europe—Economic conditions—18th century.   2. Europe—Economic conditions—19th century.   3. Europe—Economic conditions—20th century.   I. Aldcroft, Derek Howard.   II. Ville, Simon P.
> HC240,E8362   1994
> 330.94—dc20   93–27921
>   CIP

ISBN 0–7190–3598–8 *hardback*
ISBN 0–7190–3599–6 *paperback*

Printed in Great Britain
by Bell & Bain Ltd, Glasgow

CONTENTS

LIST OF TABLES

PREFACE

This project had its genesis in the late 1980s at a time when both editors felt there was a clear omission in the literature on the economic history of nineteenth-century Europe. The omission arose largely out of the lack of recent studies to take account of important progress in the literature during the 1980s and the failure of other writers to pursue Pollard's 'pan-European' interpretation. These historiographical matters are discussed in more detail in the introduction. In the light of the progress in particular specialist themes, such as business history and population studies, it was decided to recruit a team of specialists who would be best equipped to convey the flavour of these developments and their relevance to European industrialisation in a concise yet comprehensive manner. The editors wish to convey their appreciation to all the contributors for their best efforts, which were submitted punctually, and for the patience with which they have responded to demanding editorial requests. In addition, most if not all chapters benefited from the comments of fellow academics which are here gratefully acknowledged. Finally, we also appreciate the work of Jane Thorniley-Walker at MUP who has effectively built upon Ray Offord's initial support for the book and Helen Bridge for her help in the construction of the index.

D.H.A.
S.P.V.
May 1993

NOTES ON CONTRIBUTORS

Derek H. Aldcroft is Research Professor in Economic History at the Manchester Metropolitan University and Visiting Professor at the Anglia Polytechnic University. Formerly Professor and Head of Department in the Universities of Sydney and Leicester, he has published widely on British and European economic history in the nineteenth and twentieth centuries. Recent publications include *Education, Training and Economic Performance, 1944–1990* (Manchester University Press, 1992) and *The European Economy, 1914–1990* (third edition 1993). He is currently writing a book on *The Economy of Eastern Europe from Versailles to the Present*.

Roy Church is Professor of Economic and Social History at the University of East Anglia, Norwich. Formerly editor of the *Economic History Review*, he has taught widely in North American universities. His research has focused on British and comparative business and labour history in the nineteenth and twentieth centuries. Recent publications include *The Great Victorian Boom* (1975) and a prize-winning study of *The History of the British Coal Industry* 3, *1830–1913: Victorian Pre-eminence* (1986). *The Rise and Decline of the British Motor Industry* will be published in 1993/4.

P. L. Cottrell is a Professor of Economic and Social History at the University of Leicester, previously having taught at the University of Liverpool. He has been a Bye Fellow at Robinson College, Cambridge, and a Visiting Overseas Professor at the College of Commerce, Nihon University, Tokyo. His research interests lie in the field of banking and finance, recently having edited, with H. Lindgren and A. Teichova, *European Industry and Banking between the Wars* (1992) and contributed to R. Cameron and V. I. Bovykin (eds.), *International Banking, 1870–1914* (1992), and S. N. Broadberry and N. F. R. Crafts (eds.), *Britain in the International Economy, 1870–1939 (1992)*.

James Foreman-Peck, formerly Professor of Economic History at the University of Hull, is now a Fellow of St Antony's College, Oxford, and University Lecturer in Economic History. He is author of *A History of the World Economy: International Economic Relations since 1850* (1983), editor of *New Perspectives on the late Victorian Economy: Essays in Quantitative Economic History, 1860–1914* (1991) and co-author of *Tangled Networks: Public and Private Ownership since the Industrial Revolution*, to be published in 1994.

Paul M. Hohenberg was born in France. He trained as an engineer (B.Ch.E., Cornell) before taking a Ph.D. in Economics at MIT. He has taught at Stanford and Cornell in the United States and at Concordia in Canada, and has also lectured in France and Spain, the latter as a Fulbright Fellow. He has written on French and European economic history and served as editor of the *Journal of Economic History* from 1986 to 1990. *The Making of Urban Europe, 1000–1950*, which he co-authored with Lynn Hollen Lees, was published in 1985 and has been translated into Italian and French. Since 1974 he has been at Rensselaer, the oldest polytechnic in the United States, where he is Professor of Economics and has also chaired the department.

Alan Lougheed is honorary research consultant in the Department of Economics, University of Queensland. Until his retirement in July 1992 he was Reader in Economics in the department. He has published numerous articles and several books, the best known of which is *The Growth of the International Economy*, co-authored with A. G. Kenwood. One of his particular interests is certain aspects of the world gold-mining industry in the years up to the 1930s, including a study of the development of the 'cyanide process' of gold extraction. In his retirement he is conducting a study of the Westralian gold mining companies and their activities in Western Australia between 1894 and the 1930s.

Roger Price is Professor of Modern History at the University of Wales, Aberystwyth. His most recent publications include *An Economic History of Modern France, 1730–1914* (1981), *The Modernization of Rural France: Communications Networks and Agricultural Market Structures* (1983), *A Social History of Nineteenth Century France* (1987), *The Revolutions of 1848* (1989) and *A Concise History of France* (1993). He is currently writing *The French Second Empire: State and Society* and preparing a study of industrial power sources in eighteenth and nineteenth-century France.

Neil L. Tranter is Senior Lecturer in History at the University of Stirling. Formerly Lecturer in Economic and Social History at the University of East Anglia, he has published widely on the history of population and social structure and, more recently, on the history of sport in nineteenth-century Scotland. Among his recent publications is *Population and Society, 1750–1940* (1985). He is currently writing a book on *British Population in the Twentieth Century*.

Simon P. Ville is Senior Lecturer in Economic History at the Australian National University. His research interests focus upon transport and business history and industrialisation. Among his recent publications are: *English Shipowning in the Industrial Revolution, 1770–1830* (Manchester University Press, 1987) and *Transport and the Development of the European Economy, 1750–1918* (1990).

INTRODUCTION

A thematic approach to European development

There have been many general studies of European economic development of the eighteenth and nineteenth centuries. They vary considerably in length, geographical coverage and the line of approach. One of the most detailed modern studies is the *Cambridge Economic History of Europe*, spanning several centuries and published in a series of volumes which have appeared periodically in the post-war period. These volumes, written by a series of specialist authors, provide scholars with valuable detail in most key areas of economic activity for a range of individual European countries. Unfortunately, the long gestation period in publication has meant that some aspects are soon out of date in terms of either interpretation or the availability of new areas of research. In addition, while serving as valuable reference works for many graduate students and scholars, they have generally proved rather heavyweight for undergraduates comparatively new to the subject.

Fontana have published a six-volume history of the European economy written by a group of specialist authors and covering the period from the Middle Ages to the twentieth century. Volume three of the series (Cipolla, 1973) picks out some key themes for the eighteenth and nineteenth centuries, including population, demand, technology, banking, government, services and agriculture. The fourth volume is devoted to specialist country studies and has a fairly broad geographical coverage. Being of a more digestible length, the Fontana series has proved to be a valuable teaching aid. Unfortunately, the passage of time has meant that the volumes are becoming quite dated in terms of both interpretation and historical detail, since the contents are based on research undertaken in the late 1960s and early 1970s.

Milward and Saul's two-volume study (1973, 1977) provides a specific focus upon the nineteenth century, the dynamics of which are given a clear context by discussion of the economic structure and

1

extent of development in the later eighteenth century. Its value as a comparative reference source is enhanced by the systematic organization of chapters by individual countries, with standard sub-headings. As with the Fontana and Cambridge series, however, the lapse of time since publication means that the substantial new scholarship of the last decade or two is not represented. Moreover, in contrast to the former studies, the geographical focus is on continental Europe, with only occasional and passing reference to Britain. In the preface to the first volume the authors justify this decision in terms of the substantial material on Britain already in print and the need to avoid the anglocentric approach which has been a feature of much writing on European development. While Milward and Saul are doubtless correct to identify such a bias in the literature, their approach might be considered an over-reaction. New perspectives have emerged which sensibly analyse the British experience as simply one of a series of possible development paths rather than opting to ignore or over-emphasise it. It remains important to understand the impact which the experience of Britain, as the supposed first industrialiser, had on the character and pace of industrialisation in many other European and non-European countries. Furthermore, in view of recent work re-assessing the dynamics of long-run growth in Britain and the near continent, it would seem inappropriate to omit reference to the first industrial nation.

There are also several single-volume studies. These works have frequently chosen to focus upon some of the major economies, particularly the French, German, British and Russian. In place of the encylopaedic descriptive detail of some of the longer and earlier studies, the emphasis has turned towards more limited information organised around one or several paradigms. As such they appear as more appropriate teaching aids. Trebilcock's (1981) study of the con-tinental powers—Germany, France, Russia, Austria-Hungary, Italy and Spain—begins by introducing a range of economic develop-ment models and concludes with support for a modified version of Gerschenkron's theory of relative backwardness. Although omitting Britain, it provides much more detailed contextual analysis than earlier works with a similar approach. Kemp (1969), for example, in a much briefer analysis of Britain, France, German, Italy and Russia, espoused general themes and broad developments in place of detailed factual assessment.

2

A common feature of the volumes so far discussed is that they all used the individual country as a basic unit of analysis. While general themes are discussed in places, particularly in the Fontana history, and most attempt some comparative assessment, the implicit assumption is that the nature of economic development can best be measured and explained by looking at the individual nation. Even Landes (1969), who was one of the first to break away from the traditional nation-state approach in his masterly survey of industry and technology in western Europe, an updated version of his contribution to volume VI of the *Cambridge Economic History of Europe*, took the British model as a yardstick by which to measure the pace of Continental emulation. The study, as its title suggests, concentrates heavily on the manner in which industrial technology was diffused in western Europe. It offers many interesting insights into the causes and dynamics of industrial development but lacks the broader spatial perspective of many later studies. Moreover, time has again been unkind in that some of the data and material are in need of revision.

Pollard was one of the first to emphasise the broader spatial perspective of European development in an article published in 1973 and subsequently considerably amplied in, *Peaceful Conquest*, which appeared in 1981. He is one of the few writers to acknowledge the extent of 'pan-Europeanism' in the development of the European continent. Rather than identifying developed or backward countries within Europe, this approach analyses regions or enclaves of modernisation, connected to each other by transmission paths, but surrounded by large areas of traditional economic structures and limited economic growth. In other words, all or most European countries in the nineteenth century contained areas of both modern and retarded economic development. Some countries clearly possessed more or larger enclaves of modernisation than others and thus might be deemed to have been more economically advanced. Nonetheless, Pollard's work showed that a nation-state approach to European economic development revealed only part of the story. Similarly, Berend and Ranki (1982), in a narrower spatial context, explored the dynamics of the European periphery along similar lines, again illustrating the limitations of using the national context. However, Pollard's perspective remained more traditional in suggesting that Britain's experience of development remained crucial to the process in other countries. As he noted, 'Europe's industrialization occurred as an outgrowth of a

3

single root with mutations caused by varying circumstances' (1981: v). More recent survey articles by Cameron (1985) and O'Brien (1986) have questioned such potentially monolithic interpretations by suggesting that there was a range of patterns and typologies of European industrialisation.

By contrast Goodman and Honeyman (1988) rejected both political and geographical units of analysis and focused instead on industrial production. They sensibly extended their investigation back to 1600 on the grounds that important industrial changes were already taking place in the seventeenth century. This accords with the conception that modern economic growth is not wholly revolutionary but is grounded in changes which extend far back in time. While Goodman and Honeyman provide some interesting insights into manufacturing industry, the limited reference to service sectors, especially finance and transport, produces a rather artificial distinction and a somewhat narrow view of the development process. It may be argued that, in order to understand fully the nature and complexities of the development process during this period, it is essential to take account of changes in the service side of the economy and how they affected and interacted with progress in manufacturing.

Recently, Sylla and Toniolo (1991) have investigated industrialisation patterns in nineteenth-century Europe, drawing upon the collaboration of a group of economic historians with particular specialisations. The organising theme centres on one specific model or theory of economic development, Gerschenkron's concept of relative backwardness. The book examines institutional substitutes allegedly required for the prerequisites of growth which are a crucial feature of the thesis, and it also examines the experience of several individual countries, namely Britain, France, Germany, Italy, Austria–Hungary and Russia. While providing some very interesting insights into the mechanism and dynamics of growth and several revisions in interpretation, the study inevitably concentrates heavily on the issues connected with the Gerschenkron thesis, especially the role of banks and the government.

The present study pursues an essentially transnational approach to European economic development. Since Europe consisted of a series of nation states, a pan-European approach appeared to be the more appropriate perspective to adopt. The interactions between individual countries in the nineteenth century, especially in terms of trade, finance,

4

migration, transport and technology transfer, were of such magnitude as to warrant the notion of a European economy as a basic unit of analysis which can then be broken down into particular themes. It is these major themes which are analysed here rather than the economic performance of individual countries set within national political, social and cultural incentives to and constraints on growth. Nevertheless, there is no attempt to dismiss the value of national comparative studies or to deny that differences between nations did emerge as a result of the differing incentives and constraints. In any case, the predominantly national basis of statistical collection necessitates some reversion to the more traditional mode of analysis from time to time, even though one must always bear in mind the distortions this legacy gives rise to. It should also be noted that while transnational themes interacted much more widely than within the European continent alone, as Woodruff (1966) made clear nearly three decades ago, the focus of attention in this volume is limited to Europe for obvious reasons of space. Similarly, there is only brief or passing reference to the imperial and overseas interests of the major powers.

In many ways therefore, the present study seeks to build upon, update and to some degree modify Pollard's work of 1981, while at the same time taking account of developments in the literature during the intervening period. Unlike Pollard however, there is no attempt to explain the diffusion of industrial modernisation on the basis of a British prototype. And, in contrast to Sylla and Toniolo, the study does not seek to espouse a particular model or theory. Instead, individual contributors have been given the freedom to embrace competing explanations where appropriate to their arguments, emphasising, perhaps, the need to avoid a single-thesis explanation of European economic development. Within the space limitations set by the cost of publication and the need to provide a reasonably concise teaching text, the approach has been to look at the following major economic themes: the macro-economy, agriculture, population, enterprise, transport, urbanisation, foreign trade, investment and technology. In each chapter, written by a specialist in the field, the main trends in the sector are examined, together with an assessment of the manner in which they helped to shape the pattern and pace of European industrial-isation. The coverage is broad, across the whole of Europe, though within the space available it was obviously not possible to analyse developments in every country or region, or even to examine particular

5

countries in any depth. Readers who wish to expand their knowledge of an area or country should consult the references cited in each chapter.

References

Berend, I. T., and Ranki, G. (1982), *The European Periphery and Industrialization, 1780–1914*. Cambridge, Cambridge University Press.

Cameron, R. (1985), 'A new view of European industrialization', *Economic History Review*, 38.

Cipolla, C. M., ed. (1973), *Fontana Economic History of Europe* 3, *The Industrial Revolution*. London, Collins/Fontana.

Cipolla, C. M., ed. (1973), *Fontana Economic History of Europe* 4, *The Emergence of Industrial Societies* London, Collins/Fontana.

Goodman, J., and Honeyman, K. (1988), *Gainful Pursuits: the Making of Industrial Europe, 1600–1914*. London, Edward Arnold.

Kemp, T. (1969), *Industrialization in Nineteenth-century Europe*. Harlow, Longman.

Landes, D. S. (1969), *The Unbound Prometheus: Technological Change and Industrial Development in Western Europe from 1750 to the Present*. Cambridge, Cambridge University Press.

Mathias, P., and Postan, M. M., eds. (1978), *The Cambridge Economic History of Europe* VII. Cambridge, Cambridge University Press.

Milward, A. S., and Saul, S. B. (1973), *The Economic Development of Continental Europe, 1780–1870*. London, Allen & Unwin.

Milward, A. S., and Saul, S. B. (1977), *The Development of the Economies of Continental Europe, 1850–1914*. London, Allen & Unwin.

O'Brien, P. K. (1986) 'Do we have a typology for the study of European industrialization in the nineteenth century?' *Journal of European Economic History*, 15.

Pollard, S. (1973), 'Industrialization and the European Economy', *Economic History Review*, 26.

Pollard, S. (1981), *Peaceful Conquest: the Industrialization of Europe, 1760–1970*. Oxford, Oxford University Press.

Sylla, R., and Toniolo, G., eds. (1991), *Patterns of European Industrialization: the Nineteenth-Century*. London, Routledge.

Trebilcock, C. (1981), *The Industrialization of the Continental Powers, 1780–1914*. Harlow, Longman.

Woodruff, W. (1966), *Impact of Western Man: a Study of Europe's Role in the World Economy, 1750–1960*. London, Macmillan.

1 *Derek H. Aldcroft*

The European dimension
to the modern world

At a time when Europe is once again searching for a new identity and a new configuration, it is apposite to reconsider the time when she emerged from the Dark Ages to dominate the world's continents. Within the space of four centuries European states were to extend their political control over the vast majority of the earth's space, from 7 per cent in 1500 to 84 per cent in 1914 (Tilly, 1992: 183). As Carlo Cipolla (1981: 300) summed up the situation, 'The history of any remote corner of the world after 1500 cannot be properly understood without taking into account the impact of European culture, economy, and technology. . . . *Sans l'Europe l'histoire moderne est inconcevable.*' At the turn of the century Cunningham (1904: 228) had much the same frame of mind when he prophesied that 'In no territory can the rulers afford to hold aloof from the march of material progress', the origins of which lay primarily in Europe.

Since the days of Cunningham, Heaton, Knowles and Clapham our knowledge of European development has come a long way. Yet while their descriptive and institutional accounts perhaps somewhat overdramatised the dominance of the European great powers within the context of the world economy, later research has done little to dislodge the pre-eminence of Western civilization in the economic development of the past two centuries. What it has done is to provide much more quantitative detail on the structure and dimensions of development and the patterns of growth and change, but at the same time it has seemingly made it more difficult to explain precisely *why* the West triumphed over the rest of the world.

The contours of European expansion

The dimensions of growth and development in the modern world are now fairly well known and need not be rehearsed in detail. Suffice it

Table 1.1 Annual rates of growth of *per capita* GNP, 1800–1913

Country	1800–1913	1830–1913	1860–1913
Austria–Hungary	–	0·9	1·0
Belgium	1·3	1·3	1·4
Bulgaria	–	(0·3)	0·5
Denmark	1·3	1·6	2·0
Finland	0·9	1·3	1·5
France	1·0	1·1	1·0
Germany	1·3	1·4	1·6
Greece	–	(0·6)	0·7
Italy	0·7	0·8	0·9
Netherlands	0·9	1·1	1·1
Norway	1·0	1·3	1·2
Portugal	–	0·3	0·2
Romania	–	(0·6)	0·9
Russia	0·7	0·8	1·0
Serbia	–	–	0·6
Spain	–	0·6	0·4
Sweden	1·1	1·4	1·6
Switzerland	1·4	1·6	1·4
UK	1·3	1·3	1·1
Europe	0·9	1·0	1·1
USA	1·5	1·7	1·7
Japan	0·5	0·7	1·1

Source: Calculations based on data in Bairoch (1976, 1991).

to say that by contemporary standards income growth was quite modest, averaging about 1 per cent per annum on a *per capita* basis for the whole of Europe throughout the nineteenth century. The growth rates for individual countries listed in Table 1.1 should be regarded as very approximate orders of magnitude. They do show, however, that there were considerable variations in growth experience among countries, ranging from well over 1 per cent a year in the case of Belgium, Denmark, Germany, Sweden, Switzerland and the UK to around 0·5 per cent or less for Greece, Spain, Portugal, Bulgaria, Serbia and Romania. What is clearly apparent is how the growth momentum becomes steadily weaker the farther away one moves from the north-western epicentre. On the other hand, even the lagging European countries in the south and east did well by international standards, since, apart from North America, Australasia, Japan and some countries in Latin America, *per capita* incomes in the rest of the world stagnated or even declined in this period (Bairoch, 1991: 32–3).

The national aggregate figures conceal, of course, some very large regional differences, none more so than in the case of the Austro-Hungarian empire, where the Alpine and Czech lands were worlds apart from the Slavic territories as far as modern development was concerned. The former had income levels by 1913 not far removed from those of the West, whereas the lands farther east had barely begun to modernise their economies. Equally, the figures tell us little about the distribution of the benefits of growth. In the early phases of modern economic growth it is doubtful whether the mass of the population received a fair share of the rewards. Indeed, for a time the standard of living of the proletariat may well have deteriorated.

Such rates of advance were of course far better than anything recorded previously, even though income growth in some countries may well have been more robust than was once suspected (Landes, 1969: 14; Maddison, 1982: 6–7). They were more than sufficient, in any case, to create a significant gap between Europe and the rest of the world by the mid-nineteenth century as far as the distribution of global income was concerned. Estimates of world income distribution for 1860 suggest that north-west Europe alone accounted for nearly 30 per cent of world income as against a population share of 11 per cent. By 1913 the region's share had fallen slightly in the face of the rapid strides made by North America, whose income share had come to surpass that of north-west Europe. These two regions alone accounted for some 60 per cent of global income but only 18 per cent of world population (Table 1.2). To date this amazingly unequal distribution has not changed very much. While the core shares have tended to stabilise, newcomers, notably Japan, have joined the rich club. Thus, if anything, the division between rich and poor nations has deteriorated further in the present century, since high-income economies now account for over 80 per cent of world income but less than 17 per cent of the population (Aldcroft, 1991: 20–1). Even taking into account the fact that measured GNP may not always adequately reflect differences in real purchasing power and welfare between countries or regions, the gap between rich and poor is far too large to be explained away by a statistical mirage (Smith, 1993: 2–7).

Table 1.2 Population and income distribution by region, 1860–1988 (%)

	1860		1913		1988	
Region	Pop.	Inc.	Pop.	Inc.	Pop.	Inc.
North America	3·1	14·8	6·3	32·9	5·8	32·5
North-west Europe	11·1	29·3	11·5	27·6	4·9	23·0
Oceania	0·1	0·5	0·4	1·4	0·5	1·4
South-east Europe	7·9	9·8	8·2	8·5	5·5	8·7
Soviet Union	6·7	7·2	8·7	7·3		
Japan	2·9	1·4	3·3	1·5	2·5	15·7
Latin America	3·4	3·8	5·0	4·0	8·7	4·5
Far East	2·4	1·4	3·8	1·9	5·3	0·9
South-east Asia	22·3	11·8	20·3	6·9	22·9	2·4
China	40·1	20·0	32·5	8·0	23·0	2·2
Rest of the world					20·9	8·7

Sources: Zimmerman (1962), World Bank (1990).

But what of the earlier period? Bairoch's work (1981, 1991) suggests that before the upsurge in industrial development differences in international income levels were quite modest, possibly in the range 1·0 to 1·6 between the poorest and richest nations, and as low as 1·0 to 1·3 if broader regional entities such as western Europe and China are considered. Tilly (1992: 171) also doubts whether the European powers could claim to have led the world economically before the later eighteenth century. But, as we shall see, such small differentials are not wholly consistent with circumstantial evidence, nor do they fully square with the early lead in industrialisation established by western Europe.

Within Europe itself income differentials between countries were also relatively narrow initially and began to widen markedly only from the end of the eighteenth century. In 1750 the difference in income *per capita* between western and eastern Europe was probably no more than 15 per cent. By 1800 it had widened to 21·5 per cent and then leapt to 64 per cent by 1860. By the first decade of the twentieth century it was close to 80 per cent (Bairoch, 1981). However, the gap between the richest and poorest nations was by that time very much larger. The average *per capita* income of the four wealthiest countries (the UK, Switzerland, Denmark and Belgium) was some three times that of the four poorest (Greece, Poland, Bulgaria and Yugoslavia). Extending the sample to eight countries at both extremes narrows the gap somewhat but the rich were still 2·5 times better off. All the poorest countries were located in southern and eastern Europe, whereas the wealthiest ones were concentrated in the north-west corner of the continent (Table 1.3). Within countries or regions the disparities were as wide again, if not wider. For example, in the territories which later formed the state of Yugoslavia the net income per head in Slovenia in 1910 was nearly three times greater than in the south-eastern corner of Yugoslavia (Hocevar, 1965: 114–15).

Table 1.3 European income and industrialisation levels, 1913

		% of active population in:		
Country	*Per capita* GNP, 1913 (1960 US$)	Primary sector, 1909–13	Secondary sector, 1909–13	*per capital* levels of of industrialisation in 1913 (UK 1900 = 100)
UK	1,034	8·8	51·6	115
Switzerland	895	26·8	45·7	87
Denmark	883	41·7	24·2	33
Belgium	816	23·2	45·6	88
Germany	789	36·8	40·9	85
Netherlands	742	28·4	32·5	28
Sweden	705	46·2	25·6	67
Austria	681	56·9	24·2	45[a]
France	669	41·0	33·1	59
Norway	614	39·5	26·0	31
Finland	527	69·2	10·6	21
Czechoslovakia	524	40·3	36·8	
Italy	453	55·4	26·9	26
Spain	398	56·3	13·8	22
Romania	368	79·6	8·0	13
Hungary	372	64·0	17·5	45[a]
Russia	342	58·6	16·1[b]	20
Portugal	335	57·4	21·9	14
Greece	333			10
Poland	301	75·9	9·4	13
Yugoslavia	284	82·2	11·0	12
Bulgaria	284	81·9	8·0	10

Notes: (a) Austria–Hungary. (b) 1897.
Source: Bairoch (1976, 1982, 1991), Deldlycke *et al.*, (1968).

In other words, the farther one looks east and south in Europe the weaker was the impact of modern economic growth. The data in Table 1.3 provide an approximate indication of why this should have been so. By 1913 most of the rich countries had high levels of *per capita* industrialisation while employment in the primary sector was no longer the dominant form of economic activity. There were, of course, one or two exceptions, notably Denmark and the Netherlands, where the processing of agricultural produce and service activities tended to predominate. Even more significant is the contrast in structures with the remaining countries in the table. Apart from the Austrian and Czech lands and Norway, all of them had over 50 per cent, and often very much more, of their active population engaged in agriculture or primary extraction and a quarter or less in industry, while levels of industrialisation per head were but a fraction of those of the most advanced Western countries.

Patterns of development

Much of modern research and writing on the economic history of Europe has been concerned with three main issues: (1) the quantification of economic change, (2) the more neglected areas of the continent, and (3) examining patterns or typologies of development. The first effort has certainly produced an abundant array of data on incomes, structures and levels of industrialisation. Some of the statistics may be very close to guesswork but they do at least provide orders of magnitude by which to rank the performance of nations. On the second issue there has been a valiant effort to rescue some of the more peripheral regions from a mere footnote to history (Warriner, 1964: 75) and at the same time to show that modern economic growth was quite a pervasive phenomenon that was no respecter of national boundaries. Recent work on Austria–Hungary, the Balkans, Spain and Italy (Good, 1984; Komlos, 1983, 1989a; Berend and Ranki, 1974, 1982; Lampe and Jackson, 1982; Sylla and Toniolo, 1991; Harrison, 1978) has done much to deepen our knowledge of eastern and southern Europe and to demonstrate that industrial development was not solely the preserve of the western countries. However, while it is certainly true that many of the more peripheral areas of the continent experienced some economic awakening during the course of the nineteenth century (Batou, 1991), partly as a result of the infiltration of Western interests, modern capitalism was often little more than an island or two in a sea of primitivism, heavily concentrated spatially, as in the case of Budapest in Hungary and Sofia in Bulgaria (Bencze and Tajti, 1972: 19–20). Only the western sector of the Austro–Hungarian monarchy could in any way compare with the developments farther west. Agricultural systems, though by no means static, remained primitive, almost feudal, especially in the Balkans and parts of southern Europe.

In recent years there has been a revival of interest in trying to identify phases or patterns of development, including the concept of proto-industrialisation, that is, industrialisation before industrialisation (see Coleman, 1983; Clarkson, 1985). Yet what appears most characteristic about nineteenth-century European development is the great diversity of experience rather than the uniformity, a feature which most impressed Lampe (1975: 56) from his study of the Balkans. In their wide-ranging comparative analysis Morris and Adelman (1988: 78) also stress this feature above all else: 'Diversity in growth patterns, diversity in institutions, and diversity in applicable theories were the hallmarks of the process of nineteenth century development.' Not that each country should be classed as a unique case, since the authors discerned a small number of similar growth trajectories. Generally speaking, however, the work on growth patterns and typologies has not borne a great deal of fruit following the earlier attempts of Lewis (1955), Rostow (1960), Gerschenkron (1962), Kuznets (1966), Chenery (1960), Chenery and Taylor (1968) and others to impose order upon chaos and to relate the past to contemporary issues of underdevelopment (Anell and Nygren, 1980). While such efforts to systematise and synthesise the structural characteristics and patterns of growth among different countries have provided useful conceptual frameworks within which to study the development process (Siegenthaler, 1972), they cannot fully capture the intricate complexity of that process throughout an entire continent (Barsby, 1969: Gould, 1972).

For this reason we take an agnostic view on the matter—to the point of believing that there was no simple pattern of growth or single model of development which would embrace all growth trajectories (Ashworth, 1977; Cameron, 1985; Pollard, 1990). Nor were there any decisive features which made for either balanced or unbalanced growth (Geary, 1988: 357). Growth was a sprawling and uneven process which had little respect for time and space: 'Like an epidemic, it took little note of frontiers, crossing them with ease while leaving neighbouring home territories untouched' (Pollard, 1973: 647; see also Crafts, 1984; O'Brien, 1986). Perhaps therefore the most useful concept is the regional approach to European economic development which Pollard (1973, 1981) and others have done much to publicise. Indeed, one of the most striking features of European development was the very wide diversity of experience in growth and structural change between regions—even within the confines of a single country, which somewhat diminishes the significance of the national state as a unit of study (Ashworth, 1977: 152). Good (1991: 235) in fact sees regional analysis as fundamental, but at the same time complementary, to any study of national development. As he comments, 'In spatial terms, modern economic growth appeared in concentrated pockets, not evenly spread out, so regional analysis is essential for studying national economic development.'

Oddly enough, much of the recent work on European development has tended to neglect one of the most interesting questions, namely why modern growth was largely confined to western Europe and North America while the rest of the world, with one or two minor exceptions, stagnated. Or, to put the question in a different form, why didn't the whole world develop simultaneously? This raises some very broad issues, outside the European context, as to why Eastern civilisations which had once shown so much promise failed to capitalise on their fortune, and why the future Third World countries subsequently fell out of the race. In taking account of Europe's advantages we can deal only tangentially with these interesting issues.

The spread of modern economic growth is generally associated with industrialisation and the diffusion of new technology, together with associated changes in the organisation of economic activity, which allowed people to do things in better ways, thereby raising productivity levels, which in the long run are the main determinant of real income gains or better standards of living. But technology did not drop like manna from heaven, nor, had it done so, is there any reason to suppose that it would have fallen on fertile ground. In any case, even if we subscribe to single-factor proximate causation we still have to determine in the first instance why Western countries were favourably situated to exploit new opportunities which enabled them to exert economic dominance in the world arena.

14

Four possibilities seem to be worth exploring in some detail: (1) human resource development in terms of literacy and education, (2) income levels and accumulation, (3) the elimination of the population constraint, and (4) state structures and institutions.

Education and development

The relationship between education and modern development is a complex one. There is no strong correlation between educational inputs and income growth among developed countries today, though low-income countries do have high rates of illiteracy. However, development economists have argued that some threshold level of literacy is essential for countries wishing to achieve modern economic growth (McClelland 1966). This makes sense, for the spread of technology which underpins growth depends to a large extent on whether the population has acquired the aptitudes, skills and motivation necessary for the exploitation of modern technology, and this 'social capability', to use Abramovitz's phrase (1989: 46–6), can be achieved only through formal education. For this purpose education must be fairly widespread and it must also be secular and rationalistic, as opposed to narrow and ritualistic, otherwise it will not produce the desired results (Abramovitz, 1989: 25–6). A good illustration of the negative impact is the case of Spain, which experienced a considerable increase in educational provision during the nineteenth century, yet by 1900 well over half the population were still illiterate and modern economic growth was conspicuous by its absence. The reason for the failure was largely that education was under the influence of the Roman Catholic Church, which laid great emphasis on the creed and the catechism, to the neglect of secular instruction (Easterlin, 1981: 10). Similar narrow interpretations of the role of education prevailed in large parts of Latin America, the Middle East and China, where Confucian ethics stifled secular enlightenment, while Third World countries today have often been the victims of inappropriate educational strategies which have sometimes done more harm than good (Simmons, 1979).

Not all countries were handicapped in this way. According to Easterlin (1981: 10–14), it was the spread of rational education that produced the motivational response among Western nations. Using primary-school enrolments for a diverse range of countries, he

15

presented a persuasive case for the importance of education as a modernising force. The spread of mass education of a secular and rationalistic type not only helped to foster attitudes and attributes conducive to the acquisition of new technology and improved methods of production, it also heralded an important shift in political power, together with a break in traditional values and cultures which allowed greater scope for the ambitions of a wider segment of the population (cf. Anderson and Bowman, 1976). In broad terms Easterlin's case finds empirical support. Even as early as the mid-seventeenth century less than 50 per cent of the adult population of major Western cities were still illiterate, as against anything up to 95 per cent elsewhere (Cipolla, 1981: 93). Outside the West the picture had not changed very much two centuries later. Almost the whole population of the world outside north-west Europe and North America had had very little exposure to formal schooling. Literacy levels were therefore very low and well below the 40 per cent threshold considered by some development economists as essential to achieve the breakthrough in development. By the mid-twentieth century this was still generally true of Africa, much of Asia and large parts of Latin America. By contrast, in the high-income areas of North America and north-west Europe, which accounted for the major share of the world's income, literacy levels were already fairly high by 1850, formal schooling in one form or another was quite extensive, and in some cases, notably Germany and North America, it had preceded modern economic growth. It is perhaps significant in the light of later events that outside these two regions only Japan had made considerable progress in educating its populace by the latter half of the nineteenth century.

Sandberg (1982: 687–97) has also explored the longer-term relationships between education and income for a wide sample of European countries. His main contention is that literacy levels in 1850 are 'an amazingly good predictor of *per capita* income in the 1970s.' Using adult literacy rates as a proxy for human resource stocks, he finds that countries which were highly literate at the start of the period, even though poor, were generally the ones that eventually attained higher levels of *per capita* income. Conversely, the lower the initial *per capita* stock of human resources, the slower the rate of modernisation was likely to be, as in the case of the poor and illiterate countries towards the foot of Table 1.4, which is a modified version of Sandberg's, taking account of more recent estimates. It should also be noted, however,

Table 1.4 Literacy and income levels in Europe (US$ at 1960 prices)

Adult literacy c. 1850	GNP *per capita*		
	General ranking c. 1850	1913	1973
Group I (literacy above 70%)			
Sweden (90%)	Very low	705	3,411
Denmark	Low	883	2,716
Norway	High	614	3,495
Switzerland	High	895	2,661
Germany (80%)	Medium	789	2,873[a]
Scotland	High		2,284[b]
Finland	Very low	527	2,797
Holland	High	742	2,334
Group II (literacy above 50%)			
England and Wales (70%)	Very high	1,034	2,284[b]
Belgium	High	816	2,654
France (60%)	Medium	669	3,029
Austria	Medium	681	2,168
Group III (literacy less than 50%)			
Spain (25%)	Medium	398	1,179
Italy (20–5%)	Low	453	1,694
Hungary	Low	372	1,851
Romania	Very low	368	1,360
Portugal	Low	335	1,247
Yugoslavia	Very low	284	1,182
Greece	Very low	333	1,769
Bulgaria	Very low	284	1,755
Russia (5–10%)	Very low	342	1,887
Poland	Very low	301	1,842

Notes: (a) West Germany. (b) UK.
Sources: Sandberg (1982), Bairoch (1976).

that high initial income combined with a high rate of literacy, as in the case of England and Wales, Scotland, Switzerland and Belgium, did not necessarily guarantee that the original relative income ranking would be replicated at some future date. Overall, the results do suggest that early educational attainment may well have been an important prerequisite of modern economic growth. The reasoning is based on propositions similar to those of Easterlin: that, to exploit new

17

opportunities, countries require a highly articulate and mobile labour force, an elastic supply of financial services, the ability to develop and utilise new technology, a ready supply of enterprising individuals, as well as 'a more rational and more receptive approach to life on the part of the population' (Cipolla, 1969: 102). Without an improvement in the educational stock these attributes are unlikely to emerge.

The specification of the relationship between literacy and development may require further refining before we can fully appreciate the true causal links. As Nunez (1990: 135) demonstrates in showing the adverse economic effects of lagging educational provision in Spain, the ramifications of educational change can be very wide-ranging and one of its main contributions may be 'a better disposition towards change and social mobility in a very general sense'. In which case there are strong grounds for arguing that the head-start achieved by Western nations in human resource development was an important factor in their rise to economic dominance. Otherwise it might be difficult to explain the uneven application and diffusion of techniques within Europe, since these ultimately depended upon the transfer of skills and knowledge, most of which originated in and were transmitted from the West (cf. Inkster, 1990; Tortella, 1993).

Incomes and resources

Bairoch (1981), as already noted, maintains that income differences among countries or regions were probably quite limited at the dawn of modern economic growth. Does this mean then that there were no obvious leaders in the pack? We think not. The income estimates for the early period are, of course, very rough, and it could be that they are not truly indicative of the widening gap between west and east. Pedreira (1991: 349) has reminded us, moreover, that GNP figures do not always adequately reflect on-going structural changes in an economy and may therefore underestimate the extent of progress. Furthermore, as far as incomes and structures are concerned there is considerable evidence to suggest that Europe, or at least the western sector, was more advanced than any other civilised part of the world by the eighteenth century.

Some years ago Landes (1969: 13–14) argued that western Europe was already rich before the industrial revolution by comparison with most other parts of the world, the implication being that it was

18

ready for the breakthrough into modern economic growth (cf. Landes, 1991: 63). McNeill (1963: 653) also points to the superior wealth and power at Europe's command *c.* 1700, which 'clearly surpassed anything that other civilised communities . . . could muster', while Jones (1981: 41, 182) contends that a decisive gap between Europe and Asia was emerging before industrialisation. Similarly the divergence between east and west Europe in favour of the latter was already in progress by the end of the seventeenth century, if not before (Ashworth, 1974: 298; McNeill, 1979). This position was achieved not by revolutionary change but by the slow accretion of incomes over a lengthy period of time. Growth is not an invention of modern society; it has been going on for centuries, but often so imperceptibly and subject to periodic setbacks that it has not always been easy to detect (Caldwell, 1977).

This slow evolutionary process is borne out by current research findings on very long-term growth as well as by more circumstantial evidence relating to structural changes. For example, it now seems likely that income growth in pre-industrial England was more robust than was once thought possible; there appears to have been a slow but irregular upward trend in income *per capita* from as far back as Domesday, not dramatic by modern standards but significant enough to allow steady accumulation by the sixteenth and seventeenth centuries (Persson, 1988; Snooks, 1990). Other Western economies may have experienced a similar pattern over the long run. Landes (1969: 14) conjectured that income per head could possibly have tripled in western Europe in the 800 years to 1800, with some acceleration in the eighteenth century. While this scenario may be a little optimistic in the light of the evidence, even cautious students would acknowledge that incomes were more than keeping pace with population growth, barely perceptible though the improvement may have been to contemporaries (Maddison, 1982: 6–7; Snooks, 1990). The grim Malthusian picture described by some Continental historians is certainly not consistent with what we know about long-term changes in trade patterns, factor markets, technology and agrarian systems and the eventual accommodation of population changes (Matowist, 1966).

To consider England in isolation at the outset of modern growth can therefore be highly misleading, since it masks the significance of the long period of Western advances before industrialisation proper which, according to Chirot (1985: 192–3), were widely spread throughout parts of France, the Low Countries, the Germanies,

Scandinavia, Switzerland and, for a time, northern Italy (cf. Goodman and Honeyman, 1988: 9–11). These changes were many and varied, taking place over several centuries and often drawing, especially in technology, on earlier advances in Eastern civilisations (Cipolla, 1981). Without these advances, Chirot argues,

> Later industrialisation could not have occurred had markets of all sorts not achieved such a high state of development in preindustrial Europe: capital markets; land markets; labour markets; commodity markets; and even, by analogy, a kind of intellectual market for new ideas, important thinkers and artists, and technological innovations. These centered on the urban and mercantile centers of all of Western Europe, not exclusively in one nation or another. The exchange between these centers, and the mutual stimulation they gave each other, were decisive in creating a setting in which later industrial technology could flourish and revolutionize society. [1985: 193]

One of the most obvious manifestations of these changes was the expansion of mercantile activity associated with the vast extension of trading opportunities opened up by Western traders in both the East and the New World from the sixteenth century onwards. However, one should not overestimate the significance of the periphery to the development of the core in this context, since intra-European trade remained the dominant element (O'Brien, 1982: 4). This point notwithstanding, the fact remains that by the early eighteenth century Europe was the dominant force in international trade. Europe as a whole accounted for 69 per cent of world trade in 1720, and for 77 per cent by 1800, while the respective shares of western Europe were 42 and 61 per cent, with Britain, Germany, France and the Low Countries the main participants (Chisholm, 1982: 60). The New World, despite its secondary trading role, also provided Europe with an additional resource base and an outlet for surplus population. What Jones has termed the 'ghost acreages' in newly discovered lands served to augment the man–land ratios and helped to stabilise population densities at the European core (Jones, 1981: 83; Reynolds, 1985: 29). As the figures in Table 1.5 indicate, population densities in India, China and the Ottoman empire, which were already high in 1500, increased considerably over the next three centuries, whereas those of Europe and its overseas annexes subsided.

Western Europe and its overseas appendages were therefore in a much better position than either the rest of Europe or Eastern

Table 1.5 Density of population per square kilometre

Region	1500	1800
India	23	42
China	25	80
Ottoman empire	8	12
Europe plus overseas annexes	8	3

Source: Jones (1981: 232).

civilisations to accumulate capital, since expanding mercantile activities, a slow but steady rise in incomes and a favourable resource base meant that there was a margin above subsistence to allow this to take place. As Batou (1990: 464) notes, there was no social class in Asia, the Middle East or China, or for that matter in eastern Europe, comparable to the European bourgeoisie that accumulated so much movable wealth over such a long period. Such a process of accumulation was vitally important for the later exploitation of new technologies and the development of manufactures as well as for the modernisation of agriculture. It also provided the means with which to improve infra-structures and social overhead capital, including, of course, educational facilities. The European instinct to accumulate capital, albeit often very slowly, over many centuries, in contrast to the more destructive phases of many Eastern civilisations, provides an important pointer to the long-run origins of the development process, emphasising the essential continuity of that process as opposed to the concept of a dramatic structural break (Komlos, 1989b: 203–5). And, of even greater significance, it put western Europe in a strong position to spring the Malthusian population trap, to which we now turn.

Breaking through the population barrier

Many Third World countries today must no doubt envy the population problems of the early developers. From the mid-twentieth century onwards rates of population growth in Asia, Africa and Latin America have averaged between 2 and 2·5 per cent per annum, which may be compared with a range of 0·5 to 1·0 per cent during the demographic revolution in Europe (Livi-Bacci, 1992: 31, 147). Agricultural productivity has failed to keep pace with this explosion, while the growth of non-agricultural employment has been nowhere near rapid enough to absorb the excess labour on the land. This has led to diminishing returns in agriculture, thereby compounding the problem (Bairoch, 1975: 6–8, 35–8).

By contrast Western civilisation was never suffocated by the same sort of population pressure which confronts Third World countries today or which faced some Asian civilisations in the past (Ohlin, 1965: 36). Pre-industrial England, it is claimed, (Macfarlane, 1978: 3–4) was far from being a subsistence economy on the brink of starvation. She was far better developed and had a very modest population problem by comparison with today's Third World countries. As Macfarlane (1978: 163, n. 143) graphically demonstrates, had England experienced similar population pressures, her total population by the time of the Black Death could have been in the region of 250 million! It is true, of course, that in pre-industrial Europe waves of expansion did periodically run up against a population barrier, when population growth outstripped food production, and this constraint was eventually relieved through plagues, famines, wars and other Malthusian checks (Herlihy, 1971: 161–3). But Europe's main demographic break-through did not occur until the resource constraint had been lifted, or, to put it another way, Europe's population revolution took place as and when it could be accommodated (Woude, 1992: 247–8).

There was a danger of population pressure getting out of hand towards the end of the seventeenth century, with the decline in high mortality as a result of the waning impact of disease and plague owing to improved disease control. A subsistence crisis might have followed had the supply capacity of economies not improved. The reason it did not was that, as Komlos (1989a: 220–1) demonstrates in his illuminating study of the eighteenth-century Habsburg monarchy, west Europeans were able to emancipate themselves from yet another Malthusian menace because the supply capacity of their economies had improved to a point where it was possible to cope with the pressure. The Austrian example is an interesting illustration of how government was able to react favourably to population pressures in the latter half of the eighteenth century by instituting reforms which encouraged both agriculture and industry. It was in a position to do so because of the enhanced financial, military and bureaucratic power of the state and the improved social infrastructure (Komlos, 1989a: 161). Equally outstanding was the way the Dutch had responded to a doubling of their population between 1550 and 1660 with new farming methods, land reclamation and new crops, practices which eventually spread throughout western Europe in response to similar circumstances (Chisholm, 1982: 48). Dutch agriculture in fact became among the most efficient and prosperous in Europe (Mokyr, 1976: 5–6), and van Houtte (1977: 316–17) maintains that strong demographic pressure in the Low Countries was conducive to economic progress largely because early emancipation of rural society from feudal restrictions enabled the agrarian sector to respond. The main puzzle now for historians is to explain why the Dutch subsequently failed to capitalise fully on their early lead in the world economy (van Zanden, 1992: 4–5).

Komlos (1989b: 204–5) sees these developments as part of a long continuum of change involving a slow build-up of the supply capacity of pre-industrial western Europe to the point where it was able to respond successfully to population-driven expansion. The important thing to note is that both the agrarian and the non-agrarian sectors of western Europe were improving simultaneously. Agricultural productivity was increasing, albeit slowly and irregularly, well before the industrial revolution, so that food supplies, supplemented periodically with imports from the Baltic and elsewhere, were at least keeping pace with population growth (Mokyr, 1976: 23–4; Grigg, 1992: 2, 33). Bairoch's study (1989) of the delivery potential of agrarian systems suggests that those of western Europe in particular were capable, by the eighteenth century, of meeting population pressure when it came, not necessarily initially by raising the standard of living, but in preventing it from falling away as had happened under earlier population expansions. It was this ability to match food and population which turned one of the keys in the development door. Equally important in the light of later experience in the Third World, non-agricultural employment was also expanding, thus enabling inter-sectoral labour transfers to take place which meant that the agrarian sector never became swamped with manpower to the point where diminishing returns or zero labour productivity took hold.

In other words, the real significance of the industrial revolution 'is not the rates of growth that were achieved, but the fact that for the first time many European societies escaped from the Malthusian trap' (Komlos, 1989a: 205). Viewed in this light, the critical role of earlier developments becomes readily apparent. Moreover, the virtual absence of the same long-run dynamic changes in eastern Europe helps to explain its growing relative backwardness and inability to cope with population pressure (Warriner, 1965: 1–19; Berend and Ranki, 1982: 12–18). This failure to adapt was in turn associated with institutional constraints.

States, institutions and legal frameworks

The development of Western civilisation might well have been very different had states and institutions not been adapted to the needs of a modern society. There is now much greater recognition among economic historians and development economists that institutions can have a significant bearing on the rate at which a country progresses. The work of North and Thomas (1970, 1973; North, 1981) has served to remind us once again of the importance of creating an institutional and legal framework which is conducive to economic activity and commercial enterprise, that is, one which strengthens individual property rights, reduces the costs of economic transactions, and facilitates the freedom of factor markets and resource flows (Rosenberg and Birdzell, 1986: 113–40). Perhaps not an altogether novel thesis, one may add, since at the turn of the century Cunningham (1904: 152–69, 261–2) had touched upon many of these points, albeit in a less rigorous manner.

There are many examples in history of the way in which states and institutions have acted as an impediment to progress and the exploitation of new opportunities by failing to adapt to the needs of an acquisitive society. They may be restrictive and repressive towards economic enterprise, or fail to provide a proper framework to legitimise property rights and economic transactions, or at worst they may impose harsh exactions on the population through plunder, taxation or bribery and corruption. Under such conditions there is little incentive for individuals or groups to show initiative and enterprise if the rewards are not 'privatised', or if property assets of whatever kind are constantly in danger of violation by plunder or expropriation by the state or by other individuals, as was the case in medieval Europe, or if there is no proper authority to uphold the basis of economic transactions. As Batou (1990: 465) observes in another context, 'Who would have taken the risk of investing his assets in commerce and industry without being protected from the exactions of the authorities?'

In much of Eurasia state structures and institutions changed little and they remained essentially feudal and repressive. The great dynasties of India, China and the Ottoman empire were little more than military despotisms bent on preserving their power by exacting tribute from impoverished subjects who were left with little more than subsistence. Scant encouragement was given to individual initiative, since it would have undermined the basis of feudal power. The overhead costs to the state of the upkeep of the army, the central government and a parasitical aristocratic elite were heavy and tended to weaken the strength of these empires in much the same way as had occurred in the later Roman empire (Kahn, 1979: 30–1).

A not dissimilar situation can be found in the more backward parts of eastern Europe in the later nineteenth century, and incidentally in many of today's Third World countries. In the Balkans, for example, corrupt and despotic rulers imposed heavy taxes on their subjects, and the state drew more human and fiscal resources away from productive investment than it itself contributed, except for those wasted on forms of 'symbolic modernisation' (Berend and Ranki, 1982: 69–71). Bulgaria in particular was an object lesson in public corruption, bribery, financial scandals and exploitation. Liberation from the clutches of the Turks did little to improve the lot of the peasants who constituted over 80 per cent of the population. They were seen mainly as a source of revenue to meet the rapid growth of state expenditure arising from debt servicing, the armed forces, an overblown bureaucracy and ostentatious public works. A large part of the money raised through foreign loans was put to similar purposes. The peasants bore the burden and received little in return, since the small part of state expenditure devoted to 'modernisation' was 'of a decorative rather than self-sustaining variety', much of it concentrated in the cities, especially Sofia—for example, parks, public buildings, museums, trams and electric lighting to which the peasants had little access. To compound their misery, many peasants fell victim to unscrupulous usurers and were forced to pay astronomical interest rates in some cases (Bell, 1977: 8–16).

Such features were, of course, quite common in medieval Europe under the fragmented control of individual rulers. Pillage, plunder and exaction were the meat of everyday life. Fortunately, when Europe emerged from this situation it escaped falling into the hands of monolithic dynastic rule and so avoided some of the more pernicious features of the great empires of the East. Instead a system of nation states took shape. The haphazard multiplicity of political units of the late medieval period was replaced, at least in the West, by a system of

25

organised and fairly homogeneous nation states with fairly clearly defined boundaries. In this respect the history of Europe is unique in that at no time, as Cobban (1969: 30) points out, had such a considerable group of nation states survived in geographical proximity and close association over a period of many centuries. Mobilisation for war, the dominant activity in Europe throughout the present millennium, was the major factor why 'states expanded, consolidated, and created new forms of political organisation' (Tilly, 1992: 70, 74). Farther east conditions were less propitious for such developments, since the ethnic fragmentation of populations, the periodic threat of invasion and alien rule, and the absence of clearly defined geographical boundaries made the concept of the nation state something of an anachronism (Newman, 1970: 37–50).

The new states of the West were both more competitive and in time more liberal than the administrations of eastern Europe. They gave rise to greater economic security and a corresponding increase in the rights of property (P. Anderson, 1974: 420, 429; J. Anderson, 1991: 60). In time they removed or modified some of the more inhibiting features of traditional society (for example, feudal restrictions) and this in turn reduced market transaction costs and strengthened the links between effort and reward. The contrast may be seen in the different responses to market opportunities for capitalist farming. In the West the commercialisation of agriculture and the increased use of wage labour were encouraged, whereas in Eurasia and much of eastern Europe the sector was simply seen as a convenient source of revenue for the rulers.

Perhaps the most notable feature of the contrast between west and east is the differing legal framework with regard to market transactions and property rights. The emergence of the nation state in western Europe was accompanied by the revival of Roman law, one of the first systems to embody adequate safeguards for private property, and seen by many observers as the most effective instrument for encouraging capitalist transactions. The advantages of Roman law are that it facilitates title to property, provides a means of defining and enforcing contracts, and more generally establishes a systematic and coherent framework for the purchase, sale, lease, hire, loan and transfer of goods and chattels. This legal basis laid the foundations for the security of property rights and the conduct of economic transactions without which modern capitalism could not have developed. As might be expected, the evolution of comprehensive property rights, civil administration and representative institutions occurred earlier in the more capital-intensive and bourgeois-orientated societies of western Europe (Tilly, 1992: 100). Eastern Europe lagged well behind and in some respects had not progressed far from the pillage, plunder and corruption of earlier centuries. Likewise the legal systems of the East gave little support to economic agents. From the commercial point of view Islamic, Chinese and Japanese law all embodied serious impediments to economic enterprise. Islamic law was extremely vague on estate matters, Chinese law was repressive and concerned relatively little with civil or economic issues, while Japanese law was rudimentary in the extreme.

The important point is that all these changes did not occur overnight. They evolved gradually and erratically over a long period of time—several centuries, in fact—and this is partly the key to their success, as well as the lesson for others. Attempts to speed up the process of modernisation by drastic changes in economic regimes and institutions—as, for example, in eastern Europe in the later nineteenth century, in many less developed countries in the twentieth century, and possibly in eastern Europe today—have been found, to the chagrin of their instigators, not always to work as anticipated.

The reasons are obvious enough. It is virtually impossible to compress into a generation or two what took centuries to mature in the West (Ramirez-Faria, 1991: 126). By the later Middle Ages, according to Macfarlane's iconoclastic study (1978: 162–5), England was far better endowed than other countries and was well on the way to adapting its society, the majority of its ordinary inhabitants being, from at least the thirteenth century onwards 'rampant individualists, highly mobile both geographically and socially, economically "rational", market-orientated and acquisitive, ego-centred in kinship and social life'. Yet even in this case several centuries were to elapse before the real breakthrough occurred. Violent transitions engineered to telescope the process cannot easily be accommodated by a society which is basically conservative, apart from the fact that many of the elements and agents of the old order will of necessity remain in place. For example, relics of barbarous feudalism and corruption persisted in eastern Europe long after feudal restrictions had been formally abolished—well into the twentieth century, in fact—as did traditional modes of thought and behaviour, especially in the countryside

27

(Warriner, 1965: 22; Held, 1992; Berend and Ranki, 1982: 12). In Hungary, for example, despite considerable agrarian transformation from the middle of the nineteenth century onwards, the traditional way of life remained ingrained among the peasantry for many years to come, thus helping to perpetuate social rigidity, resistance to change and general backwardness. Even in the inter-war years it was still possible for a writer to comment in the following terms:

> there was a feudal, or even pagan view of the world among the peasants, and a corresponding moral view, thus, a backwardness, centuries behind modern life and work techniques. There was animal-like identification with the home, with work; backward views on health care, apathy, lack of understanding of a new way of life . . . There was only one matter on which all the peasants agreed; namely, they regarded the whole outside world, the world that surrounded and oppressed them for centuries, as hostile, alien, and one that could not be understood. [Quoted in Held (1980: 278)]

Exploitation, bribery and corruption, vestiges of feudalism, traditional modes of thought and behaviour were even more rife in the Balkans, and they lingered well into the twentieth century (Fischer-Galati, 1970; Crampton, 1987). Following emancipation in Romania 'excessive exploitation of the peasantry continued unabated and, indeed, probably increased after the emancipation there' (Blum 1978: 438). In Bulgaria the position was no better: corruption and bribery were endemic at virtually every level of administration, and the peasants were exploited mercilessly to service the spending proclivities of state officials (Bell, 1977: 8–14).

It was very difficult, therefore, to graft modern capitalism on to such an alien landscape. In the case of the south Slav lands, for example, capitalism could never come to full fruition because it

> was not an economic system which grew out of the internal structure of the economy, but rather, it was the appendage of Central and Western European capitalism and it was introduced into the South Slav lands primarily by foreigners. Whether its representatives were foreigners or nationals, capitalism in the South Slav areas remained essentially rapacious and exploitative rather than creative, a corrupting crust rather than a well-developed economic system. [Tomasevich (1955: 213)]

And while capitalism partially destroyed the old economic order of peasant society it was not robust enough to replace it completely with a new system which would improve the lot of the masses (Tomasevich, 1955: 212–13). In other words, a society takes time to adjust to new ideas and new practices and to different modes of thought and behaviour, especially if they are not indigenous, and, if the western European experience is anything to go by, the learning process is a long and arduous one.

It should not be thought, of course, that the regimes of the peripheral areas of the European east and south remained totally impervious to the modernisation that was going on elsewhere. It is true that there were pockets of containment, such as that of the Valpolicella region of Italy, which shunned what were regarded as the dubious benefits of agrarian reform in the eighteenth century in favour of a well tried system that guaranteed stability and survival. To some this might be construed as yet another case of primitive backwardness or rank conservatism, but in Musgrave's iconoclastic interpretation of the situation it was in fact a rational decision reflecting 'a very real and very realistic unwillingness to move from a system which worked and which delivered the benefits the population required to one which palpably was based on a series of lunatic gambles' (1992: 104).

At the end of the day few governments could afford to stand completely aloof from the march of material progress. By the latter half of the nineteenth century most countries on the periphery of Europe were trying to emulate the West by adopting policies to foster industrialisation and improve their archaic agarian systems. While they achieved some success, such policies could rarely guarantee both sustained progress and stability. The reason was partly that state systems and institutions could not be adapted rapidly enough to serve the needs of an emerging liberal economy, while overburdened economies and state budgets meant that the predominantly agrarian populations had to pay a heavy price to meet the costs of development (Janos, 1989; Palairet, 1979). In time this led inevitably to an alienated and rebellious peasantry in Russia, the Balkans, Hungary and parts of southern Europe, which moved governments to devise new instruments of coercion in an attempt to preserve the traditional power structure. Progress, it seemed, unleashed a challenge to existing regimes such that

> All over the European South and East, the countryside was turned into an armed camp as governments organized special forces of rural gendarmes that, with their military uniforms, equipment, and tactics,

were not so much conventional constabularies as armies of occupation within their own nations. The exact cost of this repression is hard to measure. But force and counterforce were likely links in a chain of causality that led first to stagnation, then to the decline, of agrarian production throughout the South and the East (including East Prussia and Southern France). In the long run, this decline could not be offset even by the rise of new industrial economies, and would be reflected in the persistence of the pattern of regional income distribution that had been evident since the seventeenth and eighteenth centuries. [Janos (1989: 347)]

To return to the main theme, the argument is that by the early nineteenth century only western Europe had, by a long process of evolution, adapted its institutions and legal frameworks to a point where they were no longer an impediment to modern economic growth—that is, to a point where most institutional restrictions on the development of market systems had been removed and where there was a recognised legal framework for the protection of assets and the conduct of economic transactions. The countries which readily fall into this category would include Britain, France, Belgium, Switzerland and possibly the Netherlands. Germany and Austria were still at the intermediate stage but rapidly improving (Morris and Adelman, 1988: 100–1, 209). The relationship between politics and economics is perforce a complex and nebulous one about which we still know too little. This lacuna may inadvertently lead to an underestimation of its significance. 'Once we unravel the link,' according to Good (1991: 239), 'we will understand better why the Empire disappeared in 1919 and why after 1750 some countries grew rapidly, others more slowly, and still others hardly at all.'

Conclusion

This stylised interpretation of Western development may not do justice to all the facets of modernisation, since it concentrates not on how the West achieved supremacy but on why it was the first to be in a position to do so. A number of important prerequisites have been stressed— educational attainment, income levels and resources, surmounting population barriers, and institutional change—to explain why the West succeeded whereas the East largely failed. Only countries which had undergone a long apprenticeship could hope to be in a position to unlock the door to modern development (Jones, 1988: 26, 174).

This is not to imply, of course, that the pattern of development among Western nations was identical or uniform or that countries with a head start always capitalised fully on their good fortune. The contrasting experiences of Belgium, the Netherlands and Denmark, and the relative slippage of the UK after the late nineteenth century, demonstrate how misleading it would be to try to formulate any generalised framework of development. That a strong initial position did not always guarantee leadership of the pack in the long run is beside the point, since we are not trying to assess or predict relative rankings from initial base starting positions. What we would maintain, however, is that Western countries which had achieved high income levels by the eve of the first world war, by whatever route, did so because they enjoyed clear advantages which most other countries patently lacked. Only they were in a position to reap the fruits of modern economic growth.

The advantage of this interpretation is that it does not have to invoke single factor explanations or some *deus ex machina* in the form of technology (cf. Gaski, 1982) to explain why the West was able to take the lead, nor does it need to have recourse to the thesis of colonial exploitation or economic dependence to explain either the West's achievements or stagnation elsewhere. It is true that large parts of the globe eventually became satellites or dependencies of Western civilisation, but the basis of the West's economic supremacy had been established long before dependence or colonial systems in their modern form had become a reality. There is no conclusive evidence to support the 'dependency theory' argument that the emergence of international income inequality was largely a product of Western exploitation (Ramirez-Faria, 1991: 261), even though the influence of the leading powers in the world economy was not always favourable to the development of the European and non-European periphery (Valerio, 1992: 131). Likewise, the origins of the East's relapse into stagnation are to be located well before the onset of modern economic development. But that is part of another story.

References

Abramovitz, M. (1989), *Thinking about Growth*. Cambridge, Cambridge University Press.
Aldcroft, D. H. (1991), 'World income distribution', *Economic Review*, 9.

Anderson, C. A., and Bowman, M. J. (1976), 'Education and economic modernisation in historical perspective', in L. S. Stone, ed., *Schooling and Society*, Baltimore, Md, Johns Hopkins University Press.
Anderson, J. L. (1991), *Explaining Long-term Economic Change*. Basingstoke, Macmillan.
Anderson, P. (1974), *Lineages of the Absolutist State*. London, New Left Books.
Anell, L., and Nygren, B. (1980), *Developing Countries and the World Economic Order*. London, Frances Pinter.
Ashworth, W. (1974), 'Industrialization and the economic integration of nineteenth-century Europe', *European Studies Review*, 4.
Ashworth, W. (1977), 'Typologies and evidence: has nineteenth-century Europe a guide to economic growth?', *Economic History Review*, 30.
Bairoch, P. (1975), *The Economic Development of the Third World since 1900*. London, Methuen.
Bairoch, P. (1976), 'Europe's gross national product, 1800–1975', *Journal of European Economic History*, 5.
Bairoch, P. (1981), 'The main trends in national income disparities since the industrial revolution', in P. Bairoch and M. Lévy-Leboyer, eds., *Disparities in Economic Development since the Industrial Revolution*. London, Macmillan.
Bairoch, P. (1982), 'International industrialization levels from 1750 to 1980', *Journal of European Economic History*, 11.
Bairoch, P. (1989), 'Les trois révolutions agricoles du monde développé: rendements et productivité de 1800 à 1985', *Annales*, 44.
Bairoch, P. (1991), 'How and not why: economic inequalities between 1800 and 1913: some background figures', in J. Batou, ed., *Between Development and Underdevelopment: the Precocious Attempts at Industrialization of the Periphery, 1800–70*. Geneva, Droz.
Barsby, S. L. (1969), 'Economic backwardness and the characteristics of development', *Journal of Economic History*, 29.
Batou, J. (1990), *Cent ans de résistance au sous-développement: l'industrialisation de l'Amérique latine et du Moyen-orient au défi européen, 1770–1870*. Geneva, Droz.
Batou, J., ed. (1991), *Between Development and Underdevelopment: the Precocious Attempts at Industrialization of the Periphery, 1800–70*. Geneva, Droz.
Bell, J. D. (1977), *Peasants in Power: Alexander Stamboliski and the Bulgarian Agrarian National Union, 1899–1923*. Princeton, N. J., Princeton University Press.
Bencze, I., and Tajti, E. V. (1972), *Budapest: an Industrial–Geographical Approach*. Budapest, Akademiai Kiado.
Berend, I. T., and Ranki, G. (1974), *Economic Development in East Central Europe in the Nineteenth and Twentieth Centuries*. New York, Columbia University Press.
Berend, I. T., and Ranki, G. (1982), *The European Periphery and Industrialization, 1780–1914*. Cambridge, Cambridge University Press.
Blum, J. (1978), *The End of the old Order in rural Europe*. Princeton, N. J., Princeton University Press.
Caldwell, M. (1977), *The Wealth of some Nations*. London, Zed Press.
Cameron, R. (1985), 'A new view of European industrialisation', *Economic History Review*, 38.
Chenery, H. B. (1960), 'Patterns of industrial growth', *American Economic Review*, 50.
Chenery, H. B., and Taylor, L. (1968), 'Development patterns: many countries over time', *Review of Economics and Statistics*, 50.
Chirot, D. (1985), 'The rise of the West', *American Sociological Review*, 50.

Chisholm, M. (1982), *Modern World Development*. London, Hutchinson.

Cipolla, C. (1969), *Literacy and Development in the West*. Harmondsworth, Penguin.

Cipolla, C. (1981), *Before the Industrial Revolution: European Society and Economy, 1000–1700*. London, Methuen.

Clarkson, L. A. (1985), *Proto-industrialization: the first Phase of Industrialization?* Basingstoke, Macmillan.

Cobban, A. (1969), *The Nation State and National Self-determination*. London, Collins.

Coleman, D. C. (1983), 'Proto-industrialization: a concept too many', *Economic History Review*, 36.

Crafts, N. F. R. (1984), 'Patterns of development in nineteenth-century Europe', *Oxford Economic Papers*, 3.

Crampton, R. J. (1987), *A Short History of Modern Bulgaria*. Cambridge, Cambridge University Press.

Cunningham, W. (1904), *An Essay on Western Civilization in its Economic Aspects*. Cambridge, Cambridge University Press.

Deldlycke, T., Gelders, H., and Limbor, J.-M. (1968), *The Working Population and its Structure: International Historical Statistics* I. Brussels, Université Libre de Bruxelles.

Easterlin, R. A. (1981), 'Why isn't the whole world developed?' *Journal of Economic History*, 41.

Fischer-Galati, S. (1970), *Twentieth Century Rumania*. New York, Columbia University Press.

Gaski, J. F. (1982), 'The cause of the industrial revolution: a brief single-factor argument', *Journal of European Economic History*, 11.

Geary, F. (1988), 'Balanced and unbalanced growth in XIXth century Europe', *Journal of European Economic History*, 17.

Gerschenkron, A. (1962), *Economic Backwardness in Historical Perspective*. Cambridge, Mass., Harvard University Press.

Good, D. (1984), *The Economic Rise of the Habsburg Empire, 1750–1914*. Berkeley, Cal., University of California Press.

Good, D. F. (1991), 'Austria–Hungary', in R. Sylla and G. Toniolo, *Patterns of European Industrialization: the Nineteenth Century*. London, Routledge.

Goodman, J., and Honeyman, K. (1988), *Gainful Pursuits: the Making of Industrial Europe*. London, Edward Arnold.

Gould, J. D. (1972), *Economic Growth in History*. London, Methuen.

Grigg, D. (1992), *The Transformation of Agriculture in the West*. Oxford, Blackwell.

Harrison, R. J. (1978), *An Economic History of Modern Spain*. Manchester, Manchester University Press.

Held, J. (1980), *The Modernization of Agriculture: Rural Transformation in Hungary, 1848–1975*. New York, Columbia University Press.

Held, J., ed. (1992), *The Columbia History of Eastern Europe in the Twentieth Century*. New York, Columbia University Press.

Herlihy, D. (1971), 'The economy of traditional Europe', *Journal of Economic History*, 31.

Hocevar, T. (1965), *The Structure of the Slovenian Economy, 1848–1963*. New York, Studia Slovenica.

Houtte, J. A. van (1977), *An Economic History of the Low Countries, 800–1800*. London, Weidenfeld & Nicolson.

Inkster, I. (1990), 'Mental capital: transfers of knowledge and technique in eighteenth-century Europe', *Journal of European Economic History*, 19.

33

Janos, A. C. (1989), 'The politics of backwardness in continental Europe, 1780–1945', *World Politics*, 41.

Jones, E. L. (1981), *The European Miracle*. Cambridge, Cambridge University Press.

Jones, E. L. (1988), *Growth Recurring: Economic Change in World History*. Oxford, Oxford University Press.

Kahn, H. (1979), *World Economic Development, 1979 and Beyond*. London, Croom Helm.

Komlos, J. (1983), *The Habsburg Monarchy as a Customs Union: Economic Development in Austria–Hungary in the Nineteenth Century*. Chicago, University of Chicago Press.

Komlos, J. (1989a), *Nutrition and Economic Development in the Eighteenth Century Habsburg Monarchy: an Anthropometric Study*. Princeton, N. J., Princeton University Press.

Komlos, J. (1989b), 'Thinking about the industrial revolution', *Journal of European Economic History*, 18.

Kuznets, S. (1966), *Modern Economic Growth: Rate, Structure and Spread*. New Haven, Conn., Yale University Press.

Lampe, J. R., and Jackson, M. R. (1982), *Balkan Economic History, 1550–1950: from Imperial Borderlands to Developing Nations*. Bloomington, Ind., Indiana University Press.

Lampe, J. (1975), 'Varieties of unsuccessful industrialization: the Balkan states before 1914', *Journal of Economic History*, 35.

Landes, D. (1969), *The Unbound Prometheus: Technological Change and Industrial Development in Western Europe from 1750 to the Present*. Cambridge, Cambridge University Press.

Landes, D. (1991), 'Does it pay to be late?', in J. Batou, ed., *Between Development and Underdevelopment, 1800–70*. Geneva, Droz.

Lewis, W. A. (1955), *The Theory of Economic Growth*. London, Allen & Unwin.

Livi-Bacci, M. (1992), *A Concise History of World Population*. Oxford, Blackwell.

McClelland, D. C. (1966), 'Does education accelerate economic growth?' *Economic Development and Cultural Change*, 14.

Macfarlane, A. (1978), *The Origins of English Individualism: the Family, Property and Social Transition*. Oxford, Blackwell.

McNeill, W. H. (1963), *The Rise of the West*. Chicago, University of Chicago Press.

McNeill, W. H. (1979), *A World History*. Oxford, Oxford University Press.

Maddison, A. (1982), *Phases of Capitalist Development*. Oxford, Oxford University Press.

Matowist, M. (1966), 'The problem of the inequality of economic development in Europe in the later Middle Ages', *Economic History Review*, 19.

Mokyr, J. (1976), *Industrialization in the Low Countries, 1795–1850*. New Haven, Conn., Yale University Press.

Morris, C. T., and Adelman, I. (1988), *Comparative Patterns of Economic Development, 1850–1914*. Baltimore, Md, Johns Hopkins University Press.

Musgrave, P. (1992), *Land and Economy in Baroque Italy: Valpolicella, 1630–1797*. Leicester, Leicester University Press.

Newman, K. J. (1970), *European Democracy between the Wars*, London, Allen & Unwin.

North, D. C. (1981), *Structure and Change in Economic History*. New York, Norton.

North, D. C., and Thomas, R. P. (1970), 'An economic theory of the growth of the Western world', *Economic History Review*, 23.

North, D. C., and Thomas, R. P. (1973), *The Rise of the Western World: a New Economic History*. Cambridge, Cambridge University Press.

Nunez, C. E. (1990), 'Literacy and economic growth in Spain 1860–1977', in G. Tortella, ed., *Education and Economic Development since the Industrial Revolution*. Valencia, Generalitat Valenciana.

O'Brien, P. (1982), 'European economic development: the contribution of the periphery', *Economic History Review*, 35.

O'Brien, P. (1986), 'Do we have a typology for the study of European industrialization in the XIXth century?' *Journal of European Economic History*, 15.

Ohlin, G. (1965), 'Remarks on the relevance of Western experience in economic growth to former colonial areas', *Journal of World History*, 9.

Palairet, M. (1979), 'Fiscal pressure and peasant impoverishment in Serbia before World War I', *Journal of Economic History*, 39.

Pedreira, J. M. (1991), 'The obstacles to early industrialization in Portugal, 1800–70: a comparative perspective', in J. Batou, ed., *Between Development and Underdevelopment, 1800–70*. Geneva, Droz.

Persson, K. G. (1988), *Pre-industrial Economic Growth: Social Organization and Technological Progress in Europe*. Oxford, Blackwell.

Pollard, S. (1973), 'Industrialisation and the European economy', *Economic History Review*, 26.

Pollard, S. (1981), *Peaceful Conquest: the Industrialization of Europe, 1760–1970*. Oxford, Oxford University Press.

Pollard, S. (1990), *Typology of Industrialization Processes in the Nineteenth Century*. Chur, Harwood Academic.

Ramirez-Faria, C. (1991), *The Origins of Economic Inequality between Nations: a Critique of Western Theories on Development and Underdevelopment*. London, Unwin Hyman.

Reynolds, L. G. (1985), *Economic Growth in the Third World, 1850–1950*. New Haven, Conn., Yale University Press.

Rosenberg, N., and Birdzell, L. E. (1986), *How the West grew Rich: the Economic Transformation of the Industrial World*. London, Tauris.

Rostow, W. W. (1960), *The Stages of Economic Growth: a non-Communist Manifesto*. Cambridge, Cambridge University Press.

Sandberg, L. G. (1982), 'Ignorance, poverty and economic backwardness in the early stages of European industrialization: Variations on Alexander Gerschenkron's grand theme', *Journal of European Economic History*, 11.

Siegenthaler, J. K. (1972), 'A scale analysis of nineteenth-century industrialization', *Explorations in Economic History*, 10.

Simmons, J. (1979), 'Education for development reconsidered?' *World Development*, 7.

Smith, P. (1993), 'Can we measure economic development?' *Economic Review*, 10.

Snooks, G. D. (1990), 'Economic Growth during the last Millenium: a Quantitative Perspective for the British Industrial Revolution', paper to the tenth International Economic History Congress, Leuven, Belgium.

Sylla, R., and Toniolo, G. (1991), *Patterns of European Industrialization: the Nineteenth Century*. London, Routledge.

Tilly, C. (1992), *Coercion, Capital and European States, AD 990–1990*. Oxford, Blackwell.

Tomasevich, J. (1955), *Peasants, Politics and Economic Change in Yugoslavia*. Standford, Cal., Stanford University Press.

Tortella, G. (1993), 'Causes historicas y remedios de la desigualdad', *Claves*, 29.

Valerio, N. (1992), 'Some remarks about growth and stagnation in the Mediterranean world in the XIXth and XXth centuries', *Journal of European Economic History*, 21.

Warriner, D. (1964), *Economics of Peasant Farming*. London, Cass.
Warriner, D., ed. (1965), *Contrasts in Emerging Societies: Readings in the Social and Economic History of South-east Europe in the Nineteenth Century*. London, Athlone Press.
World Bank (1990), *World Development Report, 1990*. Washington, D. C., World Bank.
Woude, A. M. van der (1992), 'The future of west European agriculture: an exercise in applied history', *Review, Fernand Braudel Centre*, 15.
Zanden, J. L. van (1992), 'Dutch economic history of the period 1500–1940: a review of the present state of affairs', *Research Notes from the Netherlands*, 2.
Zimmerman, L. J. (1962), 'The distribution of world income, 1860–1960', in E. de Vries, ed., *Essays on Unbalanced Growth*. The Hague, Mouton.

Population, migration and labour supply

In recent years it has become fashionable for students of population history to emphasise the diversities rather than the uniformities which existed in the demographic evolution of eighteenth and nineteenth-century Europe. By demonstrating that patterns of population change between and within Europe's constituent states were a good deal more varied than it was once customary to suppose, this redirection of emphasis has served as a salutary reminder not to overstate the generality of the demographic experience. At the same time, however, the significance of regional variations in population trends should itself not be pressed too far. For all the local differences that existed in rates of population growth, and in the behaviour of the mechanisms of fertility, mortality and migration which determined them, the fact remains that, at least in some of their more fundamental characteristics, the population histories of most European states between 1750 and 1914 *did* follow a remarkably similar course. If only because of their potential implications for the pace and character of economic development it is important not to allow these similarities to be wholly obscured by excessive attention to the temporal and regional differentials which undoubtedly surrounded them.

Population growth

Between 1600 and 1750 the population of Europe as a whole grew at an average rate of little more than 0·38 per cent a year (Clark, 1968: 64). In the course of the following century and a half the rate of European population growth increased dramatically, to an annual average of 0·54 per cent between 1750 and 1800, 0·96 per cent between 1800 and 1850, 0·92 per cent from 1850 to 1900 and 0·90 per cent between 1900 and 1914. With some variation in its date of inception and subsequent pace, the acceleration was common to almost all European countries. In many cases, it is true, the upturn in rates of population growth which occurred during the second half of the eighteenth century was modest or barely perceptible. In many other instances, however, it was substantial, and occasionally dramatic. Of all the countries summarised in Table 2.1, only in Italy were average rates of population growth between 1750 and 1800 lower than those of the first half of the century.

Table 2.1 Rates of population growth in some European countries, 1750–1911 (% per annum)

Country	1700–50	1750–1800	1800–20	1820–50	1850–1911
Austria–Hungary	0·77	3·64	0·62	(1789–1857)	1·14
Belgium	0·20	0·55	1·21	(1800–56)	1·18
Denmark	0·33	0·51	0·99	0·94	1·55
England and Wales	0·26	0·92	1·75	1·65	1·69
Finland	1·59	1·95	2·07	1·30	1·33
France	0·23	0·66	0·57	0·58	0·16
Germany	0·45	0·66	−0·54	1·37	1·63
Iceland	−0·19	0·14	0·52	(1801–50)	0·73
Ireland	0·38	1·32	1·44	−0·12	−0·55
Italy	0·30	0·25	0·58	0·87	0·72
Netherlands	0·00	0·21	−0·30	1·50	1·53
Norway	0·64	0·69	0·79	1·43	1·10
Portugal	0·29	0·66	0·16	0·82	0·96
Russian empire	0·89	2·9	1·85	1·37	2·24
Scotland	0·48	0·59	1·51	1·27	1·08
Spain	0·44	0·52	0·78	(1797–1857)	0·55
Sweden	0·60	0·64	0·51	1·14	0·98
Switzerland	0·33	0·43	0·79	0·71	0·95

Note: Austria–Hungary 1725–54, 1754–89. Denmark 1735–69, 1769–1801, 1801–34, 1834–50. Finland, 1721–50. France 1700–62, 1762–1801. Iceland 1703–62, 1762–1801. Ireland 1712–54, 1754–91, 1791–1821. Norway 1700–69, 1769–1801. Portugal 1700–68, 1768–1801. Russian empire 1722–62, 1762–1800. Spain 1717–68/9, 1768/69–97. Switzerland 1800–37, 1837–50. In all other cases the figures refer more closely to the whole of the period indicated.

Sources: Anderson (1988: 23), Falkus (1972: 17), Gille (1949–50: 19), Goodman and Honeyman (1988: 23), Grigg (1980: 57, 61), Lee (1979: 31, 34, 80, 124), Livi-Bacci (1968b: 525), Mitchell (1975: 19–27), Reinhard and Armengaud (1968: 227), Tomasson (1977: 406).

Temporarily, during the period of the French revolutionary and Napoleonic wars, rates of population growth in the various states of Europe followed one or other of two divergent paths. In countries like Denmark, England/Wales, Finland, Ireland, Italy, Norway, Russia, Scotland and Switzerland they remained high or even rose. In others, like Germany, the Netherlands and Portugal, they fell to low or even negative levels. Once the war years had passed, however, a broader uniformity of experience re-emerged. Except in the case of Ireland, in every European country the period between 1815 and the mid-nineteenth century was one of historically high and often accelerating levels of population increase.

During the period between the mid-nineteenth century and the outbreak of the first world war the populations of most European countries continued to grow rapidly. In some cases, rates of population increase between 1850 and 1914 exceeded pre-1850 levels. In others, rates of population growth after 1850 slipped below those of the preceding half-century or so but remained above those of the second half of the eighteenth century. Although in a number of countries the pace of population increase began to decline in the years immediately prior to the first world war, the decline was usually modest and, in any case, largely countered by the experience of countries like Italy and Spain, where rates of population growth were rising. The result was that by 1914 the population of Europe had risen to around 450 million, more than three times that of 1750. Of all European countries only Ireland, where the number of inhabitants fell at each successive census from 1841 onwards, failed to increase its population more or less continuously throughout the period and only in France were rates of population growth between 1850 and 1914 negligible and lower than at any time between 1750 and 1850. Ireland and France apart, the persistence of high rates of population increase was the dominant feature of late eighteenth and nineteenth-century demography everywhere.

Except in late eighteenth and early nineteenth-century England, where the acceleration in rates of population growth seems to have owed most to rising fertility (Wrigley and Schofield, 1981: 244–5), the demographic mechanism responsible for the sustained increase in the populations of European countries was falling mortality. To some extent this, in turn, was due to a natural decline in the virulence of some of the principal infectious diseases. In the main, however, it was the result of improvements made by man himself in his economic, political and social environment—improvements which either reduced the frequency of contact with disease viruses or enhanced resistance to them. Which improvements had the greatest influence, and how far the influence of each varied over time and from one region to another, are unresolved matters. At the moment all we can safely conclude is that the explanation for the decline in mortality lies in a combination of factors which include the effects of innovations in medical therapy such as better quarantining procedures and inoculation and vaccination against smallpox, higher standards of public health and personal hygiene, and improved levels of nutrition (Kunitz, 1983; Schofield and Rehrer, 1991).

Overseas emigration

What is particularly impressive about this hitherto unparalleled increase in numbers is the fact that it was achieved despite a massive net exodus of people to non-European destinations. This, too, was a characteristic of late eighteenth and nineteenth-century European demographic history shared by the great majority of the continent's component states.

Down to the middle of the eighteenth century, with the possible exception of Ireland, the flow of emigrants from Europe to the non-European world amounted to little more than a trickle. During the period 1750–1850 the scale of overseas emigration, though generally increasing, remained relatively moderate, confined chiefly to the populations of Ireland and, to a lesser extent, of Germany and Scotland. For most European states the age of mass overseas emigration did not effectively begin until the second half of the nineteenth century. In the course of the half-century or so after 1850 rates of overseas emigration rose markedly almost everywhere, following a pattern of peaks and troughs that was also very similar from one country to another. The exodus began from the countries of northern, western and central Europe and by the 1880s had spread to those of the south and east. Altogether, between 1821 and 1915 an estimated 46 million to 51 million people left Europe for non-European destinations, equivalent to roughly a quarter of the continent's natural excess of births over deaths. Wherever it occurred the extent of the exodus was sufficient to have significant effects on rates of population growth. In the case of

Table 2.2 Number of overseas emigrants from some European countries, 1851–1910, by decade (000)

Country	1851–60	1861–70	1871–80	1881–90	1891–1900	1901–10	1851–90
Austria–Hungary	31	40	46	248	440	1,111	1,916
Belgium	1	2	2	21	16	30	72
Denmark		8	39	82	51	73	253
Finland				26	59	159	244
France	27	36	66	119	51	53	352
Germany	671	779	626	1,342	527	274	4,219
Italy	5	27	168	992	1,580	3,615	6,387
Netherlands	16	20	17	52	24	28	157
Norway	36	98	85	187	95	191	692
Portugal	45	79	131	185	266	324	1,030
Russia			58	288	481	911	1,738
Spain	3	7	13	572	791	1,091	2,477
Sweden	17	122	103	327	205	324	1,098
Switzerland	6	15	36	85	35	37	214
UK and Ireland	1,313	1,572	1,849	3,259	2,149	3,150	13,292

Source: Mitchell (1975: 135).

Ireland, where levels of net emigration exceeded levels of natural increase in every decade from 1851 to 1914, it was so great that the absolute size of the country's population declined continuously throughout the period. Elsewhere the proportion of natural increase lost to overseas emigration ranged from a low of one-tenth in countries like Denmark and Germany to one-sixth in Austria–Hungary, between a fifth and a quarter in Sweden, a third in Spain, half in Italy and Scotland and three-quarters in Norway (Anderson, 1979: 80; Drake, 1979: 286, 288; Flinn, 1977: 448; Knodel, 1974: 258; Milward and Saul, 1973: 159; Trebilcock, 1981: 309).

Until the later decades of the nineteenth century, for the overwhelming bulk of European overseas emigrants, emigration was, and was intended to be, permanent. By the late nineteenth century, however, as reflected in the growing number of emigrants returning to Europe from overseas destinations, it had become increasingly seasonal or temporary in nature. Rates of repatriation varied considerably from one country to another, ranging from between a tenth and a fifth in cases like Belgium, England, Denmark, Germany, the Netherlands, Rumania, Russia, Scotland, Sweden and Switzerland to between a quarter and a third for Hungary, Portugal, Spain and Turkey and from half to two-thirds for Austria, Bulgaria, France, Greece, Italy,

Montenegro and Serbia, though these figures probably overstate the true levels (Baines, 1985: 128–40; 1991: 39; Gould, 1979: 608–10; 1980: 54, 57, 65; Hvidt, 1975: 177–82). Despite these differences, the phenomenon of return emigration was common to late nineteenth and early twentieth-century overseas migrant streams throughout Europe.

In their choice of destination, their age, sex and marital structures and, to a lesser degree, their socio-occupational composition, too, overseas emigrants from individual European states displayed some striking similarities. From wherever they came, the predominant destination of those who went overseas was North America, principally the United States. Except in England during the early 1770s and Ireland throughout most of the period 1841–1911, the bulk of overseas emigrants were males. In the case of Britain the dominance of male over female transoceanic emigrants decreased in the course of the later decades of the nineteenth century. For Europe as a whole, however, the surplus of male over female overseas emigrants rose over time as the main sources of emigration shifted from northern and western to eastern and southern parts of the continent.

Whatever the country of origin, overseas emigration was also primarily a movement of young adults and children. As many as 87 per cent of all emigrants from Britain to the United States in the 1770s were aged between fifteen and thirty-nine. Only 6 per cent were under fifteen and 7 per cent over forty. By 1841 the share of the fifteen to thirty-nine age group had fallen to 60 per cent while that of the under fifteen age group had risen to 29 per cent. The proportion of emigrants aged over forty, on the other hand, remained at just 11 per cent. By 1914 70 per cent of all those leaving England and Scotland for overseas destinations were under thirty, 45 per cent between eighteen and thirty-one and only 7 per cent over forty-five (Baines, 1985: 65–6, 84–5; Carrier and Jeffery, 1953: 47; Erickson, 1981: 183; 1989: 358–62). In the period 1868–1900 20 per cent of all Danish overseas emigrants were under fifteen years of age, 68 per cent between fifteen and thirty-nine and less than 10 per cent over forty (Hvidt, 1975: 73–7). On the eve of the first world war no more than 4 per cent of all Irish emigrants were aged over forty, compared with as many as 83 per cent under thirty and 70 per cent between the ages of eighteen and thirty-one (Carrier and Jeffery, 1953: 53). Overall, from two-thirds to three-quarters of all European emigrants to the United

States in the period 1840–1930 were between fifteen and forty (Baines, 1991: 43).

A further common characteristic of European overseas emigration in the second half of the nineteenth century, a characteristic reflected in a declining proportion of children and the elderly and a rising proportion of females and young adults in the composition of emigrant flows, was the growing tendency for emigrants to leave as individuals rather than in family groups (Doerries, 1987: 121, 126; Erickson, 1981: 183, 185; 1990: 21–2, 39; Hvidt, 1975: 76, 91–102; Mageean, 1991: 48–9; O'Grada, 1980: 94). Admittedly, most of the empirical evidence on this matter relates solely to emigrants from northern and western parts of the continent. High rates of repatriation among emigrants from southern and eastern European countries, however, suggest that there, too, overseas emigration in the late nineteenth century was chiefly a movement of individuals rather than families, of unmarried men and women or of married men either leaving ahead of their wives and children or always intending to return.

The great majority of those who left south and east Europe for overseas destinations were drawn from rural areas and had been employed in agriculture or its ancillary occupations. Agriculturalists of one kind or another likewise made up the bulk of transatlantic emigrants from Ireland and Norway (Carrier and Jeffery, 1953: 56, 64, 66; Drake, 1979: 308; Fitzpatrick, 1980: 133–4). The typical overseas emigrant from northern and western Europe, however, had different occupational and residential origins. Less than a third of all Danish emigrants were farmers, farm labourers or farm servants (Hvidt, 1975: 103–22). Most French emigrants were artisans or industrial workers (Reinhard and Armengaud, 1968: 398). From Denmark, England, the Netherlands, Norway, Scotland and Sweden emigrants to the New World were drawn disproportionately from people who had either been born or lived for an extended period in an urban environment (Baines, 1985: 264; Deprez, 1979: 244; Erickson, 1981: 176, 187–8; 1990: 26; Flinn, 1977: 454; Hvidt, 1975: 51–2, 55–69). In the course of the late nineteenth and early twentieth centuries, as the habit of transatlantic emigration spread to southern and eastern Europe, the overall occupational composition of overseas emigrant streams became increasingly weighted in favour of the unskilled rather than the skilled. Even in countries where a tradition of overseas emigration was longer established the ratio of unskilled workers rose, in the British case, for example, probably from at least as early as the 1830s (Baines, 1985: 73; Erickson, 1990: 22, 27). Whether or not these people came mainly from the very poorest sections of working-class society requires further investigation. Evidence for England, France, Scotland and, except during the Famine and immediate post-Famine years, Ireland, however, suggests that the majority of overseas emigrants were not drawn from the ranks of the most destitute (Baines, 1985: 73–5; Erickson, 1990: 21–2, 27–8, 30, 39; Gray, 1990: 26–7; Harper, 1988: 125, 156; Ogden, 1989b: 38; O'Grada, 1980: 96; Vugt, 1988: 411–20, 426). In spite of improvements in means of international transport and the growing availability of remittance money and other forms of financial assistance, the costs of long-distance migration were often too high for those with few or no resources of their own. More work, particularly on emigrants from south and east Europe, is needed but it seems that overseas emigrants were driven more by a desire to improve their standards of life or to avoid the *possibility* of destitution than by a desire to escape from the immediate realities of poverty.

Migration

In terms of sheer numbers, migration between Europe and the non-European world was dwarfed by the vast movements of people which occurred within Europe itself. Here, too, regional experiences exhibit a number of common traits.

While the extent of movement *inside* the borders of individual European states was more limited in Ireland and on the Continent than in mainland Britain, substantial levels of internal spatial mobility, except perhaps in predominantly peasant regions and regions where feudal ties remained strong, were the norm everywhere. Data for England and Scotland indicate that even before the middle of the eighteenth century most adults changed their place of usual residence at least once during their lifetime (Clark, 1979: 66; Whyte, 1991: 87–8, 92, 101). Rates of migration in England remained high during the period 1750–1850 and rose to still higher levels during the later decades of the nineteenth century (Kuchemann, 1973: 211; Nicholas and Shergold, 1987: 160; Perry, 1969: 124; Schofield, 1970: 274; Wrigley, 1977: 26, 28). Significant levels of internal migration have likewise been documented for France, Germany, Italy, the Netherlands,

Russia and Spain. Only in France did rates of internal mobility fail to increase in the late nineteenth and early twentieth centuries (del Panta, 1979: 210; Deprez, 1979: 242; Gatrell, 1986: 61–2, 64, 97; Klessmann, 1987: 102; Langewiesche and Lenger, 1987: 91–2; Lee, 1979b: 22; 1979c: 161; Lévy-Leboyer and Lescure, 1991: 159; Livi-Bacci, 1968a: 225; Ogden and White, 1989: 2; White, 1989: 13–33).

Similarities from country to country are also apparent in the age and socio-occupational structure of internal migrants as well as in the distances they typically covered and the directions they travelled. As in the case of overseas emigrants, most internal migrants were working-class adults aged between fifteen and thirty-five (Banks, 1967–68: 283–4; Lawton, 1979: 220–1; Tilly, 1984: 45; White, 1989: 25). In 1914, as in 1750, the bulk rarely moved more than ten to twenty miles from their place of birth, though average distances did tend to increase in the course of the late nineteenth and early twentieth centuries and were always greater among the more educated and skilled than among the less educated, the semi-skilled and the unskilled (Friedlander and Roshier, 1966: 266–8; Kuchemann, 1973: 211, 218; Langewiesche and Lenger, 1987: 94; Lawton, 1978: 33; 1979: 221; Nicholas and Shergold, 1987: 162). Down to at least the middle of the eighteenth century the pattern of internal migration was diffuse and circular, essentially an ebb and flow of people from one rural area to another, with few places consistently gaining or losing on the net balance of movement. By the late eighteenth or the nineteenth century, beginning first and proceeding furthest in mainland Britain, the geography of internal migration had become more concentrated in its direction and increasingly a movement from rural to urban areas and thus from agricultural to industrial and service occupations (Clark, 1979: 59; del Panta, 1979: 209; Drake, 1979: 307; Friedlander and Roshier, 1966: 265; Lawton, 1968: 60–5; 1978: 31–3; Lee, 1979b: 162; Nicholas and Shergold, 1987: 163–4; White, 1989: 18, 21–2).

Relatively little is known about the extent and nature of migration *between* the different countries of Europe. Two generalisations, however, are possible. Firstly, within Europe, the two principal focuses of attraction were France, which drew migrants from Belgium, Italy and, to a lesser extent, Germany, Spain and Switzerland, and, from the late nineteenth century, Germany, which attracted immigrants from Denmark, Italy, the Netherlands and, above all, from Austria–Hungary and Russia. Secondly, in common with overseas migration, the scale

45

of movement from one European country to another increased in the course of the nineteenth century (Bade, 1987b: 64, 66; Ogden, 1989b: 42; Pollard, 1974: 94).

By no means all those who moved within or between European states intended their change of residence to be permanent. On the contrary, throughout the eighteenth and nineteenth centuries much intra-European population mobility was seasonal or temporary in character. By the opening of the nineteenth century complex and extensive systems of seasonal labour migration were already well established in many parts of Europe: in the Paris basin, between Provence, Languedoc and Catalonia, in Castile, Piedmont, south Tuscany, Lazio and Corsica, from Westphalia, north-west Brabant, Liège, Hainault, Picardy and parts of Eifel and Hungruck to the coastal region between Calais and Bremen, from Ireland to the British mainland, and in Scotland from the Highlands to the Lowlands and from the western Highlands to the fishing ports of counties from Aberdeenshire to Caithness in the east. In the course of the late nineteenth and early twentieth centuries levels of seasonal migration in western European countries decreased. In Germany and southern and eastern European countries like Italy and Poland, by contrast, they probably rose. As with permanent migrants, seasonal migrants were unskilled young adults moving from one agricultural system to another and, by the later nineteenth century, increasingly between agricultural and industrial or service occupations (Bade, 1987b: 68–9; Lucassen, 1987: 29–30, 32, 34–5, 40; Ogden and White, 1989: 4).

Economic implications of population growth

The economic implications of these shared characteristics of eighteenth and nineteenth-century European demographic evolution have long been a cause of controversy. On three matters only has there been any broad measure of consensus. The first is that secular and regional variations in the amount of labour available for production were determined primarily by variations in the size and rate of growth of population and owed relatively little to differentials in age structures and labour participation ratios, the other chief determinants of labour quantity. The second area of consensus relates to the origins of Europe's growing industrial labour force, which, we are told, owed more to the persistence of relatively high rates of natural increase among industrial populations themselves than to the exodus of workers from agriculture (Levine, 1984: 111–15; Tilly, 1984: 39). Thirdly, it is agreed, even by those who see population change as more of a consequence than a cause of economic change, that demographic trends should be given at least some responsibility for what happened to the economies of Europe and its constituent states between the mid-eighteenth century and 1914.

At this point, sadly, consensus collapses. Whether the contribution of population trends to eighteenth and nineteenth-century European economic development was significant or insignificant, beneficial or detrimental, are matters on which there is clearly no general agreement. For some scholars the role of demography was crucial in shaping the character of European economic growth and its regional variations. For others, impressed by the absence of a wholly consistent regional correlation between rates of population increase and rates of economic change, its role was negligible. Some see the onset and persistence of higher rates of population growth as a stimulus to economic development, others as a hindrance to economic advance.

Much of the reason for these conflicts of opinion can be traced to the intricate nature of the relationship between demography and the economy. Considered even at a purely theoretical level, there is considerable uncertainty about the way in which variations in demographic structures affect economic systems. In part this is because, even in populations of similar size and density and subject to similar rates of increase, differences in urban–rural residential distribution, in age, sex, marital, household and family composition, and in the mechanisms of fertility, mortality and migration through which changes in the rate and structure of population growth are brought about, may have widely diverging economic consequences. In part it reflects the fact that the influence of individual demographic variables on the key determinants of economic performance—the quantity and quality of the labour supply, the level and sectoral direction of demand, rates of saving, the distribution and efficiency of investment and levels of invention and innovation—themselves frequently work in contradictory ways.

On the one hand, for instance, by reducing labour costs and thus raising rates of profit and the potential for increased investment, by facilitating greater division of labour in the production processes and by enhancing levels of application and flexibility in the work force,

47

population growth and a larger labour supply work to increase rates of production. On the other, by reducing the necessity and opportunity for introducing labour-saving technology, and by making it more difficult to maintain adequate standards of health and education among workers, additions to the labour supply work to diminish the future growth of output. Where population growth is accompanied by falling labour : land ratios and rising *per capita* real incomes it will tend to increase levels of aggregate, effective demand: where it is accompanied by rising labour : land ratios and falling *per capita* real incomes levels of demand may tend to decline. If the effect of population growth on demand is positive, rates of innovation will rise; if it is negative, they will fall. By reducing the proportion of elderly in the community, intensifying inequalities in income and encouraging parents to make more careful provision for the future and children to accumulate their own resources rather than rely on inherited wealth, population growth works to raise levels of saving, thereby increasing the supply of capital potentially available for investment. At the same time, however, to the extent that a growing population is accompanied by a rise in dependence ratios, increased pressure on *per capita* incomes and a greater tendency for income to be transferred to consumption, it may lead to a decline in savings levels. By itself an increase in population will tend to swell the pool of inventors and thus increase the likelihood that invention will be productive. If, however, larger numbers are associated with falling standards of education they may just as easily result in a decline in the size of the inventing population and the capacity for productive invention.

Even in theory, therefore, it is exceedingly difficult to predict what the consequences of demographic change will be. Generally, theorists fall into one of two groups: those who take an optimistic view of man's ability to overcome the potential hindrances to economic growth caused by demographic expansion and who, accordingly, are more inclined to see population growth as a stimulus to development; and those who are more pessimistic about man's capacity to respond successfully to the pressure of population on natural resources and who are more likely to stress the advantages of low rates of population increase. From this difference in attitude towards the power of man's 'creative imagination' stems much of the theoretical uncertainty about the economic implications of demographic change.

Confusion arising from apparent contradictions in the theoretical relationship between demography and the economy is compounded when analysis shifts from a purely theoretical to an empirical basis. Because population change is only one of the many factors which together determine the behaviour of economies, the extent and direction of its influence is largely dependent on the nature of the economic, political and socio-cultural context within which it occurs. It follows from this, firstly, that we should be careful not to overstate the independence and significance of the contribution of the population variable to economic growth and, secondly, that we should not assume that similarities in demographic experience always give rise to similar economic responses. Inevitably, in a context like that of eighteenth and nineteenth-century Europe, where environmental conditions varied greatly from one area to another, the relationship between rates of population growth and rates of economic growth was never entirely consistent. Coupled with the fact that the relatively sudden and widespread increase in rates of population growth coincided both with a more gradual pace of change in the process of economic development and with the existence of numerous alternative routes to economic advance, this should be sufficient to remind us not to oversimplify the economic consequences even of such commonly shared demographic features as are known to have existed.

On the other hand, the fact that regional economies sometimes responded in different ways to similar patterns of demography does not mean that shared demographic experiences were wholly devoid of broader economic implications. One of these, clearly, was the effect that population growth had on the size of the labour supply. Except in the case of Ireland in the period following the Great Famine, in all European countries the emergence and maintenance of higher rates of population growth resulted in a massive increase in the amount of labour available for production. In late eighteenth and early nineteenth-century England, where population growth stemmed more from rising fertility than from falling mortality, the increase in the quantity of labour was accompanied by a modest decline in the proportion of the population in the economically most productive adult age groups (Wrigley and Schofield, 1981: 443–9). Generally, however, because population growth was mainly due to falling mortality, the proportion of the most productive age groups rose over time. From the later decades of the nineteenth century it was further increased by the onset of a sustained decline in fertility. Despite the loss of so many young adults to overseas emigration and a moderate, long-term decline in labour force participation ratios, the combination of population growth and rising ratios of producers to non-producers meant that more or less throughout Europe the supply of labour invariably exceeded the demand (Crisp, 1991: 254; Kenwood and Lougheed, 1982: 93–4; Milward and Saul, 1973: 520). Exceptions were usually restricted to particular sectors or regions within individual countries. On a national level modest shortages of labour for manufacturing persisted in Britain down to the end of the Napoleonic wars. Subsequently, however, labour was always in plentiful supply. In Germany labour surplus in the first half of the nineteenth century gave way to less abundant supplies of labour in the second. But, here too, outside a few industries requiring particular skills, shortages of labour were never serious (Bade, 1987a: 6; Lee, 1978: 450, 456; Milward and Saul, 1973: 427; Pierenkemper, 1987: 40–1; Tilly, 1991: 187). Only in France, where rates of population growth were unusually low, and peasant reluctance to leave agriculture was particularly stubborn, did the demands of industry for labour more persistently exceed supply, though this was less obviously the case during the first half than during the second half of the nineteenth century (Fohlen, 1973: 26; Lévy-Leboyer and Lescure, 1991: 154; Trebilcock, 1981: 164; Walle, 1979: 139). Even here the absence of widespread contemporary complaint about labour shortages seems to imply that they did not have a severely debilitating effect on the performance of the economy (Lequin, 1978: 302–3; Milward and Saul, 1973: 313).

Such, admittedly sketchy, evidence as we have on trends in the efficiency of individual workers suggests that the increase in the quantity of the labour supply was also accompanied by improvements in its quality. Falling rates of mortality and, from the later nineteenth century, increases in the average height of populations are symptomatic of a work force whose standards of health and physique were more suited to physical labour by 1914 than they had been in 1750. From the evidence of rising levels of spatial mobility summarised above, it also seems reasonable to suppose that workers became increasingly flexible in their response to regional variations in the demand for labour. By the first world war, moreover, the work force in all European countries was better educated than ever before. In France, for example, rates of literacy between the mid-nineteenth century and 1914 rose from 50 per cent to 98 per cent among males and from 25 per cent to 97 per cent among females (Lequin, 1978: 310–1). In

England, after rising during the first two thirds of the eighteenth century, male and female literacy rates remained roughly stable and in the more industrialised and densely populated urban areas may even have declined during the late eighteenth and early nineteenth centuries. From the second quarter of the nineteenth century, however, they once more began to rise, from 70 per cent (males) and 55 per cent (females) in 1850 to 99 per cent (males and females) in 1914 (Sanderson, 1983: 10–23; Schofield, 1973: 443, 446). Assessed in terms of standards of literacy, the quality of the average British worker was certainly higher in 1914 that in 1860 or earlier. The same was probably true of workers over much of the rest of Europe. Even in Russia the quality of the labour supply available to manufacturers improved in the late nineteenth and early twentieth centuries (Trebilcock, 1981: 92–4). In Germany rising standards of basic education were accompanied by notable advances in the provision of commercial, scientific and technical education (Lee, 1978: 459; Pollard, 1989: 143–62). Elsewhere—in Britain and France, for example—though more restricted, opportunities for formal, scientific and technical education were also increasing (Baines, 1981: 174; Lequin, 1978: 314–18). Contrary to what theory suggests may sometimes occur, in the case of eighteenth and nineteenth-century Europe an increase in the quantity of labour was not incompatible with improvements in labour quality.

The economic consequences of improvements in the quantity and quality of the labour supply were not, of course, always substantial or beneficial. Whatever their value at other times and places, rising standards of literacy clearly made little or no contribution to the initial phase of industrial 'take-off' in late eighteenth and early nineteenth-century Britain, and may even have been of more limited relevance than is sometimes supposed to the achievements of the German economy in the second half of the nineteenth century. In eighteenth and early nineteenth-century England, it has been argued, the progress of industrialisation was retarded by rising rates of fertility, which increased the ratio of dependants to producers, and excessive rates of population growth, which impeded the growth of effective demand for manufactures (Crouzet, 1982: 141; Hudson, 1992: 160; O'Brien, 1985: 786; Wrigley and Schofield, 1981: 443–9). At best, the contribution of population growth to the growth of demand for manufactures during the early decades of the British industrial revolution was modest (Mokyr, 1985: 101). In less developed economies the problems caused by accelerating rates of population growth in the period 1750–1850 were sometimes more serious still. In parts of Germany, Ireland, Scandinavia, Scotland and, less so, France, for example, the extent of overpopulation and surplus labour in the early decades of the nineteenth century was sufficient to prove a major hindrance to the growth of a market for manufactures and thus to economic progress (Doerries, 1987: 121–2; Douglas, 1963: 11; Grigg, 1980: 120–3, 232; Habakkuk, 1963: 613, 616–17; Marschalck, 1987: 20; Pierenkemper, 1987: 40, 56; Pollard, 1981: 57, 152; Price, 1981: 187, 194, 199). By the later decades of the century, almost everywhere in northern and western Europe, population growth no longer had a depressive effect on demand for industrial goods. In parts of southern and eastern Europe, on the other hand, the market for manufactures often continued to be restricted by the pressure of excessive population and labour on real incomes, though, as the latest evidence for Russia indicates, even here the impairment of consumption levels caused by high rates of population growth can easily be exaggerated (Crisp, 1991: 255; Milward and Saul, 1977: 22, 281, 283, 291, 332, 447, 519; Morgado, 1979: 325–6; Nadal, 1973: 537–9; Trebilcock, 1981: 311). In the case of nineteenth-century Britain, some have argued, the pace of industrial development was also impeded by the effect of excessive supplies of labour on entrepreneurial attitudes to techno-logical innovation. According to this view, shortages of labour in the period prior to the end of the Napoleonic wars had been a key factor in encouraging employers to search out and adopt much of the technology upon which the success of Britain's industrial revolution was based (Crouzet, 1982: 139; Pentland, 1972: 183–5). After 1815, when labour shortage gave way to labour surplus, the incentive to introduce more productive, capital-intensive, labour-saving techno-logies largely disappeared. Herein, we are told, lies one of the main reasons for the failure of British industry to maintain its competitiveness in the face of the standardised, machine-based, mass-production techniques developed by industry in a labour-starved United States (Habakkuk, 1962: 91–131, 196–203; 1970: 23–76).

On balance, however, most historians take a more sanguine view of the contribution of improvements in the quality and quantity of the labour supply to economic growth in eighteenth and nineteenth-century Europe. Given the low level of skill required in most occupations, advances in the quality of labour were probably less crucial to economic development than increases in the quantity of labour (Kenwood and Lougheed, 1982: 101–2). On the other hand, the significance of the former should not be entirely overlooked.

If the initial stages of Britain's industrial revolution did not need a work force substantially more literate than that of the past, it certainly required workers who were more disciplined in their work habits than they had ever been before. In the efforts of employers like Josiah Wedgwood to raise standards of timekeeping, sobriety, skill and commitment among their employees by new methods of on-the-job training and classroom education is surely proof enough that, at least for factory enterprise, some improvement in the quality of labour was essential (McKendrick, 1961). Though sometimes exaggerated, even the early British industrial revolution required *some* increase in the application of scientific and technical knowledge to facilitate technological innovation (Musson and Robinson, 1960; Sanderson, 1983: 24, 30–1; Tunzelmann, 1981: 148–51).

In the course of the second half of the nineteenth and early twentieth centuries further advances in standards of scientific and technical education, basic literacy and formal schooling, together with the availability of on-the-job training systems, continued to play a part in ensuring that improvement in the quality of human capital which became increasingly essential to economies whose industrial and commercial activities were steadily growing in scale and complexity. As the case of Germany illustrates, the provision of scientific and technical education was clearly vital to the success of industries like chemicals and electricals which were more than usually dependent on high levels of scientific and technical knowledge among the work force. Significantly, in France and Britain, where opportunities for scientific and technical education were more restricted, the performance of such industries was on the whole less satisfactory (Landes, 1970: 150–1, 343–8; Lee, 1978: 459; Lequin, 1978: 314–18; Pollard, 1989: 130–6, 143–62). How far and in what specific ways the productivity of labour was also enhanced by improvements in standards of more basic education are questions that have still to be fully resolved. By themselves, rising rates of literacy probably made only a marginal contribution to increases in labour efficiency, and may indeed have been of little more value in the second half of the nineteenth century than they had been in the first half. In any case, their contribution was almost certainly less than that which stemmed from the effect of greater

53

exposure to the discipline of the classroom on levels of worker reliability, motivation and receptivity to instruction (Baines, 1981: 173; Pollard, 1989: 136–42). Whether or not the consequences for labour productivity of rising standards of education and more extensive participation in formal schooling were as crucial as those accruing from the skills and habits imparted by on-the-job training programmes is more difficult to determine. 'Learning by doing' practices, either in the form of institutionalised apprenticeship systems or more loosely structured procedures of observation and instruction, have always played an important part in determining levels of labour productivity, particularly in economies like that of Victorian and Edwardian Britain where the presence of unusually large numbers of skilled and experienced workers made on-the-job training procedures easier to implement and sustain. The problem is that very little detailed research has been done on the nature of these 'in-house' training techniques and the extent to which their nature varied both over time and from one economy to another. In view of this, it is impossible to comment in any meaningful, general way on the precise extent of their influence. What is clear, however, is the fact that for at least some industries the returns to efficiency generated by well established 'learning by doing' methods were considerable, and sometimes the vital ingredient in ensuring competitive success. There is no better example than that of the British shipbuilding industry, where traditional methods of on-the-job training were sufficient to produce levels of productivity far in excess of those achieved by competitors whose labour forces not only possessed superior levels of formal scientific and technical knowledge but also utilised more sophisticated technologies (Lorenz, 1991: 59–60; Pollard, 1957; Robertson, 1974).

No less essential to the successful growth of European economies in the late eighteenth and nineteenth centuries was the increase which occurred in rates of spatial labour mobility. There were, of course, occasions when migration merely worked to prop up existing economic and social systems and in doing so delayed the process of change. As attested by the migration of female workers into the silk industry of the Ardèche region of France (Ogden, 1989a: 140), this was especially the case with seasonal migration. On other occasions, as in Russia and, perhaps, France, either because of low rates of population growth or the presence of serious psychological, material or institutional barriers to mobility, levels of migration were too low to have had more than a marginally beneficial impact on the flexibility of the labour supply and thus on the pace of economic growth. Normally, however, levels of labour migration, particularly by the later decades of the nineteenth century, were high enough to have had significant and invariably positive effects on levels of output and productivity. Apart from their contribution to rising levels of aggregate demand, high and increasing rates of labour mobility facilitated the growth of European economies by adjusting regional imbalances in the supply of and demand for labour, speeding the diffusion of new technology, knowledge and skills, providing industry with essential supplies of labour at relatively low opportunity cost and advancing general levels of labour productivity through the transfer of workers from sectors with limited growth potential to sectors with a greater capacity for development (Kenwood and Lougheed, 1982: 92, 99, 101; Lee, 1979a: 22; 1979b: 162–3; Milward and Saul, 1973: 167; 1977: 44; Pollard, 1981: 147; Trebilcock, 1981: 54–5; Weaver, 1974: 74).

As illustrated by the spread of mechanisation in the agricultural sectors of the economies of Britain, France and the Netherlands, there were times, even in the second half of the nineteenth century, when the lack of an adequate supply of labour stimulated rates of technological innovation (Lucassen, 1987: 183; Mutch, 1981: 131; O'Grada, 1981: 185; Price, 1981: 212). To go beyond this to suggest that most eighteenth and nineteenth-century European economies would have benefited from slower growth in the size of their labour supplies, however, is to run the risk of distorting what was then the usual nature of the relationship between the quantity of labour and the pace of technological and economic advance. To argue, for example, that the new technologies of the British 'industrial revolution' originated solely, or even chiefly, from a desire to save on scarce supplies of labour tends to lose sight of the fact that in eighteenth and early nineteenth-century Britain rates of technological innovation were greater at times of relative labour abundance, not at times of labour shortage. In the main, the improved technologies of the industrial revolution were more a response to rising demand or deficiencies in the supply of raw materials and methods of distribution than to deficiencies in the supply of labour. *Ultimately*, indeed, the new technologies of the period of early industrialisation increased rather than decreased the demand for labour. Had the labour supply remained as constricted as in the first half of the eighteenth century, and had the size of the population not been large

55

enough to permit the degree of diversification and interaction in economic activity necessary for growth, the British industrial revolution would not have occurred when it did (Chambers, 1972: 145–57; Engelmann and Wanner, 1969: 249–51; Rostow, 1975: 16–17, 181; Sullivan, 1989: 445–6; Weaver, 1974: 90).

Recent work on the supposed advantages of labour shortage for the growth of the economy of the United States in the nineteenth century likewise largely fails to confirm the claims made for it. To confirm labour shortage as the principal cause of differences between American and British industrial technologies would require unequivocal proof that the real costs of labour, unskilled–skilled wage differentials and the costs of labour relative to capital were all lower in Britain than in the United States and that American technological supremacy was due chiefly to the substitution of capital-intensive for labour-intensive methods. For none of these assumptions, however, is the empirical evidence conclusive. Data on variations in real labour costs from one nineteenth-century economy to another are too flimsy to permit firm conclusions. Some historians believe that unskilled–skilled wage differentials in the United States were relatively small (Zabler, 1972, 1973): others that they were not (Adams, 1970, 1973). According to some the cost of borrowing was higher, not lower in the United States than in Britain, and it was therefore British rather than American entrepreneurs who had the greater incentive and opportunity to introduce capital-intensive technology (Asher, 1972; Temin, 1966). While a number of American industries did display a pronounced labour-saving bias in their choice of technologies, others chose their technologies more for their capital-saving or, given the abundance of raw materials, material-using properties. In reality, it seems, technological innovation in the United States during the nineteenth century, and the high rates of industrial growth which accrued from it, originated only in part from a need to economise on resources of labour. Much more significant was the influence of rising demand and other supply conditions, among them the richness of the raw material base, foreign investment, the role of the state in creating an environment sympathetic to private enterprise and the existence of a social structure and cultural milieu suited to productive endeavour. Nineteenth-century American economic development cannot be adequately explained without reference to the full panoply of supply and demand conditions (Lindstrom, 1983). Among these the contribution of labour shortage was probably far outweighed by that of increasing supplies of labour and the availability of a work force sufficient in size (and quality) to meet the requirements of producers. In nineteenth-century America, as in late eighteenth and early nineteenth-century Britain, the spread of improved technology, even that initially prompted by a desire to save on labour, necessitated a substantial increase in the absolute size of the labour supply. Significantly, in those parts of the United States where this was not forthcoming, the pace of technological innovation was restricted (Earle and Hoffman, 1980). The persistence of a tradition of labour-saving innovation, established during the period of high money wages and high rates of labour mobility in the early nineteenth century, certainly helps to account for *some* of the more productive advances in US technology. But it does not explain the majority. Even those innovations which originated largely as a response to labour shortage were adopted widely only when, in the course of the second half of the century, the maintenance of high rates of population growth increased the size of the work force and decreased the real cost of the labour needed to utilise them (Lebergott, 1964: 253). The development of the nineteenth-century US economy owed more to population growth, and the contribution this made to rising levels of demand and the availability of a cheaper, more flexible labour supply, than it has been customary to suppose.

In its effect on the growth and structure of output, the persistence of high rates of population increase throughout the late eighteenth and nineteenth centuries was more beneficial to the economy of the United States than to the economies of Europe. In the former, where overpopulation was never a problem, economic progress was never threatened by an excess of numbers. In the latter, as we have seen, high rates of population growth sometimes outran the capacity of economies to generate the necessary resources and employment opportunities to sustain larger numbers even at existing income levels. The part played by the demographic variable in provoking economic retardation, however, should not be exaggerated. Invariably, demographically induced periods of economic crisis were caused not so much by population growth itself as by inadequacies in cultural, institutional or socio-political arrangements which prevented a satisfactory response to population increase. What mattered most in the failure of parts of Ireland, Finland and the Scottish Highlands to avoid the famine-induced calamaties of the 1840s, for example, was not overpopulation *per se* but inequalities in resource distribution, inefficient methods of famine relief and an absence of alternative opportunities for employment outside agriculture due, *inter alia*, to shortages of raw materials, restrictive government policies or the conservative nature of prevailing social structures, systems of land tenure and attitudes to risk-taking innovation (Anderson, 1988: 68, 80; Grigg, 1980: 138–9; Mokyr, 1980: 160, 164–5). In any case, severe crises of overpopulation in Europe were rare and, as the century progressed, becoming rarer. Generally, in Europe as in the United States, higher rates of population growth in the late eighteenth and nineteenth centuries were a force for good, not ill, stimulating levels of demand, reducing the real costs of labour and thus raising levels of profit and the potential for investment, encouraging the spread of improved agricultural systems, new technologies and new industries and facilitating improvements in transport, communications, financial and other services.

The persistence of high rates of population growth between 1750 and 1914 also had implications for the sectoral composition of European economies. On the eve of the first world war, with their relatively large industrial and relatively small service sectors, the economies of the more advanced parts of Europe differed markedly from those of developed and developing parts of the non-European world. To some extent this bias in favour of manufacturing reflected the survival of traditional 'artisanal' methods of production and the greater antipathy of European consumers to standardised, mass-produced goods. But it also owed something to two distinct features of Europe's demographic experience: first, the unusually high spatial density of European populations, which worked to restrict levels of *per capita* expenditure on items like education, health, public administration and transport; and, second, the relative abundance of the European labour supply, which, in tandem with relative shortages of raw materials, encouraged a preference for labour-intensive rather than capital-intensive methods of industrial production (Kaeble, 1989).

Economic implications of emigration

That the economic consequences of European population growth between the late eighteenth century and the outbreak of the first world war were more often beneficial than detrimental owes everything to the fact that in most areas and at most times the size and rate of growth of population fell below the aggregate level and rate of growth of output. Some scholars believe that this had been the case from at least as early as the sixteenth century (Goodman and Honeyman, 1988: 13–15, 19–21): others that it emerged only in the course of the late eighteenth or early nineteenth centuries (Schofield, 1983: 270–1, 273, 275). All, however, agree that by the middle of the nineteenth century, though sometimes precarious, a surplus of output over population was the norm in most parts of Europe. In contrast to what had so often happened in the past, the result was rising, not falling, levels of *per capita* real income and even higher levels of demand and employment.

It follows that crucial to any explanation of eighteenth and nineteenth-century European economic development are those factors which together enabled output to increase more rapidly than population. Predominant among these was a complex mix of changing cultural, institutional and political circumstances which ensured that levels of productivity and output grew more quickly and persistently than ever before. There was, however, another contributory factor at work: the growing ability of European societies to curb the rate of population growth. It has often been argued that one of the chief reasons for the relatively early modernisation of the British economy was the presence in the seventeenth and eighteenth centuries of a 'low-pressure' demographic regime combining abnormally low rates of fertility and mortality. Unique to mainland Britain, this reduced the pressure of population growth on resources and helped maintain *per capita* real incomes at levels sufficient to provide the market necessary for industrial 'take-off' (Wrigley and Schofield, 1983: 184). In the course of the nineteenth century the capacity for holding fertility rates below the point at which they exceeded the capacity for generating employment and resources spread to other European societies. Albeit imperfectly, this was first achieved in the more advanced economies of northern and western Europe through the adjustment of nuptiality rates and, in a few areas, by rudimentary techniques of birth control within marriage. From the later decades of the century, in southern and eastern as well as in northern and western Europe, the ability of societies to restrict fertility rates and thus rates of population growth was further enhanced by the more widespread adoption of contraceptive methods. As fertility levels declined more and more European societies found it possible to maintain *per capita* real incomes at levels sufficient to ensure the volumes of demand, saving and investment essential for sustained economic growth.

For most of the period with which we are concerned, however, the demographic mechanism most responsible for keeping the size and rate of growth of populations more or less within the limits set by the level and growth of output was migration. It is no accident that, at precisely the time when rates of population growth rose to unprecedented heights, rates of geographical mobility both within and between European states and between Europe and the non-European world also rose dramatically.

It is generally agreed that migration is usually beneficial to the economies which gain rather than lose people. On the consequences of migration for those economies in which the number of emigrants consistently exceeds the number of immigrants there is less unanimity. For a thorough assessment of the effects of net emigration on the economies of those regions from which it occurred we require a range of information that is rarely available and a sophistication of analysis that is rarely feasible, particularly in a historical context. Ideally, data are needed not only on the number of emigrants and their age, sex, marital and socio-occupational composition but also on their levels of skill, their attitudes to work and the extent to which emigration is accompanied by repatriation of earnings, new ideas and skills and different work habits. Each element must then be considered in relation to its likely effect on the quantity and quality of the labour supply, levels of *per capita* income, saving and investment, the aggregate level and sectoral distribution of demand, rates of invention and innovation and the region's balance of payments. In the context of eighteenth and nineteenth-century Europe, an analysis of such magnitude and complexity has so far proved impossible to carry out. Inevitably, the result is an always partial, and at times inconsistent, interpretation of the contribution of net emigration to European economic growth. What follows, therefore, can do no more than identify the interpretation currently favoured by the majority of scholars.

It would be wrong to suppose that net emigration was always beneficial to the economies from which it originated. In the first place, by easing the pressure of population growth on incomes, land and other resources, net out-migration conceivably delayed the widespread adoption of modern family limitation techniques, themselves a more permanent, effective and less traumatic method of combating the threat of excessive numbers. Secondly, as may have occurred in post-Famine Ireland, by alleviating the burden of overpopulation, net emigration may have prolonged the survival of traditional methods of economic and social organisation beyond the point at which they had ceased to be productive while, at the same time, discouraging the spread of more efficient forms of production that might otherwise have emerged in response to the need to provide for larger numbers (Douglas, 1963: 15–17; Fitzpatrick, 1980: 126–17; O'Grada, 1973: 63, 71). Thirdly, as in the cases of Ireland after the Great Famine, Austria–Hungary by the 1880s and Sweden during the 1880s and 1900s, the tendency for emigrant streams to be composed predominantly of young adults and, usually, of males resulted in domestic populations whose age and sex structure were more heavily weighted in favour of the physically less productive than they would otherwise have been (Fitzpatrick, 1980: 127; Gross, 1973: 276; Milward and Saul, 1973: 168). In addition, in countries like Austria–Hungary, Ireland, Italy and Spain, to the extent that emigrant flows were increasingly composed of individuals rather than families and, more contentiously, of men and women who were not generally amongst the most destitute or least educated, skilled and enterprising, net emigration may have denuded the sending economies of at least some of those who were most receptive to change and most likely to contribute to rising levels of output and demand (Baines, 1991: 41; Hutchinson, 1970: 509; Livi-Bacci, 1977: 282; Trebilcock, 1981: 309–10). Finally, to assume that the increase in repatriated earnings and return emigration which accompanied the rise of European emigration overseas was always advantageous to the sending economies is also unwise. In some cases, like Denmark, Ireland, Italy, Finland, Norway and Sweden, the level of repatriated earnings was certainly large enough to have had substantial economic consequences. In others, such as Austria–Hungary, England, Germany and Spain, it was negligible and therefore probably of little economic significance. In any case, the economic effects of repatriated earnings depend on how they were used, and on this we have all too little information. If, as seems probable, repatriated earnings were spent largely on funding additional emigration, their direct impact on the performance of European economies would have been modest and the extent and direction of the impact restricted primarily to the effect of further emigration on the relationship between the size of the population and the level of available employment and resources.

Moreover, whether return migration was beneficial or detrimental depends on whether or not those who returned came back with the kind of newly learned skills which could be easily integrated into the requirements of their native economies. Since, especially in the case of southern and eastern European countries, repatriants were often returning to agricultural occupations from urban industrial employment overseas, this was clearly not always the case. Overall, we know too little of the character and subsequent history of return emigrant flows to be able to say for certain whether their contribution to the quality of the labour force, to the potential for innovation and to levels of effective demand was, on balance, positive or negative.

Despite these uncertainties and exceptions, the consensus of opinion among historians of the period is that, on the whole, economies with a net outflow benefited from it. Even in the case of Ireland, the most commonly cited example of the problems of mass emigration, net emigration can be seen as a stimulus rather than a hindrance to growth, reducing regional income inequalities, increasing the average size of farms and helping to raise *per capita* real wages and, through the medium of repatriated earnings, national income. Whatever its short-term disadvantages, seasonal emigration from Ireland to the British mainland, by familiarising migrants with the better opportunities available elsewhere, lessened the attachment to the motherland and encouraged emigration of a more permanent kind, with all the benefits this had both for those who left and for those who stayed. Despite the loss of so many active young adults to overseas destinations, emigration did *not* leave Ireland short of a sufficient supply of energetic and enterprising manpower. If the Irish economy failed to respond dynamically to the effect of emigration in easing the pre-Famine problem of overpopulation, the explanations are more likely to be found in non-demographic than in demographic factors.

Outside Ireland the typical impact of net emigration on the sending economies was more obviously beneficial. Directly, emigration contributed to improvements in methods of international transport and commercial organisation and stimulated exports. Indirectly, it helped overcome, or at least alleviate, the problem of excess labour that existed in various parts of Europe at one time or another during the eighteenth and nineteenth centuries and, in doing so, increased the potential for economic growth by protecting levels of income and demand from the harmful effects of what might otherwise have been unduly high rates of population growth (Bade, 1987a: 6: Gould, 1979: 667; Marschalck, 1987: 21; Milward and Saul, 1973: 167; Pierenkemper, 1987: 41; Pollard, 1981: 152–3; Trebilcock, 1981: 309–10). To suggest that net emigration left European economies short of labour and demand is to distort the normal reality. Cases like Austria–Hungary and Spain, where emigrants departed from a generally understocked labour market, were not typical. Invariably, those who emigrated came from regions where the stock of labour exceeded requirements, and this remained so even in areas which, by the late nineteenth century, were 'emigration-saturated' and in which serious imbalances between the supply of and demand for labour had long since disappeared. In spite of being weighted in favour of males rather than females, and in favour of young adults rather than children and the elderly, emigrants do not appear to have left behind economies lacking an adequate supply of labour in the most productive age groups.

Nor is it likely that levels of effective demand in European economies would have been higher had rates of net emigration been lower. Although rarely a pauper, the typical emigrant was someone who was either already hovering uncomfortably close to the poverty line or who had good reason to fear that his standard of living might be severely reduced in the near future. Without the option of emigration there seems little reason to doubt that throughout Europe the absolute and relative size of the pauper or near-pauper population would have increased and that average *per capita* levels of demand would have declined as a result.

Emigration was not, of course, solely, or perhaps even mainly, induced by a desire to escape from actual or potential material deprivation at home. For some it provided an opportunity to flee from political, racial or religious persecution and, as such, was not necessarily advantageous to sender economies. It also owed much to the lure of better economic opportunities elsewhere. Since most of those who emigrated for economic reasons did so on the basis of at least a crude comparison between material prospects at home and abroad, in most cases it is impossible to tell whether emigrants were responding primarily to the forces of push or pull. To the extent that pull considerations weighed more heavily, emigration benefited sending economies less than would have been the case had it been motivated solely or predominantly by the push of overpopulation and economic crisis at home. On the other hand, the importance of this latter

63

influence should not be understated. The fact that the correlation between levels of overpopulation and rates of net emigration was not always as close as might be expected does not mean that a desire to escape from poverty or its perceived threat was unimportant. In addition to the influence exerted by variations in the attractiveness of those economies which received emigrants, and in the significance of push factors of a non-economic type, secular and regional differences in the amount of emigration always depended on more than just the level of poverty. They varied widely in accordance with the influence exerted by variations in household structures, inheritance customs, standards of education, methods of transport, awareness of opportunities elsewhere and the extent of previous emigration. Often, too, levels of poverty were themselves too extreme to permit escape. The lack of a close and consistent statistical relationship between measures of overpopulation, on the one hand, and net emigration, on the other, should not be taken as proof that the push of actual or potential economic hardship was not a widespread motive for emigration. To the extent that emigration in eighteenth and nineteenth-century Europe *was* a flight from poverty or its immediate threat it must have played its part in lowering the barriers to economic progress in those areas from which it originated.

The relationship between migration and economic growth is an intricate, two-way process. Through its effect on rates of population increase, on the density and spatial distribution of populations, on systems of transport and communication, on levels of technological innovation and income, on standards of education and natural resource use, economic growth itself acts as a powerful stimulus to migratory movement. In turn, however, economic performance is also affected by the extent and character of migration. By rearranging the geography of population within Europe and between Europe and the New World migration played a vital role in lessening the severity and duration of regional imbalances in the supply of, and demand, for labour, and in ensuring a more efficient international distribution of capital and technology. By 1914, thanks in no small measure to the vast international flow and redistribution of population, the world economy was more extensive and more efficiently integrated than ever before, with both sender and receiver economies benefiting from the higher levels of output and income generated by an improved international alignment of natural resources and the labour needed to utilise them. Had it not been for the contribution made by international migration to lower rates of European population growth, to the development of new markets and sources of food and raw material supply overseas and to the additional wealth generated by the growing demands of the world economy for capital and commercial services, the pace of economic growth in late nineteenth and early twentieth-century Europe would certainly have been slower.

Conclusion

Despite the existence of pronounced regional differences in the details of its timing and extent, the fact that most of the constituent states of late eighteenth and nineteenth-century Europe shared a common experience of what in their terms were sustained, historically high rates of population increase cannot be denied. Much of the explanation, of course, can be traced to the direct or indirect effects of the drastic changes which simultaneously occurred in the economies of many of the countries of Europe and the non-European world. In turn, however, the persistence of higher rates of population increase itself influenced the pace and character of European economic growth. It has been argued in this chapter that, on balance, this influence was beneficial. But it might so easily have been otherwise. Had it not been for the part played by emigration in ridding Europe of much of its excess of births over deaths, a contribution made possible by a combination of rising demand for labour in the developing economies of the New World and improvements in methods of international transport and communications, rates of population growth might well have reached levels too high to do anything other than impede economic progress. To suggest that this might have been avoided by the earlier and more extensive adoption of controls over fertility than was the case is perhaps to overstate the capacity of most European societies to undertake such a fundamental transformation in their family formation practices sooner than they did.

References

Adams, D. (1970), 'Some evidence on English and American wage rates', *Journal of Economic History*, 30 (3).
Adams, S. (1973), 'Wage rates in the iron industry: a comment', *Explorations in Economic History*, 11 (1).

Anderson, M. (1979), 'Denmark', in W. R. Lee, ed., *European Demography and Economic Growth*. London, Croom Helm.

Anderson, M. (1988), *Population Change in North-western Europe, 1750–1850*. London, Macmillan.

Asher, E. (1972), 'Industrial efficiency and biased technical change in American and British manufacturing: the case of textiles in the nineteenth century', *Journal of Economic History*, 32 (2).

Bade, K. J. (1987a), 'Introduction', in K. J. Bade, ed., *Population, Labour and Migration in Nineteenth and Twentieth Century Germany*. Leamington Spa, Berg.

Bade, K. J. (1987b), 'Labour migration and the state: Germany from the late nineteenth century to the onset of the Great Depression', in K. J. Bade, ed., *Population, Labour and Migration in Nineteenth and Twentieth Century Germany*. Leamington Spa, Berg.

Bade, K. J. (1987c), 'Transatlantic emigration and continental immigration: the German experience past and present', in K. J. Bade, ed., *Population, Labour and Migration in Nineteenth and Twentieth Century Germany*. Leamington Spa, Berg.

Baines, D. (1981), 'The labour supply and the labour market, 1860–1914', in R. C. Floud and D. N. McCloskey, eds., *The Economic History of Modern Britain since 1700* 2, *1860–the 1970s*. Cambridge, Cambridge University Press.

Baines, D. (1985), *Migration in a Mature Economy: Emigration and Internal Migration in England and Wales, 1861–1900*. Cambridge, Cambridge University Press.

Baines, D. (1991), *Emigration from Europe, 1815–1930*. London, Macmillan.

Banks, J. A. (1967–8), 'Population change and the Victorian city', *Victorian Studies*, 11 (3).

Carrier, N. H., and Jeffery, J. R. (1953), *External Migration*, General Register Office Studies on Medical and Population Subjects 6, London, HMSO.

Chambers, J. D. (1972), *Population, Economy and Society in Pre-industrial England*. Oxford, Oxford University Press.

Clark, C. (1968), *Population Growth and Land Use*. London, Macmillan.

Clark, P. (1979), 'Migration in England during the late seventeenth and early eighteenth centuries', *Past and Present*, 83.

Crisp, O. (1991), 'Russia', in R. Sylla and G. Toniolo, eds., *Patterns of European Industrialization: the Nineteenth Century*. London, Routledge.

Crouzet, F. (1982), *The Victorian Economy*. London, Methuen.

Deprez, P. (1979), 'The Low Countries', in W. R. Lee, ed., *European Demography and Economic Growth*. London, Croom Helm.

Doerries, R. R. (1987), 'Gernal transatlantic migration from the early nineteenth century to the outbreak of World War II', in K. J. Bade, ed., *Population, Labour and Migration in Nineteenth and Twentieth Century Germany*. Leamington Spa, Berg.

Douglas, J. H. N. (1963), 'Emigration and Irish peasant life', *Ulster Folklife*, 9.

Drake, M. (1979), 'Norway', in W. R. Lee, ed., *European Demography and Economic Growth*. London, Croom Helm.

Earle, C., and Hoffman, R. (1980), 'The foundations of the modern economy: agriculture and the costs of labour in the United States and England, 1800–60', *American Historical Review*, 85 (5).

Engleman, H. O., and Wanner, R. A. (1969), 'Population size and industrial technology', *American Journal of Economics and Sociology*, 28 (3).

Erickson, C. (1981), 'Emigration from the British Isles to the USA in 1831', *Population Studies*, 35 (2).

66

Erickson, C. (1989), 'Emigration from the British Isles to the USA in 1841' I, *Population Studies*, 43 (3).

Erickson, C. (1990), 'Emigration from the British Isles to the USA in 1841' II, *Population Studies*, 44 (1).

Falkus, M. (1972), *The Industrialization of Russia, 1700–1914*. London, Macmillan.

Fitzpatrick, D. (1980), 'Irish emigration in the later nineteenth century', *Irish Historical Studies*, 22 (2).

Flinn, M., ed. (1977), *Scottish Population History from the Seventeenth Century to the 1930s*. Cambridge, Cambridge University Press.

Fohlen, C. (1973), 'France, 1700–1914', in C. M. Cipolla, ed., *The Emergence of Industrial Societies* I, Fontana Economic History of Europe 4. Glasgow, Fontana/Collins.

Friedlander, D., and Roshier, R. (1966), 'A study of internal migration in England and Wales' I, 'Geographic patterns of internal migration, 1851–1951', *Population Studies*, 19 (3).

Gatrell, P. (1986), *The Tsarist Economy, 1850–1917*. London, Batsford.

Gille, H. (1949–50), 'The demographic history of northern European countries in the eighteenth century', *Population Studies*, 3.

Goodman, J., and Honeyman, K. (1988), *Gainful Pursuits: the Making of Industrial Europe, 1600–1914*. London, Edward Arnold.

Gould, J. D. (1979), 'European intercontinental emigration, 1815–1914: patterns and causes', *Journal of European Economic History*, 8 (3).

Gould, J. D. (1980), 'European interncontinental emigration the road home: return migration from the USA', *Journal of European Economic History*, 9 (1).

Gray, M. (1990), *Scots on the Move: Scots Migrants, 1750–1914*. Economic and Social History Society of Scotland.

Grigg, D. B. (1980), *Population Growth and Agrarian Change*. Cambridge, Cambridge University Press.

Gross, N. T. (1973), 'The Habsburg monarchy, 1750–1914', in C. M. Cipolla, ed., *The Emergence of Industrial Societies* (1), Fontana Economic History of Europe 4. London: Fontana/Collins.

Habakkuk, H. J. (1963), 'Economic development and the population problem: population problems and European economic development in the late eighteenth and nineteenth centuries', *American Economic Review Supplement*, 2.

Habakkuk, H. J. (1962), *American and British Technology in the Nineteenth Century*. Cambridge: Cambridge University Press.

Habakkuk, H. J. (1970), 'The economic effects of labour scarcity', in S. B. Saul, ed., *Technological Change: the United States and Britain in the Nineteenth Century*. London, Methuen.

Harper, M. (1988), *Emigration from North-east Scotland* 1. Aberdeen, Aberdeen University Press.

Hudson, P. (1992), *The Industrial Revolution*. London, Edward Arnold.

Hutchinson, B. (1970), 'On the study of non-economic factors in Irish economic development', *Economic and Social Review* (Dublin), 1 (4).

Hvidt, K. (1975), *Flight to America: the Social Background of 30,000 Danish Emigrants*. New York, Academic Press.

Kaeble, H. (1989), 'Was Prometheus most unbound in Europe? The labour force in Europe during the late XIXth and XXth centuries', *Journal of European Economic History*, 18 (1).

Kenwood, A. G., and Lougheed, A. L. (1982), *The Growth of the International Economy, 1820–1960*. London, Croom Helm.

Klessmann, C. (1987), 'Long-distance migration, integration and segregation of an ethnic minority in industrial Germany: the case of the Ruhr Poles', in K. J. Bade, ed., *Population, Labour and Migration in Nineteenth and Twentieth Century Germany*. Leamington Spa, Berg.

Knodel, J. E. (1974), *The Decline of Fertility in Germany, 1871–1939*. Princeton, N. J., Princeton University Press.

Kuchemann, C. F. (1973), 'A demographic and genetic study of a group of Oxfordshire villages', in M. Drake, ed., *Applied Historical Studies*. London, Methuen.

Kunitz, S. J. (1983), 'Speculations on the European mortality decline', *Economic History Review*, 2nd ser., 36 (3).

Landes, D. S. (1970), *The Unbound Prometheus: Technological Change and Industrial Development in Western Europe from 1750 to the Present*. Cambridge, Cambridge University Press.

Langewiesche, D., and Lenger, F. (1987), 'Internal migration: persistence and mobility', in K. J. Bade, ed., *Population, Labour and Migration in Nineteenth and Twentieth Century Germany*. Leamington Spa, Berg.

Lawton, R. (1968), 'Population changes in England and Wales in the later nineteenth century', *Transactions of the Institute of British Geographers*, 44.

Lawton, R. (1978), 'Regional population trends in England and Wales, 1750–1971', in J. Hobcraft and P. Rees, eds., *Regional Demographic Development*. London, Croom Helm.

Lawton, R. (1979), 'Mobility in nineteenth-century cities', *Geographical Journal*, 145 (2).

Lebergott, S. (1964), *Manpower in Economic Growth: the American Record since 1800*. New York, McGraw-Hill.

Lee, J. J. (1978), 'Labour in German industrialisation', in P. Mathias and M. Postan, eds., *The Cambridge Economic History of Europe* 7, 1. Cambridge, Cambridge University Press.

Lee, W. R., ed. (1979a), *European Demography and Economic Growth*. London: Croom Helm.

Lee, W. R. (1979b), 'Introduction', in W. R. Lee, *European Demography and Economic Growth*. London, Croom Helm.

Lee, W. R. (1979c), 'Germany', in W. R. Lee, *European Demography and Economic Growth*. London, Croom Helm.

Lequin, Y. (1978), 'Labour in the French economy since the revolution', in P. Mathias and M. M. Postan, eds., *The Cambridge Economic History of Europe* 7, 1. Cambridge, Cambridge University Press.

Levine, D. (1984), 'Production, reproduction and the proletarian family in England, 1500–1851', in D. Levine, ed., *Proletarianisation and Family History*. Orlando, Fla., Academic Press.

Lévy-Leboyer, M., and Lescure, M. (1991), 'France', in R. Sylla and G. Toniolo, *Patterns of European Industrialization: the Nineteenth Century*. London, Routledge.

Lindstrom, D. (1983), 'Macroeconomic growth: the United States in the nineteenth century', *Journal of Interdisciplinary History*, 13 (4).

Livi-Bacci, M. (1968a), 'Fertility and nuptiality changes in Spain from the late eighteenth to the early twentieth century' I, *Population Studies*, 22 (1).

Livi-Bacci, M. (1968b), 'Fertility and population growth in Spain in the eighteenth and nineteenth centuries', *Daedalus*, spring.

Livi-Bacci, M. (1977), *A History of Italian Fertility During the Last Two Centuries*. Princeton, N. J., Princeton University Press.

Lorenz, E. H. (1991), *Economic Decline in Britain: the Shipbuilding Industry, 1890–1970*. Oxford, Clarendon Press.

Lucassen, J. (1987), *Migrant Labour in Europe, 1600–1900*. Beckenham, Croom Helm.

McKendrick, N. (1961), 'Josiah Wedgwood and factory discipline', *Historical Journal*, 4 (1).

Mageean, D. M. (1991), 'From Irish countryside to American city: the settlement and mobility of Ulster emigrants in Philadelphia', in C. G. Pooley and I. D. Whyte, eds., *Migrants, Emigrants and Immigrants: a Social History of Migration*. London, Routledge.

Marschalck, P. (1987), 'The Age of Demographic Transition: mortality and fertility', in K. J. Bade, ed., *Population, Labour and Migration in Nineteenth and Twentieth Century Germany*. Leamington Spa, Berg.

Milward, A. S., and Saul, S. B. (1973), *The Economic Development of Continental Europe, 1780–1870*. London, Allen & Unwin.

Milward, A. S., and Saul, S. B. (1977), *The Development of the Economies of Continental Europe, 1850–1914*. London, Allen & Unwin.

Mitchell, B. R. (1975), *European Historical Statistics, 1750–1970*. London, Macmillan.

Mokyr, J. (1980), 'Malthusian models and Irish history', *Journal of Economic History*, 40 (1).

Mokyr, J. (1985), 'Demand *v.* supply in the industrial revolution', in J. Mokyr, ed., *The Economics of the Industrial Revolution*. London, Allen & Unwin.

Morgado, N. A. (1979), 'Portugal', in W. R. Lee, *European Demography and Economic Growth*. London, Croom Helm.

Musson, A. E., and Robinson, E. (1960), 'Science and industry in the late eighteenth century', *Economic History Review*, 2nd ser., 13 (2).

Mutch, A. (1981), 'The mechanisation of the harvest in south-west Lancashire, 1850–1914', *Agricultural History Review*, 29 (2).

Nadal, J. (1973), 'Spain, 1830–1914', in C. M. Cipolla, ed., *The Emergence of Industrial Societies* 2, The Fontana Economic History of Europe 4. London, Fontana/Collins.

Nicholas, S., and Shergold, P. R. (1987), 'Internal migration in England, 1818–39', *Journal of Historical Geography*, 13 (2).

O'Brien, P. K. (1985), 'Agriculture and the home market for English industry, 1660–1820', *English Historical Review*, C, 397.

Ogden, P. E. (1989a), 'Industry, mobility and the evolution of rural society in the Ardèche in the later nineteenth and twentieth centuries', in P. E. Ogden and P. E. White, eds., *Migrants in Modern France*. London, Unwin Hyman.

Ogden, P. E. (1989b), 'International migration in the nineteenth and twentieth centuries', in P. E. Ogden and P. E. White, eds., *Migrants in Modern France*. London, Unwin Hyman.

Ogden, P. E., and White, P. E. (1989), 'Migration in later nineteenth and twentieth-century France: the social and economic context', in P. E. Ogden and P. E. White, eds., *Migrants in Modern France*. London, Unwin Hyman.

O'Grada, C. (1973), 'Seasonal migration and post-Famine adjustment in the west of Ireland', *Studia Hibernica*, 13.

O'Grada, C. (1980), 'Irish emigration to the United States in the nineteenth century', in D. N. Doyle and O. D. Edwards, eds., *America and Ireland, 1776–1976: the American Identity and the Irish Connection*. Westport, Conn., Greenwood Press.

O'Grada, C. (1981), 'Agricultural decline, 1860–1914', in R. Floud and D. N. McCloskey, *The Economic History of Britain since 1700* 2. Cambridge, Cambridge University Press.

Panta, L. del (1979), 'Italy', in W. R. Lee, ed., *European Demography and Economic Growth*. London, Croom Helm.

Pentland, H. C. (1972), 'Population and labour growth in Britain in the eighteenth century', in D. E. C. Eversley, ed., *Third International Conference of Economic History*. Paris, Mouton.

Perry, P. J. (1969), 'Working-class isolation and mobility in rural Dorset, 1837–1936: a study of marriage distances', *Transactions of the Institute of British Geographers*, 46.

Pierenkemper, T. (1987), 'Labour market, labour force and standard of living: from agriculture to industry', in K. J. Bade, ed., *Population, Labour and Migration in Nineteenth and Twentieth Century Germany*. Leamington Spa, Berg.

Pollard, S. (1957), 'British and world shipbuilding, 1870–1914: a study in comparative costs', *Journal of Economic History*, XVII.

Pollard, S. (1974), *European Economic Integration, 1815–1970*. London, Thames & Hudson.

Pollard, S. (1981), *Peaceful Conquest: the Industrialization of Europe, 1760–1970*. Oxford, Oxford University Press.

Pollard, S. (1989), *Britain's Prime and Britain's Decline: the British Economy, 1870–1914*. London, Edward Arnold.

Price, R. (1981), *An Economic History of Modern France, 1730–1914*. London, Macmillan.

Reinhard, M., and Armengaud, A. (1968), *Histoire générale de la population mondiale*. Paris, Domat-Montchrestien.

Robertson, P. L. (1974), 'Technical education in the British shipbuilding and marine engineering industries, 1863–1914', *Economic History Review*, 2nd ser., 37 (2).

Rostow, W. (1975), *How it all Began: Origins of the Modern Economy*. London, Methuen.

Sanderson, M. (1983), *Education, Economic Change and Society in England, 1780–1870*. London, Macmillan.

Schofield, R. (1970), 'Age-specific mobility in an eighteenth-century rural English parish', *Annales de Démographie Historique*.

Schofield, R. (1973), 'Dimensions of illiteracy, 1750–1850', *Explorations in Economic History*, 10 (4).

Schofield, R. (1983), 'The impact of scarcity and plenty on population change in England, 1541–1871', *Journal of Interdisciplinary History*, 14 (2).

Schofield, R., and Rehrer, D. (1991), 'The decline of mortality in Europe', in R. Schofield, D. Rehrer and A. Bideau, eds., *The Decline of Mortality in Europe*. Oxford, Clarendon Press.

Sullivan, R. J. (1989), 'England's Age of Invention: the acceleration of patents and patentable invention during the industrial revolution', *Explorations in Economic History*, 26 (4).

Sylla, R., and Toniolo, G., eds. (1991), *Patterns of European Industrialization: the Nineteenth Century*. London, Routledge.

Temin, P. (1966), 'Labor scarcity and the problem of American industrial efficiency in the 1850s', *Journal of Economic History*, 26 (3).

Tilly, C. (1984), 'Demographic origins of the European proletariat', in D. Levine, ed., *Proletarianisation and Family History*. Orlando, Fla., Academic Press.

Tilly, R. (1991), 'Germany', in R. Sylla and G. Toniolo, eds., *Patterns of European Industrialization: the Nineteenth Century*. London, Routledge.

Tomasson, R. F. (1977), 'A millennium of misery: the demography of the Icelanders', *Population Studies*, 31 (3).

Trebilcock, C. (1981), *The Industrialisation of the Continental Powers, 1780–1914*. Harlow, Longman.

Tunzelmann, G. N. von (1981), 'Technical progress during the industrial revolution', in R. Floud and D. McCloskey, eds., *The Economic History of Britain since 1700* 1, *1700–1800*. Cambridge, Cambridge University Press.

Vugt, W. E. van (1988), 'Running from ruin? The emigration of British farmers to the USA in the wake of the repeal of the corn laws', *Economic History Review*, 2nd ser., 41 (3).

Walle, E. van de (1979), 'France', in W. R. Lee, *European Demography and Economic Growth*. London, Croom Helm.

Weaver, F. S. (1974), 'Relative backwardness and cumulative change: a comparative approach to European industrialisation', *Studies in Comparative International Development*, 9 (2).

White, P. E. (1989), 'Internal migration in the nineteenth and twentieth centuries', in P. E. Ogden and P. E. White, eds., *Migrants in Modern France*. London, Unwin Hyman.

Whyte, I. D. (1991), 'Migration in early modern Scotland and England: a comparative perspective', in G. Pooley and I. D. Whyte, *Migrants, Emigrants and Immigrants*. London, Routledge.

Wrigley, E. A. (1977), 'A note on the lifetime mobility of married women in a parish population in the later eighteenth century', *Local Population Studies*, 18.

Wrigley, E. A., and Schofield, R. S. (1981), *The Population History of England, 1541–1871*. London, Edward Arnold.

Wrigley, E. A., and Schofield, R. S. (1983), 'English population history from family reconstitution: summary results, 1600–1799', *Population Studies*, 37 (2).

Zabler, J. F. (1972), 'Further evidence on American wage differentials, 1800–30', *Explorations in Economic History*, 10 (2).

Zabler, J. F. (1973), 'More on wage rates in the iron industry: a reply', *Explorations in Economic History*, 11 (1).

The transformation of agriculture

Farming activity can only be understood by setting it in its geo-graphical, demographic, social, political and cultural context, and, in the period which interests us, within the wider process of structural transformation known as the 'industrial revolution', a form of 'modern economic growth', achieved, according to Simon Kuznets, when a society generates 'a long-term rise in the capacity to supply increasingly diverse economic goods to its population, this growing capacity based on advancing technology, and the institutional and ideological adjust-ments that it demands' (1973: 165–6). Thus although this is a chapter about agriculture it will avoid the narrow focus of so much of the literature and especially that of the English tradition of agricultural revolution studies (Ernle, 1912; E. L. Jones, 1967; Chambers and Mingay, 1966; Mingay, 1989). The traditional concept of a rapid and continuous 'agricultural revolution' with its emphasis on the role of great innovators has largely been abandoned in favour of the concept of a long and gradual development, discontinuous in its spatial impact, varying in intensity and duration. The analytical problems are obviously considerable, involving as they do a multiplicity of variables interacting in different places and over time. Certainly statistical information will be employed as a means of achieving some idea of orders of grandeur and patterns of development but much of the data is extremely inaccurate and clearly it is impossible to quantify all the relevant economic, much less the social and cultural variables. The statistical problems of international comparison are particularly daunting. Never-theless the development of a comparative approach is another vital means of questioning existing assumptions, of challenging the precon-ceptions implicit in particular national historiographies. We need additionally, of course, to take account of geographical factors. Agricultural systems are elements within eco-systems whose structures are subject to change as a result of inputs of labour and capital, themselves representing varied adaptations to particular physical and socio-economic environments determined not only by economic factors but by the social and demographic determinants of land ownership and use.

Given the diversity of the continent, there are no neat chronological divisions. This is reflected in the organisation of this chapter. The next section examines the structures of the 'traditional' agrarian systems established since the Middle Ages, and their evolution in response to demographic and commercial imperatives during the eighteenth century and indeed in many regions throughout the nineteenth. The following one considers the characteristics of an 'agricultural revolution', beginning in some areas in the eighteenth century, which substantially, and relatively rapidly by comparison with the past, increased the productivity of both land and labour. The next two sections review the further stimulii leading to what might be characterised as a second 'agricultural revolution', beginning around the middle of the nineteenth century; the sixth section, the impact of the 'great depression' from the late 1870s; whilst in the final section some of the consequences of this epochal change are examined, particularly the virtual elimination of the age-old threat of hunger and the impact on broader processes of change associated with urbanisation and industrialisation.

'Traditional' agricultural systems

European landscapes were the product of a continuous, centuries-long evolution, and of the development of polycultural and partially commercialised agrarian systems. This was to be the context from which an 'agricultural revolution' was to emerge, and which in large part determined the potential for change. Until towards the middle of the nineteenth century, in most regions, the structure of agricultural systems was largely determined by the need to provide for local subsistence and additionally to produce a surplus for sale to acquire the means of paying taxes and purchasing necessities. The most significant exceptions were parts of southern England, the Low Countries and northern France, with superior road and especially waterborne communications, which could specialise to a greater degree in the production of cash crops and import a proportion of their subsistence needs.

73

To these ought to be added costal regions in the Baltic specialising in grain exports to the west. In contrast, in most communities, farmers, isolated from commercial opportunities by the practical difficulty and consequent cost of transport, concentrated on the production of cereals, together with some vegetables and sufficient livestock to pull ploughs and carts and provide a little meat. In France even around the middle of the nineteenth century an estimated 44·6 per cent of the arable was still occupied by cereals (Demonet, 1990: 130), constituting around three-quarters of the arable not in fallow. Historians, reflecting the concerns of eighteenth-century agronomists, have nevertheless often neglected such vital sources of food as vegetable gardens and the various local supplements to cereals such as chestnuts or livestock products as well as a wealth of ways of making ends meet which might include cash crops such as wine produced on land unsuitable for cereals, industrial crops like hemp, flax, vegetable dyes or tobacco. Such *pluriactivité* might also involve rural manufacture and seasonal or temporary migration. The varying combinations of plants and animals in polycultural systems represented a search for security against climatic variations as well as a response to wider ecological, social and commercial circumstances. However, the high cost and unreliability of food supplies from outside the community imposed pressures to safeguard local subsistence which certainly limited the ability to adapt farming to local soils. The preponderance of cereals can thus easily be explained by the fact that it takes a much greater area of land to produce a given calorific value from animal products. Moreover grain is easier to store and transport than other farm products. As population densities rose the clearance of land and extension of the arable continued, and, save where wasteland and forest provided pasture, the numbers of livestock tended to decline. Animals came to be regarded as an unfortunate necessity. Fed on waste land or fallow, their numbers were limited, and because they were not integrated into the arable system much of the manure they produced was wasted. Required for work and manure, they played an essentially subordinate, service role in an overwhelmingly vegetable agrarian system, competing with humans for sustenance.

The proportion of land under cultivation tended to decline from west to east, towards the north in Scandinavia (with the exception of Denmark and southern Sweden) and Russia, and south towards the Mediterranean as a result in the one case of a short growing season and in the other of thin soils and lack of precipitation. In compensation this might allow for a better balance between arable and pasture or the development of a more varied polyculture, with in the south the cultivation of such typically Mediterranean plants as the olive and vine and other fruits. Yields inevitably varied considerably between such different environments, with the cultivation of what twentieth-century farmers would regard as poor soils substantially reducing the average. In France, for example, in 1852—regarded as a good year—the average wheat yield was 13·5 hectolitres per hectare, varying between 30 hl/ha in the *arrondissement* of Valenciennes on the northern plains and 6·3 hl/ha in that of Castellane in the Alpine foothills (Heffer *et al.*, 1986: 1275). The essential inputs were land and labour, with productivity determined by the quality of the land, the vagaries of the climate and the amount of labour. The structures of land ownership and use were of fundamental importance. They would remain relatively stable whilst otherwise economic circumstances were changing.

From the Middle Ages, in the 'core' regions of Europe, on the basis of 'prior appropriation of land by an elite of landowners' (Offer, 1991: 12), relatively large farms with a commercial orientation had been created by a process of consolidation. In Britain at the beginning of the nineteenth century nobles and gentry are estimated to have controlled as much as 69 per cent of the land; the corresponding figures for Prussia, France and European Russia were 40 per cent, 20 per cent and 14 per cent respectively (Mingay, 1989: 546–7; Spring, 1977: 2–6; Moeller, 1986: 38). The landed estate was, of course, much more than an economic unit. Whilst differences of opportunity inevitably led landowners to use their land in different ways, land was not merely a source of income in the form of rent but the basis of social and political power. It provided its possessors with the means of exerting non-economic influence in the markets for land, labour and commodities.

The tripartite division—landlords, tenants, labourers—traditionally employed to analyse English rural society was already clearly emerging by at least the beginning of the eighteenth century. Even at its most developed, in southern England, where the process of concentration of ownership at the expense of owner-occupiers was linked with the practice of strict settlement and with enclosure, it was more gradual than historians have often claimed. Thus whilst the model effectively represents the pre-eminence of landlord–tenant relationships its limitations should also be recognised. If by mid-century half the farmland

75

was held in units of over 80 ha and only one-fifth in farms of below 40 ha, it remained the case that 42 per cent of farmers occupied less than 20 ha and did not regularly hire labour. Many of them were in effect peasant cultivators, even if the label remains unfashionable among British historians. By the 1870s, in contrast, the process of concentration had accelerated, so that around 88 per cent of the land was occupied by tenant farmers and only 12 per cent by owner-occupiers. It was claimed by agronomists that, relieved of the need to purchase land, the tenant could employ his capital to raise productivity. With over one-third of net output being paid out in rent, and wages to be paid, the margin for investment was, however, often small. Until late in the nineteenth century leases reflected the relatively weak negotiating position of tenants. To a large degree farm size also depended on ease of access to markets and on terrain. In the pastoral west the median holding in 1885 was sixty-five acres, compared with 120 in the arable and stock-rearing east. Most of Wales at the mid-point of the nineteenth century resembled Ireland, with its overpopulation, intense competition for land and undercapitalised peasant tenantry. 'John Bull's other island' might be regarded as a case apart, except that most of its land was owned by members of the same social elite regarded (often, admittedly, with some exaggeration) as favourable to innovation on the mainland. Hostility between landowners and tenants may well have inhibited investment. Absenteeism, conspicuous consumption and indebtedness were further restraints.

France, like the British Isles, exhibited numerous ecological and socio-economic contrasts. Again there was no clear correlation between the existence of large estates and large, progressive farms. The weakness of market incentives ensured that most French landlords were likely to behave as *rentiers*, subdividing the land into the smallest possible plots in order to maximise their rental income. Another sharp contrast was the fact that around four-fifths of farms were worked by owner-occupiers, most of whom were peasant farmers, primarily concerned with family subsistence. Although their land constituted less than half the cultivated area, and an even smaller proportion of the most fertile and accessible property, most tenants were also essentially peasants. Only on the fertile and urbanised plains of the Paris basin and the north did a substantial class of large-scale commercially orientated tenant farmers emerge, cultivating at least 50 ha, able to negotiate rents which were low in relation to their incomes. Continuity, often over generations, facilitated the accumulation of capital and expertise, although technical innovation was limited before the nineteenth century. Elsewhere agronomists complained about rack renting, short leases, covenants restricting changes in established farming practices to prevent overcropping, minuscule farms, shortage of capital and a lack of any incentive to change. They were even more critical of the sharecropping systems common in the Massif Central and south-west. In theory these involved close co-operation between landowner and tenant. In practice the former's share of the product rose as population pressure strengthened his negotiating position, leaving the tenant with little to sell once family needs had been satisfied, largely eliminating commercial incentives and often causing considerable tension between the contracting parties.

The essentially *rentier* mentality of landowners in most of France and much of west Germany—where, however, only about 5 per cent of the land belonged to large estates—did not extend to the whole of continental Europe. Large landowners in Germany east of the river Elbe had responded to expanding commercial opportunities since at least the sixteenth century. By the early nineteenth their estates covered at least one-third of the agricultural land, and over 50 per cent in Mecklenburg and parts of East Prussia. The direct exploitation of estates (*Gutherrsschaft*) was based initially on noble political power and a repressive labour system which through serfdom required the peasant to provide labour service in return for plots of land to cultivate. As elsewhere the size and prosperity of noble estates varied considerably, with a small minority vast in scale and a large majority of small estates. The fundamental interest of the *Junker* landlord was to sustain an adequate life style and a career in the army or bureaucracy. The preference for direct exploitation rather than rental represented a determination to maintain paternalistic forms of social authority rather than an interest in farming. Similar structures of noble dominance prevailed in other parts of central and eastern Europe—in much of Bohemia, in Poland, and above all in Hungary, where in 1867 estates of over 575 ha, including the vast latifundia of families like the Esterházy, covered 39 per cent of the land. Large-scale farming was rare, with estates generally parcelled out into both demesne and peasant allotments. The labour obligations imposed on peasants varied. In Russia this *barschina* was most intense in the fertile Black Earth region in the centre and south, with a form of quit rent (*obrok*) predominating

77

in less fertile areas. Noble landowners were again essentially *rentiers*, usually lacking any notion of book-keeping and assuming quite simply that serf labour was free. Extracting resources from their estates to finance an increasingly expensive life style, they sank deeper into debt. Only around 1,400 of the perhaps 1 million people who claimed noble status were *grands seigneurs* owning over 1,000 'souls'. The vast majority owned fewer than twenty serfs. The role of the large estate was similarly negative throughout most of southern Europe. On the northern Italian plains, stewards might directly supervise the work of large numbers of labourers, with key workers like ploughmen living under close control in large brick buildings (*boariá*) at the centre of the estate. In central and southern Italy too the availability of cheap labour promoted technical backwardness, associated with exploitative share-cropping systems. At its most extreme in the Kingdom of Naples and in Sicily latifundia were rented by absentee landlords to urban middlemen (*gabelloti*) who sub-let plots to desperate day labourers. Similar conditions prevailed through much of southern Spain.

It has often been claimed that what distinguished the Continental 'peasant' from the British 'farmer' was the latter's much closer orientation to the market. The geography of opportunity was at the root of this distinction. Where commercial opportunities presented themselves, peasants generally responded in a positive manner. However, demographic pressure, scarcity of land, and the scale on which resources were extracted from them by landlords and the state, ensured that the essential objective of the vast majority—whether owner-occupiers or tenants—was to provide for family subsistence, whilst at the same time selling something—produce or labour—in order to pay taxes, debts, rent or seigneurial dues, purchase food or other necessities, finance ceremonial expenditure like weddings, or create a cash reserve for emergencies or the eventual purchase of land, the source of security and social status. Peasant land hunger and the self-deprivation or indebtedness which often resulted from efforts to acquire land can easily be understood against this background, as indeed can prevailing agricultural practices.

The persistence of fallow, usually as part of a three or, on poorer soils, a two-year rotation, reflected this obsession with the needs of grain crops. Fallow and the grazing of animals allowed the replenishment of nitrogen levels in the soil through bacterial action and the deposit of manure, as well as the clearance of weeds. It only partly compensated for the limited availability of pasture and the consequent low density of livestock and poor supply of animal manure, although considerable efforts might be made to supplement this latter with urban waste, marl, lime or sand. Only where commercial incentives were especially strong—close to towns, the coast or navigable waterways— was a higher proportion of land likely to be reserved for alternative uses, including market gardening and pasture. In many areas the shortage of animal feed, together with inadequate housing and endemic disease, ensured that draught animals were unhealthy and weak. This in turn encouraged the use of light wooden ploughs—the *sokha* of northern Russia or the *araire* of central and southern France and all of southern Europe. These had the advantage of being easy to manoeuvre on steep hillsides and in small fields and were easily constructed. Unfortunately they only scratched the surface to a depth of 12–20 cm and their use necessitated repeated ploughing to turn the soil over and eliminate weeds. In contrast the wheeled plough (*charrue*), with coulter and mould board, and capable of deeper ploughing, required larger draught teams. Until well into the nineteenth century the high cost of iron ensured that even these were generally made by local craftsmen from wood, with the exception of the iron plough tip. The quality and size of plough teams, the major investment made by most farmers, distinguished rich from poor regions and large from small farmers. Significantly, most contemporary observers suggest that Britain already had relatively high livestock densities by the eighteenth century, supplying the manure and draught power which contributed to rising productivity.

The supply and cost of energy were clearly of crucial importance both to normal farming routines and to the possibility of long-term innovation. Pre-mechanised farming was characterised, especially on the mass of peasant farms, by the limited availability of animal power and dependence on massive human effort. The capacity for hard physical labour was a source of status and a sign of virtue. In spite of the effort, however, poor tillage resulted in inadequate drainage and weeding. The use of uncleaned and unselected seeds, sown broadcast and heavily in an effort to choke weeds, further reduced productivity. Harvesting was a similarly labour-intensive affair. Use of the sickle, a light and easily managed tool, facilitated the mobilisation of the entire community in an effort to beat the weather. The motion of the scythe, normally employed for haymaking, wasted too much precious grain and required greater skill and strength. Upland areas and those close to the northern margins of cultivation, as well as many dry and rocky Mediterranean zones, were able to integrate waste and forest into a pastoral economy, although the near drought conditions prevailing in the south limited the capacity of the land to carry livestock and necessitated the practice of transhumance, with vast movements of sheep and goats between plain and plateau for the summer months. The diverse products, especially cheese and young animals for fattening, could be exchanged in the lowlands for cereals, but could not guarantee their supply to relatively isolated regions. Thus it remained essential to produce as much as possible locally wherever the soils were even remotely suitable and almost regardless of slopes.

With subsistence as the essential aim the vital indicator of productivity was the return on the seed employed. According to Slicher van Bath, average yields had reached 4·4 : 1 in eastern Europe by the early nineteenth century, 5·4 : 1 in Germany and Scandinavia, 5·9 : 1 in France, Spain and Italy, and 11·3 : 1 in Britain and the Netherlands (Slicher, 1963: 330–3). Variations within countries were often just as wide, with soil type acting as the preponderant influence on yield. In any case, in most regions of continental Europe, a quarter to a third of each harvest (and more in a bad year) had to be retained as seed, substantially reducing the supply of food. The productivity of labour also remained low because of its habitual undernourishment and the conditions under which it was employed. Existing agrarian systems promoted sustained hard work for limited periods, so that, in spite of growing opportunities for non-agricultural work, much of the labour force was frequently underemployed. Moreover in low-wage or serf-based economies labour lacked incentives, whilst social pressures on both employers and labourers ensured that whatever work was available was shared among as many people as possible.

It would be a mistake, however, to see traditional agricultural systems as entirely unchanging. Demographic developments, climatic factors and changes in market structures ensured constant flux. Certainly in England and the Low Countries innovations resulting in rising crop yields and productivity per head occurred on an increasing scale from the middle of the seventeenth century. One recent estimate suggests that between 1600 and 1800 *per capita* output increased by some 100 per cent in England (compared with only about 20 per cent in France (Wrigley, 1987: 11). This gradual and cumulative process of growth could, however, be seen largely as a response to the basic subsistence needs of a growing population, much of it due to a fortuitous improvement in climatic conditions. It represented the upward phase of a pre-industrial economic cycle, similar to advances previously recorded in the thirteenth and sixteenth centuries, but with the advantage of more substantial 'accumulated capital, knowledge, and skills' (Komlos, 1989: 18). Nevertheless a cluster of interrelated constraints—environmental and institutional, economic and social— continued to obstruct change and to reinforce the inhibiting familistic orientation of the mass of peasant farmers.

The first 'agricultural revolution'

During the first 'agricultural revolution', lasting in most regions of western Europe from 1730–40 until at least 1820–50, and much later in the east and south, traditional agrarian systems were far more frequently perfected rather than radically transformed. Esther Boserup (1965) suggests that it was growing demand, together with changes in its structure, that provided the vital stimulus to the development of more intensive forms of cultivation. The population of Europe, including Russia, grew from some 136 million to 200 million between 1750 and 1850 and reached 410 million by 1900. Urbanisation was a major stimulus to, and was made possible by, improvements in the efficiency of the market. Some 9·3 per cent of population is estimated to have been living in towns in 1650 and 10·6 per cent in 1800, with the proportion reaching some 24 per cent in England and Wales. Major urban centres served as nodal points in communication networks, at the summit of a hierarchy of regional collector markets, providing employment for a multitude of intermediaries and acting as a wide-ranging stimulus to economic activity. The information available on the development of internal markets is fragmentary. Nevertheless in the eighteenth and early nineteenth centuries the slow improvement of waterway and road links reduced the cost of transport and consumer prices, widening the range of supply to urban centres and the stimulus they provided to farmers to improve their own efficiency. In transport-deficient areas, like much of upland Britain, natural conditions and transport costs combined to promote livestock husbandry and movement on the hoof. The demand-driven rise in prices characteristic of much of the eighteenth century lent further encouragement.

It remains extremely difficult to define the shifting balance between continuity and change. Improvement was slow, market integration gradual. For the mass of small farmers market participation could be only episodic, given the need to provide for family subsistence and to retain seed. Everywhere much of the product continued to be consumed locally. Population pressure ensured on-going efforts to clear land. In England and Wales the extension of the arable continued until the 1850s to the 1870s, in France until the 1880s. In the uplands it could be achieved only by constructing terraces on the hillsides, with massive human effort for limited returns. Often making little sense in terms of orthodox economic analysis, this effort, as well as the high purchase price of land compared with potential returns, represented a rational response to the pressing needs of household subsistence. The clearance of forest in many areas increased official concern about potential shortages of a vital fuel and construction material as well as the harmful environmental impact. The result was frequent conflict between peasant cultivators on the one hand, anxious to extend their land holdings and retain access to the woodland resources which constituted an integral part of traditional upland agrarian systems, and the state and landowners on the other, increasingly committed to the 'rational' capitalistic exploitation of the forests.

Population pressure might additionally promote the introduction of new high-yield plants from the Americas, such as maize, spreading through southern Europe from the seventeenth century, and the potato, initially regarded as animal food and then, often as a result of dearth, becoming a field crop around the end of the eighteenth century. In regions where little land remained worth clearing, especially on the west European plains, the alternative was intensification—a multiplicity of marginal improvements, making use of the abundance of labour. The practice of cultivating fodder (root crops and artificial grasses) in place of fallow, evident in Flanders in the late Middle Ages and in eastern England from the seventeenth century, 'meant that arable and pastoral farming became complementary rather than mutually exclusive' (Pounds, 1979: 204). It took time, however, to overcome the structural and psychological obstacles to the development of integrated farming systems. The introduction of fodder crops into rotation systems made an increase possible in the number of livestock and in the supply of manure. It also required more thorough preparation of the soil, which, together with the ploughing back of plant residues, increased the yields of subsequent cereal crops. The essential objective was to build up the fertility of the soil. Together with better drainage, this was essential if new rotation systems like the four-course developed in Norfolk were to be successful. Subsequently more complex rotations would include nitrogen-fixing crops and particularly legumes. All this required far more substantial inputs of both human and animal labour, and also capital, and could be implemented only slowly and partially on the less productive and smaller farms. In advanced areas of France, like the Beauce supplying the Paris market, the practice of fallow remained at the end of the eighteenth century the essential means of resting and preparing the soil. By the 1850s, however, although triennial rotation remained dominant, it was usually without fallow. Nationally fallow was reduced from about a third of the arable to something like a fifth in the first part of the century and to a seventh by 1882. The growing significance of intensification compared with clearance is revealed by the fact that whereas the area under cereals in France increased by 3·6 per cent between 1840 and 1882 production grew by 23 per cent. In the eastern provinces of the Kingdom of Prussia fallow declined from about half the arable in 1800 to one-fifth by 1878 (Mayer, 1989: 73). Farther east and south a massive increase in the cultivated area remained the primary response to population growth, with much higher proportions of the arable remaining in fallow, reflecting in the first case the obsession with producing cereals and in the second the climatic obstacles to the cultivation of fodder.

In spite of the evidence of rising production, substantial barriers to innovation survived. Even in Britain progress was to remain 'patchy' (Mingay, 1989: 969). The changes occurring in most regions were similar to the late medieval responses to the twin processes of population growth and market extension. Thus on the northern plains of France, in Hainault or the Cambrèsis, the relatively high wheat yields of the early nineteenth century—30 hl/ha—had already been achieved in the fourteenth and fifteenth centuries. It was where seed/yield ratios were particularly low, however, that the cumulative impact of even small increases was especially significant, altering the context within which farmers operated—especially the balance between family subsistence and market sales—and reducing the impact of poor harvests. Achieving, on a regular basis, a ratio of 5 : 1 appears to have been a threshold crossed by many farmers in the eighteenth century.

Historically, however, substantial innovation always tended to occur late in the cycle of population growth. By the turn of the century in most regions the symptoms of agrarian overpopulation were again evident, including the cultivation of marginal land, fragmentation of holdings, rising land prices, higher rents, underemployment, depressed incomes among most of the rural population, rising food prices and dietary impoverishment, as well as endemic social tension as conflict over scarce resources intensified. Frequent shortages revealed the continued fragility of the population/food supply balance. Particularly on the Continent, *dearth* was to remain frequent until the middle of the nineteenth century. The impact of a series of poor harvests due to excessive rain, sometimes drought or severe cold was intensified by the subsequent consumption of seed grains, market fragmentation and the inelasticity of local food supply, limited stocks (susceptible to spoilage), and widespread speculative activity, panic buying and disruptive protest. Although the poor revealed a remarkable ability to adapt to nutritional stress, that 30–40 per cent of the population which, even in the most prosperous regions, remained in a more or less permanent state of undernourishment was susceptible to the least deviation from a 'normal year'. There appeared to many contemporaries to be a real possibility that rising productivity would be terminated by another Malthusian crisis and a generalised demographic and economic downturn.

There were also, however, some reasons for greater optimism. Thus a complex of factors contributed to the declining intensity of subsistence crises. They included rising agricultural productivity, with higher yields ensuring that variations in the net product available for consumption became proportionately much less violent; further crop diversification which limited the impact of adverse weather; and broad economic growth, which created more employment opportunities in both town and country, providing the cash entitlements needed for the purchase of foodstuffs. In this context the development of rural manufacture might be considered not as 'proto-industrialisation' but, as in centuries past, as part of a desperate effort to make ends meet. More effective crisis management also contributed, involving direct governmental intervention in the market by means of the accumulation of stocks and bread subsidies, and the creation of purchasing power by employment on public works. Significantly, the long revolutionary–imperial wars, although causing substantial disruption of international markets and increasing the amplitude of the price fluctuations due to poor harvests, were not marked by the major famines and epidemics which had accompanied the movement of armies a century before. Moreover governments increasingly felt able to move from a policy of market regulation towards liberalisation intended to encourage trade.

This could prove dangerous. The ideological commitment to 'free trade', which was strongest in Britain, the most advanced economy, would result in the appalling Irish famine of 1845–48. Irish farming had diversified to meet the growing demand of the British market, and between the 1740s and 1840s had appeared to become less vulnerable to famine, despite population growth and repeated dearth. In the process, however, the poorest 40 per cent of the population had become dependent on a single high-yield crop. Potato blight resulted in a high degree of dependence on private and public welfare projects but the British government believed that market mechanisms rather than food subsidies offered the most effective solution to shortage. Its budgetary conservatism and insistence on local financial responsibility ignored the unwillingness or inability of local landowners to provide charity on an adequate scale. As a result perhaps a million people died, mainly from the spread of infectious disease amongst a weak and vulnerable population. A bitter political legacy was created. Moreover mortality rates were to be substantially lower in other stricken regions. In Flanders, where mass poverty was exacerbated by the collapse of the rural textile industry, and in the Scottish Highlands, whether from humanitarian concern or fear of disorder, the authorities continued to subsidise food and public works employment.

The significance of dearth, from the late eighteenth century to the middle years of the nineteenth, as a manifestation of the continued difficulty of balancing the supply of and demand for food should not be underestimated. The social disruption which resulted from rising prices was evidence of the fear engendered by the folk memory of famine and of widespread and genuine difficulty in making ends meet. Dearth served to inhibit risk-taking by farmers and ensured the survival of the subsistence preference. Certainly information on prices reveals a continuing decline in the amplitude of fluctuations over time and between places, reflecting both increased food production and the greater efficiency of distribution networks. This, however, remained compatible with stagnation or even deterioration in nutritional standards as a result of growing population pressure on resources and widespread poverty. Harvest failure and rising food prices had a redistributive effect which sharply reduced the real income and purchasing power of the vast majority and caused a general economic crisis, which could, and in 1789, 1830 and 1848 did, contribute to political destabilisation. Despite these reservations, the hundred years beginning around 1740 might be seen as a key transitional phase in which dearth came, in most regions, to replace the age-old menace of famine and, although it was not apparent at the time, as the prelude to an age of plenty.

Further stimuli to change

The strengthening of the various stimuli to change during the eighteenth and early nineteenth centuries has already been recognised. The process was to be broadened and intensified. The overall context of farming activity was to be drastically altered by urbanisation, industrialisation and the associated improvements in communications and in marketing systems. The institutional order was also brought into question. The various 'feudal' survivals, ranging from the mild seigneurial systems in the west which imposed dues and services on peasants to the more demanding serfdom of the east, were subjected to growing criticism on both social and economic grounds. According to critics the apparently cost-free work provided by millions of serfs was performed with such ill will that yields remained inescapably low. As demand and the opportunities for profit increased from the second half of the eighteenth century on, peasant resistance to increased labour service proved to be an obstacle to innovation. Yet fear of the unknown and of social destabilisation postponed major reforms. Only the fear of something worse and determined state action could overcome it. In France and Europe west of the Rhine the abolition of seigneurialism was part and parcel of the French revolution. Peasant unrest helped to destroy the authority of royal government and encouraged elites to save what they could. In central and eastern Europe, in the short term, the fear this engendered intensified noble conservatism. The need to alleviate rural discontent and to respond to fiscal and military weakness by engaging in Western-style modernisation was nevertheless inescapable. Governments felt obliged to impose further reforms on a usually reluctant landowning class, in Prussia through the Stein–Hardenburg reforms of 1807 and throughout the German states, and in Austria–Hungary in 1848, and in Russia following defeat in the Crimean war.

The real analytical problem is to distinguish the impact of reform from other stimuli such as population growth and market expansion. Its effects would take decades to work themselves out. Nevertheless it now seems clear that the Marxian belief that in abolishing 'feudalism' the French revolution removed the major obstacles to development is greatly exaggerated. Basic agrarian structures were not profoundly affected. Land transfers occurred essentially within the possessing classes—including the small minority of well-of peasants—with nobles losing around a fifth of their land. The number of small owner-occupiers also grew. Although the abolition of seigneurial dues and the tithe payable to the church provided peasant proprietors with a more substantial surplus for consumption or sale (as much as 10–15 per cent of the crop) it is difficult to see this as inaugurating a 'peasant route' to capitalism, which its advocates have contrasted with the 'English route'. The engagement of small farmers in commercial agriculture in such regions as northern France or north-west Germany anyway largely antedated the revolutionary years. It had been encouraged by relatively easy access to markets.

In Germany east of the Elbe the reforms of 1807–11 in many respects represented the extension of changes already introduced on the royal estates in order to encourage innovation and increase revenue. A free market in land was established, ending the previous restrictions on purchase by commoners. Personal servitude was abolished, and the legal conditions of peasant property ownership modified. The legislation was, however, shaped in fundamental ways by the entrenched political power of the landowning nobility. They were to be compensated by means of indemnities. Many, perhaps most, peasants were unable to meet the conditions laid down for emancipation and continued to fulfil a variety of obligations towards their former seigneurs until new legislation was introduced in the aftermath of the 1848 revolutions. Furthermore they were only able to obtain full title to the land they farmed provided they surrendered one-third to half, and usually the best land, as compensation to former seigneurs. The result was a massive, if seemingly unmeasurable, transfer of land to noble landowners, who additionally took most of the enclosed common land. In Prussia as a whole 40 per cent of the land was now to be noble property, rising to 62 per cent in Pomerania. The result was essentially to protect the privileged position of noble landowners, a class traditionally attuned to commercial farming and determined, to a far greater degree than the *rentier* landowners of much of western Europe, to retain both their market orientation and their direct quasi-feudal authority over the land and the people living on it.

The situation in the various provinces of the Austrian empire varied considerably. Since the 'urbarial' ordinances of Maria Theresa in 1767 Habsburg governments had attempted to protect peasants, and its own tax revenue, from excessive demands for labour service. Joseph II had given the peasants their legal freedom in 1789 but had not abolished dues or service. In 1848 emancipation was a means of satisfying liberal critics of the regime and especially peasant grievances at a moment of intense political crisis. Former lords were, of course, compensated, much of the cost being taken on by the state. The impact was further limited by the survival of large noble estates, especially in Hungary, where 64 per cent of peasants had little or no land and frequently continued to perform labour service as a form of rent in kind.

Emancipation in Russian in 1861 can also be viewed both as a stage in a process of state-inspired modernisation and as a fundamentally conservative measure. The regime was certainly determined to protect noble land ownership and to prevent the creation of a landless proletariat which might pose a threat to social and political stability. The provisions were extremely complicated. Landowners retained a substantial proportion of their property and were compensated for their losses both by the state and by the peasants through redemption payments. It has been estimated that whereas emancipation reduced the peasant allotment of land by only 4·1 per cent overall, in the sixteen fertile Black Earth provinces the proportion rose to 23·3 per cent (Blum, 1978: 395). Ownership of some 80 per cent of peasant land was vested in the *mir*, the peasant commune, rather than in individuals. Each household was given the right to a garden plot, an allotment of land, and access to the commons, with periodic redistribution of land in the fields as village population and household size changed. For this reason the average allotment in European Russia of 5·1 dessiatins per male in 1860 had fallen to 2·7 dessiatins by 1900. Many families supplemented their allocation by renting or purchasing gentry land but the rising cost, together with the burden of redemption payments and high taxes, and of redistribution, was a major disincentive to potential innovators, although recent research has pointed to increasing yields as proof that in the past an unduly pessimistic view of the restrictive impact of communal institutions has prevailed. The 1905 revolution finally persuaded the regime that individual peasant property might be more conducive to economic advance and political stability alike. The Stolypin reforms allowed the consolidation of the strips of land which households had formerly been allocated in the open fields, but only provided that two-thirds of heads of households agreed. The impact of the reforms has frequently been exaggerated. Consolidated farms were already the norm in the relatively advanced Baltic provinces. Elsewhere the peasant response was often far from enthusiastic. Nevertheless, on the eve of the 1917 revolution, some 27–33 per cent of peasant farms were held in hereditary tenure. Even then the break with the *mir* was often far from complete, and overall communal tenure remained dominant.

Farther south, in Italy and Spain from the period of French occupation in 1798–1811 and into the 1860s, the dismantlng of the seigneurial regime was accompanied by the sale of church and common land, a pattern repeated in Romania with the freeing of the serfs in 1864. Those with money to spare benefited, and large estates continued to occupy a dominant position in the rural economy. In Greece, Serbia and Bulgaria expropriation of Turkish landowners facilitated emancipation and substantial land redistribution.

Institutional change implied easing some of the restrictions on economic activity. In its various forms it had the effect of strengthening the resource base of market-orientated agriculture. It has been estimated that emancipation in Austria resulted in a once-and-for-all increase of 2·4 per cent in GNP (Good, 1984: 92–4), but, of course, all such calculations are extremely uncertain. The financial burdens on peasant farming were reduced. Deprived of apparently cost-free serf labour, landowners were increasingly forced to reorganise their estate economies. Free labour was probably more productive, whether employed on the large estate or on the family farm. Although in the short term peasant families may well have consumed rather than marketed more of their produce, in the longer term they would be better able to respond to changing market structures. Nevertheless as far as the history of agriculture is concerned a chronology based on the great dates of 1789, 1848 and 1861 is hopelessly inadequate. These essentially political turning points have to be set in the context of longer-term economic development and related to other causal factors, amongst which the market should be viewed as the key regulator of economic activity.

During the nineteenth century decisive structural changes were to occur in the markets for agricultural produce, through urbanisation, the improvement of roads and waterways, reductions in oceanic freight rates, and, from the 1830s and 1840s on, railway construction. The improvement of communications, striking in its rapidity, had the effect of reducing the cost of a product to its consumer, and, within the limits set by demand elasticity, of stimulating demand. This was particularly significant for agriculture, given the relatively low value of cereals or wine in relation to their bulk, and the loss of weight experienced by livestock moving on the hoof. Additionally the flow of information was improved by better postal services, newspapers, the electric telegraph and finally the telephone. The overall effect was to create markets which, for all their continued shortcomings, were much closer to the perfect model beloved of liberal economists. It seems clear that from *c.* 1851 farmers in Europe generally benefited from the tendency of prices to rise. In Britain waterborne transport had already promoted a substantial degree of integration, but everywhere even a marginal reduction in the cost of transport encouraged commercial activity. The stimulus was greater in areas where previously poor access to markets had depressed price levels. Thus in southern Russia grain prices doubled in the 1880s as a levelling up to west European levels occurred. The growing integration of markets was clear from the reduction in inter-regional and international price differences. It stimulated or, through intensified competition, often forced more widespread and thorough-going change on the part of farmers. The virtual disappearance of dearth, and a greater sense of security, encouraged a more pronounced orientation towards commerce and away from self-subsistence. Whilst insisting on the importance of transport as a key element in economic growth, it is, how-ever, important to stress that it was a permissive factor. The ability and willingness of farmers to respond to changing market structures depended on interactions between a complex of human and environmental factors, with results that varied widely over space and through time and according to previous levels of development (Price, 1983: Part 3).

A second 'agricultural revolution'

The context of farming was, however, decisively altered. Historically, demographic change had been the dominant factor. Farmers had responded primarily to the ups and downs of population. In most parts of Europe in the eighteenth and early nineteenth centuries a considerable increase in production had been possible, and best practice had become more widespread, but this had only repeated previous patterns of response to demographic expansion. Virtually everywhere land had been cleared and more intensive forms of cultivation introduced. However, the complex of innovations which historians have labelled the 'agricultural revolution' had been restricted to a small number of advanced farms in favoured regions, to the minority of innovators possessing the knowledge and the capital to finance investment and secure them against risks. Now the combination of political and institutional change with a communications revolution creating a world market, together with rapid industrialisation, urbanisation and the decline of rural population, resulted in a more thoroughgoing and permanent series of responses. Changes in market structures, translated by price movements, created incentives or imposed pressure on farmers. Initially the innovations which resulted remained essentially biological and labour-intensive. Increasingly, however, the use of artificial fertilisers, better hand tools and machinery revealed a perceived need to increase the productivity of labour. Innovation was especially apparent in response to the dual incentives of market widening and rising prices and of labour shortage and increases in real wages between *c.* 1850 and *c.* 1875. The extension of livestock production was particularly favoured, in marked contrast with the previous period of rising prices in the eighteenth century, when population growth had stimulated efforts to increase cereal production as the essential means of securing food supplies. The middle years of the century marked the onset of modern growth, of processes described by some historians as a second agricultural revolution but which frequently overlapped with the first.

The measurement of productivity is a hazardous business. Using estimates of wheat yields, for which information is more readily available, Bairoch has calculated that whereas in Europe (without Russia) average yields increased from 8·0 to 8·8 quintals per hectare between 1800 and 1850, i.e. an overall growth of 10 per cent or 0·2 per cent per annum, from 1850 to 1910 these rose from 8·8 to 12·3 quintals, i.e. at a rate of 0·6 per cent per annum, with the most rapid growth from 1880–90 onward (1989: 318–19). Clearly this kind of continent-wide measurement conceals massive variations, partly

Table 3.1 Wheat yields in quintals per hectare, 1800–1985 (five-year averages)

Country	1800	1850	1880	1910	1936	1985
Germany	10·0	10·3	13·3	18·5	22·9	57·9
Belgium	13·5	14·5	15·8	25·1	26·9	62·5
Denmark	–	–	22·5	31·0	30·4	63·8
Spain	5·5	–	–	9·4	9·6	22·8
France	8·5	10·9	10·9	13·2	15·6	57·3
Italy	7·3	7·0	8·0	9·6	14·4	28·8
Netherlands	14·0	15·2	15·3	23·9	30·3	73·4
Romania	–	–	9·0	11·7	10·3	27·5
UK	13·6	17·5	16·7	21·4	23·1	66·7
Russia	5·4	5·4	5·0	6·6	9·3	16·7
Switzerland	11·0	13·0	14·5	21·2	24·0	53·7

revealed in Bairoch's own calculations of national yields. This was at a time when the predominance of cereals among farming systems was beginning to decline. The official statistics thus underestimate the rise in productivity. The strength of the incentives to innovation and the capacity to respond varied. The forms of adaptation included, at the one extreme, substantial investment in seeds, fertilisers and new equipment and major changes in land use, and, at the other, piecemeal improvement of existing polycultural systems.

The impact of changing patterns of demand and variations in price levels, and then of shifts in the cost of production, can be judged from alterations in land use. Improved communications, migration and rapid urbanisation reduced the pressure to provide locally for essential subsistence needs. Farmers were better able to adapt to local natural conditions. Bairoch estimates that in the French case a minimum of one-tenth of the increase in yields between 1878–82 and 1908–12 was due to increased regional specialisation. The range of options open to particular farmers was obviously determined by location and ecology and by factor endowments. In most regions cereals remained predominant, with on-going efforts to increase productivity. In Britain the age-old effort to increase the surface under cereals continued at least into the 1840s, and in France it ended around 1851–62, involving 61 per cent of the arable. Subsequently cultivation clearly declined in the uplands and in the south, but increased in the Paris basin. Output was maintained by increasing productivity rather than the surface area cultivated. Even in European Russia, where the major cereals still made up two-fifths of gross agricultural production in 1913, extension of the sown area accounted for some nine-tenths of the increase in output in the period 1883 to 1895 but only two-fifths between 1895 and 1914 (Gatrell, 1986: 102).

More intensive cultivation continued to involve the development of mixed farming systems associating cereals, fodder crops and live-stock. These were the means of preserving soil fertility, of increasing cereal productivity and widening the range of consumable and mar-ketable products. In northern France and particularly in Germany and much of eastern Europe cereals and livestock were associated with the cultivation of sugar beet, especially on the larger farms and the more fertile loamy soils. An alternative on light and sandy soils was intensive potato cultivation, providing for domestic consumption, pig feed and processing into alcohol and starch. In both cases success depended on heavy manuring, deep ploughing and careful weeding, and thus contributed to generally improved standards of cultivation. Amongst cereals there was a switch to wheat from rye and other coarse grains, reflecting changing consumer demand and thus relative price levels. In the more humid areas of western Britain, north-western France, the Netherlands, Denmark and northern Italy the balance within mixed farming switched towards the more specialised rearing of livestock, encouraged by the rising relative price of animal products as urban demand grew. This might involve an extension of fodder cultivation or the improvement of natural pasture. Selective breeding and better feeding and care of animals at the same time led to substantial increases in their weight and in milk yields. Pigs multiplied, fed on potatoes and waste milk. In contrast, the number of sheep tended to decline in many regions as the fallow on which they had been pastured contracted and as wool prices fell. The exceptions were upland areas, where sheep were so adaptable to poor grazing, including much of the Balkans and southern Europe.

Many regions experienced a brief Golden Age which lasted for thirty to forty years before the creation of a world market led to over-supply. The railways and better roads created a two-way link with the market, both to sell and to purchase inputs like cattle cake and fertilisers, tools and consumer goods. Even in previously advanced regions like southern England farming systems and local communities had remained to a large degree self-contained, producing their own animal feed and fertiliser and consuming much of the final product. Improved communications facilitated the more widespread and heavy application of lime and marl to alter the chemical composition of soils, and of artificial fertilisers, initially crushed bones, then guano from Peru and from the 1870s chemical products. In Germany the use of artificial fertiliser can be linked with the expansion of root-crop cultivation. On the supply side, industrialisation provided growing and increasingly cheap supplies of potash, sulphate and phosphate, initially as by-products of the chemical and metallurgical industries. By 1913 farmers in Germany, where fertiliser prices fell by 55 per cent between 1880 and 1905–13, were on average applying almost twice the volume per hectare of their British counterparts (Perkins, 1981: 84–6). For best effect drainage was often a prerequisite, and from the 1850s cheap clay pipes reduced the cost. The increased application of fertilisers seemed to make it possible to produce successive cereal crops without diminishing the fertility of the soil, whilst the risk of disease was diminished by planting different varieties. Thus while the spread of intensive mixed farming increased the number of livestock, and feeding them on oilcake further improved the supply and quality of manure, recourse to artificial fertiliser was beginning to reduce farmers' dependence on animals.

Lower Languedoc provides another example of positive responses to new opportunities. Stimulated by rapidly growing urban demand for cheap wine, cultivation of the vine rapidly spread from hillsides on to the formerly cereal-growing plains. Wheat yields had always been low, and in coastal areas prices were depressed by imports. The immediate effect of the construction of a rail link between Languedoc and Paris was to reduce the cost of sending *vin ordinaire* by 45 per cent, stimulating demand and an increase in local prices from an average of only nine francs per hectolitre in 1840–55 to thirty-five francs by 1855–56 (Houssel, 1976: 279). Similar developments occurred in other vine-growing regions such as Spanish Catalonia, especially in the 1880s, when so many French vineyards were stricken by phylloxera. In more northerly climes, in contrast, the vines were rapidly replaced with cereals. Elsewhere changes in land use, although clearly evident, were more gradual and partial, restrained by existing farm structures, a residual family-subsistence preference, shortage of capital and the time needed to establish new commercial networks. The primary beneficiaries in regions of small-scale farming were frequently the small army of intermediaries. Even so a decisive shift in the balance between subsistence and commercial farming occurred. Farmers, large and small, adapted to changing patterns of opportunity with remarkable facility, although obviously not without some difficulties.

Reductions in the fallow and the introduction of root crops substantially increased labour needs. Whilst the agricultural population of western Europe fell from about 80 per cent to about 45 per cent of the total, the number of active male workers actually rose, from 22·9 million in 1800 to 28 million around 1870, but then declined—in the United Kingdom and France from the 1840s on, and in Germany from the 1880s. As migration increasingly altered the balance between the supply of and the demand for labour, so the cost of hired labour rose. In France between 1851 and 1881 agricultural wages rose by over 50 per cent. Labour accounted for perhaps one-third of the cost of producing a hectare of wheat. Efforts to increase its productivity took two forms, the improvement of hand tools and the introduction of machinery proper. Another alternative, as in Ireland, especially following the Famine, was to shift away from labour-intensive arable farming to pasture. Expansion of family farming, with little account taken of labour costs, was yet another response. Improved nourishment, and more effective education, also contributed. Higher labour productivity meant that whereas agricultural output rose by 60–80 per cent in Britain between 1830 and 1880 the work force increased by only about 17 per cent and actually fell by around 20 per cent between 1851 and 1881 (Mingay, 1981, I: 200–1).

Relatively inexpensive innovation might produce quite dramatic effects. Thus the replacement of the sickle by the scythe as the primary harvesting tool, a process begun centuries before but in most of western and central Europe finally achieved between 1850 and 1880, brought a saving on labour of 25–30 per cent. Harvesting was still sufficiently labour-intensive to provide work for most of the rural population. Ploughs could be improved. An iron tip could be added to wooden ones, or lighter ones introduced as the cost of iron fell. Deeper, more rapid and more frequent ploughing became easier, as did the elimination of weeds, aeration of the soil, and the ploughing in of manure. Such ploughs might be used in conjunction with seed drills and horse hoes to prepare the seed bed. The improved supply of fodder meant that draught animals were stronger as well as more numerous, with horses increasingly substituted for the slower and less powerful oxen, cows or mules. By the 1900s the use of improved ploughs, encouraged

95

by agricultural associations, local blacksmiths and the representatives of engineering companies like Ransome's of Ipswich or the (American) International Harvester Company was common even in central Russia.

Mechanisation proper was a much slower and episodic process, influenced as much by social as by economic factors. It was more expensive. Early machines were often unreliable and too costly for peasants just emerging from family subsistence cultivation. The wider use of machines was primarily a response to, rather than a cause of, migration. Generally, and until population densities were substantially reduced, mechanisation encountered considerable, and often successful, resistance from labourers afraid of unemployment. In Britain threshing machines, although developed in the 1780s and first employed during wartime labour shortages, entered general use only from the 1840s as intensification provided alternative work for labourers who had formerly depended on threshing with the flail for winter employment. They varied between the hand-powered variety useful on small farms and those powered by horse gins and later by steam engines, made widely available in some regions by mobile threshing contractors. By the 1880s with steam power six men might thresh 150 hl of wheat in a day, whilst a man with a flail would get through only 3 hl in spite of back-breaking effort. By 1907 threshing machines were employed on some 30 per cent of German farms, and of these around 30 per cent employed steam power (van Zanden, 1991: 233).

In most regions an agricultural revolution was achieved before mechanisation. Some innovations, including the cultivation of new crops or the use of artificial fertilisers, could be applied by every farmer on a scale appropriate to his needs and resources; others, technically more complex and costly, were more restricted in their application. In the case of mechanical reapers only fairly large farmers had a suitable field layout, could feed the necessary draught animals, and would be concerned by rising labour costs and shortages of labour during the crucial harvest period. Not surprisingly, innovations appeared first and were more generally adopted in geographically favoured areas already heavily engaged in commercial farming. Their diffusion depended on assessments of the productivity and relative cost of the new inputs. Land and labour remained the primary inputs, but clearly capital was assuming a far more significant role.

Contemporaries have left numerous descriptions of model farms, normally of over 100 ha, with carefully planned buildings, fields which were well drained and cultivated and planted with selected high-yield seeds, with housing for large numbers of well bred animals fed on concentrated foodstuffs, and tools and machines in abundance. This kind of 'high farming' was, however, costly and might be practised partly for 'non-economic' motives under the influence of fashion and the desire for social status. Its practitioners certainly influenced general standards of farming, but inevitably most farms, even in advanced regions, fell below the ideal. Landlords, tenants and owner-occupiers accumulated capital gradually, inheriting much of it, and invested cautiously. Technical education was generally lacking, and although it was possible to borrow money to acquire land, loans for the purchase of equipment were rare. In areas of large-scale tenant farming like southern England or parts of northern France the essential role of the landlord lay in setting the conditions of leases and the level of rents and in providing capital for expensive projects like drainage. The payment of rent (and of taxes) stimulated commercial activity but also drained capital away. This was even more the case where landlords behaved essentially as *rentiers*. In Russia the innovating landowner was a rare bird indeed.

Moreover landowners were increasingly attracted by the growing range of alternative investment opportunities. In many areas, particularly those with a high density of population, sales of land by large landowners, often in small lots, to maximise returns, allowed sitting tenants and former labourers to acquire land. If, as is frequently argued, the scale of farming and the awareness of and ability to introduce new techniques were directly related, this continued parcellation would certainly constitute an obstacle to future change. The marked tendency of agronomists to praise large farmers whilst condemning the practices of the small should not, however, mislead us. Certainly many of the smaller-scale cultivators were ignorant and resistant to change, preferring to avoid the risks implicit in innovation and to draw on an oral, empirical and well established code of practice. It would be a mistake, though, to ignore the innovative capacity of the family farm. Circumstances varied. Through sheer hard work, but additionally through the use of artificial fertiliser and concentrated foodstuffs, peasant farmers in much of north-western Europe (the Low Countries, Denmark, western Germany, northern France) responded positively to urban industrial demand. Intensification would usually involve greater specialisation in one element of a polycultural system, a shift of emphasis which reduced risk-taking and allowed flexible responses to uncertain markets and fluctuating prices. Thus an apparently stubborn determination to cultivate cereals might mask a switch into higher-value dairy and livestock farming, with grain used as animal feed when prices were low but sold on when they rose and replaced with cattle cake. In such circumstances the productivity of the land on a small farm, although not that of labour, might compare well with that on the large, more highly capitalised unit. Labour productivity was particularly low in southern and eastern Europe, where, if farmers certainly sought to adapt to changing circumstances, rural overpopulation and less developed market incentives ensured that family labour remained underemployed.

In most regions a dual structure emerged, with relatively large, capital-intensive units and alongside them small labour-intensive family farms. Similar distinctions could also be drawn between regions. Everywhere, however, the balance between commercial and subsistence farming was shifting, and more rapidly than ever before under the impact of improved communications, the monetisation of economic relations and technological change. Many regions experienced a levelling up as commercial incentives and technical progress spread. Thus in France in 1840 the maximum disparity between *départements* in terms of productivity per male agricultural worker was 1 : 6·4; by 1890 it was 1 : 4·0 (Bairoch, 1989: 351). Internationally, too, early developers like Britain failed to retain their lead. In contrast, the gap in productivity between western and central Europe and more peripheral regions continued to widen, despite agricultural improvement in the latter.

The 'great depression'

The 'Golden Age' was short-lived and was followed by the 'great depression'. By the late 1870s the market-widening impact of improved communications seemed to threaten the profitability of a wide range of agricultural commodities. In recent years historians have become more critical of the chorus of complaints from contemporaries, and of a traditional historiography which focused exclusively on cereals. The important contribution made by the econometricians to measuring the intensity of the crisis must, however, be balanced by an awareness of contemporary perceptions. It was these which, after all, influenced decision-making both within the rural community and by governments. The essential cause of the crisis was obvious—the over-supply of markets and the intensification of international competition following the opening up of the Russian and especially the North American plains by railway construction and falling ocean freight rates.

Between the late 1860s and the 1900s the cost of transporting wheat from Chicago to Liverpool fell by 72 per cent. Penetration inland was greatly facilitated by the construction of European railway networks and the general reduction in tariff protection. This trend, beginning with the repeal of the British corn laws in 1846, and designed to increase food security, had appeared to herald the dawn of a more optimistic age of free and expanding trade. The initial impact on world trade in farm produce had been limited by transport costs. In France imports of wheat had represented only 0·3 per cent of domestic production in the decade 1851–60, rising to 10 per cent in 1871–80 and to a peak of 19 per cent by 1888–92. In reaction prices fell gradually during the 1870s and then more rapidly until 1895, when they were one-third below the 1871–75 level. In the United Kingdom the average annual price of wheat was 55s a quarter in 1870–74, fell to a low of 28s in 1895–99, and recovered to 33s only in 1910–14 (Mathias, 1969: 474–5). Free trade and the rapid diffusion by telegraph of market information promoted an international levelling down of prices almost regardless of local variations in costs. Poor harvests were no longer dramatically compensated for by substantial price increases. Improved transport, in eliminating the dearths caused by localised shortage, to the great benefit of consumers, had established the conditions for a new type of agricultural crisis. Imports of wool and meat also increased, the latter particularly with the introduction of refrigeration in the 1880s, although home-killed produce retained a quality advantage. The value of animal products fell less drastically than that of wheat, reflecting rising dietary standards. Nevertheless the falling price of most agricultural products posed a threat to the income of most farmers and landowners, made all the more severe in some regions by such disasters as the devastation of the vines by the phylloxera beetle, which reduced French wine production from 60 million hl in 1873 to below 30 million hl in 1885. In England rents fell from an index of 106·5 in 1874–77 to a low of 71 in 1899 and in 1904, with an obvious negative effect on the value of land (Abel, 1980: 285–6).

The response to this crisis varied. Initially it was rather muted. Farmers were reluctant to accept that permanent changes had occurred in world markets. Growing pessimism led inevitably to demands for government support and especially for protective tariffs. Such had been the response when prices fell from inflated wartime levels after 1815. Once again it became the solution to every problem. Governmental action was determined by political factors. In most Continental countries large landowners and the professional politicians associated with them were able to use their own influence and to mobilise mass peasant support in favour of protection, as well as against the monopoly powers of the railway companies, whose discriminatory freight rates assisted import penetration. In France successive increases in protection culminated in the Méline law of 1892, which established a surcharge of 30 per cent on the price of imported wheat and extended protection to a wide range of produce. These moves were intended to win the countryside over to the republic. In Germany tariffs were increased five times between 1879 and 1887, and again in 1902, and grain producers were additionally assisted by low rail and water freight rates, tax concessions and export subsidies. Imports of meat and livestock were effectively blocked by veterinary controls. In both countries legislation was justified by the need to protect traditional and 'healthy' rural communities and avoid over-rapid urbanisation. Above all, protection represented a call to safeguard the social *status quo* from the impact of market forces, although the strategic implications of a secure food supply were not forgotten, either. In Germany, in particular, pressure groups frequently couched their demands in nationalist *völkisch* language. The very word 'protection' had favourable overtones which helped to overcome the hesitation of many peasants who would have benefited from the availability of cheap grain to feed their animals. Their response represented neither blind obedience to traditional leaders nor total unwillingness to adapt to changing market conditions so much as a desire for greater security in a period of instability. However, this situation certainly provided an opportunity for traditional elites to lay renewed claim to political leadership.

Where they were introduced, tariffs succeeded in their object of raising prices and land values above the level which might otherwise have prevailed. Although prices continued to fall until 1896, they tended to remain above those prevailing in free-trade Britain. In the years preceding the first world war imports made up less than 3 per cent of the cereals consumed in Spain, 12 per cent of those consumed in France, and 17 per cent of those consumed in Germany (Bairoch,

1988: 15). In Germany between 1895 and 1907, along with growing demand, protection stimulated an increase in cereal prices of 16–18 per cent. Tariff levels intended to protect the mass of peasant cultivators provided an opportunity for substantial profit taking by the more efficient among the larger farmers. By reducing international competition they also, of course, substantially eased the pressure on European farmers—large and small—to innovate, raising the price of grain relative to that of animal products and weakening the incentives to alter the product mix. In the case of Britain the balance of political power ensured that there was no return to protection. By 1909–13 Britain was importing 62 per cent of its cereal consumption, together with 75 per cent of its butter and 42 per cent of its meat, much of it from the empire. Belgian, Dutch and Danish farmers also benefited from the access their livestock products enjoyed to the British market and from cheap imported cereals to feed to their animals. Besides British farmers many in eastern Europe suffered, both from overseas competition and from the introduction of protection in western Europe, which tended to shut them out. The export price of Russian grain fell by one-third between 1871–75 and 1891–95, and owing to the resulting over-supply of internal markets prices there declined even more sharply—by 52·5 per cent (Pollard, 1981: 266).

The protectionist legislation introduced as politicians sought to conciliate the still substantial rural vote has usually been assumed, and quite reasonably so, to have slowed innovation. Certainly a higher proportion of the population remained in low-rewarding agricultural occupations than would otherwise have been the case. At the beginning of the twentieth century in France some 59 per cent of the population still lived in the countryside and 42 per cent of the labour force were employed in farming and forestry. The equivalent figures for Germany and Britain were 46 per cent and 35 per cent and 25 per cent and 12 per cent respectively. Nevertheless, judging from the British case, the preservation of free trade could be even more harmful to agriculture, if not necessarily to the economy as a whole. The precipitate decline in the importance of farming to the British economy, illustrated by the fall in its share of GNP from an already low 20 per cent in 1860 to less than 7 per cent in 1913 (Floud and McCloskey, 1981, II: 175), was accompanied by the loss of the technical lead built up earlier in the century. As in France, falling prices resulting in a substantial decline in the value of land encouraged a more land-intensive approach.

However, British farmers were also more likely to depend on relatively expensive wage labour. A switch to livestock, and, according to natural conditions and markets, specialisation in meat, cheese or butter, appeared to be the best or least bad solution, offering less depressed prices as well as the opportunity to economise on labour.

Alterations in the product mix were frequently combined with the abandonment of some of the practices associated with 'high farming' and the neglect of buildings and the land. The arable area declined from 58 per cent to 42 per cent of the agricultural land between 1866 and 1911, whilst the contribution of vegetable products to the value of total agricultural output is estimated to have fallen from 45 per cent to 30 per cent between 1867–69 and 1894–98, and that of animal products to have risen from 55 per cent to 70 per cent (Perry, 1973: 54). This meant that the predominantly livestock-rearing areas of the north and west were far more prosperous than the more arable south and east, although the contrast is very oversimplified, given the existence everywhere of mixed farming. Institutional differences were also significant. Those areas of Denmark and free-trade Holland experiencing the most substantial growth in productivity around the turn of the century combined family farming with rural co-operatives which provided credit and marketing facilities for high-value dairy and meat products. There and in Bavaria, the Rhineland and Westphalia peasant farmers used cheap grain as an animal feed. In contrast, in Russia the market for animal products, although growing, was insufficiently developed to promote substantial change, except in some particularly favoured areas—along the developing railway system in western Siberia, for example. High population densities ensured that most peasant farmers remained obsessed with providing for basic sustenance.

In general it appears to have been the small to medium-size farms dependent on family labour which were best able to adapt, particularly those of owner-occupiers with no rent to pay. The struggle to maintain income could, however, be achieved only at the cost of intense physical effort. To escape this, many small farmers joined the landless labourers in migration. Marginal land once laboriously cleared was gradually abandoned, with the cultivated area in France declining by approximately 9 per cent between 1882 and 1912. Large farmers were caught between the twin pressures of falling prices and rising costs as migration continued to reduce their ability to impose low wages. Thus whilst the number of farmers in England and Wales hardly changed, by 1911 the agricultural labour force had fallen by around 23 per cent from its peak at mid-century (Mingay, 1981: 120), forcing farmers to invest in labour-saving machinery. In regions which had been fully integrated into commerce for decades, and where capital had already been accumulated, continued investment in fertiliser, high-yield seeds, in more frequent ploughing and hoeing, and in the mechanisation of the harvest, permitted a compensatory rise in productivity. Indeed, in Britain the volume of gross agricultural product was surprisingly stable throughout the period 1870–1914 although its value could not be sustained.

Generally, price levels began to recover from the mid-1890s. The reason was not so much protection as the shifting balance between supply and demand as population growth, allied to industrialisation and urbanisation, increased domestic consumption in the New World as well as the old. Newer entrants to the export market like Romania and other Balkan countries clearly had much less impact on absolute levels of supply, although in the decade before the war many Russian farmers and landowners in their turn enjoyed something of a Golden Age. These conditions created a situation from which farmers in western Europe could benefit, particularly those family farmers with low labour costs but sufficient land to produce a commercial surplus regularly and generate profits which might be invested in improved technology. On the Continent, whilst competitive pressures and growing internal markets provided incentives, protection ensured a more secure environment for investors. In France the gross agricultural product, which had increased by 0·6 per cent a year between 1865 and 1874 and declined by 0·3 per cent per annum from 1875 to 1884, began to rise again in the pre-war decades (by 0·8 per cent in the decade 1895–1904 and by 1 per cent in 1905–11 (Ibanès, 1974: 731).

Conclusions

This is the point at which final judgements need to be made about the development of European agriculture and its impact on society at large—on the process of industrialisation, on living standards, and indeed on social and political relations. Inevitably, major regional contrasts survived. They reflected geography, of course, but also the ways in which farmers, landlords and governments had responded to changing market conditions. Throughout Europe those areas of plain and river valley which had previously enjoyed the advantage of relatively good links with urban markets and in which farmers were already committed to commercial activity were best placed to respond to the new opportunities offered by the transport revolution and accelerating urbanisation in the decades after 1830–50. North-west Europe initially benefited the most. Even small-scale cultivators were integrated into the market, both to sell produce and to purchase inputs and consumer goods. Elsewhere, in the uplands and throughout the east and south, where rural population growth continued to act as a disincentive to innovation, although commercial penetration increased, the process was more gradual and market links remained relatively weak. One would also, however, need to draw contrasts, within a vast area like Russia, between such regions of advanced farming as the Baltic, parts of the central industrial belt and western Siberia and the backward cultivation predominating in the central Black Earth region.

Agriculture represented, of course, only one aspect of the overall development of European economies. Moreover, structural change involved a transfer of resources away from farming into the more productive manufacturing and service sectors. The role of European agriculture in the process of industrialisation had been especially important in the earlier stages, when growing cities depended on local supplies of food and the rural population comprised the main market for manufactures, as well as providing much of the investment capital. That food production and subsequently importation increased more rapidly than population helped ensure the removal of the traditional Malthusian barriers to demographic and economic growth. What might otherwise have been is suggested by the difficulties experienced in the Low Countries and Austria but especially in Ireland in 1846–47. In most regions the disruptive impact of poor harvests on living standards and on markets for manufactured products was considerably eased following the serious mid-century crisis. Higher real wages, the movement of labour from low-productivity agricultural to higher-productivity industrial occupations, and the transfer of population overseas, gradually transformed the living conditions of the poor. Output consistently rose more rapidly than population, assisted by a marked slowing in the rates of demographic growth. Living standards for the mass of the population were increasingly to be determined by income rather than food prices.

This question of the standard of living has aroused considerable controversy among British historians. There seems little doubt that sustained improvement was absent before the 1840s, when food consumption again attained levels previously seen around 1760. Certainly evidence on the height of army recruits suggests a decline in the nutritional status of men born between the 1830s and 1850s. Similar evidence for Sweden suggests that, following recovery from the disruptive impact of the Napoleonic wars, living standards stagnated at eighteenth-century levels until as late as the 1870s, while in Russia improvement was probably postponed until the 1890s or more likely the 1900s (Floud *et al.*, 1990; Sandberg and Steckel, 1988). There, as in much of eastern and southern Europe, the combination of a relatively slow improvement in productivity with high rates of population growth had inevitably depressing effects.

Historians have frequently claimed that an agricultural revolution was a necessary prerequisite of industrialisation. If, however, both processes are conceived of in less 'revolutionary' terms, then it also becomes more fruitful to analyse them in terms of a complex web of interrelationships. Thus rising farm productivity meant that a smaller proportion of the total labour force was needed to provide food for a growing and increasingly urban population. At the same time industry increasingly produced inputs for farmers and absorbed the surplus rural population. Conversely, in much of eastern and southern Europe peasant poverty continued to impose severe restraints on the growth of the internal market for industrial products and on processes of capital accumulation, which in turn reduced the capacity of industry to absorb migrants from the countryside. The pace and scale of development in each sector of the economy had vital effects on the others, with improved transport and marketing facilities—the development of the service sector—intensifying the links between them. Overall, the balance clearly shifted decisively towards urban industrial predominance. The changing nature of the economic cycle was one clear indicator of this. After a lengthy period of transition the state of the harvest ceased to be the dominant element from around 1850, although, as the great depression proved, falling rural demand might still have serious consequences for industry, depending on the proportion of the overall labour force employed in farming and related activities. It also, however, through falling food prices, encouraged the diversification of diet and stimulated demand for industrial products. In France expenditure

105

on non-food items increased from 31 per cent of total consumer expenditure in the 1880s to 42 per cent by 1905–13.

Everything is relative. The level of modernity achieved by European agriculture prior to the first world war represented a massive advance on the situation a century before. Increased agricultural productivity had accompanied the creation of an urban industrial society. Yet the pace and scale of change almost pale into insignificance by comparison with the agricultural revolution of the second half of the twentieth century. The use of hunger as a weapon of war encouraged governments after 1945 to support efforts to maximise output. Subsidies, in addition to accelerated technological innovation—chemical, mechanical and more recently genetic—provided the means for unprecedented growth and, in the West at least, for the marginalisation of peasant farming. The 'agricultural revolution' banished famine from western Europe. The means now exist to end hunger throughout the world. Unfortunately the obstacles to progress are social and political rather than simply technical.

Acknowledgement

I would like to thank Colin Heywood of the University of Nottingham for his helpful comments on a draft of this chapter.

References

Abel, W. (1980), *Agricultural Fluctuations in Europe: from the Thirteenth to the Twentieth Centuries*. London, Allen & Unwin.

Agulhon, M., Désert G., and Specklin, R. (1976), *Histoire de la France rurale* III. Paris, Seuil.

Bairoch, P. (1988), 'Dix-huit décennies de développement agricole française dans une perspective internationale (1800–1980)', *Economie Rurale*.

Bairoch, P. (1989), 'Les trois révolutions agricoles du monde dévelopé: rendements et productivité de 1800 à 1985', *Annales*, 44.

Bartlett, R., ed. (1990), *Land Commune and Peasant Community in Russia*. London, Macmillan.

Berding, H., François, E., and Ullmann, H-P., eds. (1989), *La Révolution, la France et l'Allemagne: deux modèls de changement social*. Paris, Maison des Sciences de l'Homme.

Blum, J. (1978), *The End of the old Order in rural Europe*. Princeton, N.J., Princeton University Press.

Boserup, E. (1965), *The Conditions of Economic Growth*, London, Allen & Unwin.

Campbell, B., and Overton, M. (1991), *Land, Labour and Livestock: Historical Studies in European Agricultural Productivity*. Manchester, Manchester University Press.

Chambers, J. D., and Mingay, G. (1966), *The Agricultural Revolution, 1750–1880*. London, Batsford.

Chorley, G. (1981), 'The agricultural revolution in northern Europe, 1750–1880', *Economic History Review*, 34.

Clout, H. (1983), *The Land of France, 1815–1914*, London, Allen & Unwin.

Collins, E. (1969), 'Labour supply and demand in European agriculture', in E. L. Jones and S. Woolf, eds. *Agrarian Change and Economic Development*. London, Methuen.

Collins, E. (1978), *The Economy of Upland Britain, 1750–1850*, Reading, University of Reading.

Collins, E. (1989) 'The *machinery question* in English agriculture in the nineteenth century', *Research in Economic History*.

Demonet, M. (1990), *Tableau de l'agriculture française au milieu du dix-neuvième siècle*. Paris, EHESS.

Ernle, Lord (1912), *English Farming Past and Present*. London, Longman.

Evans, R., and Lee, W., eds. (1986), *The German Peasantry*. London, Croom Helm.

Floud, R., and McCloskey, D., eds. (1981), *The Economic History of Britain since 1700* II. Cambridge, Cambridge University Press.

Floud, R., Wachter, K., and Gregory, A. (1990), *Height, Health and History: Nutritional Status in the United Kingdom, 1750–1980*. Cambridge, Cambridge University Press.

Gatrell, P. (1986), *The Tsarist Economy, 1850–1917*. London, Batsford.

Good, D. (1984), *The Economic Rise of the Habsburg Empire, 1750–1914*. London, University of California Press.

Grantham, G. (1989), 'Agricultural supply during the industrial revolution: French evidence and European implications' *Journal of Economic History*, 49.

Grigg, D. (1980), *Population Growth and Agrarian Change*. Cambridge, Cambridge University Press.

Harrison, J. (1978), *An Economic History of Modern Spain*. Manchester, Manchester University Press.

Heffer, J., Mairesse, J., and Chanut, J-M. (1986), 'La culture du blé au milieu du dix-neuvième siècle', *Annales*, 41.

Holderness, B., and Turner, M., eds. (1991), *Land, Labour and Agriculture, 1700–1920*. London, Hambledon.

Houssel, J-P., ed. (1976), *Histoire des paysans français du dix-huitième siècle à nos jours*. Roanne, Horvath.

Ibanès, J. (1974), 'La répartition des exploitations dans l'agriculture français à la fin du dix-neuvième et au début du vingtième siècle', *Revue Economique*, 24.

Jones, E. L., ed. (1967), *Agriculture and Economic Growth in England, 1650–1815*. London, Methuen.

Jones, E. L. (1981), 'Agriculture, 1700–1780', in R. Floud and D. McCloskey, *The Economic History of Britain since 1700* I. Cambridge, Cambridge University Press.

Jones, P. (1990), 'Agricultural modernization and the French revolution', *Journal of Historical Geography*, 16.

Komlos, J. (1989), *Nutrition and Economic Development in the Eighteenth Century Habsburg Monarchy*. Princeton, N.J., Princeton University Press.

Kostrowicka, I. (1984), 'Change in agricultural productivity in the kingdom of Poland in the nineteenth and early twentieth century'. *Journal of European Economic History*, 13.

Kuznets, S. (1973), *Population, Capital and Growth*, London, Heinemann.
Mathias, P. (1969), *The First Industrial Nation*. London, Methuen.
Livi-Bacci, M. (1990), *Population and Nutrition*. Cambridge Cambridge University Press.
Mayer, W. (1989), 'Agriculture, société rurale et modernisation', in H. Berding, E. François and H-P. Ullmann (eds.), *La Révolution, la France et l'Allemagne: deux modèles de changement social*. Paris, Maison des Sciences de l'Homme.
Mingay, G., ed. (1981), *The Victorian Countryside*. London, Routledge.
Mingay, G., ed. (1989), *The Agrarian History of England and Wales* VI, *1750–1850*. Cambridge, Cambridge University Press.
Mironov, B. (1986), 'Le mouvement des prix des céréales en Russie du dix-huitième siècle au début du vingtième', *Annales*, 41.
Moeller, R., ed. (1986), *Peasants and Lords in Modern Germany*. London, Allen & Unwin.
Moriceau, J-M., and Postel-Vinay, G. (1992), *Ferme—Entreprise—Famille: grande exploitation et changements agricoles, XVIIe–XIXe siécles*. Paris, EHESS.
Nouschi, A., ed. (1973), *L'Anklose de l'économie méditerranéenne au dix-huitième et au début du dix-neuvième siècle: le rôle de l'agriculture*. Paris, Colin.
Oakley, S. (1990), 'The peasantry of Scandinavia on the eve of the French revolution', *History of European Ideas*, 12.
Offer, A. (1989), *The First World War: an Agrarian Interpretation*. Oxford, Oxford University Press.
Offer, A. (1991), 'Farm tenure and land values in England, *c*. 1750–1950', *Economic History Review*, 44.
O'Grada, C. (1988), *Ireland before and after the Famine*. Manchester, Manchester University Press.
Overton, M. (1990), 'The critical century? The agrarian history of England and Wales, 1750–1850', *Agricultural History Review*, 38.
Pallot, J., and Shaw, D. (1990), *Landscape and Settlement in Romanov Russia, 1613–1917*. Oxford, Oxford University Press.
Perkins, J. (1981), 'The agricultural revolution in Germany, 1850–1914', *Journal of European Economic History*, 10.
Perry, P. ed. (1973), *British Agriculture, 1875–1914*. London, Methuen.
Pfister, C. (1988), 'Fluctuations climatiques et prix céréaliers en Europe du seizième au vingtième siècle' *Annales*, 131.
Pollard, S. (1981), *Peaceful Conquest: the Industrialization of Europe, 1760–1970*. Oxford, Oxford University Press.
Pounds, N. J. G. (1979), *An Historical Geography of Europe*, Cambridge, Cambridge University Press.
Price, R. (1983), *The Modernisation of Rural France: Communications Networks and Agricultural Market Structures in Nineteenth-Century France*. London, Hutchinson.
Sandberg, L., and Steckel, R. (1988), 'Overpopulation and malnutrition rediscovered: hard times in nineteenth-century Sweden', *Explorations in Economic History*, 25.
Slicher van Bath, B. (1963), *The Agrarian History of Western Europe, 500–1850*. London, Edward Arnold.
Spring, D., ed. (1977), *European Landed Elites in the Nineteenth Century*. London, Johns Hopkins University Press.
Toutain, J-C. (1961), 'Le produit de l'agriculture française de 1700 à 1958', *Cahiers de l'Institut de Science Economique Appliquée*.
Vaughan, W. (1984), *Landlords and Tenants in Ireland, 1848–1904*. Dublin, Economic and Social History Society.

Webb, S. (1982), 'Agricultural protection in Wilhelminian Germany: forging an empire with pork and rye', *Journal of Economic History*, 42.
Wintle, M. (1991), 'Modest growth and capital drain in an advanced economy: the case of Dutch agriculture in the nineteenth century', *Agricultural History Review*, 39.
Wrigley, E. (1987). *People, Cities and Wealth*. Oxford, Oxford University Press.
Zanden, J. van (1991), 'The first green revolution: the growth of production and productivity in European agriculture, 1870–1914', *Economic History Review*, 44.

Enterprise and management

Entrepreneurship and entrepreneurs

Many of the sectoral developments described in other chapters were the result of the interactions of market or state-induced demand with the supply of productive factors; these included natural resources and the productivity-raising effects of changes in technology, knowledge and organisation. Industrialisation was the outcome of decisions taken by individuals, whether independently or in association with others, who by combining new or existing resources in new ways or by directing their use into new forms or directions—whether in production, trade, finance or urban development—displayed that 'enterprise' which epitomises the role of the entrepreneur. The importance of entrepreneurship in economic development is particularly difficult to assess. It is not susceptible to measurement separately from the quantification of such variables as the substitution of capital for labour, increased education, shifts in resources and improvements in organisation, for no single definition of entrepreneurship yields measurable precision (Geary, 1990: 284–5). Nonetheless, the centrality of entrepreneurship and of entrepreneurs to the process of economic change has been a continuing, and much debated, theme among historians and economists since the 1930s.

The most commonly cited and best-known theory of entrepreneurship is that advanced by Schumpeter (1934), who attributed to the innovative activity of entrepreneurs (which he described as 'creative destruction') the ability to make abnormally high profits, which by attracting imitators in time brought about the transformation of entire industrial sectors. Profit was seen to be the reward for innovation. Knight (1957), on the other hand, regarded profit as compensation for error resulting from the uncertainties which necessarily accompany innovating activity; profit accrued when entrepreneurial activity proved to be successful beyond the level of anticipated risk. A generation later, Kirzner, sympathetic to the notion that entrepreneurs were central to economic change, emphasised their alertness to the profitable opportunities that market imperfections, especially a widespread lack of information, offered (1973: 131).

Leibenstein (1978) also focused on the importance in the business process of the need for entrepreneurs to take decisions while possessing imperfect information, which necessarily left 'gaps' requiring the exercise of human judgement in filling them (for example, by anticipating future changes in material costs, product prices, or competitors' reactions to a certain business strategy). This approach has received reinforcement from Casson (1982), who pointed not only to the inevitability of entrepreneurs taking decisions without full information but also to the diminishing returns to which the collection of comprehensive 'objective' information was subject. For Casson the essential entrepreneurial skills, or flair, consisted of an ability to identify profitable opportunities, and the judgement and tactical awareness to exploit them effectively, in particular by securing exclusive rights to new opportunities so as to benefit to the maximum.

None of these refinements invalidates Wilson's simpler, straightforward working definition which nearly forty years ago was applied to the entrepreneur in the specific historical context of the first industrial revolution. Wilson (1955: 132) dwelt on the entrepreneur's crucial contribution in possessing, and acting upon, 'a sense of market opportunity and the ability to exploit it'. This focus on the perception of opportunities coupled with the motivation, capacity for judgement and practical ability to take initiatives embraces entrepreneurial activity of both a high and a low order. For while, for example, major technical inventions may have provided the potential for transforming an entire industry, the speed of such a development depended not only on the successful application of the invention, by the initiating entrepreneur and by imitators, but also on those engaged in continuous, less dramatic, adaptation of technical, organisational and market factors (Coleman, 1973: 112), functions which subsequently became the responsibility of managers.

In an economy in which there is substantial competition, resource mobility, and extensive knowledge on the part of entrepreneurs of alternative investment opportunities, the rationality of decision-making offers a defensible criterion by which to judge the quality of entrepreneurship.

111

Rationality has formed the basis of the judgements passed by some historians, but others have emphasised the constraints imposed on rational choices by the historical reality of imperfect flows of information, the effects on decision-makers of the law, government activity and the behaviour of other economic institutions, as well as of the unanticipated consequences of decisions taken by other firms or organisations. This approach favours the use of 'bounded rationality' as a criterion (Arrow, 1974: ch. 1; Williamson, 1985; Nelson and Winter, 1982: 35–6), opening up the analysis of international differences in the timing and patterns of industrialisation. It accords importance to institutions and to people as well as to costs, prices and profits as relevant explanatory factors.

The continuing debate on the relative importance to industrialisation of entrepreneurship compared with other factors does not alter the reality of economic change, which involves decisions made by people whose perceptions, motivation, origins and actions are therefore of interest. How, when and with whose involvement industrialisation occurred are matters which are of no less interest than the broader question of why that process took place. Furthermore, international comparisons of the quality of entrepreneurship and the forms it took have been employed by historians to explain differences in the pace and patterns of economic development, and of divergent national performance.

The years between 1750 and 1914 saw industrialisation proceeding at various and variable speeds yet dominating the course of economic development. Partly for that reason, industrial entrepreneurs have been the principal focus in historians' attempts to illuminate the character and contribution of enterprise. The novelty which the industrial entrepreneurs represented, however, derived neither from a new, nor even from a more intense, 'spirit of enterprise', nor from greater willingness to accept risk as compared with former times. The novel factor was the appearance of profit opportunities relatively more favourable to industrial, as distinct from commercial and financial, investment. Moreover, growing industrial activity increasingly required the investment of larger amounts of fixed capital in plant and the establishment of factory production, which presented new problems of organisation and management, not least the recruitment, discipline and control of a new factory labour force. Before sustained industrialisation, bringing with it recognisably modern forms of business, had begun, markets were overwhelmingly local and limited in extent. Monopolies and privileges shaped and restricted capital investment, while the structure of land ownership and political regulation were additional inhibiting influences on entrepreneurial activity other than of a traditional kind.

Institutional structures and incentives: markets and the state

By the eighteenth century British businessmen were least hampered by state regulations and restriction. In part this was because of the weakness and inefficiency of local administrations responsible for enforcement, though the greater freedom from restrictions also reflected the advanced penetration of market and commercial influences into internal and external trading. By contrast, in many parts of central and eastern Europe, and also in France, during the eighteenth century state ownership and strong state influence in the form of concessions, tariffs, subsidies and privileges continued to discourage long-term industrial investment undertaken by private entrepreneurs employing mainly market criteria. So long as business opportunities were heavily shaped by princely courts and governments, through controls, intervention and subsidies, the officials themselves exercised quasi-entrepreneurial functions. Under such circumstances the survival and success of business enterprise rested more on continued official support and favour than on rational business decisions in response to market factors. Kocka (1978: 506) described the skills required of the successful entrepreneur in much of Germany in the eighteenth century as political as much as economic, requiring 'a talent for intrigue, corruption and adaptability to authority'.

From the late eighteenth century, first in Britain, though also in other regions within Europe, market opportunities increasingly favoured the entrepreneur who 'organised production, . . . who brought together the capital (or somebody else's) and the labour force, selected the most appropriate site for operations, chose the particular technologies of production to be employed, bargained for raw materials and found outlets for the finished product' (Flinn, 1966: 179; Kocka, 1978: 502–3); they thus exercised managerial as well as strictly entrepreneurial functions.

Where no convergence of market, social, institutional and technical factors stimulated industrial investment traditional forms of enterprise continued to predominate during the early nineteenth century, in France, to a greater degree in many of the German states, and even more widely in territories lying farther east. The favoured avenue to profit in those areas continued to be the exploitation of commercial and financial opportunities which were the result of market imperfections due to state intervention, inadequate communications and lack of knowledge. Public finance continued to offer profitable lending opportunities in those countries in which limited natural resources, or corrupt, aristocratic government, or both, were least equipped to industrialise. In southern Italy, for example, loans to the Bourbon government attracted the attentions and financial resources of local entrepreneurs, who by controlling credit and perpetuating poverty in the region further diminished the possibility of economic progress (Davis, 1981: 26–7).

From the mid-eighteenth century the growth of rural industrial and other larger-scale centralised production was easier to accomplish in those countries in which the powers and privileges of the older corporate manufacturing industries and of the guilds which controlled them were weakened. Restrictive regulations concerning the location, quantity and quality of production, and guild control over entry to the crafts, presented barriers to enterprise which were either disregarded or removed, first in Britain, in France from the mid-century, and in the 1780s in the Low Countries (Milward and Saul, 1973: 34–7; Pilbeam, 1990: 35–7).

Landes has also pointed to the inhibiting effects of Continental customs and laws on the involvement of the nobility in business enterprise. Commercial enterprise had traditionally entailed derogation from noble status, and Landes argues that even after the Napoleonic wars the efforts of Louis XVIII to remove the stigma attached to trade and industry, by issuing decrees to that effect, could not overcome established social values. In Germany the different spheres of activity of noble, burgher, and peasant were more rigidly delineated and for longer with the force of law, a stratification which became even more rigid farther east. 'The effect of this invidious social segregation of business enterprise,' Landes (1969: 129) concluded, 'was to discourage talent and capital from entering the field and to draw out the most successful of those already engaged.'

There is evidence, however, to suggest that neither traditional institutional structures nor law and custom affecting different social groups seriously inhibited the emergence of industrial entrepreneurship or were so central in influencing the social composition of entrepreneurs during the eighteenth and early nineteenth centuries. In some of the more economically backward German states mercantilist policies affecting industry and trade were accompanied by the award of noble titles, one effect of which was to render business success a legitimate aspiration among the nobility. This helps to explain the mining and other industrial activities of an increasing number of landed aristocrats during the eighteenth century (Kocka, 1978: 500–12).

In other parts, notably the Rhineland and Westphalia, where state intervention was minimal, a strong business tradition emerged independently among a number of bourgeois families, which in the course of the nineteenth century developed dynastic dimensions. Examples of such dynasties include the families Stumm, Hoechst, Krupp and Scholler (Kocka, 1978: 509–11). Furthermore, Milward and Saul suggest that the relaxation of traditional controls was as much a consequence as a cause of early industrialisation, for it was the growth of rural manufactures outside the towns which led the French government to withdraw support from the guilds. In the Austrian Netherlands Emperor Joseph II's assault on the guilds occurred when the growth of manufacture made the enforcement of the myriad monopolies and privileges claimed by producers increasingly problematic (Milward and Saul, 1973: 36–7).

In the German states, too, evasion and inefficiency in the enforcement of mercantilist restrictions in a period of expanding economic activity in many parts of Europe warn against any exaggeration of the inhibiting effects either of the guilds or of social disapproval upon the timing and character of entrepreneurial activity and its contribution to industrialisation. In Russia friction between the court and the old mercantile elite proved both a stimulus and a constraint on entrepreneurial activity. During the eighteenth century the growing strength of the established merchants, buttressed by the traditional guild system, was increasingly counteracted by the court, which, jealous of merchants' increasing status and influence, introduced a wide range of court monopolies and protection. One result was that by the end of the century nobles produced 85 per cent of the country's pig iron and 85 per cent of its copper; by 1813, 64 per cent of mines, 80 per cent of potash capacity, 78 per cent of wool cloth production, 66 per cent of glassworks and 60 per cent of paper mills were owned by nobles, some of them ennobled merchants. Those merchants who remained outside the court were compelled, therefore, to assume a strictly trading role (Pilbeam, 1990: 28–30). By comparison with the role of the aristocracy in the rest of continental Europe the Russian nobility exercised a considerably greater influence on industrialisation and, though under very different circumstances, in this respect may be compared with the British landed aristocracy.

The social origins of entrepreneurs

Exploration of the occupational origins, social composition and prospects of the early generations of industrial entrepreneurs has presented particular difficulties. One is the lack of statistical data, another the tendency for studies to be biased, inevitably, towards successful entrepreneurs whose firms endured over a lengthy period, and of whom some record has survived. Well documented longevity, however, has not been characteristic of the evidence on businesses during the pioneering period of industrialisation (Payne, 1988: 22; Lévy-Leboyer, 1976: 102). The contribution of landed aristocrats to the development of mining and metallurgy is acknowledged to have been substantial, both in the presence and in the absence of state intervention, in Britain and in many parts of continental Europe (Pilbeam, 1990: 28), but on a broader front the social composition was more diverse.

The social origins of British industrialists have received much attention, most recently from Crouzet, whose 'sample' of over 500 leading factory employers active some time between 1750 and 1850 revealed few aristocrats and few working men. Most entrepreneurs originated from trade and industry, though, unlike previous critics of the 'rags to riches' thesis, notably Honeyman (1982: 166–70), he underlined the social mobility of managers, shopkeepers, craftsmen and others emerging from the lower middle class (Crouzet, 1985: 116–42). Evidence for the post-1850 period points in a similar direction, suggesting that a prosperous background, above-average education and career entry through the family business typified the British business elite (Jeremy, 1984: 3–22).

There are, however, some important international differences in the social composition of entrepreneurs, not least in Russia, where the rise of craftsmen and peasant traders and industrialists is evidence that, in one European country at least, the self-made man made an appreciable contribution to industrialisation (Pilbeam, 1990: 28–30). This has been attributed to the success of some peasant entrepreneurs in exploiting the antagonism between the merchants and those among the nobility who by the late eighteenth century had come to dominate business activity through monopolies granted by the court. While the peasant entrepreneur continued to be unusual in other parts of Russia, many merchants trading in Moscow were peasant entrepreneurs by origin. After taking advantage of official permission, granted in 1824, to settle in towns, many commuted their serf status for cash in order to share trading rights identical to those enjoyed by merchants, subject only to the purchase of guild membership (Rieber, 1982: xxi–xxv, ch. 10). Pilbeam (1990: 35–6) describes how in 1825 'fifteen Ivanovo industrialists bought their freedom and turned Ivanovo into a Russian Manchester'. Nonetheless, a new entrepreneurial middle class did not emerge on a sufficient scale to overcome the serious economic, socio-political and institutional barriers to industrialisation which continued to check the process until the end of the century.

While there is some evidence of Russian nobles having invested in industry, applying new technology and controlling production, they represented a small minority which displayed an unusual disregard for the low esteem attaching to business activity of this kind [30]. In France, too, industrial activity among the nobility was largely confined to a minority who, despite custom and tradition, seized the opportunity to exploit mineral resources found on their estates, sometimes to the extent of production and manufacture, whether as sleeping partners or by direct involvement (Palmade, 1972: 62). This was a common feature in the development of the mining and metallurgical industries of France, Russia, the Rhineland and Silesia. Mineral resources usually belonged to the state, which imposed leasing terms typically beyond the means of those lacking wealth (Landes, 1969: 130). In Britain, where landowners owned the minerals, many were active both in mining and in metallurgical manufacture. They also contributed to canal and road development as well as to other forms of industrial invest-ment (Ward and Wilson, 1971: 1–16). Such activities have prompted one description of a number of Britain's aristocrats as having been 'among the foremost risk-takers, and through their agents among the most imaginative entrepreneurs of their time' (Thompson, 1984: 200).

Another difference in the composition of entrepreneurs in conti-nental Europe was the greater proportion recruited from the higher

117

civil service, a feature linked partly with the earlier rise of bureacracies in France and Prussia before industrialisation and partly to the direct involvement in entrepreneurial activities of some departments of public administration, a reflection in Germany of the degree of economic backwardness then prevailing. Outside Russia, however, there are few indications that industrialisation during the early phases enabled many from outside the middle classes to turn opportunity into business success and to substitute rags for riches (Kaelble, 1980: 406–8). This is because by family background (in many cases families involved in trading or putting-out production of some kind, notably textiles), and by education, entrepreneurs appear to have been advantaged in comparison with the average person. Most of those whose educational record is known attended secondary school.

The narrow and diverse chronological, sectoral and regional basis of the available statistical evidence for attendance at institutions of higher education suggests that the claim that in the nineteenth century 50 per cent of the French business elite proceeded to higher education compared with 33 per cent in Britain and over 25 per cent in Germany (Pilbeam, 1990: 37) should be treated with caution. In any case, higher education, and specifically scientific and technical education, for entrepreneurs and managers assumed appreciable practical importance only from the late nineteenth century, when the emergence of new and increasingly technically complex industries and large corporate structures increased the importance of technical, scientific, specialist and managerial skills (Landes, 1969: 60–2, 323–6).

What *can* be said is that by 1880 there was a widespread perception among informed British opinion that whereas the object of the British system of technical education generally was to educate workmen the French and German systems displayed more interest in educating the scientist or manager, particularly the latter (Floud, 1982: 56–7). How far by 1914 these differences had been removed and had affected comparative economic performance is considered below. It is less easy to establish the validity of the suggestion made by some historians that in the course of the nineteenth century the German bourgeois elite underwent a process of 'feudalisation', cultivating connections and adopting aristocratic patterns of behaviour in an attempt to legitimise their social position. Kaelble and Kocka accept that a change in bourgeois–aristocratic relations occurred, but interpret closer identification with the nobility as a sign of a new bourgeois loyalty to the state (Kaudelka-Hanisch, 1991: 89–90).

From an economic standpoint, the important question is whether what has been described as the 'feudalisation' of the German bourgeoisie also represented a weakening of the business ethic. Pierenkemper's analysis of the business elite reveals a self-perpetuating process, while Kaudelka-Hanisch (1991: 92–7) has shown how, in Prussia at least, after the reforms of 1807 the conferment by the state of the title 'Commercial Councillor' accorded public recognition of success in business and status for businessmen. Highly valued by the business community, these awards proved an effective antidote against aspirations to aristocratic status or leisure, for most Councillors' sons became active industrialists rather than *rentiers*.

Apart from this feature peculiar to Germany, Kaelble detected a convergence of family background and education among the business elites in the three major industrial countries: an increase in the importance of entrepreneurs and managers from wage-earning rather than salaried or independently wealthy families, and an increasing proportion of business leaders possessing higher educational experience (Kaelble, 1980: 404–20). However, in Britain in those industries typified by relatively large size and capital intensity, such as iron and steel and coal, shipbuilding, textile manufacturing and brewing, families in business continued to provide most of the business leaders and there is evidence to suggest that the social composition of the business elite actually narrowed (Erickson, 1959: 9–49, 79–122; Church, 1986: 465–6; Howe, 1984: 88–9). This trend would run counter to Kaelble's claim that the characteristics of French and German business leaders converged to resemble those of their British counterparts (Kaelble, 1980: 419).

The 'entrepreneurial spirit' and the business environment

In search of the rise of capitalism and the enterprise spirit historians and sociologists have long debated the connections between religion and business enterprise. Max Weber focused in particular on the Protestant ethic, which stressed diligence, hard work and thrift, each indicative of values and behaviour likely to find acceptance in societies already experiencing the weakening of feudal and other traditional structures, and the expansion of trade and industry. They were seen to sanction and encourage effective business behaviour (Samuelson, 1964: 25–6). Kocka drew a similar conclusion, stressing that the rationale for endeavour of an entrepreneurial kind offered by Calvinist ideas gave business activity and achievement a religious meaning which was easily incorporated into a philosophy of service for family and for firm (Kocka, 1978: 529–30).

Critics of the Weber thesis have variously pointed to examples of economic success in non-Calvinist regions and among Catholic merchant and banking dynasties, and have questioned the assumed homogeneity and uniqueness of Puritan thought in relation to wealth and business conduct. They have also raised the possibility of a two-way relation between capitalism and religion, suggesting that the persecution of religious minorities, rather than the Puritan ethic, may explain the greater participation of such groups in European economic progress (Samuelson, 1964; Pratt, 1985: 1–11, 129–40). Greater emphasis upon religious groups as merely one type of minority seeking 'status respect' was followed by McClelland's analysis of successful human endeavour as the outcome of the 'need for achievement'. This approach was different from, but not inconsistent with, the notion that similar early parental influence, preparation and training, which stressed standards of behaviour, self-discipline and independence, tended to encourage aspirations to achieve (possibly regardless of profit or wealth), and to develop the abilities to realise ambitions (Pratt, 1985: 11–12).

Certainly Hagen presented some evidence, though on a sample of dubious representativeness, to suggest that innovators in British manufacturing during the industrial revolution included a disproportionate number of dissenting Protestants (1962: 294–309). While the severity of Methodist upbringing ruled out the operation of the achievement-inducement process outlined by McClelland, his hypothesis, though refocused upon business communities rather than mainly on religious beliefs, has received some support from historians knowledgeable about Eurpean entrepreneurs (Flinn, 1966; Landes, 1969; Redlich, 1944: 121–48). The tendency for entrepreneurs to be part of informal communities sharing religious and cultural affiliations has been emphasised by both Pilbeam and Chapman (Chapman, 1992: 288–92). Examples are the Protestant cotton manufacturers of Alsace, the Old Believer textile producers of Moscow and Jews in western Russia, the Quaker ironmasters of Shropshire, and the ubiquitous Jewish merchant and financial communities which shared a different language as well as a different culture and religion.

120

In Rhineland-Westphalia nearly three-quarters of all Commercial Councillors, comprising the business elite, were Protestants. In the German empire as a whole, even in those areas where the Catholic population was numerically dominant, Protestants were disproportionately represented among the Councillors (Kaudelka-Hanisch, 1991: 101). All these groups exemplify the close, and sometimes closed, communities which might nurture entrepreneurial values and enterprise. The same was true of the Poles, Germans, Greeks, Armenians and Tartars who flocked to Russia in response to Peter the Great's encouragement of foreign technology, settling in ethnic enclaves throughout the empire (Pilbeam, 1990: 40–3). In mid-eighteenth-century London more than three-quarters of all merchants were of foreign origin or descent, while, of the twenty leading merchant banks in 1914, twelve were of foreign origin (Chapman, 1992: ch. 1).

There is, therefore, abundant evidence of entrepreneurial communities, whether geographically concentrated or linked by race or religion, which derived mutual strength from proximity, connection and intermarriage. It is possible that the force which canalised their energies may have owed something to a self-confidence fostered by a shared system of beliefs (Pratt, 1985: 140). But this might have been equally plausible for the Catholic manufacturers of the twin cities of Roubaix–Tourcoing, where the disadvantages of location seem to have been overcome by the ethic of enterprise generated by the business leaders within the community in response to perceived pressure to conform (Landes, 1976: 43–7, 68–79). Less debatable are the real advantages of belonging to kinship and extended family socio-cultural networks in an age when limited communications, underdeveloped financial and trading institutions, and a general lack of business information, resulted in high levels of uncertainty and risk surrounding business transactions. An examination of the activities of Quakers in England during the industrial revolution showed how on a trading basis they provided each other with ready access to capital, became leaders in banking and wholesale provisioning, were pioneers in the iron and steel industry, and took part in early transport improvements and the switch to factory-made cotton textiles (Pratt, 1985: 140).

Even outside the kinship network and the congregation, connections and proximity resulting from the localisation of economic activity could generate that which would now be described as a culture of enterprise—what the economist Alfred Marshall called an 'industrial

121

atmosphere' which encouraged innovation, one of the major tests of entrepreneurship. In 1841 a Nottingham manufacturer of machine-made lace articulated the advantages of localised specialisation: '. . . it is not the machines themselves in which the value exists, but the great practice we (in Nottingham) have had, and the ideas we have from being congregated together, that enable us to apply our various improvements to the machines . . .' (quoted in Church, 1966: 78). It seems fruitful not only to analyse industrialisation in Europe as a regional process (Pollard, 1981: 198), but also to appreciate the tangible and intangible contributions offered by the external economies of urbanisation, which directly affected the exercise of the principal entrepreneurial functions: the mobilisation of capital and labour, the development of markets and distribution, and technical and organisa-tional innovation. During the early stages of industrialisation, before the widespread adoption of joint-stock form or limited liability, each of these functions tended to reside in a single person (Wilson, 1955: 132), the classic entrepreneur.

While the adoption of the factory system was an important organisational innovation which presented new problems, particularly of labour and personnel management and capital accounting, factory production was slow to affect entrepreneurs, managers and workers outside the textile industries; even in Britain, where the textile industry was the first to be transformed by steam-powered centralised manu-facture, the rest of industry lagged well behind until after 1870 (Musson, 1976: 430–9). New techniques of production based on minor innovation, specialisation and the division of labour, however, were much more pervasive, operating within traditional workshops and in the homes of workers. It was a system which also facilitated the introduction of new products. A less tangible form of innovation was the application of 'know how'.

For the merchant entrepreneur involved in wholesale and foreign trade, whose capital typically was very largely tied up in stock and credits to customers, the relevant 'know-how' related to his ability to exercise close financial control in order to maintain cash flow. Upon this rested the pivotal position of the merchant in European trade and industry. Increasingly during the nineteenth century merchants dele-gated or devolved the business of buying and selling to correspondents or agents in other countries and drew on the knowledge and experience of specialist brokers, but the extension of credit and the maintenance of financial liquidity, on which success crucially depended, could not be delegated (Chapman, 1992: chs 1–2). For the entrepreneur engaged in producing as well as selling, the critical know-how was also partly financial but also involved the organisation and operation of plant at maximum efficiency—whether through planning the scale of production to facilitate low costs, by identifying, through flair, judgement or market intelligence, a potential demand for existing, improved or new products, or by creating credit links to minimise discontinuities in supply or demand.

Invention, innovation and the diffusion of technology

How far Britain's lead as the first industrial nation was based on theoretical and scientific know-how related to the development of new technology, which many historians have placed at the centre of the industrialisation process, is at least arguable. Inkster's view (1990: 423) is that the new British technology was not the product of a superior scientific and technical culture, and that on balance it seems probable that before the second half of the eighteenth century the continent of Europe was the main source of specific techniques. Most industrial innovators possessed limited, if any, knowledge of science and depended, where necessary, on practical mechanical skills; they were 'the "tinkerers" that made the Industrial Revolution' (Landes, 1969: 324).

The key innovations (notably those of Newcomen, Abraham Darby, Richard Arkwright and James Watt) which during the late eighteenth century first transformed the British textile and metallurgical industries, and later those on the Continent, were exceptional, in that they were the result of major technologically creative—rather than imitative—entrepreneurship (Payne, 1974: 13). Yet to a considerable extent industrialisation depended upon the effective application of new inventions (and new ideas) and their adaptation to suit local, even firm-specific, conditions, which depended on such considerations as costs, the quality of raw materials and labour, the power source available, and the type and condition of the plant and machinery in use (Coleman, 1973: 112). Once adopted, small alterations—affecting machine speeds, factory layout, the mix of inputs, product range and quality—each minor in its effect by comparison with the major inventions, were nonetheless innovations which cumulatively contributed to entrepreneurial success or failure, with implications for the industries of different countries and regions.

Furthermore, evidence of patents in England between 1660 and 1800 suggests that the proportion registered by 'industrial producers' rose from roughly 30 per cent at the beginning of the eighteenth century to 76 per cent during the second half of the century, a development which McLeod described as the 'industrialisation of the patent system' (1988: 134). She concluded that patents were most frequently taken out in areas where the 'modern' manufacturing industries had developed among highly competitive, capitalist enterprises. During the second half of the eighteenth century industrial producers accounted for a higher proportion of patentees. Within that category 'artisan patentees' were overtaken by entrepreneurs, both those in out-working trades and those involved in centralised production, and by engine makers (135, 143). Manufacturers' holdings of multiple patents indicated a growing recognition of the financial justification for limiting risk and protecting investment in this way, incurring patent costs for each successive modification or improvement. The rise of an 'invention industry' towards the end of the eighteenth century, with quasi-professional inventors patenting numerous inventions for use in a variety of different industries (Dutton, 1984: 108, 125; McLeod, 1988: 141), may be interpreted as a further movement of entrepreneurial effort away from invention and technical innovation towards organisation and marketing.

The conversion of inventions into commercially successful innovations even without high levels of techno-scientific theoretical knowledge or creativity was a reflection of the more favourable economic climate for industrial investment in England and of the alertness of entrepreneurs to opportunities resulting from expanding demand. Because the major inventions and innovations in Britain after 1770 were those which brought about the mechanisation of the textile industry, the development of large-scale metal fabrication, and deep mining—the three sectors which to a greater or lesser degree spearheaded industrialisation throughout Europe—British entrepreneurs assumed a major international role. After 1815 industrialists from the Continent were also instrumental in the international diffusion of those innovations, a process which often involved the entrepreneur in supplying not only the technical skills required to operate plant and machinery but the managerial know-how needed to organise production effectively.

In many instances the initiative for transfer was not that of the entrepreneur but of Continental governments seeking to modernise their states and principalities by offering inducements of various kinds. Whether in the form of subsidies, guaranteed profits or high salaries, accompanied by monopoly or special privileges of some kind, inducements were more than a reward for risk, they were an incentive to British entrepreneurs to indulge in the illegal activity of exporting machinery and artisans. Though the prohibitive legislation was not repealed until 1825 as it affected workers, and 1842 for machinery, its effectiveness was much less than complete. A combination of evasion and lax implementation, which allowed the movement of blueprints and components, failed to stop the international transfer of ideas, technology, entrepreneurial and managerial know-how and labour skills (Mathias, 1979: 31). Few of the British entrepreneurs contributed more to the process of international transfer of technology, engineering and entrepreneurial skills than the Cockerills, who created a modern wool textile industry in Belgium, before establishing with the aid of a government loan the ironworks at Seraing which until the 1850s were the largest and most modern plant throughout the entire Continent (Milward and Saul, 1973: 182, 443).

The regional character of state initiative or support for enterprise is clear from the history of government–industry relations in Germany, where in this respect, even after economic liberalisation, no sharp discontinuity has been detected before unification in 1870. Minimal state intervention affecting industry in the Rhineland and in Saxony contrasted with the strongly interventionist policies of Prussia, especially immediately following the Napoleonic wars (Kocka, 1978: 504–8). Patents there were free, and protected by the state, which also sometimes pirated foreign patents for use by Prussian industrialists. By funding travel scholarships and bursaries to promote the transfer of ideas and technology, especially in metal manufacturing and steam engine technology, entrepreneurs in this region established a comparative advantage over those in other parts of Germany (Redlich, 1944: 144).

This is not to say that best practice was uniformly adopted as a result. In all countries after the initial introduction of the most modern technology the diffusion process, which required adjustments in operating practices to such factors as the relative costs of capital and labour, the availability of skilled labour for maintenance as well as supervision, the location and quality of raw materials and supplies of parts, and transport costs, was a protracted process (Fremdling, 1992:

119–24). State support in this way, as well as by establishing technical institutes and schools to create a trained work force, enabled entrepreneurs in Prussia to keep pace with developments in Britain, Belgium and France (Lee, 1991: 9).

The various independent states adopted policies which differed in the degree of intervention and the form they took, and in their effectiveness. Lee (1991: 4–7) has suggested that the multiplicity of state forms that existed at both local and regional levels of authority allowed the evolution of varied strategies of state–industry relations, which resulted in a diversity of experience. Nowhere, however, was the scale of penetration by the ideas, technology and business skills of foreign entrepreneurs greater than in Russia, where because of the strategic and enclavist nature of the state-dominated sectors the activities of foreign entrepreneurs were at the same time more induced yet more restricted than in western Europe (Inkster, 1990: 427). Under Catherine the removal and travel expenses of foreign entrepreneurs and technicians were met from state coffers (Bartlett, 1979: 179). Later, encouraged by the policies of Peter the Great, foreign merchants and manufacturers came to dominate first trade and later industry in some parts of the country.

As in other parts of Europe, the famous Carron ironworks in Scotland and the Baird business dynasty were the source of migrant entrepreneurship focused on new technology in the form of a large iron foundry and machine works built in Russia during the 1790s. This venture was subsidised by the state through direct orders, wages were paid by the state, and permission was granted to purchase peasants as factory workers. The ennoblement of William Baird's son in 1852 marked the recognition of his family's long record of industrial activity in Russia, and of the son's position as leader of the nation's metallurgical and machine construction industries, and as adviser to the government on military and civil engineering (Bartlett, 1979: 179; Inkster, 1990: 418–28).

At the beginning of the nineteenth century British and German firms dominated the foreign trade of St Petersburg; by the mid-century almost half the city's factories, then the industrial capital of the Russian empire, were owned by foreigners. So too were almost a third of the largest cotton factories, the oil industry of the Caucasus, and the coal and metallurgical industries of the Ukraine. The steel mill built by John Hughes in the Donbas region marked the beginning of the steel

126

industry in Russia (Bartlett, 1979: 164 ff.; Blackwell, 1965: 407–24; Milward and Saul, 1977: 182). Enclave development, whether the result of indigenous or foreign enterprise, artificially induced by state or principality, extended the process of industrialisation into the indigenous market environment. After the Napoleonic wars the entrepreneurial exodus from Britain, short and long-term, diminished sharply, though the international movement of skilled workers to supervise and carry out maintenance continued to increase (Mathias, 1979: 39–40).

In the reverse direction, sometimes under official sponsorship, visitors from continental Europe, who included bureaucrats and entrepreneurs or their sons or key employees, wishing to effect their own transfer or to improve technology and organisation journeyed to the workshops, mines and factories where they might observe best practice in the country of origin, though the technical details and costs of certain processes, as at the important Carron ironworks, might be kept secret from them (Mathias, 1979: 29). Up to 1870 almost a third of entrepreneurs in the Rhineland and Westphalia had visited Britain on business or to study (Kocka, 1978: 532). In the metal manufacturing and engineering industries, where technical knowledge was of particular importance to business success, the *Wanderjahhre* was often spent abroad by aspiring entrepreneurs who familiarised themselves with the latest ideas and practice before setting up their own small workshops or factories in Germany (Kocka, 1978: 522).

Industrial capital and finance

Industrial investment in the new technology and factory organisation faced entrepreneurs with the need to secure funds to finance their ventures. Pollard described English capital markets before the mid-nineteenth century as local and regional rather than national, personal rather than corporate (1964: 299–314); the same can be said of Europe generally. In merchanting and industrial enterprise, mobilising capital by securing initial finance or trading credit depended much upon mutual trust between lender and borrower, information on sources, and familiarity with the risks and prospects of particular industries or enterprises. In England (though not in Scotland), for more than a hundred years after the Bubble Act—introduced in 1720 in reaction against disastrous speculation—the law prohibited the joint-stock form

127

of company in manufacturing and commerce. Sleeping partnership arrangements, legal in France, were prohibited in England, which meant that launching an enterprise in that country was a matter of personal or family provision of starting capital. Where sizeable fixed assets were needed, and the entrepreneur was in possession of a title deed that he could pledge, it usually necessitated borrowing on the security of property.

Even in those countries where joint-stock or *en commandité* sleeping partnerships were legal the financing of industry before the mid-nineteenth century was mostly similar, and as diverse in the forms it took as in England. In France even large firms were mostly organised as limited partnerships (Lévy-Leboyer, 1978: 272–5). The legal form adopted by a firm, however, did not necessarily alter policy, with regard, for example, to the 1867 law which required new (but not existing) public companies to issue balance sheets for shareholders. The famous Saint-Gobain glassmaking company, for example, established more than a century before 1867, did not produce a financial statement for its shareholders until 1907. Such giant mining enterprises as Anzin also avoided the controls imposed by commercial law because in France mining companies came under the civil law; mining was not regarded in law as a commercial activity (Lemarchand, 1992: 6–9).

The freedom and flexibility which the partnership offered to owner-managing entrepreneurs of the ubiquitous small and medium-size firms guaranteed the overwhelming predominance of this form of organisation throughout Europe until 1914. Networks of friends and family were the main sources of starting capital, after which profits ploughed back into the firm, merchant credit from suppliers and to some extent bank credit provided the financial basis of growth and survival. Even such exceptionally large firms as the Compagnie d'Anzin, which in 1850 supplied half the coal produced on the northern coalfield, and Wendel's metallurgical enterprise in Lorraine favoured the partnership until the late nineteenth century. In Germany, too, until the last quarter of the nineteenth century, when—unusually, compared with other countries—banks began to play an important role in industrial finance, few firms outside the transport sector were large enough to necessitate substantial financial provision from outside sources. The massive Krupp works in the Ruhr remained a partnership until the 1890s (Fohlen, 1978: 354–62; Feldenkirchen,1991: 118–20; Kocka, 1978: 538).

128

Belgium, however, was different. The rapid growth of the metal-based and machine-building industries from the 1830s was achieved by newly formed joint-stock companies which to a considerable extent drew the capital for development from the Banque de Belgique and the Société Générale (Cameron *et al.*, 1967: 147–50). For a time, so close were the financial and strategic links between industry and the new state-sponsored Belgian investment banks that Milward and Saul (1973: 451) refer to the 'captain of industry' being replaced by the bank. These twin developments—joint-stock organisation and dilution of the entrepreneurial role through bank intervention—occurred somewhat later in Germany, beginning in the 1850s. This followed the conjuncture of the successful transfer of coke-smelting technology from Britain, the discovery of black-band high-quality coal and ore deposits in the Ruhr, the revision of Prussian mining law, which facilitated mining enterprise, and the demand for coal and iron generated by the railways. As in other European countries, the railways improved access to resources and markets, dominating the new large company formation by the adoption of joint-stock limited liability status (Tilly, 1986: 146–7; Feldenkirchen, 1991: 119).

Since the 1770s mining in Prussia had come under state administration, the role of private participants being limited to providing capital and electing representatives to the bureaucratic structure responsible for the management of mines. In 1851 this system of state control, direction and management in the Ruhr began to be replaced by private enterprise (Kocka, 1978: 540–2). Joint-stock company organisation became necessary for the new enterprises then required to embark on large-scale exploitation and economically efficient production. To this development the bankers of Cologne contributed by assisting in the founding of enterprises, acting as agents for entrepreneurs by placing all or part of share issues through their connections, though some banks also made loans to industry (Feldenkirchen, 1991: 119–20).

The joint-stock banks, however, set the pace. The Bank für Handel und Industrie's proclaimed policy was to promote 'sound and big business by investing the bank's and other people's money'. Until the late nineteenth century virtually the entire profits made by the bank derived from company formations, especially in the textile industry in south-west Germany, from shareholdings in industrial companies and from stock market transactions. At the centre of the massive industrial

129

development of the Ruhr, however, was Prussia's single joint stock bank, the A. Schaaffhausen'sche Bankverein, which maintained a leading position in the coal, iron and steel industries of the Ruhr throughout the period (120–1). This bank, however, was exceptional, for most of the capital raised to finance companies in Prussia during the mid-century came from other German states or from foreign countries, notably France and Belgium, through the new Crédit Mobilier banking enterprise (Cameron *et al.*, 1967: 127–8).

Nonetheless, as in France and Britain, despite growing capital requirements, particularly in the heavy industries which increasingly favoured joint-stock organisation to enable firms to attract external finance for expansion, most new company formations consisted of family partnerships of some kind. While securing the protection offered by joint-stock limited liability, at the same time such companies retained a high proportion of equity enabling owner managers to maintain control (Feldenkirchen, 1991: 123; Kocka, 1978: 540–1). During the period of depressed industrial prices between 1874 and 1895 the dependence of large businesses on the banks increased. By holding shares and extending them loans and overdrafts to avoid share issues at unfavourable times banks supported many of Germany's major companies through the 'great depression' of the mid-1870s and 1880s (Feldenkirchen, 1991: 126–7, 131–3).

Their influence in encouraging and helping to finance greater integration and concentration of production into fewer, larger firms in German heavy industry had enduring effects. The scale of several of the mergers that took place between 1880 and 1913, creating large firms in the electrical engineering industry as well as in coal, iron and steel, involved multi-bank financing and greater representation on company boards, which legislation in 1884 facilitated. The first result of such developments, which were less in evidence in general engineering and chemicals, was industry's growing dependence on the banks during the 'great depression'. This, however, was followed by a degree of inter-dependence as the growth in the size of the merged companies, coupled with inter-bank competition, led to a more balanced relationship between entrepreneurs, managers and bankers. By 1914 industry–bank co-operation was still a distinguishing feature of German industry, even though industrialists had recovered their pre-depression strength *vis-à-vis* the bankers (Feldenkirchen, 1991: 133–4).

Neither in Britain nor in France did the banks penetrate firms to a comparable extent, not even in the heavy industries in which the strategic influence of German banks was greatest (Fohlen, 1978: 367–73). The French investment banks were active in financing railways, in helping the diffusion of new technology and the development of the mining and metallurgical industries, but these involved exports of capital and know-how, and left the structure and organisation of French firms largely unaffected. In each of the three major, most advanced, industrialising countries, joint-stock limited liability legislation had the effect of strengthening rather than undermining large family firms (Fohlen, 1978: 350–5; Brockstedt, 1984: 240–50; Payne, 1988: 17–20).

Industrial and business organisation

Managerial responsibility, whether concerned with production, organisation or marketing, was normally taken on by sons, nephews and cousins, an extended family business structure which through familial loyalty was similarly intended to minimise the risk of lack of effort and application at best, of commercial duplicity or fraud at worst (Mathias, 1979: 101–3). The reliance on family to fill the managerial positions was accompanied by widespread adoption of subcontracting, which meant that problems of labour management were hived off to foremen or gangers who were closer to the work process, and by the use of factors distributing products in the home market or of merchants selling overseas. The concentration of production within a sizeable factory and the increasing integration of managerial functions under the centralised control of the entrepreneur was a feature of industrialisation, but in all countries and in most industries it remained exceptional until well into the second half of the nineteenth century.

Even in Germany, where the development of industrial concentration from the 1880s has received particular attention from historians, most enterprises were small single proprietorships or partnerships of medium size. Typically they were engaged in one branch of activity, even the relatively large firms, manufacturing such items as yarn, cloth, hardware, machinery or paper. The numbers employed could normally be counted in tens or hundreds rather than thousands— no more than could be managed through oral command by an 'ever-present, ubiquitous, and all-seeing employer', an 1868 description of the ideal management system (quoted in Kocka, 1978: 550; Caron,

1979: 163–71; Clapham, 1932–39, II: 35). Outside mining, in which subcontracting survived until well after 1900, the increasing complexity of manufacturing and metallurgical processes, the expansion, internationalisation and diversification of demand, and the emergence of business cycles, together increased entrepreneurs' incentive to exercise greater direct control over the methods, volume and quality of production, and later to greater direct involvement in marketing.

The extension of control, however, was a slow process, never more so than in adapting the long-established double-entry method of accounting to the needs of enterprises employing substantial amounts of fixed capital. The mining and metallurgical sector was among the first to adopt improved accounting systems, though the pace of diffusion of best practice is difficult to judge. Neither the distinction between capital and revenue, nor the concept of depreciation as a charge before striking a profit figure, were widely acknowledged even in relatively large firms during the second half of the nineteenth century. To the extent that improved methods were introduced they reflected the greater capital intensity of industry, the shift to joint-stock organisation and the introduction of businessmen—and, in Germany, bankers too—from outside the former family partnerships. Railway organisation and methods were another influence towards more systematic accounting practices, though the pace at which the role of the professional accountant and the utilisation of accounts for management decision-making developed is a matter of debate (Pollard, 1965: 209–49; Fleischman and Parker, 1991: 361–75; Fohlen, 1978: 378–9; Kocka, 1978: 544–56).

On the basis of research into the textile industry, two reasons for the neglect of double-entry and of systematic management accounting have been put forward: entrepreneurial obsession with secrecy and the burden of preparing detailed accounts (Hudson, 1991: 236). Evidence from British and French firms in other industries supports this view. By the last third of the nineteenth century, public companies in the major European economies (which excludes Russia and the southern European countries) were required to issue shareholders with financial statements. However, the legal requirements were couched in such general terms that companies were able to present only the information it suited the directors to reveal. Typically, even in public companies, that choice was made by a small number of large shareholders, declared profits and dividends being determined by their interests, which in normal times included deterring people from buying shares in the company, unless there was a desperate need to raise capital on the financial market, and the avoidance of taxation (Lemarchand, 1992: 9–20; Baldwin *et al.*, 1992: 20–63).

The specialist marketing function integrated with production in a corporate structure was also slow to develop in countries, notably Britain, France and Italy, where centuries of internal and overseas trade had built up a network of wholesaling factors and merchants through whom, for much of the nineteenth century, most producers distributed their goods. The transaction costs of conducting business through such specialist institutions were lower than the costs entrepreneurs would incur by taking on those functions themselves. Even in 1914 the proportion of exports sold overseas direct by British producers was less than half (Payne, 1988: 41–2; Chapman, 1992: 304). Elsewhere, especially in Germany, which lacked a similar continuity of industrial and trading enterprise, localised cultures of mutual business experience and trust, production and selling were more integrated (Kocka, 1978: 550–2).

One feature common to the industrial strategies of several large firms, particularly in mining and metallurgy but also in textiles, was the approach to relations with workers, though what proportion of the labour force was affected is impossible to estimate. Often described as 'industrial paternalism', it took the form of private welfare systems set up by employers, especially those operating in rural districts and therefore facing particular difficulties in recruiting labour. Houses, schools, shops and places of worship together formed a social infra-structure designed to create and nurture communal life revolving around workplace and employer, who in many instances before the late nineteenth century dominated the life and labour of the workers. Sickness benefit and rudimentary provision were often other elements in the paternalist strategies intended not only to attract workers in the first place but to retain them, and their families, in the future.

Indebtedness, whether arising from rent arrears or dealings with the company shop, was often a material barrier to labour mobility. However, by providing education, opportunities for apprenticeship or more limited forms of training, through religious instruction, the encouragement of innocent pastimes, the works brass band and other subsidised social events, employers forged communities in which they projected their role as benevolent provider rather than autocratic

133

capitalist. Typically, as a corollary of housing and welfare provision, employers showed intense hostility towards trade unions, the most extreme, the most enduring and most politically charged of all being that demonstrated by German industrialists. Paternalism and the kind of control which it achieved over workers weakened during the nineteenth century as industrialisation was accompanied by urbanisation and the growing strength of trade unions (Pollard, 1979: 45–67; Geary, 1991: 140–52; Reid, 1985: 579–607). Industrial paternalism varied in character, in degree of control, and over time, which makes generalisation on its effects difficult. Some historians minimise the benefits gained by employers, whereas others have stressed its contribution to the stability, skill and loyalty of the work force (Lévy-Leboyer, 1984: 217–22; Joyce, 1980: ch. 4).

There were other important influences affecting the rapidity with which, beginning in the 1870s, functional integration and specialisation was adopted. They included the size and complexity of business organisation, the scale and character of production or the services provided, single or multi-product, the role of fixed capital, the number of workers employed and whether activities were centred on a single plant or dispersed. In each of these respects the size and complexity of the new joint-stock railway companies were greater than in any other sector, which explains why in all countries the railways were first to tackle the problem posed by the need to raise very large amounts of capital from the public and to design management structures which reconciled the widespread dispersion of ownership with the imperative of managerial control over complex, diverse and geographically widespread operations.

Corporate and managerial structures

The solution devised in order to manage large-scale business organisations was to devolve power from the board of directors to departmental committees which operated at various levels of the organisation (Gourvish, 1986: 189; Fohlen, 1978: 374–8; Kocka, 1978: 555). This hierarchical managerial structure heralded the clearest separation of the entrepreneurial from the managerial role. It led to the gradual professionalisation of salaried managers and to the evolution of more advanced accounting techniques. In Europe, as in the United States, the nature of railway business, diverse and geographically extended, for which precision was necessary to ensure safety and punctuality, placed communication to achieve co-ordination in a central role. The networks of railway and telegraph lines which were built up facilitated the physical connections and scheduling, so combining production and distribution in a single enterprise capable of supplying a national, and later an international, market.

This model, described by Chandler (1977: chs 3–4) in the American context, while applicable to the evolution of the organisational structures and managerial practices of European railway companies from the mid-nineteenth century, is much less applicable to the manufacturing, mining and service sectors before 1914. Similarly, business organisations in Europe were on the whole smaller and less diversified in their output than those in comparable sectors in the United States. These differences in scale and scope, which in themselves, Chandler argued, through organisational innovation of the kind begun by the railway companies—though more scientific in conception and more professional in execution from the 1880s—he employed as a benchmark, against which other national models of entrepreneurial and managerial performance may be compared. The international comparisons between industrial enterprise led him to distinguish between the 'competitive managerial capitalism' of the United States from that which he called the 'organised' or 'co-operative capitalism' of Germany and the 'personal capitalism' of Britain (Chandler, 1990: chs 3–8).

The differences between the patterns of industrial development Chandler explained in terms of the size of markets, the application of capital-intensive production technologies and the legal environment affecting inter-firm relations (89). In the United States each of these factors was conducive to the development of the 'managerial firm' and the multi-divisional structure, in which all but the most major strategic decisions became a matter of routine. The 'organisational capabilities' of the enterprise as a whole (the physical facilities and the human skills organised within the enterprise) increased the probability that investment in production, distribution and management would maximise efficiency and counteract bureaucratic inertia (230).

The concept of 'organisational capability' and the international comparisons drawn to assess its character and strength in different countries has a counterpart in the debate about the quality of entrepreneurship and the differences in national cultures which may explain

135

divergent entrepreneurial performance. In the European context these concepts have been employed to explain the greater success of German industrial performance between 1880 and 1914 as compared with the contemporary record of Britain and of France.

In terms of the size, degree of integration and extent of diversification of firms in the heavy industries, German 'co-operative' or 'organised capitalism' is considered to have developed some of the features of the American form of competitive managerial capitalism in that period. Because of Germany's position as a latecomer to industrialisation, in the era of steel rather than iron, of the emergence of chemicals and electricity, the environment in which businessmen conducted their affairs—which in Britain, and to a lesser degree in France, included a well developed network of financial institutions, market development and an extensive system of distribution—differed in Germany, notably in the role of government and of the banks. The tacit political alliance between the Prussian nobility and the new industrialist elite, dominated by heavy industry, resulted in government favourable to entrepreneurial interests. One tangible outcome was the reintroduction of tariff protection in 1879. Furthermore, German law not only allowed collusion between firms but from 1897 recognised cartel agreements as binding contracts in the courts (Fremdling, 1992: 144).

The cartelisation of German heavy industry had its origins in the severe depression of the 1870s, when investment in the vertical integration of coal, iron and steel production by such firms as the Thyssen 'Combine' and the Gelsenkirchener Bergwerksverein was one strategy designed to secure greater control of the market (and in this respect was ahead even of American industry). Another strategy which contributed to industrial concentration and firms' exercise of market power was horizontal combination through mergers and take-overs. The formation of two very large holding companies, Siemens and Allgemeine Elektrizitäts Gesellschaft (AEG), between 1890 and 1914 transformed the electrical engineering sector (Tilly, 1974: 149–153). The trend towards cartelisation intensified during the 1890s, the formation in 1893 of the Coal Syndicate in Rhineland-Westphalia representing one of the most complete and effective of the German cartels (152). In many cases the initiative behind mergers, acquisitions and cartelisation came from the banks. This constitutes another difference, compared with Britain and France: the relations between banks and bankers on one hand and industrial firms and industrialists on the other. German industrialisation occurred at a time when the technology of iron and steelmaking and the scale of production of coal, iron and steel required large-scale investment if British pre-eminence was to be challenged (161). This explains why German banks not only functioned as intermediaries in issuing shares but held shares as well as providing both long and short-term loans.

This relationship gave bankers an incentive to promote cartelisation and to finance rationalisation by helping to implement concentration and vertical integration to secure greater efficiency (Fremdling, 1992: 143; Feldenkirchen, 1991: 116–35). In central and eastern Europe deficient markets and the lack of a network of market and financial institutions in effect forced entrepreneurs to compensate by internalising more functions and to use formal organisation to achieve market power (Kocka, 1978: 536–60). Other industries—engineering and chemicals, for example—and small family firms typically reliant on internal financing were much less reliant on the banks and so not susceptible to comparable banking influence on business policies. The bulk of investment undertaken by German enterprises, large and small, was internally generated. Nonetheless, the degree of industry's dependence on the banks contrasts with the more distant relations general in the rest of Europe (Tilly, 1974: 156–61; Feldenkirchen, 1991: 135).

It remained the case, even when that dependence gave way to increasing interdependence as the growth of retained earnings strengthened the position of firms *vis-à-vis* the banks. The boardroom influence of the latter was in decline after about 1900, especially during the years immediately preceding the war. Another difference was the greater degree of intensive inter-firm co-operation in Germany by comparison with other countries. Among the most extensive of these business arrangements were the links between AEG and Siemens. Through investment banks allied to them, Germany's two leading electrical enterprises provided finance for the construction of utility power plants. A comparable constellation was the autonomous but interdependent iron and steel, coal and electrical utility enterprises under the managerial control of Hugo Stinnes. Such firm-transcending enterprises, which in other instances also involved some form of state participation, generated a powerful stimulus to regional industrial development. They also involved management in evaluating performance, planning long-term strategy, allocating funds, facilities and

137

personnel, of which they became suppliers (Kocka, 1990: 714–15; Schaefer, 1991: 200–15).

One of the implications for the growth in the size and complexity of enterprise lay in the extensive managerial hierarchies and organisational routines required in the large firms and joint enterprises which evolved in Germany. That country's long tradition of bureaucratic management and a highly respected civil service combined with willingness among German entrepreneurs to hand over executive management to salaried managers. This situation has been contrasted with a tendency in Britain and France for entrepreneurs to continue participation in managerial decision-making (Hannah, 1976: 8–26; Chandler, 1990: 499–501; Lévy-Leboyer, 1984: 212–16). Greater managerial demands were also made on German enterprises because of the relative limitations of the market in Germany, which made exporting a priority, and led to corporate policies consistent with risk-spreading and to product diversification in a greater degree than occurred among large British companies (Kocka, 1980: 107–10; Chandler, 1990: 644–713).

The history of the electrical equipment manufacturers Siemens, thought to have been the first firm in the world to develop the multi-divisional structure, affords an important example of a major enterprise in transition. During the 1880s the partnership of Siemens & Halske, though dominated by the strong personality of Werner Siemens, was losing competitive advantage. After his death in 1892 the firm became a corporate organisation under salaried managers. The reformed organisation featured devolved decision-making and decentralised operations, followed by external finance and growth (Kocka, 1971: 133–57; Tilly, 1974: 154). Such developments, like those at the Rhenisch-Westfälisches Electrizitätswerk, towards integration, diversification and managerial hierarchies, compare well with developments in the United States. However, Brockstedt (1984: 249) concludes that even in the iron and steel, electrical, engineering and mining industries, where the large-scale integrated firms were to be found, entrepreneurial families continued to dominate or retain a very strong influence. Just how much more widespread such managerial enterprises were, even in heavy, large-scale industry, is difficult to assess, though their number did increase (Tilly, 1974: 156; Kaelble, 1986: 77–9).

In Britain firms which became large enough to allow full exploitation of the technological economies of scale and scope, which invested in marketing to balance the volume of production with sales, established a multi-divisional organisation with extensive managerial hierarchies, and employed scientific management techniques, were the exception. Among the few that did were Brunner Mond, Dunlop, Guinness, Lever, Metropolitan Carriage and Nobel. A further difference between many of the large British companies which were formed through amalgamation was that, unlike their German counterparts, they functioned not as an integrated organisation but as a federation of firms under a holding company, each legally controlling its small, personally managed operating divisions (Hannah, 1976: 8–26).

The level of industrial concentration in the heavy industries was higher in France than in Britain, though, as in Britain, the process was achieved more through internal expansion than by merger; for example, the firms of Decazeville, Wendel, Le Creusot and Fourchambault, which in 1840 produced 6·2 per cent of iron and steel, accounted for 21 per cent in 1869. In 1912 the ten leading iron and steel producers supplied 70 per cent (Caron, 1979: 169–70). The potential for a small number of very large companies to affect the market through collusion was greatest in basic chemicals and aluminium, though the scope for independent—or collusive—manoeuvre was constrained by legislation on cartels designed to avoid excess dispersion but to prevent monopolistic behaviour. Cartels were fewer and less powerful in France than in Germany, though price-fixing agencies, mostly short-lived, resembled the many trade associations in Britain, where business leaders proved no more successful in dominating the market, either by controlling output or prices, for more than short periods (Caron, 1979: 169–71; Lévy-Leboyer, 1980: 116–18).

Differences between corporate development in the mining and heavy manufacturing sectors in Britain and Germany to a considerable extent reflect their contrasting histories of market development and distribution, and importantly the existence in Britain of a well developed network of financial institutions even early in the nineteenth century. Several historians have stressed that the emergence of large-scale business structures and complex managerial hierarchies was important to industrialisation because of their contribution to efficiency and growth. In the personal or entrepreneurially dominated firm performance depended on the entrepreneur. Some historians have argued that over and above the entrepreneurial and management skills involved in corporate decision-making, responding to market signals and shaping and influencing market incentives, the large corporation developed a momentum of its own, through 'organisational capability'. This quality was achieved by investment in large-scale production, distribution channels and management structures, a combination which generated an internal dynamic ensuring the continuing growth of an enterprise (Chandler, 1990: 8–9).

Alternative models of industrial growth

Throughout western Europe, even in Germany, this dynamic, managerial corporate sector was relatively limited in extent; the small and medium-size family firm and flexible craft production continued to dominate large areas of the economy. The fact that 54 per cent of the largest German manufacturing and mining firms in 1887 no longer figured among them twenty years later (Chandler, 1990: 722–32) is indicative not only of the extent of mergers among big businesses but of the capacity of smaller firms to compete and grow large. The dualistic structure of industry which persisted throughout even the most industrialised countries has been explained by the resilience of small and medium-size firms, partly owing to their success in supplying specific products to markets in which local and individual preferences limited the scale and scope of businesses. Their survival throughout the nineteenth century, as independent workshop producers or as subcontractors reliant on large undertakings, reflects their ability to exploit the external economies available through the development within localities and regions of specialist production, technical, financial, marketing and distributive skills (Caron, 1979: 166).

For example, O'Brien and Keyder compared the greater importance, by comparison with Britain, to French producers of a domestic market less affected by international trade and urban demand and more by the traditional tastes and preferences of a highly dispersed rural society. They noted a continuing regard for relatively high-quality products, associated with craft and fashion, especially in textiles, one of the most important industries in most countries (1978: 164–8; Caron, 1979: 143–6, 164). Except in countries where the state intervened to develop heavy industry, that consumption pattern applied to most of continental Europe. In Italy the introduction of tariffs in

140

1887 was accompanied by state subsidies to assist the development of steel, shipbuilding, railway equipment and armament firms (Webster, 1975: 40–2, 51–4; Piore and Sabel, 1984: 151–2). For most of the nineteenth century Italian entrepreneurs were unable to prosper without the support of local politicians or, in some instances, of large landowners active in industry. Insulated to a greater degree than countries in north-western Europe from the penetration of market forces, narrow opportunities for industrial entrepreneurship fostered traditional values and limited entrepreneurial horizons. Not until the 1880s, when nationalist ideology, protectionist drive and a measure of state involvement combined to create an 'ideological stimulus' to economic advance, was capital (including foreign investment) and entrepreneurship directed into manufacturing on an appreciable scale (Federico and Toniolo, 1991: 209–10). Even so, a handful of large, privately financed Italian firms, notably Fiat, established before 1914 possessed managerial hierarchies comparable to those of some of the major German enterprises (Webster, 1975: 40–2, 51–4; Piore and Sabel, 1984: 151–2).

Industrialisation in Russia also benefited from state policies aimed at modernisation, even though the 'byzantine' complexity of the Russian bureaucracy responsible for implementing policy was often inefficient, obstructive and sometimes corrupt (Kirchner, 1981: 372; Gregory, 1991: 74; Munting, 1992). However, with the major exception of railway building, which the government itself undertook during the second spurt of railway investment in the 1890s, state involvement with industry was indirect. In the 1870s railway building by private enterprise benefited from government loan guarantees to private investors, regardless of origin, and the opportunities for entrepreneurs were widened through the derived demand for engineering and metallurgical production, and by opening access to hitherto underutilised natural resources which led to the development of new industrial regions as well as new industries.

Tariffs were introduced in the 1890s, for revenue purposes rather than protection, which was nonetheless real, while official encouragement was shown towards cartelisation, which was deemed to be in the national industrial interest (Kaser, 1978: 432–72; Gregory, 1991: 73–4). The logic of government policy in welcoming foreign enterprise and capital through direct and indirect investment from the 1880s was explained in a memo by Sergei Witte, the Minister of

Finance, in 1899. The effect, he thought, was 'to knock down the excessively high level of profits to which our monopolistic businessmen are accustomed and force them to seek profits through technical improvements . . .'. Direct investments, he maintained, 'educate, change attitudes and infuse a missing dynamism' (quoted by Kaser, 1978: 472–3).

The combination of cartelisation with foreign capital and entrepreneurial aggression was a formula intended to bring about large-scale, technologically advanced private enterprises. Trends in this direction occurred in the engineering and metallurgical industries, where the main contribution came from France, and in the chemical and electrical industries, which depended much on German capital and expertise. Britain was a major contributor to the development of oil extraction. Even more spectacular was the introduction through foreign connections of entirely new industries producing telephonic and telegraphic equipment, sewing and agricultural machinery (McKay, 1970). Changes in the law regularising the status of joint-stock companies led to the creation of a market for equities in 1874. After 1890 one of the features of faster industrial growth was a sharp increase in company formation (Gregory, 1991: 73–4). Such developments lend plausibility to Rieber's observation that 'indigenous capitalists contributed as much to the great industrial spurt as did foreign entrepreneurs and the state' (1982: 415).

Historians are not agreed, however, on the effect of changes in the legal, economic, social and political context facing entrepreneurs and enterprises. Gerschenkron and McKay have argued that one effect of the injection of foreign capital and enterprise into the Russian economy was to initiate a transformation of values and attitudes towards business activity, and to affect the motivation and conduct of Russian entrepreneurs. Systematic reinvestment of profits, the training of workers, and the recruitment of managers from among non-Russian nationals were some of the manifestations of this shift in cultural attitudes (Gerschenkron, 1968: 77–97; McKay, 1970: 379–90; Kaser, 1978: 474). At the same time, a network of producers' committees were able to voice their industrial interests through a congress of trade and industrial representatives which acted as spokesman. Associations such as these, together with local industrial societies which were also established, helped to promote greater social approval of entrepreneurs and managers (Kaser, 1978: 479–80).

This process may have been assisted to some extent by the participation in business of the gentry. In the 1860s and 1870s many were to be found among the leading concessionaires developing the sugar-beet processing industry on their estates, whose factories, producing a variety of products, increased in number. By 1900 the number of gentry directors on the boards of joint-stock companies suggests that changing economic opportunities—resulting in part from state policies, notably towards capital imports, but also from a conjunction of rising population and increasing real incomes (Munting, 1992)—were at least as important in the flowering of Russian entrepreneurship as the demonstration effect of the presence of foreign entrepreneurs and greater social acceptance of indigenous business activity.

The perception that a cultural change in public attitudes towards business was necessary indicates the probability that for many years business activity had been identified especially with minorities, religious sects shut out from the mainstream of professional life in Russia (Blackwell, 1968: 407–24). In the late nineteenth century merchants who had earlier become involved in the manufacture of cotton textiles reinvested profits in the new metallurgical sectors. Like the coal and steel producers in southern Russia, they formed pressure groups to influence government policy, the most ambitious association of this kind hitherto having been the Russian Industrial Society, founded in 1867 (Owen, 1985: 587–606). The activities of this group might be interpreted as evidence to support McKay's claim that by the late nineteenth century a marked trend towards 'entrepreneurial self-sufficiency' is discernible (1974: 368). Owen regards this as an overstatement of the degree to which entrepreneurial progress had been achieved before 1914. 'For every competent Russian manager . . . we can infer the existence of hundreds of bearded merchants in the provinces who clung to their abaci and pursued the old goal of maximum profit through minimum honesty' (Owen, 1991: 210).

However extensive the entrepreneurial and managerial cadres that developed during the late nineteenth and early twentieth centuries, historians have disputed the degree to which corporate development was helped or hindered by the state. Gerschenkron's view was that as a consequence of the 1905 revolution traditional attitudes, and certainly by 1907 expectations and conventions as they affected business activity, had disappeared, and that the massive bureaucratic

143

involvement which had inhibited industrial development in the nineteenth century came to an end (1968: 126). A detailed study of the development of the business corporation in Russia since 1800 by Owen, however, showed how the law of 1836 aimed at protecting investors from 'speculators and capitalist crooks' consigned the fate of each new company to state bureaucrats. Moreover, subsequent amendments, which Owen describes as based on 'pre-modern ethnic, religious and national prejudices', represented even greater restrictions on business activity (1991: 198).

During the course of the nineteenth century the growth of a strong corporate sector was impeded by the often arbitrary decisions of a centralist, autocratic and fundamentally anti-capitalist regime. Even Witte's commitment to economic development resulted in reforms which observed the principle adopted by successive Tsars and Tsarist bureaucrats, that private economic activity should continue to depend on the needs of, and service to, the state and that the state should be the principal initiator. The effect was to cripple any sense of dynamic independence in the corporate sector (201–3). A contemporary critic of the system before 1917 referred to the frustration and discouragement experienced by Russian entrepreneurs, whose business potential was persistently neutralised by the intellectual efforts of a bureaucracy dedicated to creating 'hindrances, obstacles and restrictions' (Ozeroff, quoted by Owen, 1991: 209).

New evidence of the incompatibility of the modern corporation with the nature of autocracy presented by Owen adds support to the view, presented in more general terms by Kahan (1967), who challenged the thesis that in the absence of a capitalist ethos and indigenous capitalists the state undertook the role of the entrepreneur in Russian industrialisation. The limited corporate sector survived and grew, it seems, despite, and not as a consequence of, the anti-capitalistic legal and bureaucratic framework. The long-established conventional wisdom that the state filled the role of the entrepreneur in industrialisation is now seen to be flawed. The lack of research into Russian firms and the late and rapid emergence of other industries in which large-scale corporate organisation was typical, where they existed, in the rest of Europe makes generalisation and international comparison alike difficult. It seems likely, however, that the characteristics of Russian industrialisation between 1880 and 1914 meant that such organisational capacity as existed relied neither upon a tradition of effective bureaucracy and training such as contributed to German industry, nor upon an even longer tradition of personal capitalism such as is central, many historians have argued, to an explanation of the relative decline of British industry from at least the beginning of the twentieth century. This argument is similar to that which has been adduced to help explain slow growth in the French economy during the second half of the nineteenth century (Landes, 1969: 528–9; Kindleberger, 1964: 115).

Differential performance: enterprise and management to 1914

In contrast with Germany, both Britain and France experienced a fall in their percentage share of industrial output in Europe between 1860 and 1913 (Bairoch, 1982: 296). For this the persistence of the family firm—which, all historians agree, in the early stages of industrialisation was an appropriate institution to promote business enterprise and industrial success—has been accorded a large portion of blame. During the late nineteenth and early twentieth centuries, the argument runs, large business corporations administered by extensive, professionally trained managerial hierarchies on the American model were required to achieve international competitiveness. These developments, it is argued, were inhibited in Britain by 'personal capitalism'. Family firms, those which Chandler describes as controlled and managed by family, were not conducive to effective entrepreneurship and successful competition in international markets. Rather than reinvestment in innovation and long-term growth, the priorities of the owners of family firms included retention of ownership and control, management participation, and a dividend policy which placed rewards to shareholders above profit retention for reinvestment (Chandler, 1990: 236–94). Entrepreneurial firms, which although by definition were neither family-owned and managed nor dominated in their decision-making by a managerial hierarchy, were also included in Chandler's definition of 'personal capitalism'.

Chandler's view of the reasons why German economic performance, reflected in growth rates and the rapid development of metallurgical, electrical and chemical industries, was superior to that of Britain or France, the other major European economies, may be challenged. Evidence on the structural characteristics of German, compared with British, industry reveals greater similarities than are evident in Chandler's analysis. German cartels did operate more co-operatively than the looser associations formed between firms in Britain and in Germany, achieving higher levels of integration and organisation. Even in cartelised industry, however, it has been suggested, the degree of inter-firm rivalry that arose has been understated.

Among the companies engaged in heavy industry were some of the largest family and entrepreneurially dominated firms in Germany, including Krupp, which became a joint-stock company in 1903 but remained entrepreneurial in its managerial structure (Brockstedt, 1984: 256). Brockstedt's assessment of the characteristics of the mining, iron and steel, engineering and electrical industries in 1907 is that Krupp's history in this respect was far from exceptional. The legal form of joint-stock organisation often made little difference to control, which was frequently also accompanied by the exercise of high-level managerial power by family or salaried 'entrepreneurs', managers who showed loyalty to the controlling family and who themselves in many instances became part of the dynasty. Whether overtly or covertly, he concludes, at least until 1914, even in the heavy industries, entrepreneurial families were either dominant or retained a strong influence. Except for shipbuilding, which he describes as mixed in its characteristics, family and entrepreneurial firms continued to dominate German industry, as they did the industries of its European competitors (Brockstedt, 1984: 241–50). The differences in corporate structure and organisation have been accorded an exaggerated role in explaining the divergent pace and pattern of industrialisation in Europe before 1914.

International comparisons between the industrial performance of European countries have often been critical of the quality of entrepreneurs, in France throughout the nineteenth century and well into the twentieth, and in Britain from the second half of the nineteenth century onward. Emphasising the social influences on the priorities, motivation, attitudes and behaviour of those sections of the population from which entrepreneurs emerged, Sawyer, Landes (who later modified his view) and Kindleberger conclude that French entrepreneurs were peculiarly ill suited to the kind of innovating industrial activity characteristic of the early British industrialists. Aristocratic values and aspirations were kept alive, among them disdain for business and the pursuit of conspicuous consumption (Landes, 1949: 45–61; Sawyer, 1952: 7–22; Kindleberger, 1964: 115). Social and institutional influences included a strong centralised state which favoured policies of protection aimed at national power, a strong bureaucratic tradition and the artificial perpetuation of petty-bourgeois activity with limited horizons, no ambition and small production units. From the mid-nineteenth century the evolution of anti-capitalist ideologies tended to reinforce, so it has been argued, the lack of industrial dynamism in France. Among the consequences of this matrix, according to those critical of the character and outlook of the typical French entrepreneur, were a sense of social inferiority on the part of the bourgeoisie and lack of entrepreneurial vigour. Marriage was a favourite escape route from business (Palmade, 1972: 12–13).

Before considering the validity of the entrepreneurial interpretation of French industrial history it is well to note that not all historians accept this picture of French business and businessmen after the revolution. The bourgeoisie were one of the principal elements in the struggle in 1789, and again in 1830 when the nobility were dealt a final blow. Thereafter the bourgeoisie are seen to have been so socially and politically supreme over the economy (Kemp, 1971: 213) as to justify the description 'a kind of "industrial nobility"' (Kemp, 1971: 182). However, the characteristics to which Landes attached so much importance in explaining French retardation persisted; the family enterprises the bourgeoisie owned and managed have been described as typically small-scale, averse to investment for expansion and to the development of new markets, and cautious towards international competition (Kindleberger, 1964: 115; Caron, 1979: 167–8; Landes, 1969: 336–9; Pollard, 1989: 165–7).

British entrepreneurs seem to have lacked the status and political influence of their French counterparts, who are also seen to have suffered a decline during the late nineteenth century. Businessmen in Britain (particularly in England) have also been portrayed in an adverse light. They have been accused of aspiring to gentrification through the purchase of land and an aristocratic life style, ultimately seeking escape from industrial activity. Another specific criticism levelled at English businessmen has been their neglect of science and innovation (Pollard, 1989: 153–5). Whereas upward revisions of French growth rates suggest that the debilitating effects of the weaknesses attributed to French entrepreneurs on the nation's economic performance have been at least exaggerated, the debate over the record of English entrepreneurship and the role of family firms continues.

Evidence has been presented to challenge the reassertion that there was 'a decline in the industrial spirit' (Wiener, 1981) in England after the mid-nineteenth century, evidence which points to a history of success in the new mass consumer goods such as bicycles, cigarettes, soap, margarine, confectionery and newspapers (Sigsworth, 1969: 125–9). In the staple industries of iron and steel, coal, shipbuilding, cotton, in branches of engineering and armaments, British entrepreneurs have been described as behaving rationally within the context of relative factor costs and technical market opportunities (McCloskey, 1971: 459). This meant that in some branches of all these industries British entrepreneurs performed well. In part this was because, contrary to the conventional wisdom that in Britain education and science suffered from neglect, particularly in meeting the needs of industry, the lag behind the education offered by German universities and technical colleges that existed before 1900 was rapidly made good in British universities thereafter (Sanderson, 1972: 118–20, 212–13; Pollard, 1989: 156). In any case, while in the long run science was to become increasingly important to industrial production, until the late nineteenth century the prevailing need in industry was a knowledge of technology rather than science. Until about 1900 technologically relevant teaching in Germany was catching up best practice in Britain, learned mainly through apprenticeship in British companies at a time when British industry was recruiting science-trained Germans (Pollard, 1989: 155).

The anti-industrial prejudice attributed to entrepreneurs educated in English public schools has been adduced as one contributory factor to the relative decline of British industry. They are said to have nurtured a culture favouring landed aristocratic values which led to a 'haemorrhage of talent and perhaps capital' from industry, with deleterious effects (Ward, 1967: 47, 52). Several reservations caution against attaching to this factor the importance which some historians have accorded it. In the first place, finance, and particularly merchant banking, was an occupation much favoured by public school leavers, either before or after university, a sector which showed considerable enterprise in this period. Second, the sons of industrialists entered the public schools in any significant numbers only towards the end of the century, and would have made their impact, therefore, only after 1914 (Pollard, 1989: 157). Third, an apposite comparison can be drawn between the English public schools and the *Gymnasien* which were likewise schools for the country's elite and favoured classical and literary rather than modern or practical studies (James, 1990: 109).

148

As for wider social attitudes to business, particularly towards industrial entrepreneurs and to profit-making, the verdict is to be found in the literary traditions of the two countries, which both contained strong negative elements (James, 1990: 95–103). Bourgeois values in Germany are now seen to have been subordinated to those of the nobility and senior bureaucrats to a much greater extent than was the case either in France, where bourgeois democratic values suffused society, or in Britain. It was Germany, it seems, that was disadvantaged in the inhibiting social influences which aspiring entrepreneurs had to face (Pollard, 1989: 164–5). James concluded his comparison of English and German literature by emphasising that both reflected similarly hostile or sceptical attitudes towards business, and elitist attitudes towards education (1990: 122). Such a view undermines the stereotype entrepreneurs presented by those who have emphasised contrasting institutional and broader cultural influences on men in business as the most important factor explaining differences between the pattern and pace of industrial development in European countries.

The answers to such questions are more likely to be found by concentrating attention on the chronology and dimensions of changes in demand and the effects on the structure of incentives, paying particular attention to basic resource endowments and the supply and quality of productive factors—human capital especially, but also the influence of the legal framework and the role of the state. In all societies before 1914 the role of entrepreneurs and enterprises, whether individual proprietorships, partnerships or corporations, was the key agent in determining the pace and extent of industrialisation. In western Europe the differences between the motivation and capacity of entrepreneurs and the legal, institutional development of the firm were not sufficiently large for us to attribute to them the crucial role in determining different paths to, and the chronology of, industrialisation. East of Germany, and in the southernmost parts of Europe, the social and political context reinforced the disadvantages of economies which lacked comparable wealth, resource endowments and financial institutions, and which were hampered by populations ill-prepared to acquire the basic skills which industrialisation, especially from the later nineteenth century, required.

References

Arrow, K. (1974), *The Limits of Organization*, New York, Norton.

Bairoch, Paul (1982), 'Industrialisation levels from 1750 to 1980', *Journal of European Economic History*, II.

Baldwin, T., Berry, R. H., and Church, R. A. (1992), 'An examination of the accounts of the Consett Iron Company, 1864–1914', *Accounting and Business Research*, spring.

Bartlett, Roger P. (1979), *Human Capital: the Settlement of Foreigners in Russia, 1762–1804*. Cambridge, Cambridge University Press.

Bater, James (1976), *St Petersburg: Industrialisation and Change*. London, Edward Arnold.

Blackwell, W. L. (1965), 'The old believers and the rise of private industrial enterprise in early nineteenth-century Moscow', *Slavic Review*, XXIV.

Blackwell, W. L. (1968), *The Beginnings of Russian Industrialisation, 1800–60*. Princeton, N.J., Princeton University Press.

Brockstedt, J. (1984), 'Family enterprise and the rise of large-scale enterprise in Germany, 1871–1914' in Akio Okochi and Shigeaki Yasuoka, eds., *Family Business in the Era of Industrial Growth*. Tokyo, Tokyo University Press.

Cameron, Rondo (1983), 'French economic growth: a radical revision', *Social Science History*, 7, 3.

Cameron, Rondo, Crisp, O., Patrick, H., and Tilly, R. (1967), *Banking in the early Stages of Industrialisation*. Oxford, Oxford University Press.

Caron, F. (1979), *Economic History of Modern France*. London, Methuen.

Carter, E. C., Forster, R., and Moody, J. N. (1976), *Enterprise and Entrepreneurs in Nineteenth and Twentieth Century France*. Baltimore, Md., Johns Hopkins University Press.

Casson, M. (1982), *The Entrepreneur: an Economic Theory*. Oxford, Blackwell.

Casson, M. (1987), *The Firm and the Market*. Oxford, Blackwell.

Chandler, Alfred D., jnr (1977), *The Visible Hand: the Managerial Revolution in American Business*. Cambridge, Mass., Harvard University Press.

Chandler, Alfred D., jnr (1990), *Scale and Scope: the Dynamics of Industrial Capitalism*. Cambridge, Mass., Harvard University Press.

Chandler, Alfred D., jnr, and Daems, Hermann, eds. (1980), *Managerial Hierarchies: Comparative Perspectives on the Rise of the Modern Industrial Enterprise*. Cambridge, Mass., Harvard University Press.

Chapman, Stanley (1992), *Merchant Enterprise in Britain*. Cambridge, Cambridge University Press.

Church, Roy (1966), *Economic and Social Change in a Midland Town: Victorian Nottingham*. London, Cass.

Church, Roy (1986), *The History of the British Coal Industry* 3, *1830–1913: Victorian Pre-eminence*. Oxford, Oxford University Press.

Clapham, J. H. (1932–39), *An Economic History of Modern Britain* I. Cambridge, Cambridge University Press.

Coleman, D. C. (1973), 'Gentlemen and players', *Economic History Review*, 2nd ser., XXVI.

Coleman, Donald C., and McCleod, Christine (1986), 'Attitudes to new techniques: British businessmen, 1800–1950', *Economic History Review*, 2nd ser., XXXIX.

Crouzet, François (1985), *The First Industrialists: the Problem of Origins*. Cambridge, Cambridge University Press.

Davis, J. A., (1981), *Merchants, Monopolists and Contractors: a Study of Economic Activity in Bourbon Naples, 1803–1914*. New York, Arno Press.

Dutton, H. (1984), *The Patent System and Industrial Activity during the Industrial Revolution, 1750–1852* Manchester, Manchester University Press.

Erickson, Charlotte (1959), *British Industrialists: Steel and Hosiery, 1850–1950*. Cambridge, Cambridge University Press.

Federico, Giovanni, and Toniolo, Gianni (1991), 'Italy', in R. Sylla, and G. Toniolo, eds., *Patterns of European Industrialization*. London, Routledge.

Feldenkirchen, Wilfred (1991), 'Banking and economic growth: banks and industry in Germany in the nineteenth century and their changing relationship during industrialization' in W. R. Lee, ed., *German Industry and German Industrialization*. London, Routledge.

Fleischman, R. K., and Parker, L. D. (1991), 'British entrepreneurs and pre-industrial revolution foundations of cost management', *Accounting Review*, 66.

Flinn, M. W. (1966), *The Origins of the Industrial Revolution*. London, Longman.

Floud, Roderick (1982), 'Technical education and economic performance: Britain, 1850–1914', *Albion*, 14.

Fohlen, Claude, (1978), 'Entrepreneurship and management in France in the nineteenth century', in Peter Mathias and M. M. Postan, eds., *The Cambridge Economic History of Europe* VII, 1. Cambridge, Cambridge University Press.

Fremdling, R. (1992), 'The German iron and steel industry in the nineteenth century', in Suzuki Yoshita, ed., *The Rise and Decline of Steel Industries*. Tokyo, Tokyo University Press.

Geary, D. (1991), 'The industrial bourgeoisie and labour relations in Germany, 1871–1933', in David Blackbourn and Richard J. Evans, eds., *The German Bourgeoisie*. London, Oxford University Press.

Geary, Frank (1990), 'Accounting for entrepreneurship in late Victorian Britain', *Economic History Review*, 2nd ser., XXXIX.

Gerschenkron, A. (1953), 'Social attitudes, entrepreneurship and economic development', *Explorations in Entrepreneurial History*, I.

Gerschenkron, A. (1968), *Continuity in History and other Essays*. Cambridge, Mass., Belknap Press.

Gourvish, T. R. (1986), 'The railways and the development of managerial enterprise in Britain, 1850–1939', in Kesaji Koboyashi and Hidemasa Morikawa, eds., *Development of Managerial Enterprise*. Tokyo, Tokyo University Press.

Gregory, Paul (1991), 'The role of the state in promoting economic development: the Russian case and its general implications', in R. Sylla and G. Toniolo, eds., *Patterns of European Industrialization*. London, Routledge.

Guroff, L., and Carstenson, F., eds., (1983), *Entrepreneurship in Imperial Russia and the Soviet Union*. Princeton, N.J., Princeton University Press.

Hannah, Leslie (1976a), *Management Strategy and Business Development: an Historical and Comparative Study*. London, Macmillan.

Hannah, Leslie (1976b), *The Rise of the Corporate Economy: the British Experience*. London, Methuen.

Hagen, Everitt (1962), *On the Theory of Social Change*. Homewood, Ill., Dorsey.

Harder, K. P. (1969), 'Major factors in business formation and development: Germany in the early industrial period', in L. J. Kennedy, ed., *Papers of the Sixteenth Business History Conference*. Lincoln, Nebr., University of Nebraska.

Henning, Hansjoachim (1981), 'The social integration of entrepreneurs in Westphalia, 1860–1914', in *Business History Yearbook*. Berlin, Springer.

Honeyman, Katrina (1982), *The Origins of Enterprise: Business Leadership in the Industrial Revolution*. Manchester, Manchester University Press.

Horn, N., and Kocka, J., eds. (1979), 'Law and the formation of the big enterprise in the nineteenth and early twentieth centuries', in Norbert Horn and Jürgen Kocka, eds., *Studies in the History of Industrialization in Germany, France, Great Britain and the United States*. Göttingen, Vandenhoeck & Ruprecht.

Hudson, Pat (1991), *The Genesis of Industrial Capital*. Cambridge, Cambridge University Press.

Howe, A. C. (1984), *The Cotton Masters, 1800–60*. Oxford, Oxford University Press.

Inkster, Ian (1990), 'Mental capital: transfers of knowledge and techniques in eighteenth-century Europe', *Journal of European Economic History*, 19.

James, Harold (1990), 'The German experience and the myth of British cultural exceptionalism', in Bruce Collins and Keith Robbins, eds., *British Culture and Economic Decline*. London, Weidenfeld & Nicolson.

Jeremy, David (1984), 'Anatomy of the British business elite', *Business History*, XXVI.

Joyce, Patrick (1980), *Work, Society and Politics*. London, Methuen.

Kaelble, Hartmut (1980), 'Long-term changes in the recruitment of the business elite: Germany compared to the US, Great Britain, and France since the industrial revolution', *Journal of Social History*, 13.

Kaelble, Hartmut (1986), 'The rise of the managerial enterprise in Germany, *c.* 1870 to *c.* 1930', in Kesaji Kobayashi and Hidemasa Morikawa, eds., *Development of Managerial Enterprise*. Tokyo, Tokyo University Press.

Kahan (1967), 'Government policies and the industrialization of Russia', *Journal of Economic History*, XXVII.

Kaser, M. C. (1978), 'Russian entrepreneurship', in Peter Mathias and M. M. Postan, eds., *The Cambridge Economic History of Europe* VII, 1.

Kaudelka-Hanisch, Karin (1991), 'The titled businessman: Prussian commercial councillors in the Rhineland and Westphalia during the nineteenth century', in David Blackbourn and Richard J. Evans, eds., *The German Bourgeoisie*, London, Routledge.

Kemp, Tom (1971), *The French Economy, 1913–39: the History of a Decline*. London, Dobson.

Kindleberger, Charles, F. (1964), *Economic Growth in France and Britain, 1815–1950*. Cambridge, Mass., Harvard University Press.

Kindleberger, Charles, F. (1976), 'Technical education and the French entrepreneur', in E. C. Carter *et al.*, *Enterprise and Entrepreneurs in Nineteenth and Twentieth Century France*. Baltimore, Md, Johns Hopkins University Press.

Kirchner, W. (1981), 'Russian tariffs and foreign industries before 1914; the German entrepreneurs' perspective', *Journal of Economic History*, 45.

Kirzner, I. M. (1973), *Entrepreneurship and Competition*. Chicago, University of Chicago Press.

Knight, H. J. (1957), *Risk, Uncertainty and Profit*, London, LSE Reprints.

Kocka, Jürgen (1971), 'Family and bureaucracy in Germany industrial management, 1850–1914: Siemens in comparative perspective', *Business History Review*, XIV.

Kocka, Jürgen (1978), 'Entrepreneurs and managers in German industrialization', in Peter Mathias and M. M. Postan, eds., *The Cambridge Economic History of Europe* VII, 1. Cambridge, Cambridge University Press.

Kocka, Jürgen (1980), 'The rise of the modern industrial enterprise in Germany', in Alfred D. Chandler, Jnr, and Herman Daems, eds., *Managerial Hierarchies*. Cambridge, Mass., Harvard University Press.

Kocka, Jürgen (1981a), 'The entrepreneur, the family and capitalism', in *German Yearbook of Business History*. Berlin, Springer.

Kocka, Jürgen (1981b), 'Capitalism and bureaucracy in German industrialization before 1914', *Economic History Review*, 34.

Kocka, Jürgen (1981c), 'The entrepreneur, the family and family capitalism: some examples from the early rise of industrialism in Germany', in *German Yearbook of Business History*. Berlin, Springer.

Kocka, Jürgen (1990), 'Germany: co-operation and competition', *Business History Review*, 64.

Landes, D. S. (1949), 'French entrepreneurship and industrial growth in the nineteenth century', *Journal of Economic History*, IX.

Landes, D. S. (1954), 'Social attitudes, entrepreneurship and economic development: a comment', *Explorations in Entrepreneural History*, II.

Landes, D. S. (1960), 'The structure of enterprise in the nineteenth century: the case of Britain and Germany', *XI Congress of Historical Sciences*. Uppsala, Rapports.

Landes, D. S. (1969), *Prometheus Unbound*. Cambridge, Cambridge University Press.

Landes, D. S. (1976), 'Religion and enterprise: the case of the French textile industry', in E. C. Carter *et al.*, *Enterprise and Entrepreneurs in Nineteenth and Twentieth Century France*. Baltimore, Md, Johns Hopkins University Press.

Laux, James M. (1975), 'Managerial structures in France', in Harold Williamson, ed., *The Evolution of International Management Structures*. Newark, N.J., University of Delaware Press.

Lee, Robert (1991), 'The paradigm of German industrialization: some recent issues and debates in the modern historiography of German industrial development' in W. R. Lee, ed., *Germany Industry and German Industrialization*. London, Routledge.

Leibenstein, H. (1968), 'Entrepreneurship and development', *American Economic Review, Papers and Proceedings*, LVIII.

Lemarchand, Yannick (1992), 'The Dark Side of the Result: Self-financing and Accounting Choices within XIXth Century French Industry', discussion paper, ABFH conference, Cardiff.

Lévy-Leboyer, Maurice (1976), 'Innovation and business strategies in nineteenth and twentieth-century France', in E. C. Carter *et al.*, eds., *Enterprise and Entrepreneurs in Nineteenth and Twentieth Century France*. Baltimore, Md, Johns Hopkins University Press.

Lévy-Leboyer, Maurice (1978), 'Capital investment and economic growth in France, 1820–1914', in P. Mathias and M. M. Postan, eds., *Cambridge Economic History of Europe* VII. Cambridge, Cambridge University Press.

Lévy-Leboyer, Maurice (1980), 'The large corporation in modern France', in A. D. Chandler, jnr, and H. Daems, eds., *Managerial Hierarchies: Comparative Perspectives on the Rise of Modern Industrial Enterprise*. Cambridge, Mass., Harvard University Press.

Lévy-Leboyer, Maurice (1984), 'The large family firm in French manufacturing industry', in Akio Okochi and Shigeaki Yasuoka, eds., *Family Business in the Era of Industrial Growth*. Tokyo, Tokyo University Press.

McCloskey, Donald M. (1973), *Economic Maturity and Entrepreneurial Decline: British Iron and Steel, 1870–1913*. Cambridge, Mass., Harvard University Press.

McKay, J. P. (1970), *Pioneers for Profit: Foreign Entrepreneurship and Russian Industrialisation, 1885–1913*. Chicago, University of Chicago Press.

McKay, J. P. (1974), 'Foreign enterprise in Russian and Soviet industry: a long-term perspective', *Business History Review*, XVII.

MacLeod, Christine (1988), *The Patent System and Inventive Activity during the Industrial Revolution, 1750–1852*. Cambridge, Cambridge University Press.

Mathias, Peter (1979), *The Transformation of England*. Methuen, London.

Milward, A., and Saul, S. B. (1973), *The Economic Development of Continental Europe, 1780–1870*. London, Allen & Unwin.

Milward, A., and Saul, S. B. (1977), *The Economic Development of Continental Europe, 1850–1914*. London, Allen & Unwin.

Munting, Roger (1992), 'Industrial Revolution in Russia'. Unpublished paper.

Musson, A. E. (1976), 'Industrial motive power in the United Kingdom, 1800–1870', *Economic History Review*, 2nd ser., XXIX.

Nelson, Richard R., and Winter, Sidney G. (1982), *An Evolutionary Theory of Economic Change*. Cambridge, Mass., Harvard University Press.

O'Brien, Patrick, and Keyder, Caglar (1978), *Economic Growth in Britain and France, 1780–1914*. London, Allen & Unwin.

Owen, Thomas, C. (1985), 'The Russian industrial society and Tsarist economic policy, 1867–1905', *Journal of Economic History* XLV.

Owen, Thomas, C. (1991), *The Corporation under Russian Law, 1800–1917: a Study in Tsarist Economic Policy*. Cambridge, Cambridge University Press.

Palmade, Guy, R. (1972), *French Capitalism in the Nineteenth Century*. Newton Abbot, David & Charles.

Payne, P. L. (1978), 'Industrial entrepreneurship and management in Great Britain', in Peter Mathias and M. M. Postan, eds., *The Cambridge Economic History of Europe* VII, 1. Cambridge, Cambridge University Press.

Payne, P. L. (1988), *British Entrepreneurship in the Nineteenth Century*. London, Macmillan.

Pilbeam, Pamela, M. (1990), *The Middle Classes in Europe, 1789–1914*. London, Macmillan.

Piore, Michael J., and Sabel, Charles, F. (1984), *The Second Industrial Divide*. New York, Basic Books.

Pohl, H. (1982), 'On the history of organisation and management in large German enterprises since the late nineteenth century', in *German Yearbook of Business History*. Berlin, Springer.

Pollard, Sydney (1964). 'Fixed capital in the industrial revolution in Britain', *Journal of Economic History*, 24.

Pollard, Sydney (1965), *The Genesis of Industrial Management*. London, Edward Arnold.

Pollard, Sydney (1979), 'Management and labour in Britain during the period of industrialization' in Keichiro Nakagawa, ed., *Labour and Management*. Tokyo, Tokyo University Press.

Pollard, Sydney (1981), *Peaceful Conquest: the Industrialization of Europe, 1760–1970*. Oxford, Oxford University Press.

Pollard, Sydney (1989), 'Reflections on entrepreneurship and culture in European societies', *Transactions of the Royal Society*, 40.

Pratt, David, H. (1985), *English Quakers and the first Industrial Revolution*. New York, Garland.

Redlich, F. (1944), 'The leaders of the German steam engine industry during the first 100 years', *Journal of Economic History*, IV.

Reid, Donald (1985), 'Industrial paternalism: discourse and practice in nineteenth-century French mining and metallurgy', *Comparative Studies in Society and History*, 27.

Rieber, A. J. (1982), *Merchants and Entrepreneurs in Imperial Russia*. Chapel Hill, N.C., University of North Carolina Press.

Samuelson, Kurt (1964), *Religion and Economic Action*. New York, Harper & Row.

Sanderson, Michael (1972), *The Universities and British Industry, 1850–1970*. London, Routledge.

Sawyer, J. (1952), 'The entrepreneur and the social order: France and the United States', in William Miller, ed., *Men in Business: Essays on the Historical Role of the Entrepreneur*. New York, Harper & Row.

Schaefer, Hermann (1991), 'New industries and the role of the state: the development of electrical power in south Germany, from *c*. 1880 to the 1920s', in W. R. Lee, ed., *German Industry and German Industrialization*. London, Routledge.

Schumpeter, J. A. (1934), *Theory of Economic Development*. Cambridge, Mass., Harvard University Press.

Sigsworth, Eric M. (1969), 'Some problems in business history, 1870–1914', in Charles J. Kennedy, ed., *Papers of the Sixteenth Business History Conference*. Lincoln, Nebraska.

Thompson, F. M. L. (1984), 'English landed society in the nineteenth century', in P. Thane, G. Crossick and R. Floud, eds., *The Power of the Past*. Cambridge, Cambridge University Press.

Tilly, Richard (1974), 'The growth of large-scale enterprise in Germany since the middle of the nineteenth century', in H. Daems and H. van der Wee, *The Rise of Managerial Capitalism*. Cambridge, Mass., Harvard University Press.

Tilly, Richard (1978), 'Capital formation in Germany in the nineteenth century', in Peter Mathias and M. M. Postan, eds., *The Cambridge Economic History of Europe* VII, 1. Cambridge, Cambridge University Press.

Tilly, Richard (1986a), 'Financing industrial enterprise in Great Britain and Germany in the nineteenth century: testing grounds for Marxist and Schumpeterian theories', in H. J. Wagner and J. W. Drukker, eds., *The Economic Law of Motion of Modern Society: a Marx–Keynes–Schumpeter Centennial*. Cambridge, Cambridge University Press.

Tilly, Richard (1986b), 'German banking, 1850–1914', *Journal of European Economic History*, 15.

Ward, David (1967), 'The public schools and industry in Britain after 1870', *Journal of Contemporary History*, 11.

Ward, J. T., and Wilson, R. G. (1971), *Land and Industry*. Newton Abbot, David & Charles.

Webster, R. A. (1975), *Industrial Imperialism in Italy*. Berkeley, Cal., University of California Press.

Williamson, O. E. (1985), *The Economic Institutions of Capitalism*. London, Macmillan.

Wilson, Charles (1955), 'The entrepreneur in the industrial revolution in Britain', *Explorations in Entrepreneurial History*, III.

Alan Lougheed

Industry and technical change

Technological change was an important factor in the industrialisation of Europe, since it gave rise to the need for centralised production in factories. It spelt the decline of domestic or cottage industry, which, by the mid-eighteenth century, was generally approaching the limits of expansion. To the extent that technical change embodied new production processes, factory production evolved in order to use non-human power.

Technological advances increased and then sustained output *per capita* and output per worker, thus contributing substantially to the process of modern economic growth. Its impact was greatest upon the productivity of labour (output per worker). However, it is difficult to separate this influence from that of capital accumulation, for much of the new technology was embodied in new or improved capital goods. There was thus a close relationship between investment, technological progress and increased output (Hartwell, 1967: 68).

Its contribution to the changing location and the size of industry, altering the roles of various raw materials, the social patterns of work and the quality of life itself, must also be noted (Milward and Saul, 1973: 171). Moreover, 'one thing that is clear about modern economic growth is that it depends on, more than anything else, a continuing process of technical change' (Deane, 1965: 118).

In this context, it is *manufacturing* industry with which we are mainly concerned—the production of commodities in a central location by means of non-human power. This chapter is devoted to the growth of such manufacturing activities from their origins in the mid-eighteenth century, largely in response to technical change and its spread across the European economy, affecting one country after another.

156

The nature of technological change

Technological change involves the development of new products and their production, the invention, adoption and spread of new processes for the manufacture of a product or a service, and of improvements in the organisation of production processes. It normally follows a distinct pattern involving invention, innovation, diffusion within a country or an industry and transfer abroad. Invention involves the discovery of something new, be it product or process. Some inventions occur in isolation, others respond to economic pressures or production bottlenecks, that is, challenges requiring solutions. Some inventions are simple in nature and, if they fill or create a potent demand, may be adopted rapidly. Others, because of their complexity and/or the lack of potential demand, may not be adopted at all. An invention has no importance until it is innovated, that is, put into production. Innovation is '. . . the heart and core of technological production. It is this that enlarges the possibilities of production, requires new combinations of factors of production, and creates new cost structures' (Deane, 1965: 95). Innovation is undertaken by the inventor or someone else, generally a factory owner, especially if a large amount of capital is required. Innovation may be fast or slow, depending on several factors.

Diffusion includes the spread within a country from one firm or industry to another and from one geographical centre to another. It also involves the transfer of a new idea, commodity or process from the country of origin to others. The popularity of a new product, the importance of an innovation, its ability to bypass or eliminate production bottlenecks, or its cost-reducing potential, will determine the rapidity of spread, within or from a country.

Adoption and spread

Given that the development of a product or a process is often derived from a need for something of the kind, its adoption is virtually certain. Nevertheless, until it has been subjected to trial its success cannot be guaranteed. New consumption goods may not become as popular as was assumed; new capital goods or processes may have teething troubles which may take a long time to overcome. Thus the greater the acceptance of a new product, or the more efficient a new machine or process, other things being equal, the faster will be the adoption and spread of the innovation.

157

The simpler the innovation, the faster will be its diffusion. A complex innovation may require specialist knowledge of its operations or uses to overcome mechanical and other difficulties, Also, before an innovation can spread it may have to be adapted to meet local conditions. For example, it may need changes in ancillary machinery or in the layout of the factory floor, the introduction of associated equipment, or the supply of cheap raw materials. Moreover, the spread of an innovation may depend on the existence or emergence of a diversified machine tool industry, for such is central to the acquisition and diffusion of the skills and techniques required in a modernising economy (Rosenberg, 1963: 416–17).

The size and scope of the innovation are important. A new idea which requires large capital investment, such as most of the technological advances after 1850, will depend on the presence of large firms to undertake the heavy expenditure necessary. Large firms often respond to a new idea faster than small ones because they have readier access to financial and product markets and because technological conditions within the large firm often favour the adoption of new technology—replacing the old with the more modern.

Deane notes the importance of the bunching of innovations in Britain for promoting modern economic growth in that country, for it demonstrates the 'technological dynamism' of the country's entrepreneurs (1969: 95–6). It must be stressed that, in addition to the well known inventors, there would be many unknown ones making vital discoveries or devising essential additions to or alterations of the major innovations (Mathias, 1969: 136).

The speed of diffusion may be greatly affected by how big an advance the new technology is over the old. If a new process reduces the existing unit cost or increases productivity substantially, replacement of the old technology could be rapid. If not, replacement may not occur until the old technology wears out. The introduction of the early spinning machines, for example, raised productivity so quickly that they soon replaced the spinning wheel.

In general terms, the rate of diffusion depends upon the strength of the demand for the product or process, on the availability of relatively cheap raw materials, skilled labour, managerial staff, capital (including risk capital) to finance its adoption, the existence of a suitable transport network if necessary to move greater volumes of materials and commodities, and the degree to which the innovation

158

may overcome production bottlenecks or to which it complements another product already in great demand (Rosenberg, 1972–73: 21). The speed of diffusion may also depend upon how quickly *secondary* improvements of the primary innovation can be effected (1972–73 6).

Government attitudes towards technology may promote or limit the expansion of markets or the protection of rights in inventions—for example, towards customs duties, patent law, the exporting or importing of machinery, or the emigration or immigration of skilled workers.

The absence of one or more of these factors may retard or prevent the diffusion of an important innovation. Other factors whose presence may have the same effect include the failure of early trials for lack of awareness of local conditions, inability to incorporate modifications to suit local requirements, or lack of foreign specialised knowledge.

The role of technological progress in the industrialisation process

Technological progress usually has an important impact upon the growth of manufacturing. Its influences are many and varied. Innovations in the eighteenth century produced a central location for manufacturing activity, the central workshop or 'manufactory', the distinguishing feature of which was by mechanical power. Once the factory had developed as a firm's production centre, further innovations would increase the firm's productivity. Even so, initially, not all activities required non-human power; nor could all the activities involved in turning out a particular product be incorporated in a factory. Production comprised both factory and domestic forms of labour or, if a product became purely factory-made, activities supplying materials for it might be carried on as a domestic industry—in nearby workshops. It is thus important to note that the establishment of factories did not necessarily preclude all domestic-type industry.

Technological change does not occur simultaneously across all industries. As eighteenth-century experience has shown, it can be highly discriminatory in its impact. For example, woollens formed the most important section of textiles in 1700, from 1800, and increasingly after 1820, cottons rose from insignificance to dominate the sector and become Britain's major export, because the major textile innovations favoured cottons. In addition, iron and steel production benefited from major discoveries and, if the steam engine is added, this sector also rose in prominence during the period.

159

Rarely did technological change fail to raise productivity or improve efficiency in the sectors in which it was concentrated. The greater productivity, and the ability to cultivate widening markets for output and new sources of inputs, allowed manufacturing industry to expand quite rapidly. With major innovations in transport and communications, distant markets were brought much closer to the factory. In addition, the accumulation of savings, which increasing productivity tends to encourage, facilitated the growth of the firm so that its expansion from the productivity benefits of the innovations and the improved efficiency from economies of scale could occur unfettered by shortage of capital.

Technological progress broadens the range of products available for consumption or increases the opportunities available to firms for improving their productive efforts, that is, it aids the expansion of a capital goods industry, the production of the new machines and of machine tools. It can alter the whole industrial structure of a country. During the early days of Britain's industrialisation the number of innovations increased substantially, changing the nature of economic activity and turning it into a continuous, if fluctuating, flow (Deane, 1965: 118). That is what distinguishes this period from previous periods where single innovations did not maintain their momentum. It was this continuous flow, stimulating productivity in various fields, which made modern economic growth self-perpetuating. In turn, industrialisation greatly increased the flow of innovations. Hughes (1970: 62) adds:

> The factories . . . grew in size because of internal economies. But they grew up close together because of external economies. . . . the forge masters moved to the neighbourhood of the blast furnaces once they no longer needed to use charcoal for fuel. The blast furnaces were located near their fuel, raw materials, and transportation. Men moved near their work. . . . In a sense the new cities grew on their own impetus out of the primary specialities, ports, trading centres, . . . as industry grew the conurbations appeared . . .

Industry and technical change in the early industrialisation of Britain, 1750–1850

The technological discoveries in eighteenth-century Britain did not spring suddenly from a vacuum but formed part of an on-going process which had proceeded slowly over time, some say from the early Middle Ages (Lilley, 1973: 187). 'Domestic' production in villages and small towns of woollen cloth, iron, ships, houses, carriages, printing, paper, glass and copper developed over the centuries. By the mid-eighteenth century, gloves, stockings, lace, nails, chairs, refined sugar, alum and brass, were also produced there (Court, 1954: 43–4).

An acceleration in technical change occurred around 1750 which had an enormous impact upon the growth of manufacturing and eventually brought the work force out of the villages into central locations. The use of non-human power (at first, the waterwheel) to drive the new factory machines and the need for greater and continuous supervision of the many production stages were important influences in the development of the factory. But small-scale production in town workshops still remained throughout the modernising of the economy, often using the final output of the factories as their inputs or efficiently providing the factories with some of their needs. The overall result was a large improvement in labour productivity.

The areas of industrial endeavour between 1750 and 1850 to attract the greatest attention are textiles (especially cottons), iron and steel and coal. One way of explaining the new innovations is in terms of challenge and response—that in Britain it was largely the response of supply factors to the rising demand challenges, both internally and externally, which prompted research into the problems. Increasing the number of cottage workers was no more than a temporary answer to the rising demand; a more permanent one was the substantial raising of labour productivity through technological advance. Recent commentators are unsure about the strength of such demand forces and question the interplay of demand and supply in some instances (von Tunzelmann, 1981: 143–58).

Once the innovatory process had begun, greater productivity in one stage of production of a commodity could create a bottleneck at another, a new problem requiring a solution. One striking feature of the time was the number of people with the creativity and training to invent something new and introduce it into production, including 'amateurs', among whose ranks may be counted the inventors of the new textile machines (Lilley, 1973: 193).

Few innovations entered the production lines in their final form. Initially, the new machines were crudely made of wood and broke down frequently. Their shortcomings were rectified by trial and error.

161

Only after several decades and the change-over to precision-made iron machines was it possible to maintain some quality control over production. By that time, the evolved machine often bore only a slight resemblance to the rudimentary prototype, as it was the outcome of many small modifications whose significance was cumulative (Rosenberg, 1982: 6–7). Such changes often came from artisans experienced in the working of the machines who saw ways of improving them.

The major textile innovations included John Kay's flying shuttle in the 1730s, widely used by cotton weavers in the 1750s and 1760s, and Lewis Paul's carding machine of 1748, both contributing to a lag in spinning behind weaving. In response to the lag came Hargreaves's spinning jenny around 1765, Arkwright's water frame (1769) and Crompton's mule (1779), the mule incorporating features of the other two. The flying shuttle and the jenny could be used in cottages but the water frame was a factory machine from the start, allowing cotton cloth to be produced free of linen (Deane, 1965: 87). The jenny was the first successful improvement over the spinning wheel but was itself obsolete by 1800, unable to compete with the mule.

The large technical advances in spinning prompted machine makers to overcome the consequent bottleneck in weaving. Cartwright's power loom of 1787 went some way towards providing an answer, but it was not widely adopted until design faults were corrected in the 1820s (Hughes, 1970: 58). By the 1840s the days of the domestic hand-loom weavers were over, the operators of the new machines being able to produce many times their daily output. Also in the 1820s Richard Roberts developed the self-acting mule, further advancing spinning techniques.

Factory production did not supplant the old domestic system straight away; for several decades it supplemented and strengthened it as the somewhat labour-intensive jennies and looms entered the cottages (Deane, 1965: 90). Deane also noted that manufacturing made no progress until technology developed equipment specifically aimed at factory production, for example the water frame and power loom (1965: 87).

Despite the rudimentary, often clumsy, nature of the early innovations, and the constant repairing and refining, they began the transformation of cotton textile production into a factory system, and from 1760 to 1787 raw cotton consumption rose from 2·5 million lb to 22 million lb (Landes, 1970: 44–5), largely because of these inventions. They also created large price reductions between the mid-1780s and 1800 (on very fine yarn by a quarter), despite the general price increases of the time (Milward and Saul, 1973: 189–90). In terms of productivity, Landes notes that the mechanical advantage over hand spinning was enormous even with the earliest machines: anything from six to twenty-four to one for the jenny and several hundred to one for the water frame (1970: 85–6). The water frame and the mule were also more than mere labour-saving devices; they were substitutes for human skill, allowing the production of a stronger, finer yarn by relatively unskilled labour (Deane, 1965: 93).

There were many other innovations. The revolution in spinning was possible only because of improvements in cleaning and roving the raw materials; the demand for the output of the looms would have been lower had the improvements in bleaching and printing in finishing not occurred.

Finally, the growth of cotton production in Britain between 1750 and 1850 owed much to the drive of the country's entrepreneurs (Deane, 1965: 95). Innovation is the province of the entrepreneur. He had to adapt an invention to its particular role in the firm and improve its efficiency. Moreover, the entrepreneur had to assume whatever financial and other risks were involved in adopting the new machines.

Many of the above innovations were also used in the woollen and other fibre industries with a lag but, generally, not with the same speed of operations as in cottons. In addition, much of the early development of the chemical industry too came from the demands of the textile sector. Chemical advances arose out of extensive scientific research, and a number of Continental discoveries were adopted in Britain. Research concentrated on cleaning, bleaching and dyeing, reducing the production costs of acids and alkalis and increasing their efficiency so as to provide the textile industry with much cheaper and more effective inputs.

Sulphuric acid production had been improved by Joshua Ward, John Roebuck and Samuel Garbutt by the 1740s, reducing the price from as much as 1s 6d and 2s 6d an ounce to 3½d a pound (Haber, 1958: 3–4). Hydrochloric acid and chlorine were developed on the Continent in the 1770s, the latter being used as a somewhat unsatisfactory bleaching agent. In 1799 Charles Tennant in Glasgow discovered 'bleaching powder', calcium hyperchlorite, by saturating slaked lime with chlorine. It became very useful in the textile industries, especially after its price had fallen from £140 a ton in 1800 to £14 a ton in 1850 (Haber, 1958: 9, 15).

In alkalis, while potash was used to make soft soap for scouring and fulling in the woollen industry, for bleaching and cleaning cloth and for softening leather, it was Frenchman Nicolas Leblanc's development of soda in 1789 from salt and limestone which was the major advance at the time. British textile producers did not use soda for cleansing until the 1820s but, when they adopted it, the local price fell sharply (Landes, 1970: 110).

Important technological advances also occurred in iron and steel, which had been used for centuries by European blacksmiths in making tools, implements and weapons. The foundries and furnaces converting iron ore into the bar iron they used required large amounts of carbon (charcoal), both to heat the iron ore and to treat it. It has been argued, however, that, by the eighteenth century, the expanding use of timber for making charcoal had begun to deplete the forests and increase charcoal prices, underlining the need for a substitute. Although coal had already been used as fuel in a number of production processes (Harris, 1991: 11–12), such was not the case with iron. In 1709 at Coalbrookdale, Shropshire, Abraham Darby became the first person to use coke in smelting iron. Even so, coke smelting was not to spread until the 1760s, largely because coke was more costly to use than charcoal at the time (Hyde, 1972–73: 398). The shortage of timber argument has been questioned by some who agree, however, with the relative costs argument for the 1750s (von Tunzelmann, 1981: 147). The use of coal as fuel was also related to the close location of plentiful supplies of the mineral and its superiority in heat per ton over its rival, wood (Harris, 1991: 11).

Further developments included the production of wrought iron in 1766 by Thomas and George Cranage, using coal as fuel and a reverberatory furnace, a combined puddling and rolling process by Henry Cort in 1784, allowing the large-scale production of wrought iron using coal, breaking the link between iron and water power for the rolling mill and allowing the use of steam power in producing refined bar and rolled iron. From then on, the iron industry moved to the sources of coal and iron (Mathias, 1969: 123–4), from Shropshire into Staffordshire, having already moved into Scotland in 1759 and South Wales (Dowlais) in 1760. The switch from charcoal to coke also allowed economies to be derived from using large coke furnaces (Deane, 1973: 182).

'Charcoal' steel had been used for some time in making weapons, clocks and cutlery, but in the early 1740s Benjamin Huntsman used coke fuel to cast steel in crucibles and moulds. Its high quality and lower price accelerated the production of Sheffield cutlery and other commodities (Court, 1954: 52).

The innovations of the early ironmasters led to iron becoming the raw material of mechanical and civil engineering and to its substitution for timber in the new textile machines, improving their performance and prolonging their lives. But for engineering the development of steam power and the Boulton & Watt engine were also crucial. The early prototypes, Thomas Savery's 'fire engine' (1695) and Thomas Newcomen's steam pump (1712), used in pumping water out of mines, were useful but technically inefficient despite later improvements in the latter. Watt's changes to the steam engine, the introduction of a separate steam condenser and its rotative nature, were patented in 1769 and his engine was used commercially from 1776 (von Tunzelmann, 1981: 156–7). Its success was partly due to the use of John Wilkinson's 1774 invention of a cannon-boring device to produce an accurately bored cylinder (Mathias, 1969: 135). Landes notes that the saving of the energy previously dissipated in reheating the cylinder at each stroke was the breakthrough to the 'Age of Steam' (1970: 102). Boulton & Watt opened their Soho works near Birmingham in 1795. The steam engine was improved and its use extended by other innovators such as Wilkinson, who is credited with being the first to use steam to blow blast at the furnace, to work a forge hammer, and to slit and roll iron. Arthur Woolf in 1804 produced the first commercially successful compound engine, using high pressure and a separate condenser (Landes, 1970: 103). Nevertheless, as Musson points out (1978: 112), the use of the steam engine up to the 1780s was limited to drainage and pumping, while in the 1790s it made great advances in cotton spinning and, to a lesser extent, in iron smelting and forging. But by 1800 factory power still came mainly from the water wheel. The use of steam power grew only slowly, and even by 1850 it was still mainly confined to textiles, iron and coal (Musson, 1978: 68).

The combination of steam power and coke in the smelting of iron stimulated coal mining, which used steam pumps to reduce flooding, while the substitution of iron for timber in the rails of the pony-powered 'tramways' bringing out the coal was due mainly to Richard

Reynolds in Shropshire and Richard Trevithick in South Wales. Few other innovations appeared in the coal industry until 1815, when Sir Humphrey Davy invented his safety lamp.

Transport in Britain had improved considerably by the 1820s. In 1779 the first iron bridge had combined iron, steam power and the first machine tools in its construction over the river Severn, and the new canals, roads and bridges were the products of the emerging engineering trades. The next major achievement in transport appeared in respose to the growing volume of commodities requiring carriage. The efforts of Trevithick (in 1804) and George Stephenson (up to 1829), illustrated that the railway could be used for fast travel as well as hauling goods and livestock. From the late 1820s the steam locomotive ushered in a new era in land transport (Musson, 1978: 114). The demand for railway technology rose very quickly and by the 1840s railways were being built in many parts of Britain and the Continent (see Chapter 6 below).

The development of machine tools accelerated the pace of industrial progress (Landes, 1970: 105–7). By 1800 the need for increased operating speeds to raise productivity, as in textile machines, demanded greater precision in machine tools and in planning and manufacturing. In addition to Clement's self-regulating lathe and double-driving centre chuck, Nasmyth's self-acting nut milling machine and steam hammer and, in planing, the turret lathe and milling machines were developed (Musson, 1957–58: 121–7). Standardisation in the design and manufacture of machine tools, advocated extensively by Joseph Whitworth in the 1830s, including the size and pitch of screw threads, nuts and bolts, did not take on until the 1850s, when the use of templates and jigs also became popular for repetitive operations. In addition, some Manchester engineers introduced interchangeable parts to reduce further the manufacturing costs of their operations, while Nasmyth set up perhaps the first production assembly line (Musson, 1975: 114–20).

Britain's industrialisation was wider-based than the above suggests and encompassed other industries in which important innovations occurred. The modernisation of the glass and pottery industries, led by James Keir and Josiah Wedgwood respectively, for example, largely imitated Continental technical advances such as Dutch Delft ware in the Staffordshire pottery industry. Moreover, the glass industry relied for many years on Continental (mostly French) skilled workers (Musson, 1978: 126–8).

The close relations existing between firms and industries, often the result of technical advances in one leading to the need for changes in others, had an agglomerative effect on certain geographical regions and accounted for much of the growth of local populations, such as Manchester, Birmingham, Glasgow and Newcastle.

Finally, pure science played a much smaller role in the development of modern technology up to 1850 than in later decades; practical men and trial-and-error contributed more in the earlier decades than later (Milward and Saul, 1973: 179).

Technological progress on the Continent to 1789

Despite Britain's technological lead in the eighteenth century, several major innovations occurred on the Continent, such as in the production of iron and steel by Reaumur, cast steel by Clouet, Jacquard's silk loom, chlorine bleaching by Berthollet, a cloth printing cylinder by Oberkampf and Widmer, artificial soda by Leblanc (Henderson, 1967: 8) and the discovery of chlorine in 1774 by Karl Scheele (Lilley, 1973: 229). In Germany a water-pressure engine was developed by Winterschmidt, new dyes by Diesbach and Barth, and the world's first beet-sugar refinery was constructed by Achard (Henderson, 1967: 8). Government patronage played an important part in the adoption of new technology in armaments and in such luxuries as silks, porcelain, glassware, carpets, curtains and tapestries (Henderson, 1967: 11–12). Some of these innovations were taken up in Britain.

The western Continental countries experienced similar economic conditions over the centuries to those of Britain. The rural (cottage) industry developed in a similar way, using the same technology. But, despite many early changes, it was not until after 1815 that technological advance accelerated (Henderson, 1967: 10), many of the new ideas coming from Britain. Then, when industrialisation began, Continental inventors and innovators followed the British in producing their own innovations. As Pollard notes (1981: 84–5): '. . . the transformation of the British economy jerked the Continent out of its existing paths and, instead of developing out of its own traditions, it had to react, adapt, and adopt'. Yet, Cameron argues (1985: 1–23), each country pursued its own road to industrialisation, with few strictly following 'the British model'.

The European economy

Technology transfer

How were the major British innovations after 1700 diffused to other countries, and to which countries? First, it must be recognised that the rate of diffusion was much higher in neighbouring countries (or regions) than in those farther removed, in the east and south of Europe. It should also be noted that the countries susceptible to the adoption of new technology were those in which social, economic and cultural conditions placed few barriers in the way of its importation.

It was mainly the diffusion of the new techniques in textiles, iron and steel, the steam engine and later the railway which accelerated the modernisation of Continental economies. Despite legal restrictions until the 1820s, machinery and skilled workers from Britain continued to cross the Channel. Technology was also transferred by exporting under licence (Hughes, 1970: 72), migrant British entrepreneurs, visitors to Britain returning home with machines or blueprints, smuggling, industrial espionage and the copying of descriptions in the British scientific literature (Henderson, 1971: 4–9; Harris, 1991: 13–27). The development of a second-hand market for textile machinery created another means of transfer.

After transfer, the technology was adapted for local use or, if plans only had been obtained, the machinery was constructed from first principles. Not all attempts succeeded, but the attraction of skilled workers and entrepreneurs from Britain offered a greater chance. Some successful transfers comprised complete packages of entrepreneurship, specialised skills and government aid which often led to the spread of the transferred technology from one location to others and from one form of industry to others (Inkster, 1991: 53).

> There is no single important industry in any of the major Continental regions that did not have British pioneers as entrepreneurs, mechanics, machine builders, skilled foremen and workmen, or suppliers of capital (and usually several of these combined) to set them going. [Pollard (1981): 145]

In addition to the dozens of knowledgeable British people who introduced the new technology to Continental firms, many Continentals spent time in British workshops learning enough to set up their own establishment at home.

Some transfers involved no adaptation but constituted fully British machines—steam engines, spinning mules and blast furnaces.

But even more evident at times was the complete adoption of the whole British factory organisation or railway layout. Transfer was sometimes slow because of inability to adapt the technology to local Continental conditions, lack of expertise on the part of the adapter, or other reasons. The earliest French attempt at coke smelting was undertaken by Gabriel Jars in 1769, while Wilkinson was brought to France by de la Houliere in 1777 to 'blow in' the first coke-fired blast furnace on the Continent at Le Creusot in 1785 (Milward and Saul, 1973: 91). When the works failed, charcoal returned for a further lease of life (Hughes, 1970: 72), coke smelting not being used generally before 1850.

Belgium was the first country to adopt British technology widely. Rich in coal and iron ore, Belgium had an industrial tradition partly based on the Flanders linen industry, as well as the ingredients of modernisation (Dhondt and Bruwier, 1973: 329). The first Newcomen pump arrived there in 1720, and because of its low operating cost several remained in use on the coalfields even after the introduction of the steam engine (Pollard, 1981: 87). The first Boulton & Watt engine was introduced in 1785 at Jamappes, but because of maintenance problems was replaced by a Newcomen pump in 1818 (Dhondt and Bruwier, 1973: 333). It was not until the 1830s that the steam engine became generally accepted. The greatest early progress in iron and steel occurred at Liège, where twenty-five rolling mills were installed between 1800 and 1815, mostly water-powered (Pollard, 1981: 88). At Charleroi, Paul Huart-Chapel invented a reverberatory furnace for melting scrap in 1807 and set up the first puddling furnace in 1821 to convert pig iron into wrought iron and the first blast furnace in 1827 (Dhondt and Bruwier, 1973: 339). William Cockerill and his sons arrived in Belgium in 1799 to manufacture textile machinery. In 1813 they added the steam engine to their production line, and in 1817 John Cockerill transferred the plant from Liège to Seraing. It became one of the largest and most modern plants of its kind in Europe. From 1834 the main changes in the iron industry were connected with railway construction (Pollard, 1981: 89–90).

In the early eighteenth century the Ghent textile industry switched from linens to printed cottons, first by domestic production and after 1780 in mechanised factories. Two spinning mills had been set up at Ghent by 1803, both equipped with mules manufactured there. After 1819 the Belgian cotton industry modernised rapidly. Steam superseded water and in 1827 the first power looms appeared, some made in Ghent by British artisans, some imported and, later, most made locally (Dhondt and Bruwier, 1973: 349–50). By the 1860s Belgium was highly industrialised, largely in line with British technology.

The new British ideas were also favoured in the Nord and Pas-de-Calais *départements* of France, economic extensions of the Belgian industrial belt. Here mining of the important coal reserves occurred with the use of Newcomen pumps from 1732 but the coal was expensive to mine and not economically viable until after 1850. The Cockerills and William Douglas mechanised the woollen industry in Sedan and Amiens, using British technology, while in cotton production in Normandy, Picardy and the Nord the spinning jenny was in general use before 1789. It was being manufactured locally, largely by English artisans, subsidised by the French government (Price, 1975: 103). The water frame and mule jenny, introduced in the 1780s, spread more slowly, and cotton spinning was not completely mechanised until after 1830. In weaving, the flying shuttle appeared in 1747 but was little used until after 1820, at Roubaix, in Normandy, until 1825, and at Alsace until 1830. The adoption of the power loom was slower than in Britain because of the failure to adapt it to light cloths until around 1830.

Rural weavers were employed longer in France than in Britain, and water power persisted in Alsace and Normandy even after 1850, while steam engines were introduced in the Nord, around Lille, in the 1820s. Mechanisation was more rapid in the 1870s (Price, 1975: 104–5), when there was also a marked movement towards industrial concentration (Caron, 1979: 151). The French silk industry was located around Lyons. Despite Jacquard's invention of a silk weaving loom, it was mainly domestic until the 1840s, by which time mechanisation had limited domestic production to the very delicate operations a machine could not accomplish (Fohlen, 1973: 27).

Despite the early energies of British and French entrepreneurs in the establishment of the French iron and steel industry, based on British practice, some of the innovations were not widely adopted before 1830, including coke smelting, puddling, rolling and the hot blast, largely because of their high cost (Henderson, 1967: 100). Le Creusot, set up in 1782 by royal charter, obtained its first Boulton & Watt steam engine that year and soon after one from Perier of Chaillot, who in 1781 gained from Watt a fifteen-year concession to build steam engines (Fohlen, 1973: 47). Other large establishments existed but techno-

170

logical progress in metals remained slow until the demand for rails rose after the laying of the first French railway line in 1827. Steel was made by means of the German cementation and the British Huntsman processes.

German industrialisation in the British mode extended to the lower Rhine and the Ruhr, favoured by an abundance of coal and iron deposits. Iron and steel goods, such as cutlery, arms, wire, sickles and scythes were produced. Textiles began to benefit from the successful copying of British machines by local makers, and a steam-driven cotton mill, the first of its kind, was established at Elberfeld (Pollard, 1981: 97–8). The transfer of British technology to Germany occurred in the usual way, and British artisans and industrialists visited the region— the Cockerills in the 1860s to build woollen mills in Brandenberg, and Wilkinson from Le Creusot to Breslau to establish an iron foundry. German chemists also went to France to study (Kindleberger, 1978: 192–3). But the German textile industry remained backward. Although cotton spinning had been mechanised in factories before 1850, the modernisation of weaving occurred only later. Despite the many innovations, factory production was not the norm in cotton until after 1873, later still in wool, and in silk only after 1890 (Borchardt, 1973: 132). In 1882 about a third of all textile employees were still working under the putting-out system (Henderson, 1967: 30–2). Moreover, it was not until the 1860s that coal overtook wood as a source of power. Yet the sewing machine was introduced as early as 1854 (Borchardt, 1973: 130–2).

In 1830 coal mining in the Ruhr was still limited. Some iron and engineering works existed, the first puddling furnace had been set up in 1826, but coke blasting began only in 1849, at Mulheim, although earlier coke blast furnaces had been established in Upper Silesia (Henderson, 1967: 21). Until 1849 the Ruhr imported pig iron from Britain, having changed from bar iron when the tariff structure of the Zollverein was established. Importing British iron products acted as a technology transfer, for they were copied, adapted, improved and eventually manufactured in Germany. That the Germans borrowed technology selectively (Fremdling, 1991: 50–2) is very apparent in railway locomotive construction, which commenced in 1841 with an engine which immediately outperformed a British rival (Kindleberger, 1978: 203).

Alsace, partly French and partly German, established itself as an

171

important producer of cottons and textile machinery. At first a water-powered cotton spinning mill was constructed at Wesserling in 1802 but cotton printing of calico predominated at Mulhouse and Wesserling until the locally developed power loom arrived in 1826 to stimulate factory weaving. Even so, the need for bleaching produced an even earlier innovation of local origin in the form of Berthollet's chlorine bleach in 1791. Engineering also became important in Alsace, producing textile machinery and, later locomotives, while the wool industry was enhanced by the local development of wool-combing machinery in 1845–46 (Pollard, 1981: 100–1).

Before unification in 1860 the major technical advance in Italy was the development of a silk throwing machine in the north in the early eighteenth century, enhancing the growth of exports of raw and spun silk. The machine was adopted in 1719 by Thomas Loombe in Derby (Mathias, 1969: 128). Other textile activities were also developed, based on British technology and using water power from the Alpine streams.

Before 1850 British technology also reached Switzerland, Saxony, the upper Loire valley, Paris, Berlin and parts of the Habsburg monarchy, all substantially affected in some field of manufacture. In Switzerland textile development began early, initially as an adjunct to agriculture during the harsh winters. Up to 1820 cotton yarn was all imported from Britain but by 1830 it was being supplied locally. Spinning technology was borrowed from Britain but the mechanisation of weaving was largely local in character, first in an adaptation of Jacquard's silk loom in 1821, and then in the 1830s in Altherr's broadstitch loom and the chainstitch loom, allowing coloured designs and embroidery patterns to be incorporated in the weaving. The production of watches and clocks eventually moved into workshops for stricter supervision, while the development of new precision watch-making tools by Georges Leschot in 1839 allowed production to switch from high-priced to low-priced timepieces to cater for the growing need. By 1850 there were several machine-making factories in Switzerland, turning out cotton-spinning and hydraulic machinery and, later, locomotives and rolling stock for export (Milward and Saul, 1973: 455–63).

In Austria–Hungary the Czech lands and Lower Austria adopted cotton spinning and finishing techniques by 1840 but hand weaving still predominated. Chemical advances had been introduced in printing.

172

The processing of wool in patterning and printing, using imported yarn which was hand woven locally, was also well advanced by the 1840s in Moravia. Water power dominated at this stage. The coal (in Silesia) and iron industries received an impetus from the introduction of the railway but by 1840 pig iron was still charcoal-smelted. Technological advances were partly aided by state encouragement of the transfer of foreign technology and the attraction of immigrant workers (Gross, 1973: 242–5).

By 1850 Continental industrialisation was well under way in several regions, largely as a result of the diffusion of British technology. During the next two decades, however, Continental progress led to greater mechanisation, partly from the use of previously developed technology and partly from new improvements. The Continent was catching up with Britain in many fields of industry and, because modernisation was happening later than in Britain, manufacturers could adopt the latest technology without having to go through the various stages followed by their British counterparts. During this time the British model became less relevant. After 1870 many technological advances issued from the Continent or the United States.

The second technological acceleration

After 1850, in textiles, the adoption of an American invention, the condenser, by the British woollen industry displaced the last large number of hand textile workers in the country. On the Continent it was Alsace which led the way in the mechanisation of cottons production while, in woollens, the French worsted centres of Roubaix and Fourmies in the Nord and Rheims in Champagne modernised rapidly in the 1860s to become the Continental leaders. The previously slow movement towards mechanisation and factory production of textiles gave way to accelerated change, including the replacement of the mule and hand loom by the self-actor and power loom. In the iron industry occurred the major shifts from charcoal to coke fuel and from the waterwheel to the steam engine. The chemical industry became firmly established, and the machine spread—into nail-making and cutlery, the stamping of heavy metal forms, tailoring, paper manufacture and many other fields (Landes, 1970: 193–5). There was also massive investment in the railways, reducing land transport costs considerably and adding to the speed and reliability of land travel. At the same time, steam locomotives and other railway equipment were made increasingly by Continental producers—a major stimulus to many industries.

Another major cluster of innovations occurred in the decades after 1850, promoted by an acceleration in inventive capacity and innovative ability with the appearance and generally rapid adoption of cheap steel, electricity, electrical power, lighting and motors, organic chemicals and synthetics, internal combustion engines and automotive devices, and the bicycle, while precision manufacture and assembly-line production were adopted (Landes, 1970: 235).

While Britain was almost completely wedded to coke blasting by 1800, it was not until much later that the Continental iron industry turned away from charcoal, once again because of the rising cost of using it. Belgium was first, followed by France, but in Germany coke blasting began on the Ruhr only in 1849, even though it then expanded very rapidly. Nevertheless, the puddling furnace remained the bottleneck of the industry at that time, limiting furnace size and thus the gains in productivity. There were three major developments in steel production which, in the course of thirty years, completely transformed the industry, the Bessemer (1856), the Siemens–Martin (1861–64) and the Gilchrist–Thomas (1879) processes. Together they had reduced the cost of producing crude steel by some 80–90 per cent by the mid-1890s and increased production some eighty-three times (Landes, 1970: 259). Nevertheless, it was mainly in Britain that the first two were readily adopted, though not until the 1870s was much interest aroused abroad because of the need for further refinements. In Germany before 1870 it was in the Ruhr that pig iron and steel production rose rapidly, partly perhaps with some use of the Bessemer converter and the Siemens–Martin open hearth. The first Bessemer plants were established on the Continent in France and Sweden for experiments in 1858, at Krupp's at Essen in 1862 and in Austria in 1866 (Milward and Saul, 1973: 200). But their use was still retarded largely because, it is argued, German puddled iron was superior to that obtained by the new processes. When they were later adopted, however, steel output rose more rapidly and, later still, the Gilchrist–Thomas process allowed the opening up of the industry in Lorraine and Luxembourg (Henderson, 1967: 36–7).

The Bessemer process, cheap, consistent in quality, produced in larger plants, was used mainly for rails; Siemens–Martin, more homogeneous, closer to specification, better suited to custom work, able to reclaim scrap, was used largely for making plates (Milward and Saul, 1973: 200). On the other hand, the Gilchrist–Thomas process, useful in overcoming the presence of phosphorus in ores, was adopted across Europe in a matter of four years, mainly in those countries with phosphoric coal such as France. The first users of the new types of steel were the military, the railways and shipbuilders. Wrought iron was not completely eclipsed at first, and only after the major cost reductions of the new steel did it bow out.

The supply of coal on the Continent was extended by the development of newly found or newly exploited deposits, the deep beds in Westphalia and the Pas-de-Calais section of the French Nord field, which was opened up mainly during the 1850s, and the deeper Ruhr beds of coke-producing coal, with iron ore also available. In the 1850s exploitation of the Ruhr deposits began in earnest and the rate of coal extraction accelerated up to 1873 (Borchardt, 1973: 130). Coke-blast iron at last prevailed, overcoming the technical retardation of half a century.

In the second half of the nineteenth century there were important technological innovations in chemicals, including alloy steels, in non-ferrous metals such as aluminium, in glass-making, papermaking, cement and rubber manufactures and ceramics (Landes, 1970: 269). Some appeared as improvements in furnaces and kilns, while sulphuric acid production rose as further uses for it were found in producing fertilisers, explosives and dyes and in petroleum refining. In the mid-1870s Ernest Solvay, a Belgian, developed a process to replace the somewhat unsatisfactory Leblanc method of producing alkalis (Haber, 1958: 100–1). The latter virtually disappeared on the Continent but not in Britain, where it had become more entrenched, continuing there, through cost savings without profits, until 1914 (Haber, 1958: 122).

Synthetic dyes became available from 1856 when William Perkin patented his aniline purple. From 1860 on, numerous aniline dyes were discovered and put into use in the textile sector, especially in France and Germany. The discovery of other synthetic dyes occurred in Germany, and by 1900 German producers covered up to 90 per cent of the world market, Switzerland controlling most of the rest. Other products, mostly discovered in Germany, included those based on cellulose, artificial silk, viscose and Bakelite. Optical goods and precision instruments closely connected with scientific institutions and the military, such as clocks, watches, cameras, surgical and scientific instruments, were improved and produced in Germany during this period (Borchardt, 1973: 135–6).

The new discoveries after 1870 were adopted rapidly in the advanced countries. The country of origin, by this time, enjoyed little advantage in the form of initial protection against foreign adoption or adaptation. Moreover, the growing number of transnational corporations became important in the international transfer of new technology, while technological development was favoured also by the standard of technical education reached in many countries. Diffusion was rapid internationally and adoption was also fast, if in varying degrees.

Further innovations occurred in power. The steam engine was improved with the development of the compound engine and its introduction into large ships. The steam turbine was developed in 1884 by Charles Parsons to run electric generators but he had to develop his own generator as well, introducing a very efficient electric power industry. Another important advance was the appearance of the internal combustion engine. From Etienne Lenoir's experiments of 1859 progress went via de Rochas's four-stroke cycle of 1862 to Otto's practical gas engine of 1876, the latter offering an efficient, relatively cheap, form of power and eventually running on petroleum. With it came the motor car in the 1890s (Landes, 1970: 280).

Electric power had the advantages among others that it could be taken to the workplace and into the home. As Landes noted (1970: 284), many innovations were made in this field, including the electro-magnetic telegraph in 1837, undersea cables (from 1851), Bell's telephone in 1876 and Marconi's wireless in 1895. Werner von Siemens constructed electrical works in Germany in 1847 to produce telegraphic equipment, electro-plating was begun in Birmingham in 1840, and the incandescent filament lamp was invented in the United States by Edison. Electric lighting led to the development of the central electrical power-generating source, the first being set up at Godalming in Surrey in 1881 by the Siemens brothers. Improved systems were introduced in many countries before the end of the century, bringing electric light into the home, the factory, the office and the shop. To provide the electricity, coal and steam were used widely, while in countries with the required water resources on the Continent relatively cheap hydro-electric generation was adopted. Extensions of electric power included the electric railway, demonstrated by Siemens in Berlin in 1879 (Henderson, 1967: 71–2), electric tramways, the industrial use of electrical chemistry, the electric furnace of Sir William Siemens in 1878, and the fixed electric motor with its multitude of applications in the 1890s. The importance of this innovation can be gauged by the vast number of innovations its use generated, many—including household appliances—not developed fully until after the first world war. It also changed industrial practice by saving space in the layout of factory plant and by replacing the belting needed by other forms of energy for movable tools, machinery and electric lighting.

All these innovations in electricity and electrical products suggest that a huge volume of funds was required for industrial investment during the period of extensive world economic growth at the time. In Germany, in particular, such investment created another area of cartelisation, dominated by a few large firms. By then, too, German entrepreneurs had changed from being copiers and improvers to technological initiators and efficiency experts (Kindleberger, 1978: 226–9).

Landes (1970: 296–305) refers to other important innovations associated with the drive for greater production speed, efficiency and productivity. Hard steel alloys emerged to improve the cutting of metals, innovations ranging from the high carbon steel of the late 1850s through the tungsten vanadium and manganese self-cooling alloys to the high-speed chromium–tungsten steel of F. W. Taylor and Maunsel White in 1900, increasing cutting speeds from 40 ft a minute in 1860 to 300 ft a minute by 1914. Faster-operating machinery was also sought and involved the substitution of steel for wrought iron, the use of lubrication to reduce wear and heat, and the ball bearing (patented by William Brown of Birmingham in 1877). Machines also grew in size, especially in the manufacture of electrical equipment, reaping economies of scale in making dynamos, motors, generators and transformers. With greater speed came the need for accurate measurement and standardisation of parts which saw the appearance of the turret lathe, milling and grinding machines and materials. At first in watches and small arms, later in the manufacture of bicycles, sewing machines, typewriters and motor vehicles, interchangeable parts reduced manufacturing costs as specialist firms concentrated on certain products with multiple applications. Accurate measurement was also essential.

In this period of massive technological advance, rarely was the amateur discoverer evident, for by then the link between science and technology had grown strong. As firms grew in size, so too did the amounts spent internally on research and development. Scientists experimented, discovered and perfected new commodities and processes. It is apparent that innovation occurred rapidly in all branches of industry after 1870, affecting the development of several European countries, especially the latecomers.

The latecomers

After 1870 Sweden achieved outstanding success, adopting the latest foreign technology and developing some of its own, including the cream separator. By the 1900s the country's manufacturing was turning out an increasing volume of turbines, internal combustion engines, electrical machinery, gas accumulators, ball bearings, matches and timber industry equipment, largely for export (Jorberg, 1970: 89–90). Denmark and Norway were also among the fastest-growing countries in Europe in terms of output and *per capita* income. Free-trade Denmark modernised through high-technology agriculture (Pollard, 1981: 235), while Norway was able to set up its manufacturing industry using hydro-electric power, closely allied to her natural resources, mainly timber.

Lacking both coal and iron, the Netherlands still achieved partial industrialisation with little concentration on heavy industry. There were some developments in textiles, using the latest machinery, food processing as in sugar-beet factories, engineering, shipbuilding, steam engines, smelting works, potteries and diamond cutting (Dhondt and Bruwier, 1973: 355–61).

Austria was said to be level with Germany in industrial development until 1860, with Sweden until 1880, and always ahead of Russia (Ashworth, 1977: 144). After 1850 the Czech provinces became the most industrialised region. Pig-iron production rose but was still predominantly charcoal-smelted in 1883, even though the Bessemer process had been introduced in Vilkovice in 1866. In textiles and other light industries, mechanisation proceeded rapidly from 1851 to 1873, power looms being increasingly adopted and factory production predominating in wool. Beet sugar received a boost when refining technology improved after 1867. Steam power, however, was little used until the 1890s, when further advances took place and textiles, metallurgy, sugar, engineering, the new electro-technology and chemicals became growth industries. In eastern Europe, as in Denmark and Holland, technological advance tended to favour the growth of industry closely associated with agriculture. This was particularly so in Hungary and the Balkans (Berend and Ranki, 1974: 62–4). In Hungary industrial growth proceeded much more slowly and in a different way from the developments in the Austrian provinces. A spurt at the turn of the century led to the food sector accounting for about 40 per cent of manufacturing production, particularly the treatment of grain, using some of the technology being developed in Budapest by the Ganz engineering company. This firm gained an international reputation for its technical advances, producing metal rollers for modern grain mills and electrical products (Berend and Ranki, 1974: 54–9).

In Italy, another late developer, a sharp distinction persisted between the modernising north and the agricultural south. It was not until the 1880s that some mechanisation took place when the protectionist and patronising policies of the state laid the groundwork for an industrialising stage after 1900. In those years the iron and steel works at Terni, textile machinery, cotton textiles and engineering were developed. After 1900 the machine industry advanced rapidly, as did motor vehicle production. At the same time the textile industry was modernised at long last, and electrical (largely hydro-electric) power was introduced. The growth of steel production using the Martin process was slow but those industries using steel grew rapidly—modern engineering, bicycles and cars, typewriters and motor cycles. The chemical industry was another important sector which expanded during this period, especially in artificial fertilisers (Cafagna, 1973: 279–328).

Most of the rest of Europe was still predominantly agricultural. Russia began to acquire an industrial sector after 1880, but by 1913 agriculture still accounted for around 66 per cent of the population and almost half of national income (Goldsmith, 1961: 442). Railway expansion, from 1,000 miles in 1860 to 40,000 miles, was at the forefront of economic development. While industry grew rapidly, it was starting from a low base and—despite the influence of foreign capital in the early phases, foreign technology and state promotion (a feature of eastern Europe)—by 1913 manufacturing employed little over 5 per cent of a rapidly growing labour force and contributed only about 20 per cent to national income. Most striking was the growth of heavy industry (coal, iron and steel, oil) but the textile and other consumer goods industries, though relatively slow growers, started from a stronger base and remained more important. The weakness of Russian growth shows up in the lack of unimportance of most industries producing machinery, electrical, chemical and mechanical equipment.

Taking Europe as a whole, the diffusion process of technological advance appears to have moved from western European countries most rapidly and extensively as far as Austria. Even so, economic development farther east and south tended to follow somewhat the experience of such countries as Denmark and Holland, where agriculture was still important and very advanced. The British example was less apparent in such countries, and textiles, iron and steel were not always greatly prominent in their development. Furthermore, among the latecomers in Scandinavia, Austria–Hungary, Italy and Russia, some of which were not very far along the development path by 1913, either the latest technology in engineering, chemicals, electrical goods and hydro-electricity tended to become paramount, or development programmes were more closely related to the primary sectors (food and raw materials) and attempts to increase productivity there. Industrialisation, despite the degree to which it had been achieved by the first world war, was not universally committed to the British model, as Ashworth (1977: 140–159) and others have stressed.

Conclusion

So it was that the acceleration of technical change, combined with other favourable influences, appearing first in Britain, increased productivity in a number of manufacturing industries, leading to self-sustaining modern economic growth. Through several avenues the new technology moved across the Channel, alighted on fertile ground in parts of the European continent and diffused from one region to another. It was not just the new British technology that was absorbed on the Continent but the desire to emulate the British inventors and create new technological advances.

From 1850 on, the number of centres from which new ideas were emerging had grown on the Continent and in the United States, many of the ideas being inspired by scientific investigation, fewer by amateur research. Because of the nature of the discoveries and the massive improvements in communications between countries, their spread among nations also accelerated, some aided by the growing number of transnational corporations coming into existence.

The latecomer to industrialisation, confronted with a whole range of technological possibilities to choose from, a range which was growing rapidly, with each choice depending on a certain resource mix of labour, raw materials and capital, tended to opt for the most advanced technology at the time most appropriate for the country's factor endowments. Nevertheless, by 1914 the spread of industrialisation was still limited to a handful of countries, many others not enjoying the economic conditions at the time which would have allowed them to follow the example of their more successful neighbours.

Accelerated innovation, never before experienced, not only contributed to sustained economic growth but, through the higher productivity it engendered, led to higher living standards. Technological change, crucial to modern economic growth in its impact upon productivity, depended for its effect upon the presence of several other factors working in combination to ensure that economic growth became a certainty.

Finally, taking the whole period into account, it is evident that the appearance, growth and spread of industrialisation was partly at least due to the massive additions to technological knowledge, which itself accelerated substantially after 1850, creating a multitude of opportunities for profitable investment and for further extensive research.

References

Ashworth, W. (1977), 'Typologies and evidence: has nineteenth-century Europe a guide to economic growth?' *Economic History Review*, XXX.

Barker, T. C., Dickinson, R., and Hardie, D. W. F. (1956), 'The origins of the synthetic alkali industry in Britain', *Economica*, 23.

Berend, I. T., and Ranki, G. (1974), *Hungary: a Century of Economic Development*. Newton Abbot, David & Charles.

Borchardt, K. (1973), 'Germany', in C. Cipolla, ed., *The Fontana Economic History of Europe* 4, 1. London, Collins/Fontana.

Brittain, J. E. (1974), 'The international diffusion of electrical power technology, 1870–1920', *Journal of Economic History*, XXXIV.

Cafagna, L. (1973), 'Italy, 1830–1914', in C. Cipolla, ed., *The Fontana Economic History of Europe* 4, 1. London, Collins/Fontana.

Cameron, R. (1985), 'A new view of European industrialization', *Economic History Review*, XXXVIII.

Caron, F. (1979), *An Economic History of France*. London, Methuen.

Chambers, J. D. (1961), *The Workshop of the World*. London, Oxford University Press.
Cipolla, C., ed. (1973), *The Fontana Economic History of Europe*. London, Collins/Fontana.
Clapham, J. H. (1961), *The Economic Development of France and Germany, 1815–1914*. Cambridge, Cambridge University Press.
Court, W. H. B. (1954), *A Concise Economic History of Britain*. Cambridge, Cambridge University Press.
Crouzet, F. (1980), 'Toward an export economy: British exports during the industrial revolution', *Explorations in Economic History*, 17.
Deane, P. (1965), *The First Industrial Revolution*. Cambridge, Cambridge University Press.
Deane, P. (1973), 'Great Britain', in C. Cipolla, ed., *The Economic History of Europe* 4, 1. London, Collins/Fontana.
Dhondt, J., and Bruwier, M. (1973), 'Belgium and Holland', in C. Cipolla, ed., *The Fontana Economic History of Europe* 4, 1, London, Collins/Fontana.
Falkus, M. E. (1972), *The Industrialisation of Russia, 1700–1914*. London, Macmillan.
Floud, R., and McCloskey, D. (1981), *The Economic History of Britain since 1700*. Cambridge, Cambridge University Press.
Fohlen, C. (1973), 'France', in C. Cipolla, ed., *The Fontana Economic History of Europe* 4, 1. London, Collins/Fontana.
Fremdling, R. (1991), 'Foreign competition and technological change: British exports and the modernisation of the German iron industries from the 1820s to the 1860s', in W. R. Lee ed., *German Industry and German Industrialisation*. London, Routledge.
Gerschenkron, A. (1977), *An Economic Spurt that Failed*. Princeton, N.J., Princeton University Press.
Goldsmith, R. W. (1961), 'The economic growth of tsarist Russia', *Economic Development and Cultural Change*, 9.
Gross, N. T. (1973), 'The Habsburg monarchy, 1750–1914', in C. Cipolla, ed., *The Economic History of Europe* 4, 1. London, Collins/Fontana.
Haber, L. F. (1958), *The Chemical Industry during the Nineteenth Century*. London, Oxford University Press.
Harley, C. K. (1982), 'British industrialization before 1841: evidence of slower growth during the industrial revolution', *Journal of Economic History*, XLII.
Harris, J. R. (1991), 'Movements of technology between Britain and Europe in the eighteenth century', in D. J. Jeremy, *International Technology Transfer*. Aldershot, Edward Elgar.
Hartwell, R. M., ed. (1967), *The Causes of the Industrial Revolution*. London, Methuen.
Henderson, W. O. (1967), *The Industrial Revolution on the Continent*. London, Cass.
Henderson, W. O. (1971), *Britain and Industrial Europe, 1750–1870*. Leicester, Leicester University Press.
Hoffman, W. G. (1965), *British Industry, 1700–1950*. London, Oxford University Press.
Hughes, J. (1970), *Industrialization and Economic History*. New York, McGraw-Hill.
Hyde, C. K. (1972–73), 'The adoption of coke-smelting by the British iron industry, 1709–1790', *Explorations in Economic History*, 10.
Hyde, C. K. (1977), *Technological Change and the British Iron Industry, 1700–1870*. Princeton, N.J., Princeton University Press.
Inkster, I. (1991), *Science and Technology in History*. London, Macmillan.
Jeremy, D. J., ed. (1991), *International Technology Transfer: Europe, Japan and the USA, 1700–1914*. Aldershot, Edward Elgar.

Jorberg, L. (1970), *The Industrial Revolution in Scandinavia, 1850–1914* 4, 1. London, Collins/Fontana.

Kemp, T. (1969), *Industrialization in Nineteenth Century Europe*. London, Longman.

Kenwood, A. G., and Lougheed, A. L. (1982), *Technological Diffusion and Industrialisation before 1914*. London, Croom Helm.

Kindleberger, C. P. (1978), *Economic Response*. Cambridge, Mass., Harvard University Press.

Landes, David S. (1970), *The Unbound Prometheus: Technological Change and Industrial Development in Western Europe from 1750 to the Present*. Cambridge, Cambridge University Press.

Lee, W. R., ed. (1991), *German Industry and German Industrialization*. London, Routledge.

Lillog, S. (1973), 'Technological progress and the industrial revolution, 1700–1914', in C. Cipolla ed., *The Fontana Economic History of Europe*, 4, 1. London: Collins/Fontana.

MacLeod, C. (1992), 'Strategies for innovation: the diffusion of new technology in nineteenth-century British industry', *Economic History Review*, XLV.

Mathias, P. (1969), *The First Industrial Nation*. London, Methuen.

Milward, A. S., and Saul, S. B. (1973), *The Economic Development of Continental Europe, 1780–1870*. London, Allen & Unwin.

Musson, A. E. (1957–58), 'James Nasmyth and the early growth of mechanical engineering', *Economic History Review*, 10.

Musson, A. E. (1975), 'Joseph Whitworth and the growth of mass-production engineering', *Business History*, XVII.

Musson, A. E. (1978), *The Growth of British Industry*. London, Batsford.

Pollard, S. (1981), *Peaceful Conquest*. Oxford, Oxford University Press.

Pollard, S., and Holmes, C., eds. (1972), *Documents of European Economic History* 2. London, Edward Arnold.

Price, R. (1975), *The Economic Modernisation of France, 1730–1880*. New York, St Martin's Press.

Robinson, E. (1974), 'The early diffusion of steam power', *Journal of Economic History*, XXXIV.

Robinson, E. (1986), 'Matthew Boulton and Josiah Wedgwood, apostles of fashion', *Business History*, XXVIII.

Rosenberg, N. (1963), 'Technological change in the machine tool industry, 1840–1910', *Journal of Economic History*, 23.

Rosenberg, N. (1972–73), 'Factors affecting the diffusion of technology', *Explorations in Economic History*, 10.

Rosenberg, N. (1982), *Inside the Black Box*. Cambridge, Cambridge University Press.

Saul, S. B. (1970), *Technological Change: the United States and Britain in the Nineteenth Century*. London, Methuen.

Tann, J. (1979), 'Arkwright's employment of steam power: a note of some new evidence', *Business History*, XXI.

Tunzelmann, G. N. von (1978), *Steam Power and British Industrialisation in 1860*. Oxford, Clarendon Press.

Tunzelmann, G. N. von (1981), 'Technical progress during the industrial revolution', in R. Floud and D. McCloskey, eds. (1981), *The Economic History of Britain since 1700*. Cambridge, Cambridge University Press.

Webb, S. B. (1980), 'Tariffs, cartels, technology, and the growth of the German steel industry, 1879 to 1914', *Journal of Economic History*, 40.

Transport and communications

While historians continue to debate the nature of and the reasons for rapid industrial progress in many parts of Europe in the century and a half prior to the first world war, it is worth remembering that the qualitative and quantitative changes occurring in transport over this period were at least as great. Transport's share of GDP doubled in many European countries during the nineteenth century. In France, Britain and Belgium, among the most successful industrialisers of the period, freight output grew at more than double the rate of commodity output between 1830 and 1913 (O'Brien, 1982: 339). Toutain, for instance, has estimated that transport output in France rose at a rate of 3·3 per cent per annum, 1840–1913, compared with 1·4 per cent for commodity output (Lévy-Leboyer and Lescure, 1991: 157). While little is known about the growth of transport output in less advanced European countries, qualitative evidence points to a similar ratio for Spain and Russia at least. Besides rapid growth of transport output, the mode of conveyance and the organisation of services both experienced a series of major changes, mostly as a result of the introduction of new technologies. The transformation of the road and inland waterway infrastructure, the coming of the railway, the displacement of the small wooden sailing vessel by the large steel steamer, and the early years of the motor industry were all features of this period. The professionalisation of transport operations manifested itself most clearly in the development of scheduled services by specialist companies. While much has been written about these developments in the transport sector, such work has focused mainly upon a descriptive case-study approach. This chapter outlines the major changes in transport, explains how these mostly capital-intensive technologies were financed, and analyses the manner in which these developments affected the economic progress of European countries, a topic which remains comparatively neglected.

Developments in European transport

Road systems and services. We know little of the size of road networks in the eighteenth century, since most were little more than unmaintained mud tracks or bridle paths. Responsibility for their upkeep frequently lay with negligent local authorities. In Britain an Act of 1663 authorised the collection of a toll to finance the upkeep of the Great Irish Road connecting London and Holyhead. This set a precedent for many turnpikes, each administered by a trust. By 1750, 143 trusts had been established, covering 3,000 miles of roads (Albert, 1983: 60). Road networks continued to expand after 1750, with construction concentrated in 'manias' in 1750–72, the early 1790s, 1809–12 and the mid-1820s. Improvements in road planning and construction also occurred in France, including Napoleon's *routes impériales*. Further progress between 1815 and 1850 saw 7,000 km of main highways and 23,000 of departmental roads completed (Price, 1983: 37). Road-building technology improved from the end of the eighteenth century, when Metcalfe, Telford and McAdam applied more scientific methods. A convex surface, strengthened with tightly packed broken stones, permitted effective drainage. New materials were introduced in the nineteenth century to strengthen and preserve roads, including concrete and tarmacadam in Britain and asphalt in France.

Improved technology and the 'demonstration effect' of progress in Britain and France stimulated activity elsewhere in Europe. Belgium, using a system of tolls, extended its highways in the decades after the French Wars: 3,000 km of maintained roads had been completed by 1830, with a doubling of this by 1850 and slower growth to 1880 with coverage of minor routes. A small Dutch road system was built in the eighteenth century complementing the extensive waterways, with slow progress continuing through the first half of the nineteenth century (Milward and Saul, 1973: 112, 441). In Germany Frederick the Great's belief that roads would aid invaders delayed progress. After about 1815 Bavaria and Westphalia expanded road provision. The formation of the Zollverein in 1834 encouraged inter-state co-operation in highway building. In Spain a system of royal highways remained incomplete by 1830 but its size had doubled by mid-century. Limited attempts were made at road-building in Italy before unification, but after 1860 it was subordinated in the budget to railway construction. Few worthwhile roads existed in Scandinavia, which relied mainly upon coasting and inland waterways for transport services. Except for several main routes such as the Siberian highway of 1781 connecting Moscow with Perm, Tobolsk and Irkutsk, roads remained few and primitive throughout Russia in the nineteenth century.

Road services were provided by the professional common carrier and the local or peasant carrier, which distinguished the full-time, long-distance specialist from the part-time, local and occasional carrier. The professional carrier's activities were often governed by regulations relating to freight rates and the nature of services which were adhered to in return for certain privileges. Improvements in road surfaces enabled more and larger coaches and carts to be used, carrying heavier loads and gradually displacing pack animals. Thus the volume and range of services provided and the average and maximum permissible loads all expanded. In Britain the provision of inter-city and suburban passenger services grew rapidly in the second half of the nineteenth century while in France the variety of service is indicated by the distinction between *roulage ordinaire* and *roulage accéléré*.

A major fillip to road transport efficiency resulted from the introduction of motorised transport at the end of the nineteenth century. Electric trams were introduced into American cities in the late 1880s, spreading to France and Germany in the following decade and thence to other European countries by the turn of the century (McKay, 1976: 67–74). It was not until after the first world war that the lower-cost and more versatile motor bus began to supersede the tram in many cities. The popularity of electric cars was more short-lived because of such disadvantages as their short range, need of frequent battery recharging and excessive weight for pneumatic tyres. The internal combustion engine provided the solution to these problems. In 1883 Daimler patented his design for a high-speed light internal combustion engine. Accompanying necessary advances occurred in metalworking, chassis design, electrical apparatus, tyres, suspension and lubricants, many of which drew upon the technological precedents set by the bicycle boom during the 1880s and 1890s.

While many of the earliest technical developments originated in Germany, France was the leading European producer before the first world war, with 45,000 vehicles in 1913, followed by Britain, with 34,000; the only other significant manufacturers were Germany (23,000) and Italy (8,000) (Laux, 1976: 196). The United States was far and away the leading producer, with an output ten times that of the French, achieved by adopting mass-production techniques uncommon in Europe before 1914. The delay in adopting 'Fordism' in Europe was rational, since neither the market nor the manufacturing environment suited its adoption. Vehicle manufacturers tended to draw upon specialist suppliers rather than resort to vertical integration because they offered greater operational flexibility at a time of rapid technological change and the policy reduced fixed capital costs.

The smaller and less homogeneous European market militated against mass production of a few standard designs. France's leading position was achieved through a large volume of exports, especially to Britain, which had the largest number of vehicle registrations in Europe, although sales also reached countries as geographically diverse as Algeria, Germany and Argentina. Exhibitions, motor shows, clubs, catalogues, races and improved infrastructure all helped to expand ownership, but not to mass proportions by 1914. The marketing techniques of the modern mass-production industry such as instalment buying, trade-ins and dealerships were in their infancy.

The earliest vehicle manufacturers came from various commercial backgrounds, especially engineering or cycle production. Among pioneer French firms, Darracq, Peugeot, Clément, Chenard & Walcker, Rochet-Schneider and Richard began as cycle firms while Decauville (railway equipment), Lorraine-Dietrich (railway rolling stock builders), Delaunay-Belleville (ships' boilers) and Mors (electrical equipment) all originated in engineering. A similar pattern was apparent among early British firms, with Humber, Rover, Swift and Singer all from the cycle industry, while Crossley, Ruston, Hornsby (engine makers), Vauxhall (marine engineering), and Royce and Brush (electrical engineering) all began in engineering. Diversification into motor vehicle production was more commonly a matter of necessity than part of a long-term strategy. Rover, for example, diversified into motor cycles and then into vehicles in the first decade of the twentieth century as a result of declining prices and profits (Foreman-Peck, 1983: 187).

Inland waterways. River improvements and canals existed as far back as the Middle Ages and in the seventeenth century the Dutch built an extensive system. Increased activity from about the later seventeenth century reflected demographic and economic pressure for improved inland transport. In Britain about forty rivers were improved between 1660 and 1750, to be followed by extensive canal building, beginning with the Mersey & Irwell Nagivation in 1757 and the Bridgewater

Canal in 1761, both designed to improve the transport of coal in the north-west of England. In the following decade and a half at least fifty canals and navigations were authorised, including several long-distance trunk routes (Duckham, 1983: 101). The Forth & Clyde Canal, designed to give Edinburgh merchants access to the Clyde, was begun in 1768 and not completed until 1790; the Leeds & Liverpool took longer.

Few canals were built in Britain after the French Wars, the notable exception being the Manchester Ship Canal in 1894. In France, where waterway development was also concentrated upon the industrialising regions, many canals were built between 1815 and 1850. The Canal de la Sensée (1820), the Canal d'Aire à la Bassée (1825) and the Canal de Saint-Quentin (1828) were all designed to improve the market links of the northern coalfields. Construction continued after 1850, such as the Canal de l'Est (1882), linking the Nancy region with Belgium to the north and the Rhône–Saône corridor to the south. Most waterway development in Germany postdated the railway system. By 1850 only 750 km of canals existed in the German states; between 1873 and 1914 the length of canals and canalised rivers doubled to 6,600 km (Milward and Saul, 1977: 43). The Kiel Canal of 1895 was a wider and deeper version of the Eider Canal to connect the Baltic and North Seas, and the Dortmund–Ems in 1899 linked the coalfields of the Emscher valley with the port of Emden. Equally important for the German states was the abolition of various tolls and prescriptive rights on the Rhine which culminated in the Mannheim Convention of 1868, declaring free navigation on the river from Basel to the open sea.

The Dutch extended their waterway system in the nineteenth century, mainly to improve port access. The North Holland Canal (1824) connected Amsterdam with Den Helder to the north but the continuous growth in ship sizes led to its supersession in 1876 by the North Sea Canal, taking the shorter westward sea route. Amsterdam's link with the Rhine was improved withe Merwede Canal in 1892 while the New Waterway connected Rotterdam westwards to the sea. The waterway communications of Middleburg and Zwolle were also improved (van de Woud, 1987: 118, 134). Improvements in Belgian waterways were designed to improve port access and facilitate the coal trade. They included the Pommeroeul–Antoing Canal in 1823 and a series of canals linking the Meuse and Scheldt river systems by way of Brussels, Charleroi, Liège and Antwerp. The waterways of southern

Europe were mostly unsuitable as trade routes owing to their shortness and unnavigability. Exceptions were the Douro, Tagus, Guadalquivir and Ebro, which enabled part of the latter to be canalised. Except for the Castile and Aragon canals, much of Spain was geologically unsuited to waterborne transport. In Italy there were few effective waterways beyond the Po valley. Eastern Europe fared little better except for the long and navigable Volga and the waterway link between the Black Sea and the Baltic, completed by the 1820s. It was not until 1898 that canalisation of the Danube at the Iron Gate overcame a major hurdle to long-distance navigation (Hajnal, 1920: 189–91).

At the end of the eighteenth century transport on inland water-ways was by man or horse-powered barges or small sailing vessels. This made for slow and intermittent progress. Steamboats began to appear after the French Wars but were not common before the 1830s or 1840s. Waterway output continued to grow through the nineteenth century. There was only limited competition between road and waterway, as the latter concentrated upon higher bulk and lower-dispersion traffic. Rail competition, in similar markets, was more serious: the construction of a rail link could have drastic effects. Traffic on the Rhône collapsed from 634,000 tonnes in 1855 to 273,000 tonnes four years later, owing to the completion of the Paris–Lyons–Marseilles line (Price, 1983: 284). Such competition was most severe in Britain, where private enterprise set its face against waterways in the early nineteenth century. In other countries, especially Germany (Kunz, 1992: 19–32) and France, waterway transport survived and continued to expand. Between the mid-1880s and 1905 the volume of tonnage on French waterways grew by 73 per cent, on Belgian waterways by 114 per cent and on German ones by 274 per cent but only 8 per cent growth occurred in Britain despite the opening of the Manchester Ship Canal (Waterways Association, 1913: 15). French waterways increased their share of total traffic volume over this period and grew more rapidly than rail (Lévy-Leboyer and Lescure, 1991: 159).

Shipping was the most important and effective mode of transport in the eighteenth century. The extensive coastlines of Britain, France and Scandinavia provided the opportunity for extensive coastal communica-tions by sea. Overseas, British and French shipping was the main beneficiary of the growth of the colonial trade with the American continent, India and the East Indies. Thus by the end of the eighteenth century Britain accounted for more than a quarter of European-owned shipping and France a fifth.

A succession of technological changes led to the replacement of the small square-rigger of 1800 with the large steel steamer a century later. Experiments with steamboats took place on the Clyde in the first decade of the nineteenth century and they were shortly in use as river craft. By the 1820s and 1830s larger engines and more efficient paddles had brought steam into coasting. In the 1840s paddles were replaced by the more efficient screw propellers and in the following decade the compound engine of Elder & Randolph was patented. Further improvements in engine efficiency with triple and quadruple expansion engines and the turbine, together with the use of high-pressure boilers, surface condensers and reliable Siemens steel, revolutionised the efficiency of the steamship in the second half of the nineteenth century. Successive increases in boiler pressure (Graham, 1956–57: 82–8) and reductions in coal consumption (Henning and Trace, 1975: 365–8; Fletcher, 1958: 557) made the steamship efficient on most of the ocean trade routes. Iron and then steel possessed advantages over wood in ship construction in terms of strength, safety, space, malleability and tensility. The problems of magnetic deviation and sweating cargoes were soon overcome, although that of marine fouling proved more enduring. In the years leading up to the first world war the internal combustion engine was introduced into shipping, which meant a smaller engine, no boiler and fuel which was lighter and could be more easily stored. Specific vessel types were developed, including 'reefers', tankers and ore vessels. Infrastructural developments resulted from the new technologies, including a network of bunkering stations, improved port facilities to hasten the turn-round of capital-intensive steamers and the reorganisation of shipyards.

The new technology extended British maritime dominance. Strong coal, metal and engineering industries and a large domestic market helped British shipbuilders to dominate output before 1914 (Table 6.1). Only Germany presented a modest challenge to the yards of Clydeside, Belfast and the north-east. Traditional wooden shipbuilding, particularly in Scandinavia, was destroyed by the rapid technological change in British shipbuilding. Scrapping by British owners seeking the latest improvements provided an active international market in second-hand ships, especially for Norwegian and Greek owners. By the early 1880s more than half the British fleet was steam-powered and,

Table 6.1 Output of major European shipbuilding countries, 1892–1914 (annual averages, 000 tons)

	UK	Germany	Netherlands	France	Norway	Italy
1892–1895	986	83	10	21	18	9
1896–1900	1,262	163	26	74	23	33
1901–1905	1,394	215	52	123	44	50
1906–1910	1,300	218	65	61	48	31
1911–1914	1,790	371	104	132	48	34

Sources: Pollard and Robertson (1979: 249), Fayle (1927: 416).

through a range of channels, this technology was rapidly transferred to many other countries (Ville, 1991: 76–82). By 1900 Finland, Greece, Italy and Norway still owned more sail than steam shipping, but this was a rational choice based upon the higher opportunity cost of adopting steam (Gjölberg, 1980: 141).

From 1780 to 1914 the volume of European-owned merchant shipping grew from less than 3·5 million tons to around 23 million, mainly as a result of the increased demand for shipping generated by industrialisation, migration and the accompanying international specialisation (Ville, 1990: 68–71). Britain dominated shipowning throughout the nineteenth century, with its share of the European total rising from a quarter in the late eighteenth century to half a century later. France's share contracted, owing to slower industrial development, as did that of the Dutch until the recovery of Amsterdam and Rotterdam in the late nineteenth century. The German North Sea ports, on the other hand, gained in importance, helped by industrial expansion. This growth was based largely upon Hamburg and Bremen, which benefited from the operations of several major liner companies, particularly the Norddeutscher Lloyd and Hamburg–Amerika. Other significant maritime nations, including Denmark, Greece, Spain, Sweden, Italy and Norway, maintained smaller and more stable shares of European shipping.

The organisation of shipowning went through important changes: increased concentration and specialisation of shipowning firms in the first half of the nineteenth century and a gradual division of the industry into liner companies and tramp owners in the second half. Specialisation represented an organisational advance which enabled the industry to meet the large increase in demand for shipping associated with industrialisation and free trade. The later change was largely due to the advent of steam and the electric telegraph, and represented a distinction between fast, regular, timetabled services of mixed consignments on particular routes at fixed freight rates and slower conveyance of a specific cargo on almost any route at a negotiated rate. The polarisation of types of shipping operation brought enhanced competition between the sectors which produced rate fixing by the liner companies after 1875 under the conference system (Moore, 1981).

Patterns of deployment shifted regularly and became more diverse as the period progressed. At the end of the eighteenth century most European shipping was deployed within the continent, with smaller volumes in the Atlantic and whaling trades and the chartered companies trading with Asia. The nineteenth century brought extended deployment to Latin America, Africa, south-east Asia and Australasia. In spite of the coming of the railway, coasting remained important throughout the nineteenth century. As late as 1910 British coasting, helped by lower rates, accounted for a greater volume of output, measured in ton miles, than the railways (Armstrong and Bagwell, 1983: 173–4; Armstrong, 1989: 196).

Railways. Britain also led in railway construction, beginning in the 1820s and 1830s. By 1850 almost 10,000 km had been built—nearly double the extent of second-place Germany, with the French network only half as large again. Delayed construction in Russia, Spain and Italy resulted from economic backwardness, these countries having neither the capital and expertise to build a system nor the traffic for it to carry. For several countries, particularly Denmark, Norway and Switzerland, smallness or the nature of the terrain inhibited the construction of an extensive network. By the first world war, many systems had been completed; the largest were those of Austria–Hungary, France, Germany, Italy, Spain, Sweden and the United Kingdom. Belgium built the most dense network, followed by Germany, Switzerland, the United Kingdom and the Netherlands (Milward and Saul, 1977: 541; Ville, 1990: 115).

The pattern of the network varied between countries. The major trunk routes were generally built first because of their greater economic importance and profitability. France, Britain and Spain each developed a radial network in which most main lines connected directly with the capital. A multi-nodal feature characterised Germany's railways, while Belgium produced a transit network handling through traffic from

Table 6.2 The growth of the European railway network, 1830–1910 (km)

Country	1830	1840	1850	1860	1870	1880	1890	1900	1910
Austria–Hungary	–	144	1,357	2,927	6,112	11,429	15,273	19,229	22,642
Belgium	–	334	854	1,729	2,897	4,117	4,526	4,562	4,679
Bulgaria	–	–	–	–	224	224	803	1,566	1,897
Denmark	–	–	30	109	770	1,584	2,005	2,914	3,445
Finland	–	–	–	–	483	852	1,895	2,650	3,356
France	31	410	2,915	9,167	15,544	23,089	33,280	38,109	40,484
Germany	–	469	5,856	11,089	18,876	33,838	42,869	51,678	61,209
Greece	–	–	–	–	12	12	697	1,033	1,573
Ireland	–	21	865	2,195	3,201[a]	3,816	4,496	5,125	5,476
Italy	–	20	620	2,404	6,429	9,290	13,629	16,429	18,090
Netherlands	–	17	176	335	1,419	1,841	2,610	2,771	3,190
Norway	–	–	–	68	359	1,057	1,562	1,981	2,976
Portugal	–	–	–	67	714	1,144	1,932	2,168	2,448
Romania	–	–	–	–	248	921	2,424	3,100	3,437
Russia	–	–	501	1,626	10,731	22,865	30,596	53,234	66,581
Serbia	–	–	–	–	–	–	540	571	892
Spain	–	–	28	1,649	5,295	7,490	10,002	13,214	14,684
Sweden	–	–	–	527	1,727	5,876	8,018	11,303	13,829
Switzerland	–	–	25	1,053	1,421	2,571	3,243	3,867	4,463
UK	157	2,390	9,797	14,603	21,558[a]	25,060	27,827	30,079	32,184

Note: (a) 1871.
Source: Mitchell (1975: 581–4).

north to south and east to west. Italian railways followed the contours of the peninsula, with an intensive local network in the Po valley. The Russian network formed several superimposed patterns: a radial system operated around Moscow, other nodal points included St Petersburg and Warsaw, whilst major east–west lines followed the American transcontinental configuration.

Finance and the role of government

In Britain transport improvements were largely initiated, financed, planned, built and operated by private enterprise. The role of government was restricted to minimal regulation, although by the later nineteenth century a more extensive body of shipping legislation began to emerge. New canals, railways and turnpike trusts required a private Act and thus Parliament became a battleground for competing economic interests, with distinct pressure groups emerging in the railway and shipping industries (Alderman, 1973; Palmer, 1990). Promoters were often entrepreneurs, hence Wedgwood's promotion of the Trent & Mersey Canal for the movement of coal, clay and pottery and the Duke of Bridgewater's canal to move coal from his Worsley mines to Manchester. Alternatively, a syndicate of local businessmen and farmers might promote a scheme. Periodic government grants towards the construction of roads, bridges, harbours and similar works constituted only a tiny proportion of transport finance. In the eighteenth century the British shipping industry had been one of the largest users of fixed capital. This expenditure had been financed through fractional share-holding sometimes referred to as the sixty-fourth system. Although liability was mostly unlimited, owners of a ship were tenants-in-common, able to buy and sell their holding without reference to other investors. In the nineteenth century specialist private shipping firms and joint-stock companies emerged which provided alternative funding methods. The only notable exception to private finance was temporary government mail subsidies to selected shipping lines in the second half of the nineteenth century. However, until their repeal in 1849, Britain's navigation laws provided a preferential operating system for national shipping. Railways required substantially more capital than shipping because of the cost of constructing and maintaining the track, extensive civil engineering works and the grandiose style of many terminal buildings. The repeal of the 'Bubble Act' in 1825, which had con-strained joint-stock company formation, arrived in time for the early booms in railway investment. The use of low-denomination shares attracted a wide investing public, while the resort to loan stock sustained investment when the profitability of many railways fell short of expectations.

In much of mainland Europe the state played a more active role. In France the *Corps des Ponts et Chaussées*, established in 1716, was the first government body of civil engineers in Europe and was closely involved with construction and maintenance. In 1842, for example, the Legrand plan for a national rail system was devised by the Director General of the *corps*. The government then bought the land and its engineers built the main engineering works, selling the rights (conces-sions) of completion (rails, stations and rolling stock) and operation for a fixed period by tender. Intervention also included standardisation of dimensions and tolls on the waterways, and some canal ownership and rate regulation to promote fair competition between transport modes. Finance was a combination of private and public. The state was largely responsible for the financing of the *routes nationales* while local roads received support from local government. French governments provided £56 million for waterway construction between 1830 and 1900 (Waterways Association, 1913: 15) and encouraged private railway investment by guaranteeing minimum rates of return (*garantie d'intérêt*) on securities and inducing the major companies to cross-subsidise the development of minor lines (Franqueville conventions). Further state support for transport came under the Freyçinet plan of 1879. Major Parisian bankers, particularly Rothschild, also supplied finance. The requirements of railway financing led to the creation of the Crédit Mobilier in 1852 to channel private savings into industrial investment through the sale of low-denomination shares to the public. It played a pioneering role in mixed banking and led to the development of many similar financial institutions in France and other countries. French shipping, as in most countries, was predominantly financed by private investors, with trends similar to those experienced in Britain. French governments introduced a series of building and navigation bounties in the last two decades of the century but they were ineffective as they did not sufficiently distinguish sail from steam or domestic from foreign shipping.

A mixture of public policy and private initiative characterised transport development in Germany. Road expansion in Westphalia in the quarter-century after the French wars owed much to the policies of the state's president, von Vincke, who raised a loan during the economic downturn of the early 1820s, kept costs down by putting work out to competitive tender and hired the unemployed as a form of winter relief work. State capital, particularly Prussian, also went into waterway construction and maintenance. Mail subsidies, preferential railway rates and immigration control stations were designed to enhance the competitiveness of German shipping and shipbuilding against British rivalry, although they affected only a small percentage of the industry. Railway policy varied between states: in Hanover, Brunswick, Baden and Württemburg the railways were state-owned while in Prussia and Saxony they were privately owned but with a regulatory hand. From the mid-1870s there was a significant move towards public ownership so that by 1913 only 6 per cent of German lines remained in private hands. This had more to do with raising

195

revenue than notions of unification and rationalisation. Private finance was thus more significant in the early period; by the 1840s railway shares were being traded on the Berliner Börse. Major entrepreneurs such as Strousberg and Camphausen were also heavily involved in railway promotion and finance for strategic purposes.

In later-developing countries governments played an important role. This was particularly the case with railway construction because of contemporary advocates such as Friedrich List, who viewed railways as a panacea for economic backwardness. Many of the earliest lines in Austria–Hungary were state-built or drew upon the initiative of foreign investors and entrepreneurs such as Baron von Hirsch. Spanish and Russian governments also enlisted foreign support. The Spanish railway law of 1855 offered incentives to foreign investors, including tariff concessions, subsidies and favourable company status. The result was that 40–67 per cent of railway investment came from abroad (Platt, 1984: 131; Gomez-Mendoza, 1980: 126). With railway investment constituting 90 per cent of gross domestic capital formation in the decade after the railway law (Harrison, 1978: 50) foreign investment eased the risk of crowding out manufacturing. Foreign capital from Britain was important in the growth and modernisation of the Spanish mercantile marine in the later nineteenth century (Valdaliso Gago, 1992: 203–13). The picture was similar in Italy, where English contractors like Brassey were closely involved in construction and French banks in financing. The Russians were most successful at securing foreign investment and attracting foreign entrepreneurs by making transport improvement part of a wider industrialisation policy.

Some of the smaller European countries also sought foreign support. Sweden turned to foreign investors when a domestic sale of railway bonds fell flat in 1854. State policy concentrated on loan rather than risk capital in order to minimise foreign influence. A similar attitude was taken by Belgian governments; concessions were awarded to foreign companies but frequently as part of a syndicate with Belgian firms in order to restrict the power of the likes of the Compagnie du Nord. Dutch railways were financed by the state and local business interests, supported by capital from France, Belgium and England. Swiss railways were built and financed largely by the state, domestic enterprise and French bankers.

196

Transport and European industrialisation

It has been shown above that there was a profound change in the extent and efficiency of transport in many European countries in the eighteenth and nineteenth centuries. Although these developments often coincided with rapid economic progress, drawing a precise causal link is made difficult by the widespread impact of transport. This led early post-war analysts such as Rostow (1960) and Jenks (1944) to adopt a somewhat exaggerated all-embracing interpretation. Fogel (1964) and his followers in the 1960s offered a more cautious reinterpretation. Disagreement has also ranged over which developments have been most important: Szostak (1991) emphasised eighteenth-century improvements in roads and waterways, while Freeman (1988) held that it was the application of steam transport from the mid-nineteenth century which gave transport such an important role.

The diffusion of transport innovations, and hence their impact, was a lengthy process inhibited by conservatism, the unreliability of new technologies, and mistakes in their application. In addition, organisational developments in transport were to have a more gradual impact. The process was also extended by competition between modes of transport. In many cases second-best technology continued for many years, sometimes complementing the new, as is indicated by the use of sailing ships to carry bunker coal and the development of horse-drawn road haulage services connecting with rail terminals. The economics of transport also dictate that the relative efficiency of different transport modes varies according to the length of haul, with shipping being at its most effective on long hauls, railways on medium and roads on short hauls. Thus complementarity as well as competition existed between different transport technologies.

It is helpful to regard transport as two distinct types of economic activity: a construction industry in building and maintenance and a service industry in operation. Transport tends to be capital-intensive, as is indicated by infrastructure such as railway track, port facilities and road systems, together with the means of conveyance—ships, locomotives, motor vehicles. Thus one might expect to find a significant stimulus, or backward linkage, to supply industries such as heavy goods and processed raw materials. The operation of the transport service will generate lateral linkages in relation to the labour, material and organisational features of transport enterprises. More diverse are the economic

197

consequences of the provision of new or improved transport, particularly in terms of market integration and improved resource allocation, which may be analagous to the idea of forward linkages. Thus, while Rostow's euphoric interpretation has rightly been modified, elements of his methodology remain probably our best means of analysis and produce a more encompassing assessment than Fogel's social savings methodology.

While transport contributed to industrialisation, the causality might also operate in the opposite direction. Steam power was initially developed for use in mining and manufacturing. Development economists have become interested in whether social overhead capital, such as transport, drives industrialisation or vice versa. Hirschman (1958) developed the paradigm that development occurs either by an excess (DBE) or by a shortage (DBS) of social overhead capital. In the case of DBE, transport or similar social overhead capital takes a leading role by creating opportunities for increased investment in directly productive activities. With DBS, social overhead capital adopts a secondary or permissive role, responding to needs created by manufacturing investment. While DBE implies a more dynamic role for transport, its ability to respond effectively to perceived needs under DBS also suggests an important developmental role. The study of European transport in this period indicates that both DBS and DBE occurred regularly. We often find DBE in backward countries when the state takes a leading role in inducing accelerated development by infrastructural investment. It is more difficult to decide whether one option consistently promises a more effective path of economic development.

Construction and maintenance linkages. Backward linkages were most important to industries supplying materials and know-how for transport construction, particularly coal, iron and steel, engineering and building materials. The capital intensity of many transport projects additionally influenced the development of financial institutions and markets. In order to raise capital many projects were floated in economic upturns, although this risked 'crowding out' in capital markets. The large size of many projects, on the other hand, created long investment gestation periods which exerted a countercyclical influence on factor markets.

Road improvements in the eighteenth and early nineteenth centuries were only a mild stimulus to economic activity: small amounts of capital and materials were used, and labour was often secured

198

through the employment of paupers or the fulfilment of labour duties. No innovative forms of finance emerged, although it was probably one of a number of sectors where passive middle-class savings were attracted into commercial ventures. By the late nineteenth century the more substantial road surfaces probably entailed more significant backward linkages. By then, however, the motor vehicle industry was having an important impact. In spite of Landes's assertion that 'no other product yielded so rich a harvest of forward and backward linkages' (1969: 443), little work has been completed on the topic. While much of the capital invested in railways occurred during construction, the cost of road transport was more continuous and recurrent, reflecting the increasing number of road vehicles and the resulting road repairs. Total investment in the industry before 1914 was much less than in railways; in Britain, for example, it took up only a few per cent of the value of new share issues. However, its stimulus was concentrated on a few sectors and regions. The former included the new industries of steel, rubber, aluminium and electrical systems, where the motor vehicle gave a significant boost to output and investment and an incentive to technological innovation. The motor industry took up around 20 per cent of domestic aluminium consumption in France. Only 2 per cent of French steel output went to the motor industry but it was a principal customer for steel alloys and encouraged research into the growing field of alloys (Laux, 1976: 206). On the eve of the first world war France was the leading aircraft manufacturer, which led Laux to conclude that 'such achievements . . . rested primarily on the foundation of the large automobile industry' (1976: 206). By 1909 Renault, Panhard & Levassor, De Dion–Bouton, Mors, Darracq and Clément were all building aero engines. In Britain the car industry was concentrated in the Midlands, together with Manchester and London. This was particularly important for employment: in Coventry in 1911 cycle and car makers accounted directly for 20 per cent of the city's labour force, many others being employed in component and related industries (Thoms and Donnelly, 1985: 44–5). The initial Parisian domination of vehicle production was probably much less important for such a major city but the industry was more significant for regional centres like Lyons, Montbéliard, Le Mans and Lunéville.

The construction and maintenance of inland waterways yielded few backward linkages. The demand for labour and the products of the major industries such as coal and iron was quite limited. Canal construction obliged engineers to confront many of the problems of major works such as tunnels, bridges and embankments, setting a precedent for similar challenges to be faced by railway builders. Major canal projects of the nineteenth century such as Manchester's involved greater supply linkages. Although in many countries finance was organised by the state, in Britain canal building encouraged the wider use of preference shares and debentures, thereby helping to lay the ground for the more widespread use of such securities by railway companies (Ward, 1974).

Shipbuilding had drawn mainly upon traditional materials such as wood, pitch, flax and tar. By the second half of the nineteenth century, however, the industry was characterised by the heavy use of coal, steel and engineering products. British shipbuilding reached its zenith in the later nineteenth century, helping to sustain the demand for the output of heavy industry at a time when railway building had passed its peak. Regional concentration of shipbuilding allowed transaction cost economies through vertical integration with local metallurgy and engineering firms which fostered economies of localisation, as in the growth of a local pool of skilled labour (Ville, 1993). The result was efficiency gains for both shipbuilding and heavy engineering and close co-operation in technological progress. This example also illustrates that transport developments could be a product of industrial progress as well as a contributor to it.

Railway building entailed a strong demand for the products of heavy industry (Table 6.3). The technology gap meant that most countries initially imported British railway equipment, with the rate of substitution varying between countries. During the railway building boom of 1844–51 around 39 per cent of British iron output went into the railways, a figure which excludes its use in rolling stock. Over the same period, 6–10 per cent of coal output was consumed in producing iron for the railways (Gourvish, 1980: 24, 25). In the late 1830s and 1840s railways took up about 20 per cent of engineering output, particularly in rolling stock. The mature system still required the products of the heavy industries for maintenance and occasional extension but, with the exception of periodic re-equipping, such as with steel rails from the 1880s, this was mostly a lower level of demand than previously.

Slower and more orderly French railway construction produced a less dramatic but longer-term stimulus. In the four decades from 1845 railway orders took up 12–18 per cent of iron and steel output. This

Table 6.3 Output of major industries delivered to the railways, 1830–1914 (%)

Country	Pig iron	Steel	Coal	Bricks	Wood	Engineering
England and Wales	39 (1844–51)	–	2–14 (1865)	30 (1840s)	–	20 (1830–50)
Spain	6·0 (1890–1914)	8·5 (1890–1914)	18–29 (1865–1914)	–	–	–
Germany	22–37 (1840–59)	–	3 (1860s)	–	–	–
France	–	12–18[a] (1845–85)	–	13–18[b] (1845–85)	1 (1875–84)	–
Italy	–	12–13[c] (1861–1913)	–	16–23[d] (1861–1913)	–	5–11 (1861–1913)
Belgium	6 (1860–1913)	20–60[e] (1890–1913)	10 (1913)	4–10 (1865–1913)	–	–
Russia	–	59[a] (1895–99)	–	–	–	–
Sweden	–	–	–	–	–	17–30 (1870s)

Notes: (*a*) Iron and steel, (*b*) Building materials, (*c*) All ferrous materials, (*d*) Construction materials, (*e*) Proportion of finished steel output used in rails and sleepers.
Sources: O'Brien (1983: 16), Gatrell (1986: 153), Holgersson and Nicander (1968: 21), Laffut (1983: 220–1), Gourvish (1980: 24), Mitchell (1964: 327–8).

longer-term stimulus helps to explain the technological linkages: the perfecting of iron processes in the 1840s and 1850s, the diffusion of the Bessemer process in the 1860s and of the Gilchrist–Thomas method from the 1870s were all 'direct consequences of the pressure exerted by the railways on their suppliers' (Caron, 1983: 37). Five-year contracts with iron companies provided the stability and certainty needed for investment in new plant. Caron makes a similar case for developments in steel and electricity. Coal demand has not been calculated but may have necessitated increased imports from Britain. The domestic engineering industry soon began production of loco-motives and rolling stock. Gouin & Co., for example, became the Société des Batignolles and began building locomotives.

While French tariff policy sought to exclude Belgian rails and British locomotives and stimulate domestic production, Germany, aware of the inadequacy of the domestic iron industry, imported rails and locomotives duty-free in order to begin building a railway system cheaply and quickly. It then began to impose tariffs on processed iron products while allowing pig iron in duty-free in order to stimulate domestic production of rails and locomotives. Import substitution proved successful: German industry's share of rails supplied to Prussian railways rose from 10 per cent to 85 per cent in 1843–63, and its share of locomotive production in 1840–52 rose from 8 per cent to 97 per cent. By the mid–1850s rails and rail fastenings alone accounted for 37 per cent of domestic iron production (Fremdling, 1983: 125–8). While the value added was less than in Britain, which also exported much greater quantities of railway equipment, there is some validity in Fremdling's model of a leading sector complex in terms of the substantial input–output flows between railways and the heavy industries. Import substitution was even more rapid in Belgium, which, like Britain, became a major exporter of railway equipment. By 1840 eighty-one of 123 locomotives in operation had been domestically built (Laffut, 1983: 209–10). Engineering firms adapted to railway production; Marcinelle were producing 30,000 tons of rails by 1845 (Milward and Saul, 1973: 444). The steel industry also benefited; by 1890 rails and sleepers represented 60 per cent of domestic output (Laffut, 1983: 209–12).

Most other countries relied heavily upon imported rails and rolling stock for most of the nineteenth century, including Spain, Italy, Sweden, Bulgaria, Romania, Greece and Switzerland. British and Belgian products predominated in Spain until the 1890s, when a depreciating exchange rate and a protectionist policy fostered import substitution. By the following decade domestic industry was supplying 75 per cent of rails, although this represented only 8 per cent of pig iron and steel production (Gomez-Mendoza, 1983: 159). In Italy half of the cost of construction was manual labour, while mining and natural resources constituted only 17 per cent and engineering and metal-working 8 per cent. However, maintenance of the mature system, especially in terms of repair shops for rolling stock, drew on engineering and metalworking in the proportion of 30 per cent of costs. Maintenance demands were particularly important to domestic industry after the 1905 nationalisation, when the government modernised the system and placed many orders with Italian firms (Fenoaltea, 1983: 66–9). In Sweden reliance upon imports of rails was greater than in the case of rolling stock, which reversed the pattern of most countries, where establishing the technology of rail production was regarded as the easier option. In the 1870s railway orders constituted 17 per cent of the output of the engineering industry, although the figure was as high as 30 per cent in some years (Holgersson and Nicander, 1968: 50–1).

Russia presents a picture of a backward country which managed to build a rail system quickly while also achieving rapid import substitution of materials. What distinguished the Russian experience from that of others such as Spain and Italy was the inclusion of import substitution as part of a wider policy of forced industrialisation. The charters of many railway companies required that a proportion of rails and rolling stock should be purchased from domestic suppliers, and incentives were offered to engineering firms to convert to producing railway equipment. This pressure was reinforced by tariff protection and a development policy which provided a more stable infrastructure and attracted much foreign investment and entrepreneurship. Railway building was a key element of the development programme in terms of both backward and forward linkages.

Operational linkages. The main operational linkage of transport innovations was to the coal industry. Surprisingly little has been done to calculate the amount of coal consumed by transport systems, although Laffut estimates that by 1913 10 per cent of Belgian coal output was consumed by locomotives (1983: 213). Palmer (1979: 337–9) has estimated that bunker coal represented 20 per cent of British coal exports by the end of the nineteenth century. While improvements in engine efficiency led to reduced coal consumption the saving was offset by the expansion in steam shipping. By 1914 the demand for fuel in both road and sea transport was already beginning to shift towards oil by-products. While specialist oil tankers were being used from the 1880s, the main growth and most organisational developments in distribution and sale occurred later.

The impact on labour was probably quite limited; most transport innovations involved the substitution of capital for labour. However, this implied an important lateral linkage. In the eighteenth century shipping had been among the most fixed-capital-intensive of industries. In the nineteenth century railways and steam shipping used much more fixed capital and expanded in size. There were clear implications for the operation of such enterprises. In contrast to labour, capital was a permanent asset of the business which could not be laid off when trade was poor. Stability of operations was thus implied, together with careful accounting for these assets. Railway companies were among the earliest business enterprises to adopt more sophisticated capital accounting methods, understanding, for example, the need for depreciation and amortisation. The development of shipping lines and the organisation of price rings was also a reflection of the need to keep capital fully and efficiently employed. Large transport companies also operated over extensive distances, which required careful co-ordination, particularly where regular timetabled services were being operated (Gourvish, 1970).

Profits from transport operations created lateral linkages through reinvestment. Until at least the middle of the nineteenth century, most investment was locally based. Since the land-based operations of the maritime industries were geographically concentrated, they brought notable benefits to the locality of a thriving port. Many of the most rapidly growing regions of Europe in the eighteenth century surrounded major ports; such was the case at Liverpool, Bristol and Bordeaux. For some countries shipping also provided a significant surplus on invisible earnings, especially in Britain, for which country this and earnings generated in related areas, such as marine insurance, maritime law, commodity markets and shipbroking, helped to offset a persistent imbalance on visible trade.

Service linkages. Quicker, cheaper, more regular and more comprehensive transport can contribute to the integration of markets. It stimulates the widening of markets, the breakdown of local monopolies and other restrictions on competition, the decline of subsistency, the opening up of new areas to production and improvements in the information flows on which producers and markets rely. It can also concentrate markets by assuring food supplies and facilitating the residential expansion associated with urbanisation. Similarly, improved transport impacts upon institutions operating within those markets. Wider markets create the opportunity for larger-scale production and economies of scale. Greater regularity of transport makes inventory reductions possible, thus enabling circulating capital to be converted into fixed capital to finance such expansion. A more flexible and efficient location of production may result and so afford the opportunity for geographical expansion nationally and even internationally by individual firms. Improved information flows, increased personal mobility and easier monitoring all facilitate geographical expansion.

There are several notable studies of the relationship between transport services and economic development. Chandler (1977) traced a link between the coming of the railways and the growth of large-scale, vertically integrated business in the United States. Railways, and the stimulus they imparted to the coal trade, facilitated internal co-ordination of large institutions and the development of national markets. The institutional structure described by Chandler, however, does not fit the pattern of business enterprises in nineteenth-century Europe in spite of the coming of the railways. Nor should failure to adopt such a structure be regarded as a retarding factor in a country's economic development (Elbaum and Lazonick, 1986). It may be argued that in America the railways more often broke into virgin territory and so their impact is likely to have been greater, although this conflicts with the conclusions of Fogel (1964) and Fishlow (1965) that inland waterways were already providing a good internal transport system for American businesses.

Fogel and Fishlow are also responsible for applying the concept of social savings: they set up a counterfactual model to calculate the extra costs of carrying goods by alternative transport if the railways were closed for a year. They concluded that the railways' impact upon American economic development had been exaggerated. Estimates for a number of European countries have since been put forward involving a range of methods, conclusions and interpretations, discussed in detail elsewhere (Ville, 1990: 166–71). While attempts to specify and quantify more closely the impact of the railway, or other innovations, is laudable, the criticisms of the methodology and the evidence used are considerable. In particular, if the railway had not emerged, transport services would have developed in some other way and with different freight rates, thus largely invalidating the already fragmentary extant evidence. Even if an accurate calculation could be made it would still exclude most of the benefits of increased speed, flexibility and reduced seasonality.

Szostak (1991) establishes a complex but well considered flow diagram of the possible links between improved transport and industrialisation from which he argues that eighteenth-century transport changes led to an industrial revolution in Britain but not in France.

Elegant and helpful though the model is, it is less clear that the evidence is sufficiently detailed and sophisticated to confirm many of the flows and to distinguish transport's pivotal role in the differing growth experiences of France and Britain. Transport services were becoming progressively cheaper and more efficient in the eighteenth and nineteenth centuries, particularly in terms of speed, regularity, cost and coverage. Thus Chandler and Szostak are offering just part of a wider and longer picture. The remainder of this chapter analyses the progressive impact of transport upon markets and enterprises throughout the period.

Better roads, more carts, tighter schedules, longer periods on the road and more regular changes of horses all increased speeds. Journey times by coach fell by between two-thirds and three-quarters in Britain between 1750 and 1830, while average speeds rose from 3 m.p.h. to 10 m.p.h. (Aldcroft, 1980: 38–9). In France speeds rose from 3·4 km/hr to 9·5 km/hr between 1800 and 1848 (Price, 1981: 10). In spite of such improvements, waterways remained cheaper for most bulk goods. At the beginning of the nineteenth century coal could be carried only short distances overland before the cost became prohibitive. It was on the conveyance of passengers and information that roads had their greatest impact. Faster and more extensive passenger and mail services provided better contact between business associates and between producer and consumer. It also served to standardise tastes and fashions across a broader area, thereby providing scope for longer, more homogeneous production runs.

Inland waterway improvements brought transport costs down for many heavy industrial goods; for example, the Bridgewater Canal halved the price of coal in Manchester, while the Oxford Canal extended the market for Staffordshire coal to Reading and that of North Wales to Shrewsbury. Canalisation of the Moselle aided the expansion of the iron and steel industries of the Ruhr by improving access to sources of iron ore. Waterways were particularly important in linking major port cities to emerging industrial hinterlands. This is clearly illustrated with the revival of Amsterdam and Rotterdam in the later nineteenth century; arrivals at the former grew from 0·7 million tonnes to 2·6 million tonnes between 1879 and 1911, and at the latter from 1·6 million tonnes to 11·3 million tonnes for the latter (Milward and Saul, 1977: 196). In Britain the Aire & Calder Navigation linked Selby's coastal trade with the rich textile hinterland of the West Riding.

Perhaps the best example is the flowering of many industries, including iron and steel, engineering and chemicals, along the banks of the Rhine in what developed as a major area of industrial concentration. Riverside industries were in effect located at the point of major trans-shipment, rather than being close to the market or raw material source. This implied a significant cost saving in trans-shipment which was important in an era before mechanised handling and containerisation. The Manchester Ship Canal effectively brought many of that city's industries to the point of major trans-shipment and led to remarkable growth of imports from £2·8 million to £30·4 million between 1894 and 1907 (Farnie, 1980: 26, 53).

In some countries the efficiency gains were very modest, particularly where technology or geology restricted the location of transport. Construction was sometimes defective or designed for non-economic needs, such as the Spanish military highways, which connected Madrid with coastal ports but bypassed major towns like Valladolid and Toledo and did little to open up backward areas of the inland economy. Transport supply and cost were further complicated in Spain by government requisition of many professional carriers (Ringrose, 1970: 84). Although road communications were quite good on the northern plains of Italy, elsewhere there were few roads and people continued to rely upon Roman roads unsuited to the economic infrastructure. Even in western Europe regularity, although improved with developments in road technology, was still constrained by climate and the small and varied nature of freights. Road freight rates between Marseilles and Lyons jumped 250 per cent in 1816 when flooding of the Rhône at a time of heavy grain imports created a much expanded demand for road transport (Price, 1983: 44). Regularity was also adversely affected by the number of part-time or seasonal carriers.

While waterway hauls were generally longer than those by road, their context remained primarily regional, bringing together markets and centres of production on a regional basis. Localised finance and control of transport was a further geographical constraint. The increased risk of being unable to find a return cargo put upward pressure on long-haul rates. Improved road services in England led to the decline of many local markets and their replacement by fewer, larger regional centres (Pawson, 1977: 323). This view has been reinforced for waterways by Turnbull, who argues that the economic impact 'was heavily local and regional' (1987: 540). He notes that the major regions of industrial expansion by 1800 were coalfield areas with a canal network. Most freight movement was over comparatively short distances and long hauls were restricted by the slow development of trunk routes and the 'extreme parochialism of most canal companies' (1987: 541). A similar situation existed in the Netherlands, where the waterway system consisted mostly of a series of regional networks with few connections between them (de Jong, 1992: 5).

The service impact of the introduction of the motor vehicle was minimal before 1914. Railways continued to dominate long-haul services while the superiority of motor over horse-drawn vehicles had yet to be fully established. Certainly electric trams had led to a large rise in urban passenger transport by the first world war, creating 'streetcar suburbs' in cities such as Manchester and Brussels (McKay, 1976: 94). While this may have helped to ease inner-city congestion and the problems of ribbon development it is unlikely that trams had a major economic impact during this period.

By contrast with waterway and road services, railways mostly influenced long-distance transport costs within individual countries. In Germany, Britain, France, Belgium and Russia extant data suggest a substantial decline in freight rates, generally by more than half in the nineteenth century (Ville, 1990: 155). Regularity improved, owing to less susceptibility to climatic interruption than waterways and better protection from banditry than the highways. Railway systems were more comprehensive than waterways, while road haulage was reorganised into complementary short hauls. Great increases in speed resulted: the fastest road services in mid-nineteenth-century France covered 60–80 km in a day, a distance which could be covered by the railway in only a few hours. Similarly with the waterways: from Amsterdam to Utrecht took seven hours by barge but only seventy minutes by train (de Jong, 1992: 12–13).

The integration of national markets through the railway can be seen in the decline of regional price differences between producing and consuming areas. Metzer's study of the market for rye and wheat in Russia revealed that 83 per cent of the decline in price differentials between Odessa and St Petersburg in the second half of the nineteenth century was due to 'railroad-induced decline in transportation costs' (1974: 548). He argued that railways promoted regional specialisation, increased the proportion of output marketed and reduced uncertainty by improved arbitrage. Kelly (1976) uncovered similar results for

Russian oil and grain, which he attributed to government rail tariff subsidies. Low rail tariffs to the ports on grain, butter and sugar encouraged exports of such goods and helped build up reserves to support the rouble on the gold standard. Lower unit rates on long than on short hauls also encouraged interregional trade and the economic development of Siberia. German governments used rail tariff subsidies to enhance market integration. The Berlin textile industry benefited from the city's central position in the rail network. Larger and more standardised demand fostered the expansion of firms such as Herzog and Gerson. In the 1850s the *einpfennigtarif* reduced the cost of bringing coal to Berlin from Upper and Lower Silesia. As a result, British coal's share of the Berlin market fell from 100 per cent in 1846 to 21 per cent in 1865 (Fremdling, 1983: 135). From its nadir in the 1870s the British share grew once more in the final two decades of the century owing to lower sea and inland waterway rates relative to rail and the restrictive policies of the Rheinisch-Westfälische Kohlensyndikat which offset the benefits of lower transport costs (Fremdling, 1989: 184).

Gomez-Mendoza's optimistic interpretation of the impact of the railway in Spain derives largely from its major effect upon transport costs, which, he estimates, were reduced by a factor of nine. Railways removed the transport bottleneck and enabled greater marketing of produce and the widening of markets. By 1913 rail carried 47 per cent of domestic consumption of grain, 34 per cent of flour, 64 per cent of wine and at least 46 per cent of coal (1983: 165). However, railways continued to be poorly utilised, owing to a disappointing entrepreneurial response, the poor quality of the infrastructure and the inappropriate routing of lines, bypassing major towns and industrial areas. The Italian system was hampered by poor construction and high state-regulated freight rates. Thus it did little to integrate markets or create a national economy but perpetuated the economic dualism of the country by aiding the development of the industrial triangle of Turin, Milan and Genoa. Even there, industrial localisation and vertical integration suggested a limited need for transport.

In the Balkans the railways, together with the expansion of shipping, promoted market integration while also attracting much-needed foreign capital and expertise. Rail competition helped reduce freight rates on the Danube while also providing complementary services to and from major ports. The Sofia–Varna line of 1897 encouraged grain exports through Varna and Ruse, together with sales in the urban market of Sofia. In Serbia the competition of the Paračin to Zaječar railway in 1912 linked the valleys of Morava and Timok and facilitated copper ore mining at Bor and Vrska Cuka. However, the benefits of the railway were restricted to a few localities while the region as a whole remained the most backward in Europe before 1914.

The impact of railways in Britain and France may be seen in a somewhat different context, since both countries already had quite good transport systems and neither resorted to freight subsidies. Railways often extended a process of market integration begun by the roads and canals. Between 1859 and 1878 the difference in corn prices between nine French regions fell from 4·6 to 1·7 francs. However, in the thirty years from 1817 the differential had already fallen from 45 to 20 francs (Price, 1981: 72). With all the major networks linked to Paris, expansion of the capital was facilitated by an extension of the supply area from 50 km to 250 km (Price, 1981: 80) and increased competition. The integrating effects also influenced the extension of regional specialisation, including the vineyards of Languedoc, stock rearing in Thierache and Charentes, fishing off Boulogne, the production of sugar, oil, iron and steel in northern and eastern France and the mechanical and food processing industries around Paris. The railway also had a trade-diversionary impact by intruding upon the heavily regionalised nature of the French economy. The ancient markets of Mulhouse and Rouen declined, as did the textile industry of Limousin, metallurgy in Poitou and steel in Berry.

While French governments did not pursue tariff subsidies, intervention influenced the economic consequences of railway services in other respects. Sustained support for waterways enabled them to survive the railway era and play a valuable role as competitor and complementer. In Britain the canal system largely collapsed during the railway age. This was partly due to the inappropriateness of much eighteenth-century infrastructure but also because governments allowed many take-overs by railway companies. The careful planning of a national rail network in France minimised the duplication of the British system and the consequently wasteful investment. However, by ensuring that each locality was provided with a similar network irrespective of its economic potential this created artificial marketing conditions, halted regional migration and restricted the localisation of industry which became a central aspect of British economic growth (Lévy-Leboyer and Lescure, 1991: 159).

In Britain, in the absence of network planning, the railways mostly reinforced existing patterns of settlement and industrial location and sustained a drift towards increased regional concentration. By the later nineteenth century the economies of localisation in the major heavy industries were substantial. The railways extended these opportunities by providing wider markets without altering the balance of industrial location away from established areas. Thus South Wales, Clydeside and the north of England reinforced their emerging dominance. This is perhaps best illustrated by the example of the dominant British shipbuilding industry, mentioned earlier.

While railways helped to integrate national markets, the shipping industry played a major role in the emergence of international markets and institutions. A secular trend of rising productivity and declining freight rates (Ville, 1986; Walton, 1967; Harley, 1988) caused the freight factor to decline and thereby encouraged an extension of international trade and specialisation. There was an increase in the foreign trade ratio of many countries, and world trade *per capita* grew at over 30 per cent per decade, compared with 20 per cent for industrial production, in 1850–1913 (Kuznets, 1967: 4). Ships carried a widening range of goods, including low-value bulky ones, to and from many regions of the world. Helped by mail subsidies as well as falling transport costs, British shipping lines operated frequent and regular services to Asia, Australasia and South America. With the arrival of steam and metal, regular services were provided by liner companies whose large size and organisational structure enabled them to publicise regular sailings, store consignments and ensure speedy delivery within a specified date. For business enterprises receiving and sending goods, fast and regular services yielded benefits in terms of greater certainty of throughput and reduced stocks.

Wider international markets provided the opportunity for expansion in firm sizes although this was offset, to some degree, by increased protectionism in the second half of the nineteenth century. Wilkins (1977) has argued that the growth of European multinationals in the period can be traced to faster and more regular transport services. This view would appear to be supported by the fact that foreign direct investment provides a means of jumping tariff barriers. The reasons for multinational expansion at the time have generated much debate. Even if improved transport efficiency was not the principal explanation, it nonetheless contributed indirectly, given the communication benefits—better

211

transfer of technologies, more effective monitoring of employees and reduced uncertainty regarding conditions in overseas markets.

Summary

The remarkable growth in the extent and efficiency of transport systems in the eighteenth and nineteenth centuries is a story too extensive to relate in detail here. Instead, this chapter has paid more attention to assessing the economic impact of these developments, something which still requires much more attention by economic historians. Studies of transport and economic development have emphasised a specific period (Szostak, 1991; Freeman, 1988) or a particular aspect of the impact (Fogel, 1964). A more holistic approach recognises that the multifarious developments frequently built upon and indeed often complemented one another. As the period progressed competition between the different modes gradually gave way to greater complementarity as each increasingly specialised: road services gradually concentrated upon the short hauls, leaving the railway to the medium and shipping to the long hauls, each best suiting the economics of its operation. This development accords well with the economic impact of each mode: roads and waterways stimulating regional, railways national and shipping international growth and integration of markets and enterprises.

References

Albert, W. (1983), 'The turnpike trusts', in D. H. Aldcroft and M. J. Freeman, eds., *Transport in the Industrial Revolution*. Manchester, Manchester University Press.

Aldcroft, D. H. (1980), 'Aspects of eighteenth-century travelling conditions' in *Der Curieuse Passagier*, ed. M-L. Spieckermann. Heidelberg, Carl Winter.

Alderman, G. (1973), *The Railway Interest*. Leicester, Leicester University Press.

Armstrong, J. (1989), 'Freight pricing policy in coastal liner companies before the first world war', *Journal of Transport History*, 3rd ser., 10.

Armstrong, J., and Bagwell, P. S. (1983), 'Coastal shipping', in D. H. Aldcroft and M. J. Freeman, eds., *Transport in the Industrial Revolution*. Manchester, Manchester University Press.

Bagwell, P. S. (1974), *The Transport Revolution from 1770*. London, Batsford.

Bardou, J-P, Chanaron, J-J., Fridenson, P., and Laux, J. M. (1982), *The Automobile Revolution*. Chapel Hill, N.C., University of North Carolina Press.

Caron, F. (1983), 'France', in P. K. O'Brien, ed., *Railways and the Economic Development of Western Europe*. London, Macmillan.

Chandler, A. D. (1977), *The Visible Hand*. Cambridge, Mass., Belknap Press.

Duckham, B. F. (1983), 'Canals and river navigations', in D. H. Aldcroft and M. J. Freeman, eds., *Transport in the Industrial Revolution*. Manchester, Manchester University Press.

Elbaum, B., and Lazonick, W., eds., (1986), *The Decline of the British Economy*. Oxford, Clarendon Press.

Farnie, D. A. (1980), *The Manchester Ship Canal and the Rise of the Port of Manchester*. Manchester, Manchester University Press.

Fayle, C. E. (1927), *The War and the Shipping Industry*. London, Oxford University Press.

Fayle, C. E. (1933), *A Short History of the World's Shipping Industry*. London, Allen & Unwin.

Fenoaltea, S. (1983), 'Italy', in P. K. O'Brien, ed., *Railways and the Economic Development of Western Europe*. London, Macmillan.

Fishlow, A. (1965), *American Railroads and the Transformation of the Ante-bellum Economy*. Cambridge, Mass., Harvard University Press.

Fletcher, M. E. (1958), 'From coal to oil in British shipping', *Journal of Transport History*, new ser., 3.

Fogel, R. W. (1964), *Railroads and American Economic Growth*. Baltimore, Md, Johns Hopkins University Press.

Foreman-Peck, J. (1983), 'Diversification and the growth of the firm: the Rover Company to 1914', *Business History*, 25.

Freeman, M. J. (1988), 'Introduction', in M. J. Freeman and D. H. Aldcroft, eds., *Transport in Victorian Britain*. Manchester, Manchester University Press.

Fremdling, R. (1977), 'Railways and German economic growth: a leading sector analysis with a comparison to the United States and Great Britain', *Journal of Economic History*, 37.

Fremdling, R. (1983), 'Germany', in P. K. O'Brien, ed., *Railways and the Economic Development of Western Europe*. London, Macmillan.

Fremdling, R. (1989), 'British coal on Continental markets, 1850–1913', in C. L. Holtfrerich, ed., *Interactions in the World Economy*. New York, New York University Press.

Gatrell, P. (1986), *The Tsarist Economy, 1850–1917*. London, Batsford.

Gjölberg, O. (1980), 'The substitution of steam for sail in Norwegian ocean shipping, 1866–1914: a study in the economics of diffusion', *Scandinavian Economic History Review*, 28.

Gomez-Mendoza, A. (1980), 'Railways and Western economic development', *Transport History*, 11.

Gomez-Mendoza, A. (1983), 'Spain', in P. K. O'Brien, ed., *Railways and the Economic Development of Western Europe*. London, Macmillan.

Gourvish, T. R. (1970), 'Captain Mark Huish: a pioneer in the development of railway management', *Business History*, 12.

Gourvish, T. R. (1980), *Railways and the British Economy, 1830–1914*. London, Macmillan.

Graham, G. S. (1956–57), 'The ascendancy of the sailing ship, 1850–85', *Economic History Review*, new ser., 9.

Hajnal, H. (1920), *The Danube: its Historical, Political and Economic Importance*. The Hague, Nijhoff.

Harley, C. K. (1988), 'Ocean freight rates and productivity, 1740–1913: the primacy of mechanical invention reaffirmed', *Journal of Economic History*, 48.

Harrison, R. J. (1978), *An Economic History of Modern Spain*. Manchester, Manchester University Press.

Henning, G., and Trace, K. (1975), 'Britain and the motor ship: a case of the delayed adoption of new technology', *Journal of Economic History*, 35.

Hirschman, A. O. (1958), *The Strategy of Economic Development*. New Haven, Conn., Yale University Press.

Holgersson, B., and Nicander, E. (1968), 'The railroads and economic development in Sweden during the 1870s', *Economy and History*, 11.

Jenks, L. H. (1944), 'Railroads as an economic force in American development', *Journal of Economic History*, 4.

Jong, H. J. de (1992), 'Dutch inland transport in the nineteenth century: a bibliographical review', *Journal of Transport History*, 3rd ser., 13.

Kelly, W. (1976), 'Railroad development and market integration in Russia: evidence on oil products and grain', *Journal of Economic History*, 36.

Kunz, A. (1992), 'La modernisation d'un transport encore préindustriel pendant l'ère industrielle: le cas des voies navigables de l'Allemagne du nord, 1850–1913', in M. Merger, ed., *Les Transports terrestres en Europe continentale*. Paris, CDU and SEDES.

Kuznets, S. (1967), 'Quantitative aspects of the economic growth of nations', *Economic Development and Cultural Change*, 15.

Laffut, M. (1983), 'Belgium', in P. K. O'Brien, ed., *Railways and the Economic Development of Western Europe*. London, Macmillan.

Landes, D. (1969), *The Unbound Prometheus: Technological Change and Industrial Development in Western Europe from 1750 to the Present*. London, Cambridge University Press.

Laux, J. M. (1976), *In First Gear: the French Automobile Industry to 1914*. Liverpool, Liverpool University Press.

Lévy-Leboyer, M., and Lescure, M. (1991), 'France', in R. Sylla and G. Toniolo, eds., *Patterns of European Industrialisation*. London, Routledge.

McKay, J. P. (1976), *Tramways and Trolleys: the Rise of Urban Mass Transport in Europe*. Princeton, N.J., Princeton University Press.

Metzer, J. (1974), 'Railroad development and market integration: the case of tsarist Russia', *Journal of Economic History*, 34.

Milward, A. S., and Saul, S. B. (1973), *The Economic Development of Continental Europe, 1780–1870*. London, Allen & Unwin.

Milward, A. S., and Saul, S. B. (1977), *The Development of the Economies of Continental Europe, 1850–1914*. Cambridge, Mass., Harvard University Press.

Mitchell, B. R. (1964), 'The coming of the railway and United Kingdom economic growth', *Journal of Economic History*, 24.

Mitchell, B. R. (1975), *European Historical Statistics, 1750–1970*. London, Macmillan.

Moore, K. A. (1981), *The Early History of Freight Conferences*. London, National Maritime Museum.

North, D. C. (1958), 'Ocean freight rates and economic development, 1750–1913', *Journal of Economic History*, 18.

O'Brien, P. K. (1982), 'Transport and economic growth in western Europe, 1830–1914', *Journal of European Economic History*, 11.

O'Brien, P. K., ed. (1983), *Railways and the Economic Development of Western Europe 1830–1914*. London, Macmillan.

Palmer, S. (1979), 'The British coal export trade, 1850–1913', in D. Alexander and R. Ommer, eds., *Volumes, not Values*. Newfoundland, Memorial University of Newfoundland.

Palmer, S. (1990), *Politics, Shipping and the Repeal of the Navigation Laws*. Manchester, Manchester University Press.

Pawson, E. (1977), *Transport and Economy: the Turnpike Roads of Eighteenth Century Britain*. London, Academic Press.

Platt, D. C. M. (1984), *Foreign Finance in Continental Europe and the USA 1815–70*. London, Allen & Unwin.

Pollard, S., and Robertson, P. (1979), *The British Shipbuilding Industry, 1870–1914*. Cambridge, Mass., Harvard University Press.

Price, R. (1981), *An Economic History of Modern France, 1730–1914*. London, Macmillan.

Price, R. (1983), *The Modernisation of Rural France: Communication Networks and Agricultural Markets*. London, Hutchinson.

Ringrose, D. R. (1970), *Transport and Economic Stagnation in Spain, 1750–1850*. Durham, N. C., Duke University Press.

Rostow, W. W. (1960), *The Stages of Economic Growth*. Cambridge, Cambridge University Press.

Szostak, R. (1991), *The Role of Transportation in the Industrial Revolution: a Comparison of England and France*. Montreal, McGill–Queen's University Press.

Thoms, D., and Donnelly, T. (1985), *The Motor Car Industry in Coventry since the 1890s*. New York, St Martin's Press.

Tolliday, S., and Zeitlin, J., eds., (1986), *The Automobile Industry and its Workers*. Cambridge, Polity/Blackwell.

Turnbull, G. (1987), 'Canals, coal, and regional growth during the industrial revolution', *Economic History Review*, 2nd ser., 40.

Valdaliso, Gago, J. (1992), *Los navieros vascos y la marina mercante en España, 1860–1935*. Bilbao, Instituto Vasco de Administración Pública.

Ville, S. (1986), 'Total factor productivity in the English shipping industry: the north-east coal trade, 1700–1850', *Economic History Review*, 2nd ser., 39.

Ville, S. (1990), *Transport and the Development of the European Economy, 1750–1918*. London, Macmillan.

Ville, S. (1991), 'Shipping industry technologies', in D. J. Jeremy, ed., *International Technology Transfer: Europe, Japan and the USA, 1700–1914*, Aldershot, Edward Elgar.

Ville, S., ed. (1993), *United Kingdom Shipbuilding in the Nineteenth Century: a Regional Perspective*. Newfoundland, International Maritime Economic History Association/ Merseyside Maritime Museum.

Vries, J. de (1981), *Barges and Capitalism: Passenger Transportation in the Dutch Economy, 1632–1839*. Utrecht, HES Publishers.

Walton, G. M. (1967), 'Sources of productivity change in American colonial shipping, 1675–1775', *Economic History Review*, 2nd ser., 20.

Ward, J. (1974), *The Finance of Canal Building in Eighteenth Century England*. Oxford, Oxford University Press.

Waterways Association (1913), *Digest of the Report and Recommendations of the Royal Commission on Canals*. Birmingham, Waterways Association.

Wilkins, M. (1977), 'Modern European economic history and the multinationals', *Journal of European Economic History*, 6.

Woud, A. van de (1987), *Het lege land: de ruimtelijke orde van Nederland, 1798–1848*. Amsterdam, Meulenhoff.

Foreign trade
and economic growth

Small eighteenth-century seaports, such as Whitby in Yorkshire, promised adventure and escape from rural drudgery to young men like James Cook. Cook went on to discover Australia, and to explore Antarctica and the Arctic before being killed in Hawaii in 1779. However, for most seamen of the period, operating out of the burgeoning ports of Liverpool and Bristol in England, Bordeaux and Nantes in France, Copenhagen in Denmark and long-established Amsterdam in the United Provinces, the demands of trade were sufficiently challenging. Through these docks they imported the exotic goods of the rapidly growing colonial trades: sugar, tobacco, tea, coffee, cotton, muslins. Long-distance foreign trade supplied novel foods, stimulants, drink and clothing that added to the spice of eighteenth-century life. Portugal and Spain imported gold and silver from colonies in Latin America. Also into European seaports were brought materials for naval stores: pitch, tar, hemp and timber. Many of this second group of products, however, originated in northern Europe, exported through the Baltic ports. Basic foods were traded on a large and increasing scale. Salted herrings from Scandinavia, and flour, wheat and rice from as far away as North America were sent especially to southern Europe and Britain.

Mercantilists and many later writers thought that so prominent an activity must have been central to national economic growth and development (Hecksher, 1955; Coleman, 1969; O'Brien, 1991). They held to a doctrine popular in France and Britain during the late seventeenth and eighteenth centuries which emphasised that national strength required bullion imports to create employment. Exports were necessary to obtain gold, but imports, especially of basic foods, were dangerous, for they undermined self-sufficiency in time of war. Success in war also turned on bullion, to pay for naval stores, for mercenaries

216

and for subsidies to foreign allies. Not only did foreign trade offer the lure of gold, and supply the prerequisites of naval security, but it also generated government revenue from taxes on imports (those that were not smuggled). Despite all this, eighteenth-century foreign trade may not have been an engine of economic growth, as so many have believed. An object of the present chapter is to assess that belief.

Later, nineteenth-century apostles of liberalism, like the mercantilists, also saw trade as vital. They preached that the path to prosperity and peace was through free trade, and undoubtedly European growth accelerated at the same time as European international commerce. As liberals recognised, free trade was a doctrine applicable to domestic as well as foreign business. The difference was that in the second case, where commercial relations crossed national boundaries, issues of international law and order and state policy could arise. Moreover the greater distances generally traversed by foreign trade created special problems of transport and communication that required different forms of organisation. Trade between European countries, particularly western European countries, was less distinguished from domestic transactions by the challenges of distance, though those stemming from different political jurisdictions were, if anything, more prominent.

During our period, almost all the factors bearing on foreign trade changed—transport and communication technology, political boundaries, state commercial policies, endowments of human capital and the technology that could make use of natural resources. The greatest *political* inhibitor of European trade came towards the end of the eighteenth century. For almost a quarter of a century after 1792 the French revolutionary and Napoleonic wars devastated Europe. The Congress of Vienna brought a lasting peace in 1815 and ushered in a period of deflation and political repression, restraining liberalising tendencies. Over the ensuing decades British economic power coupled with political liberalism proved increasingly persuasive for the Continental powers. By 1850 the European picture had been transformed. Free trade and cheap food were attractive slogans for urban workers and manufacturers. The market they created for overseas farmers and landowners spread prosperity. Rising affluence gave an incentive to cut tariffs and remove trade prohibitions. Access to cheap British coal encouraged the diffusion of steam power on the Continent. National currency links with precious metals and falling transport costs ensured

217

closer integration of national and world markets. Southern Europe remained poor while Britain increased her economic lead over many countries, raising the question (addressed in this chapter) of how much freer trade contributed to intra-European inequality.

With by far the largest share of world trade and the steam shipping fleet, in retrospect Britain has been represented as the guarantor of economic and political stability, the essential pre-condition of flourishing European trade and economic growth (Kindleberger, 1973: Imlah, 1954). This hypothesis, formulated in the light of the US hegemony in the Western world after 1945, is investigated below.

The arrival of cheap food *en masse* from the New World in the last quarter of the nineteenth century was too much of a shock for those European countries with a large agricultural population and influential landowners. Restrictions on trade began to increase again. Just before, victory in the Franco-Prussian war and political unification dramatically announced the economic and political rise of Germany. Germany's economic size, its natural resources and rate of economic growth threatened the previous European balance of power. Was slow British growth caused by competition from Germany, and other new industrialisers? Or was European prosperity intertwined with the development of the young giant through trade and technology transfers? Answers to these questions, and appraisals of other issues already stated, must be grounded in an appreciation of the causes and nature of European foreign trade.

The basis of trade

Trade is voluntary exchange, undertaken because traders with different preferences, resources or capacities, believe the exchanges will make them better-off. Any one of these three bases of trade will generate price differences between the regions not linked by trade. When regions are linked, changes in demand or supply conditions, in either territory, can boost trade. So also will falling transport costs or other trade barriers. Both reduce what buyers have to pay and raise prices sellers can command. Trade within Europe, and between Europe and the rest of the world, was based upon marked differences in natural and human resources between places, and constrained by human and natural barriers. Institutions such as slavery and serfdom also mattered. Slaves were bought from African rulers or traders in exchange for manufactures.

Often the forts of the chartered Africa companies served as collection centres. The slaves were transported to plantations in the Americas, where they produced sugar, cotton, indigo and molasses, the processing of which created new industries in western Europe. The maintenance of the slaves and their owners on the plantations provided another market for British and French industry, New England agriculture and the Newfoundland fisheries. French overseas investments and trade were no less concerned than British with slavery. When Haitian slaves rebelled in 1791 they demolished a system that had absorbed two-thirds of French foreign commercial interests (Wolfe, 1982: 151). Very considerable Polish exports of grain at the end of the eighteenth century were based upon huge exploitative estates. A different pattern of land ownership may have given rise to another less extreme form of specialisation.

Human capital offered a basis for trade, for endowments varied enormously within Europe. Protestant north-western Europe attained far higher levels of literacy than the south or the east. With Britain holding a small lead in the nineteenth century, she and France were similarly placed, both in the geographical pattern and in levels of literacy. Natural differences between European territories that generated trading possibilities included climate. January temperatures in 1860 ranged from $-4\cdot6°$C in Helsinki to $7\cdot9°$C in Rome, while January rainfall in the same year was 172 cm in Berlin but only $1\cdot8$ cm in Madrid (Smithsonian Institute, 1927). Later in the nineteenth century differences in mineral endowments, especially coal, contributed to European specialisation and trade.

Some, like the Victorian economist W. S. Jevons, then argued that Britain owed her prosperity entirely to her abundant coal resources, which provided cheap fuel for railways and steamships. Certainly the central importance of coal largely explains the pattern of French trade and technology. French engine drivers were paid a bonus according to their fuel saving, while British and German engine drivers were merely required to arrive on time. French ironmasters used less fuel per ton of pig iron smelted than British ironmasters throughout the second half of the nineteenth century. Mid-nineteenth-century French trade utilised the different resource endowments within economic reach in other nations. France's most important trading partners were Britain, the United States and Belgium. In trade with the United States, France, like Britain, bought products that used a great deal of the abundant

219

land in America, but because of the paucity of her coal deposits, her imports from Belgium and Britain were coal-intensive products. Over 60 per cent of British exports to France in 1854 consisted of raw materials or intermediate goods, including coal, wool, iron, copper, semi-finished textiles particularly woollen products; while over half of French exports to Britain took the form of finished manufactured goods and processed foodstuffs, such as silk, leather and cotton manufactures, wine, spirits, refined sugar and flour. British industry sent machinery and intermediate goods to French industry, which sold finished manufactured goods to British consumers. The French, with a comparative disadvantage in coal-intensive products, possessed a comparative advantage in skill-intensive processes (despite a lower literacy rate) which tended to involve finishing rather than basic manufacture (O'Brien and Keyder, 1978: 162).

In addition to natural and human endowments, another basis for trade is technology differences between nations. Technology adapted to one country's factor endowments may not be appropriate to the relative resource costs of another country. The fast-flowing waters of Switzerland allowed the Swiss textile industry to use water-powered machinery as efficiently as the British textile mills used steam power. In that case technology has adapted to endowments and is not itself a basis for trade. National differences in technology may also have arisen because investment in new techniques was unprofitable until either the old equipment was so worn out it had to be scrapped, or the variable costs of generating a given sales revenue with the old technique exceeded the total costs of earning the same money with the new methods of production. But the durability of old equipment cannot explain technology differences persisting over decades. More credible is the third possibility, that the size of the market accounted for different national technologies. Profitable employment of the new techniques may require a larger number of higher-income customers within an economic distance of the manufacturer. If this were so, the improvement of transport facilities was a prerequisite for the profitability of the other innovations. In Germany the establishment of a free-trade area, the Zollverein, from 1834 reduced the economic distance between buyer and seller. A fourth reason why a technological lead may persist is the lapse of time necessary for the discovery and exploitation in the 'follower' economies of the natural resources on which the new technology is based. Until the middle of the nineteenth century the coal and iron ore deposits of the Ruhr were unexploited. Then between 1850 and 1855 coke production trebled; iron ore output rose fifteen times in the decade after 1852 (Milward and Saul, 1973: 406, 409).

British railway exports and construction in mid-nineteenth-century Europe are consistent with the third (market size) explanation above. British contractors were heavily engaged in building the French railway system as Napoleon III pursued a vigorous policy of developing the French economy. At the same time British engineers, navvies and operatives were working in Piedmont, Switzerland, Austria, Spain and, after the Crimean war (1854–56), in Russia and Turkey. In Denmark and Scandinavia Morton Peto had virtually a monopoly of railway construction in various projects intended to improve the transport of Swedish iron and Danish butter to the English market.

British contractors in Europe tended to order capital goods from Great Britain. Countries that were investing most heavily in their transport systems increased their British purchases by the greatest amounts. Exports of iron and steel from Britain doubled in volume during the years 1850–53. Britain early created the largest market for railways, and those supplying it acquired experience and capacity that allowed them to sell more cheaply than the nationals of other countries. These observations are also consistent with the British advantage stemming from coal-intensive industries, which included railways, as well as iron and steel.

Differences between regional endowments, technologies or preferences alone were not sufficient to generate specialisation in production and trade. The cost of moving the goods between factory and market had to be low enough. Wind and water supplied the essentials for the lowest-cost forms of eighteenth-century transport and therefore coastal or navigable river locations possessed trading advantages over inland sites that might often be geographically closer to markets and sources of supply. During the eighteenth century the most dynamic sector of overseas trade in mainly high-value commodities from different climatic zones across the Atlantic favoured the ports of Liverpool and Bristol, Bordeaux and Nantes, Amsterdam and Copenhagen. Cadiz and Lisbon maintained their position as gateways to Latin America but very much for foreign, rather than Iberian, produce. At the end of the eighteenth century the enormous metropolis of London drew in two-thirds of total British imports. German states did not participate directly in the colonial trade until the 1770s, when Hamburg and Bremen extended their earlier redistribution of products originally imported via Amsterdam and Bordeaux. Frankfurt was an international entrepot and centre of finance and exchange rather than of manufacture. Trieste became the outlet for German and Austrian manufactures exported to the Levant and for importing raw cotton from that area. Austria exported manufactures to Hungary in exchange for primary products (Milward and Saul, 1973: 106–11).

For geographical reasons, trade and economic development in the German states were much more dependent on canals and roads. Not only did the higher cost of these modes constrain trade but the impact of geography was deepened by political barriers. Even within Prussia there were tariffs supplementing those between German states. Different currencies in circulation provided another inconvenience for traders and another restriction on trade. With the coming of steam the pace of trading accelerated within Europe as railways offered cheap overland transport for the first time, and the steamship, not economical for bulk intercontinental freights until the 1870s, cut costs in the Baltic and Mediterranean trades from the 1850s.

Trade and economic growth in the eighteenth century

Trade must necessarily have been linked with eighteenth-century economic growth by changes in at least one of the bases of trade. Mercantilists maintained that foreign demand pulled exports up, in the absence of any change in transport costs or tariffs. Where smaller economies supply larger ones, the pattern may be common. Much of the Danish economy in the later nineteenth century was driven by British demand for dairy produce exports. But in the eighteenth century, outside Europe, only the Americas were an important industrial export market. African imports were restricted to firearms and linen, while Asia was impenetrable. Hatton *et al.* (1983) contest the implication for Britain; they argue that exports did not drive eighteenth-century economic growth. They point out that, with less than full employment, fluctuations in export demand must have affected the level of domestic economic activity. In order to test the relationship between exports and economic growth Hatton *et al.* adopt the assumptions that temporal precedence indicates causality and that imports are a measure of domestic economic activity. They go on to find that variations in time series of retained imports did not systematically precede variations in exports. When no special allowance is made for the effects of war, the evidence points in the opposite direction. They conclude that exports caused fluctuations in British income. Contrary to this claim, their findings are consistent with the domestic generation of economic growth. Exports may rise because of productivity growth in the domestic exporting industries as well as because of overseas demand. In the first case, the result that export variation preceded import variation could be explained by the delay in export industry productivity growth spreading through to domestic spending. Export industries, not export markets, were leading sectors.

A compelling point against the primacy of export markets is that, within Europe for much of the century, state efforts were devoted to ensuring that their nationals' demand should not boost other European economies. Foreign, extra-European, demand growth was a minimal influence on European economic growth. The demand-side route by which trade encouraged economic growth therefore seems unpromising. Nonetheless a possible demand-side scheme can be given a supply-side interpretation. During the eighteenth century the notion was popular that exports stimulated the economy by taking up spare production on capacity ('vent for surplus'). The supply-side view of the stimulatory effects of trade turns on wider consumption possibilities. In 1750 sugar, tea, coffee and perhaps tobacco were not available from indigenous suppliers in Europe for climatic reasons. They competed with domestic honey, beer and spirits but provided a much greater range of opportunities and, so far as they offered alternatives to heavy gin drinking, were probably less debilitating. They became items of mass consumption in the eighteenth century not because they became cheaper. From the 1730s the course of their prices relative to the general price level indicates that European demand was rising faster than colonial supply. A reduction in shipping losses through wrecking or piracy and larger, faster ships lowered freight charges and allowed higher prices in the colonies at the same time as unchanged prices in Europe. Tobacco prices in Amsterdam in the twenty years after 1750 fluctuated around a virtually stationary trend, while the Philadelphia price rose (Shepherd and Walton, 1972). The colonials, not Europeans, apparently gained most of the advantage from falling transport costs. But the ability merely to buy a greater range of produce may well have increased the willingness to work in Europe. With more rewards available for effort, greater effort was likely to be supplied and therefore more European output was produced because of trade.

Trade undoubtedly produced 'multiplier' effects through learning by doing and economies of scale in this period, as well as through more conventional specialisation according to comparative advantage. The Dutch economy, already in relative, if not in absolute, decline by 1750, demonstrated these effects in an extreme form. At its peak the Dutch fleet was half the world's shipping, Dutch industry became highly specialised and productive, bidding up wages above any others in Europe (or the world) so that Dutch agriculture was forced to become the most productive in Europe (although agriculture was helped by a good portion of the land being effectively a region of recent settlement, unrestricted by tradition) (Israel 1989).

An alternative view to mercantilism, favoured here, is that growing economic power at home created a tax base that enabled British governments to pursue successfully the mercantilist policies they did. Trade, as well as victory in the imperial struggle, was a reflection of the productive capacity of a domestic economy that could regularly pay and equip warships, troops and foreign allies, while at the same time providing goods wanted by the rest of the world. Without the same economic support French governments were handicapped over the long term. Causation runs in the opposite direction, according to this second hypothesis (Kennedy, 1988). For British exports during the industrial revolution, growth also was domestically generated. Technical progress drove the price of domestic industry's products down, so that exports expanded at the expense of a deterioration in the terms of trade, as for British cotton manufactures.

A third trade-growth configuration was extremely pervasive. Between 1750 and 1914 organisational and technical progress in transport raised trade within and outside Europe continuously, except in time of war. Two periods of rapid trade growth were the last two decades of the eighteenth century and the two decades after 1820. Both, broadly, were years of peace. Nearly all British imports of colonial goods came from plantations in the West and East Indies in the first period and from the plantation states in the United States in the second. Both domestic and foreign trade will have gained from such improvements, although it is likely that advances in shipping benefited foreign more than domestic business. However, in this third case, as in the second, trade is not the driving force behind the economic growth, it is a response.

224

Trade policy and power, 1750–1850

Consisting as it did of transactions that crossed national borders, foreign trade was inextricably intertwined with state policy, especially as war was a normal state of affairs in the eighteenth century. The perceived profitability of the entrepot or carrying trade and the desire to boost national wealth gave Britain and France an incentive to employ their greater military and naval power to wrest this source of income from the Dutch.

The British Navigation Acts were intended to capture entrepot trade profits for Britain. The Acts specified enumerated commodities which the colonies might manufacture or import only from England. They also laid down preferential rates of duty upon some colonial products exported to England. People of New England were expected to consume Jamaican molasses and West Indians should use English manufactures and American grain, according to official British policy. The ultimate object was mutual advantage within a framework of national or imperial security. A second objective of requiring that commodities of inter-imperial trade should sail in British 'bottoms' was to guarantee a supply of sailors for the Royal Navy in times of war.

Like most weapons of war the effects of restrictive trade legislation were probably a net burden on those who imposed them, Britain and France, if a necessary one, given the political constraints. British prices of tobacco were lower than they otherwise would have been but only 15 per cent of enumerated commodities (those imported from the United States amounting to £1·5 million) were retained. If UK prices were one-third lower, the gains were $1/3 \times 0·15 \times £1·5$ million = £75,000, whereas the defence and administrative costs of North America were five times this maximum benefit figure (Thomas and McCloskey, 1981: 97). Turning to the West Indies, according to one estimate 8–10 per cent of UK income came from the West Indies at the end of the eighteenth century, but the British return on the capital invested in the West Indies was 2 per cent. Since capital invested in Britain could earn a safe 3·5 per cent, the British economy suffered an annual loss of £600,000 (Thomas, 1965). West Indian sugar in the UK cost more than world sugar because of preferential duties, and so West Indian landlords gained at the expense of British consumers. Only ginger was sold below world market prices. There were no benefits from a monopoly of West Indian exports because of competition within Britain. And the 4·5 per cent West Indian export tax covered only part of the costs of defence and administration. The net cost of the West Indies was £1 million, about 10 per cent of British government revenue (Thomas and McCloskey, 1981: 98). If these calculations are anywhere near correct, mercantilist trade did not matter anything like as much as the mercantilists and some later historians suggested.

This conclusion is reinforced by the mercantilist emphasis on bullion. Contrary to some mercantilist claims, bullion itself was not the key to national prosperity. Portugal received almost as much Brazilian gold annually in the first half of the eighteenth century as the Mexican and Peruvian shipments of the late sixteenth century. Most of it flowed out to pay for foreign, primarily British, manufactures, to the detriment of native industry, but to the benefit of multilateral European trade. In the early 1760s gold mining began to decline, and a state campaign to promote Portuguese industrialisation met with some success. In wartime bullion was essential for paying foreign allies and for importing naval and military stores. At all times bullion was needed to settle eighteenth-century trading accounts with Asia, for while Europe demanded spices and muslins, little could be offered in return that Asia wanted apart from gold and silver. For Europe, then, Latin American precious metals were highly desirable as a means of conducting international transactions, unlike Asia, where they were demanded for purely internal purposes. Asia's demand for bullion must have constrained its well-being and economic development because resources that could have supplied consumer or producer goods instead were sunk in personal stores of value. Underlying Asia's bullion demand were institutions inadequate to channelling savings into more socially productive uses. Europe locked up proportionately fewer resources.

The foreign sector may have mattered to European economic growth even though trade *per se* did not very much. Perhaps it was not trade, in the sense of voluntary exchange, that benefited western Europe but theft from, and exploitation of, non-Europeans. Unilateral transfers from them, or trade at prices dependent on theft (in particular slavery, the theft of labour), allowed western Europe to become wealthy, according to this view (O'Brien, 1982; Foreman-Peck, 1989). It is natural to think that if members of one group steal from another the first must gain, and the greater the theft the bigger the advantage. But that is not necessarily so with competitive markets. For the slave owner, slaves were an investment. If funds were not committed to slaves they would be diverted into other productive assets. As much as nine-tenths of the capital of a Caribbean sugar plantation excluding the land itself might be invested in slaves, each with an expectation of life of no more than ten years, in 1750. At the margin the returns on slave investment are likely to have been similar to other opportunities. European gains from investment in slavery took the form of lower prices for slave-produced products than would have ruled in the absence of slavery. If we are to assess these benefits we must know the margin by which, say, slave sugar could undercut 'free' sugar produced with the same resources. The second necessary statistic is the volume of slave products consumed in Europe. The product of the margin and consumption then gives a rough (upward-biased) estimate of the European gains from slavery. Because the proportion of slave goods in total consumption was low, European gains were unlikely to have been large, even though for some individuals they were.

Other expropriations included bullion from Latin America. Eighteenth-century Iberian history suggests no great direct benefit from these inflows. The gold and silver allowed Iberian governments to buy domestic resources and other European goods, but neither country built up its economy with this purchasing power. Analogously with slavery, the hardships inflicted to acquire the bullion were not necessarily commensurate with the European advantage. Though the bullion lubricated the wheels of European commerce, the rise of the bill of exchange indicates that other, substitute means of facilitating international transactions would have been found had Latin American gold and silver not been available.

Given their links with slavery and forced mining of bullion, it is not surprising that colonies have widely been seen as a generally exploitative institution. But in the mercantilist world of the eighteenth century no single nation could conduct much legitimate international trade without colonies. In the later nineteenth-century liberal economic order, colonies were neither necessary nor sufficient for economic development. During the nineteenth century Germany and Belgium showed they were not necessary and Spain and Portugal that they were not sufficient. But if in the eighteenth century colonies were necessary, they were similarly not sufficient. Denmark demonstrated the advantages of entrepot colonies. On the other hand, most of the goods in the eighteenth-century Spanish colonial trade were foreign. Cadiz's monopoly of the Latin American trade was that of an entrepot, for foreign, not Spanish, goods. Spanish industry did not prosper from exports to Latin America. Even the finance of trade was partly in the hands of the French and Swiss.

The case of Holland shows that small eighteenth-century economies, unable to undertake the investment that Britain did, could be half strangled by their rivals. Formerly Amsterdam could count on attracting a large part of the Atlantic and Eastern trades for redistribution around Europe, earning from shipping insurance and banking services as well. Enforcement of nationalistic trading laws diverted this trade to Britain and France. Over 90 per cent of the tobacco imported into Great Britain was re-exported in 1768–72. Sugar from the French colonies was at first re-exported from Bordeaux, Nantes and Marseilles mostly to Amsterdam and Hamburg for refining. Amsterdam was the principal refiner of sugar until the beginning of the eighteenth century, when the industry shifted to France, Germany and England.

Prussia squeezed Poland in much the same way as Britain and France ground down the United Provinces, as is shown by the changing fortunes of the respectively Prussian and Polish ports of Stettin and Danzig (Gdansk). That indicates that trade and colonies may have mattered to small countries, but for large ones, better able to compete militarily in trade and colonial wars, they may have been less central precisely because the home market was so much larger.

Very soon after 1750 began the slow recognition of the irrationality of much of the trade legislation enforced to enhance national power. Liberalisation was proceeding in Spain under Carlos III. The Spanish *flota* system was slowly abandoned in favour of allowing direct contact betwen the merchants of Lima, Mexico City and Buenos Aires, on the one hand, and Cadiz on the other. Once the French threat was removed by British action, the North American colonists decided they had no further use for the restrictions of the 'Old Colonial System'. In 1786 came the short-lived Eden treaty between Britain and France, apparently inaugurating an era of freer trade and coexistence between the traditional enemies. If the French revolutionary and Napoleonic wars had not devastated Europe, evolution towards a more co-operative regime would have occurred earlier. Instead Napoleon introduced his 'Continental System' of 1806, intended both to throttle British trade and to boost French economic pre-eminence in continental Europe. It wa unsuccessful. Not so dissimilar in its nationalistic aim— to promote the economic and political development of Germany—but more positive, the Zollverein (customs union) achieved a great deal more than the Continental System. The formation of the Zollverein in 1834 widened the market sufficiently to initiate Germany's nineteenth-century catching-up.

Liberalisation anyway took tentative steps in Britain, despite the war. The East India Company's trading monopoly was eroded by successive Acts of Parliament until by 1831 the company had entirely lost its commercial functions. In 1820 London merchants petitioned Parliament for free-trade policies, Lancashire exporters increased the pressure to abolish trade monopolies, and reciprocal trade treaties were negotiated by Canning and Huskisson between 1823 and 1830. Declining terms of trade suggested the lack of opportunity for primary producers to sell to Britain. The Anti-Corn Law League's campaign for cheap food from 1839 was supported by the exposure in the report of the Committee on Import Duties of 1840 of the irrationalities of revenue tariffs being employed for protection and so not generating much revenue. This revelation heralded Peel's free-trade budgets, for which income tax in 1841 paved the way by making an alternative source of revenue available. Finally free trade was symbolically inaugurated five years later when the Irish famine precipitated the abolition of the corn laws, followed in 1849 by the Navigation Acts.

French trade liberalisation was far more hesitant. In 1822 iron goods imported into France carried duty equal to 120 per cent of the price of English iron (Caron, 1979). Imports of cotton and woollen goods were prohibited. Pyramiding of tariffs provoked some manufacturer reaction, for fine fabrics were dependent on the inadequate supplies provided by French spinners. Limited tariff reductions were made between 1836 and 1841, but railway companies and Napoleon III's political designs were responsible for the major mid-century policy shift. In 1847 railway companies wanting cheap iron and steel pressed for tariff cuts. The average French tariff fell from 17·3 per cent in 1847–49 to 4·2 per cent in 1865–69 (Lévy-Leboyer and Bourgignon, 1990: table A-VI).

Industrialising Europe and trade, 1850–1914

By far the bulk of Europe's trade was conducted within Europe throughout the period, even though intercontinental trade has received more attention (Table 7.1). The exception to this rule was Britain, which began to expand extra-European trade rapidly in the mid-eighteenth

Table 7.1 The European focus of European exports, 1830–1910: the percentage of European exports destined for Europe

Area of origin	1830	1860	1910
Europe	72	68	68
Britain	47	34	35
Continent	82	82	78

Source: Bairoch (1974).

century. By 1850 her two most important trading partners were the United States and India. Because this reorientation occurred prior to the diffusion of steam transport, it cannot be attributed to the technology in which Britain at first held such a tremendous advantage. Initially trade was associated with 'the flag' of empire, though whether as cause or effect is less clear.

Steam shipping merely continued the falling trend in sea freight cost but railways transformed inland carriage charges. Intra-European trade from the mid-nineteenth century therefore increased disproportionately more by land than by sea. At the same time as railway building enhanced the integration of internal markets, tariff reductions, exemplified by the Cobden–Chevalier treaty of 1860 and the repeal of the corn laws, encouraged greater intra-European specialisation. Manufactured exports accelerated, first textiles then metal and machinery products, transforming the composition of trade. Whereas in 1800 Europe accounted for perhaps little more than a quarter of world manufacturing output, by 1860 its production was more than half the world total and continued rising (Bairoch, 1982). French, primarily intra-European, overseas trade grew rapidly in the first two-thirds of the nineteenth century, from 13 per cent of GNP in 1830 to 41 per cent in 1870. Between 1815 and 1875 export growth averaged 4·5 per cent a year at an accelerating rate—reaching 6 per cent in 1845–65 (Lévy-Leboyer and Bourgignon, 1990: table A-IV). And this despite the pressure on the Restoration government to become more protectionist and even prohibitionist. Imports were mainly industrial materials, especially coal and wool. With the 1860 treaty manufactures and food imports rose, helped by falling transport costs. The French economy as a whole clearly gained from the British shift to free trade until 1866 (Caron, 1979). Tariff reductions stimulated foreign demand, raising

230

French economic growth so as more than to offset the harm to some domestic industries wrought by the greater volume of imports (Lévy-Leboyer and Bourgignon, 1990: 240). After the 1870–71 Franco-Prussian war, the loss of the industrial *départements* of Alsace and Lorraine, missing out on the boom and the emigration of the silk industry, all contributed to a deterioration in the performance of the French economy. On the other hand, chemical producers increased their share of exports, as did car manufacturers after 1900, and these modern sectors possessed great growth potential, in contrast to textiles. Whether because of trade expansion or independently, during the 1850s national European income gaps tended to widen (Bairoch, 1976). Britain, the richest country, was the second fastest growing economy, while Russia, with the lowest income, experienced the lowest growth rate. The next decade showed more signs of convergence. France and Germany both attained growth rates greater than those of the much more open economies which took the top four places in the income per head league (Crafts, 1983). That these countries—Britain, Belgium, Switzerland and the Netherlands were clustered together may itself be taken as evidence of the effects of trade: since they were small, regional differences within them may have been less persistent and the cost of trading with their neighbours relatively low.

European income growth rates diverged primarily because of coal availability and because national institutions and political developments limited the extent to which economies could take advantage of the new opportunities at home and abroad. The poor performance of the Spanish economy owed much to widespread banditry and endemic civil war, which culminated in the fully fledged revolution of 1868, followed in turn by nearly a decade of anarchy and civil war. Austria–Hungary also remained backward. Only in 1850 was the customs frontier between Austria and Hungary abolished, and the new tariff of 1852 merely replaced outright prohibitions on importing many articles with high duties. Unsuccessful wars with Piedmont and France in 1859 and with Prussia in 1866 similarly did not encourage economic development. On the other hand, from 1853 Austrian trade with the Zollverein was boosted by large tariff reductions. Even after political unification in 1861, Italian economic development was slow and the relatively small size (and unprofitability) of the railway system reflected the poor prospects for economic growth.

In the 1870s, the pattern of comparative advantage in manufactures

231

shifted as Germany, the United States and other countries industrialised. In no commodity was this more apparent than in iron and steel. By 1913 German iron and steel exports exceeded British, with American exports not far behind, and Britain had become a major importer of steel. Had Britain dominated the world iron and steel market in 1913 as she did before 1870, she would have supplied the exports actually provided by Germany and America. In so doing the relative output levels of Britain and Germany would have been reversed, with British production half as large again as that of the German iron and steel industry (Allen, 1979).

The change in relative coal prices since the period of Britain's industrial supremacy shows one cause of shifting comparative advantage. By 1900 the price lead that British coal possessed in the 1860s had disappeared. Pennsylvanian coal was cheaper, and German coal was no more expensive (see Table 7.2). The advantages that British industry had gained from power and heat cheaper than elsewhere in the world had disappeared. Britain's production possibilities resembled more closely those of her European partners, diminishing the scope for trade of the mid-century's pattern.

The high concentration of British exports on coal and cotton textiles offered little opportunity for productivity increases based upon the available science and technology. That concentration is more likely to have been a consequence of Britain's relatively weak formal scientific and technological base than a cause of it. By contrast, German exports of chemicals and machinery were proportionately much more important, and textiles and coal less so. British economic growth, which reached its nadir in the decade after 1900, suffered accordingly. But structural change was taking place. As Table 7.3 demonstrates, British exports did show some of the changes that are more usually attributed to the German economy. Chemicals quadrupled their export share over the twenty-year period 1880–1900, and machinery exports also increased at a rate faster than total exports. When ships are included in the iron and steel manufactures category for 1900 there is also a slight increase in the share of that class. Textiles, on the other hand, especially cotton, showed a marked decline in export value share, though not in total value. Thus, although British exports were still less diversified than German in 1900, the difference was narrowing. In 1900 78 per cent of British merchandise exports were manufactures, whereas the proportion for Germany had risen from only 26·4 per cent in 1880 to 39·2 per cent in 1900 (UK Statistical Abstract for Foreign Countries).

232

Table 7.2 The pithead price of coal in various locations, 1861–1901

State	*c.* 1861	1901 (average)
France	6s–14s	12s 7½d
Germany	7s–10s	9s 4¼d
England	6s–10s	9s 4¼d
Pennsylvania	n.a.	8s 4¾d
Pennsylvania (anthracite)	8s–9s	2s–4s

Source: Jevons (1906: 343).

Table 7.3 The changing composition of British exports, 1880–1900 (%)

Type of product		1880	1900
Primary			
	Coal	3·7	13·3
Manufactured			
	Cotton and woollen textiles	43·1	32·1
	inc. Woollen manufactures	7·7	8·2
	Wool yarns	1·5	
	Cotton manufactures	28·5	23·9
	Cotton yarn	5.3	
	Iron, steel and manufactures	12.7	10.8
	Machinery	4·1	6·7
	Linen manufactures	2·6	2·1
	Chemicals	1·1	4·5
	Ships	—	2·9
	Wearing apparel	1·4	2·7
Total export value		£223 million	£291.2 million

Source: Statistical Abstract for the United Kingdom, London: HMSO.

Germany remained to a much greater extent a primary producer, with 35 per cent of the employed population—over 10 million people—officially still working in agriculture in 1913. Because of protective tariffs, there was virtually no reduction in the area of arable land, in marked contrast to Britain, although there was a decline in the land area devoted to pastoral farming. Food exports fell in absolute

233

value as well as in market share because of rising population and capital accumulation on a relatively fixed agricultural area (see Table 7.4). Sugar exports are an exception to this generalisation because of the payment of an export subsidy. The low cost of water transport meant that Ruhr coal could often be sold cheaper in western Europe than in Berlin and north-eastern Germany. Consequently, these latter regions imported British coal.

Within the total of German manufactured exports, cotton textiles greatly increased their share, and the proportion of woollen textiles declined. But cotton and woollen textiles together slightly raised their percentage between 1880 and 1900, moving Germany towards the British pattern of specialisation. Machinery, iron and steel manufactures, dyestuffs and books all increased dramatically. In machinery both Germany and Britain exported their own specialities to each other and the trade was almost balanced. The steel industries of the two countries also developed complementarily, each country exporting semi-manufactures to the other (Milward and Saul, 1977).

Precocious German economic development has often been suggested as a cause of Britain's deteriorating international competitiveness in manufactures and slow economic growth. One explanation draws analogies between the slowdown in advanced economies during the 1970s and the relative decline of the British economy in the nineteenth century (Beenstock, 1983). In the later period there was rapid industrialisation in middle-income countries and higher energy prices. Maizels (1963) shows that (middle-income) Germany gained the most trade from an improved competitive position at the beginning of the twentieth century. Britain lost almost exactly the amount Germany won, because of a deteriorating comparative advantage in manufactures. But, as already mentioned, there was a good deal of complementarity between the late nineteenth-century British economy and the newly industrialising Germany. The arithmetic relation does not necessarily indicate a causal link. Could declining British competitiveness in manufactures be the 'normal' pattern of development of a mature economy in which an increasing proportion of resources is allocated to services because of their high income elasticities of demand? French national income per head was close to Britain's, and France might therefore reasonably be expected to have experienced a similar shift in comparative advantage away from manufactures, but the French decline in competitiveness was smaller even than that of the United States.

Thus a 'normal' process of development of the economy is less satisfactory as an explanation of Britain's declining trade in manufactures than is low productivity growth in manufacturing shifting her comparative advantage towards natural resources, in particular towards coal. That leaves unexplained the question why British productivity growth should have been comparatively slow.

Inflexibility of institutions concerned with production is consistent with a comparison of British, French and German 'revealed comparative advantage' (Table 7.4) in 1899 and 1913. The fastest-growing country, Germany, changes industry rankings the most (Crafts 1989). Britain loses out on growth sectors; cars and aircraft in France and electricals in Germany. Underlying this pattern may well have been Britain's distinctive emphasis upon 'on the job' industrial training. British informal training created a large work force skilled in particular trades but one that was perhaps unsuited or resistant to new industries. By the end of the nineteenth century industrial development abroad perhaps combined with this inflexibility to give Britain a comparative disadvantage in high-wage, high-skill, research and development-intensive industries (Crafts and Thomas, 1986).

Organisation of foreign trade

A nation's ability to take full advantage of foreign trade required suitable institutions and markets. During the eighteenth century and earlier, a premium was placed upon the defensive ability of trading organisations, for national governments could not or would not

Table 7.4 European revealed comparative advantage, 1899 and 1913 rankings

UK			France			Germany		
1899 rank		1913 rank	1899 rank		1913 rank	1899 rank		1913 rank
1	Rails and ships	1	1	Alcohol and tobacco	1	1	Books and films	2
2	Iron and steel	3	2	Apparel	3	2	Fancy goods	7
3	Textiles	2	3	Books and films	4	3	Metal manufactures	6
4	Industrial equipment	5	4	Cars and aircraft	2	4	Chemicals	5
	Alcohol and tobacco	4					Electricals	1
							Wool and textiles	3
							Industrial equipment	4

Source: Crafts (1989).

guarantee security of intercontinental trade. National monopoly chartered companies were therefore assigned prominent roles. A relative
latecomer was the Danish Asiatic Company, founded in 1732, which
rapidly grew into a trading giant as the British, French and Dutch East
Indies companies had previously. Chartered companies could justify
their trade monopoly privileges by the need to provide the 'public
good' of defence. Without a monopoly they would be unable to finance
this activity, on which other traders would 'free ride'. Policing any form
of taxation would have been extremely expensive and unreliable. The
defence obligation of chartered companies also deprived their capital
of liquidity. Consequently, to reduce the risk borne by investors,
companies were organised as joint-stock associations. Intra-European
trade did not lock up funds in the same way and therefore associations
of private merchants predominated (Davies, 1957: 16–38). Smaller
trading ventures subscribed for particular voyages and were disbanded
at their completion. Trade was a risky business, and individual merchants generally preferred not to commit a great deal of their money
to any one voyage, even when they could afford it. Ship ownership
was therefore traditionally divided into sixty-fourths, and capitalists,
sometimes including the ship's captain, would buy a number of these
shares.

As the European world became more co-operative and piracy was
reduced, there were more opportunities for small merchants to maintain and build up permanent organisations. International sales and
purchases of goods made special demands on credit, information and
trust. Because of their overseas connections foreign merchants were
often at an advantage, especially if they had settled long enough to
build up domestic contacts in the more commercially open countries.
Foreign merchants did not control trade only in low-income states.
They formed a world-wide 'cosmopolitan bourgeosie' by the mid-
nineteenth century (Jones, 1987: 27–9, 66–9). A large part of British
trade with Europe was carried on by German families with branches in
Manchester, Bradford and Liverpool. Odessa's trade was conducted
largely by Greeks and German Jews; in 1865 Germany superseded
Britain as Russia's premier trading partner. By 1870 the number of
Greek firms in Manchester exceeded the number of German ones
primarily because they were able to find markets for British cotton piece
goods in parts of the world where British representation was weak—
Turkey, Egypt and Africa. They imported grain through the Black Sea

236

ports, especially Odessa, and to a lesser extent the Baltic, helped by the repeal of the corn laws. The Ralli brothers, who also operated in India, were pre-eminent, reputedly employing 4,000 clerks and 15,000 workmen in the 1850s (Chapman, 1992: 157–8).

Probably the largest cotton buyer in the world in 1875 was Ludwig Knoop, a German merchant with extensive mill interests in Russia and branches in all the cotton markets in Europe and America. His father, Julius Knoop, began his New York career as a pedlar and sent Ludwig to an apprenticeship with De Jersey's, in Manchester. When De Jersey, specialising in the export of yarns and later machinery to Russia, went bankrupt in 1847, Ludwig Knoop effectively took it over, along with the Russian agency for Platt Bros, the textile machine builders. Knoop built and managed Russian cotton mills (122 spinning concerns in total by the 1890s) but also was active in the cotton trade with the United States and in banking (Chapman, 1992).

Manufacturers large enough to engage directly in foreign trade originated from the smaller economies of western Europe far more often than the GNPs of the latter would at first sight lead one to expect. Their domestic markets were too limited to support the overhead costs without exports, and so in that way trade contributed to their countries' higher living standards. Foreign investment replaced trade when tariffs or other barriers threatened export markets. Swiss chemical companies, electrical companies such as Brown Boveri, dairy goods manufacturers such as Nestlé, all depended substantially on overseas business. Sweden gave birth to L. M. Ericsson and other major hi-tech multinational companies, the Netherlands was home to the electrical giant Philips and shared parentage with Britain of Unilever and Shell (Hertner and Jones, 1986).

Commodities new to international trade called for new forms of trading enterprise. In the middle of the nineteenth century Siemens, selling electric telegraph equipment, were a family multinational that merged old and new organisations. Crude oil and rubber trading also required new forms to cope with their distinct characteristics, including integration backwards to production. Rapid growth in sales sometimes necessitated organisational changes as well—in grain, tea, meat, sugar. Bunge & Born, a German firm operating mainly in Argentina after 1876, was the most successful Continental company in the grain trade, opening collection centres in the interior and building silos and elevators at ports. Edouard Bunge became broker to King Leopold II of Belgium. British firms like Ralli's lost out to continental Europeans and later Americans because powerful British millers such as Rank's took a direct hand in the trade themselves, further reducing the role of middlemen. The fragmented British staple industries generally left an opportunity for merchant houses. These houses may have exercised a harmful long-term influence over exports compared with what sales departments might have achieved in larger firms. Within a unitary organisation the flow of information back from the customer to the producer is likely to have been greater, and so also therefore would have been responsiveness to the market.

Commercial policy, 1850–1914

Judged by tariff policies, the twenty-five years after 1850 may be described as the era of free trade. But tariff cuts were rarely guided primarily, or even substantially, by a desire to reap the maximum gains from trade, which economic liberals maintained would be forthcoming (Foreman-Peck, 1983; O'Brien and Pigman, 1992). From the government's point of view, the use of tariffs as a source of revenue often vied with their potential use as instruments of foreign policy. In some cases the government merely responded to pressure groups who stood to gain, or thought they did, from the imposition of a particular tax on imports. Beneficiaries were producers expecting to sell at higher prices behind the tariff barrier. The losers, including the ultimate consumers and the buyers of intermediate goods and raw materials, were obliged to pay the higher prices. In addition mercantile interests suffered from the reduction in the carrying trade.

French liberalisation of trade led continental European policy, but was implemented for quite different reasons from the earlier British move. Ideas played some part, and Michel Chevalier was an influential intellectual advocate of economic liberalism. Most significant in overcoming the weight of vested interests in protection was Napoleon III's foreign policy. Only the emperor was empowered to conclude treaties, including those dealing with trade. The British disapproved of his desire to rid Italy of Austrian rule by force. They were intended to be mollified by the Anglo-French commercial treaty of 1860. Thereafter France, the Zollverein states, Italy and Britain negotiated a whole series of reciprocal trade treaties with 'most favoured nation' clauses.

In Germany freer trade united authoritarian East Prussian landed aristocrats, selling agricultural exports, with the liberal western and urban classes who had unsuccessfully challenged their political control in the 1848 uprisings. Changes were made to reduce the Zollverein tariff after 1850 and continued until 1879. The objectives of Prussian foreign policy coincided with *Junker* interests. Foreign policy was directed towards establishing a unified Germany with Austria–Hungary excluded. A trade treaty with France served to isolate Austria. Considerable financial concessions were made in order to achieve unification, Hanover, for instance, was bribed to enter the Zollverein customs union by being offered more revenue from the customs than she would get on the basis of population, the usual method of allocating receipts. In addition to the policy object of unification, the importance of the British market to German food grains required some attention to be paid to the sensibilities of the British government about the taxation of British exports to Germany. The British managed to foil proposals for a higher external tariff on textiles by referring to the benefit conferred on Germany by the repeal of the corn laws.

A major policy shift came in the last quarter of the nineteenth century when the huge agricultural resources of the regions of recent European settlement were pulled into the world economy. Most of western Europe was not prepared to accept fully the further shifts in economic structure that lower world food prices implied, and raised tariffs. The depression of 1873 also supported a political response. Industrial interests reacted to lower prices by demanding tariff protection and by forming cartels to restrict output in order to maintain prices. Higher tariffs provoked retaliation and the ensuing tariff wars reduced trade.

Under pressure from industrialists and agrarian interests, Bismarck introduced a new German tariff in 1879 which placed relatively low duties on a wide range of imported manufactures and heavier duties on agricultural produce. No major charge occurred in the 1880s, but in 1890 higher rates were imposed on many articles. In 1893 a tariff war with Russia broke out. Both sides eventually concluded that the resulting paralysis of trade was dangerous to the peace of Europe, and reached agreement.

France began to embrace protectionism at the same time as Germany, when the flood of US wheat increased agricultural agitation for a tariff in 1878, and the 'American peril' became a subject of popular debate. The 1881 tariff raised rates on manufactures by an average of

24 per cent, but only as a basis for negotiation with other countries. At the same time the French introduced state subsidies for shipbuilders and for owners of ships engaged on long voyages. The agricultural interests were disappointed in the tariff of 1881 and managed to raise rates on various agricultural products during the 1880s. The French duty on cattle imports annoyed the Italians, who in any case in their search for revenue proposed to revise upwards their tariffs to an average level of 60 per cent *ad valorem* in 1886. Negotiations between France and Italy over the new tariffs broke down in 1888, and each country successively increased duties on the others' products until 1892.

French exports to Italy approximately halved, although they were recouped in other markets. Italy suffered much more, its exports to France falling by more than half, and the decline was not compensated for by increased sales elsewhere. The 1892 French tariff raised duties further—on agricultural produce to an average level of 25 per cent, and on textile manufactures. A two-and-a-half-year tariff war with Switzerland followed this increase (Ashley, 1904).

Britain remained loyal to free trade despite the founding of the Fair Trade League in 1881. When in 1906 the Conservative Party fought the election on a platform of protectionism, they lost. The prospect of higher food prices for the greater part of the electorate employed outside agriculture was sufficient to sway their vote. Those parts of the empire without tariff autonomy were therefore obliged to follow suit.

Earlier in the nineteenth century Britain had led Europe by demonstration. By the last quarter of the nineteenth century the British example was less compelling. Instead a spontaneous international order began to emerge in European economic relations, as free-traders expected. International institutions were established covering communications (the International Telegraph Union in 1865, the Universal Postal Union in 1874) and trade. This second group included the 'most favoured nation' clause. Agreements were reached to avoid trade wars (the beet sugar subsidy conferences, 1887 and 1898) and a common monetary base was adopted (the Latin Monetary Union, 1865; the Scandinavian Monetary Union, 1875; the International Monetary Conferences, 1867 and 1878). Trade and economic growth were facilitated by free movement. Russia, Rumania and Greece were distinguished among European countries in requiring travellers entering their territory to hold passports. (Turkey did too). For other European states passports were unnecessary. A form of liberal international economic order was created without leadership or hegemony.

Increasing protectionism in the later nineteenth century must have reduced world trade relative to free trade, though it is less clear that economic welfare consequently declined. There is a positive association between the revenue raised from imports as a proportion of import value and national income in these years, which may be taken as an indication of the harmful impact of protection, but causation could run in the opposite direction (Foreman-Peck, 1994; Capie, 1983). Protection in Germany reduced the relative decline of the agricultural sector and therefore cut migration from the country to the towns. Such migration was not necessarily beneficial if it was taking place at a rate faster than could be accommodated by the expansion of social overhead capital—schools, roads, sewers. In the British case the economy might have benefited from protection by utilising economies of scale or learning in some of the new industries in which Britain was weak. Had tariff protection been given to the young motor industry early in the twentieth century it might well have driven costs down as a result of the greater capacity permitted by increased home market sales. These lower home costs might have offset the higher imported motor vehicle prices forced up by protection.

Later nineteenth-century trade and colonisation

In addition to tariff policy, a second area of European economic conflict arose from trade and colonisation. Colonisation as a means of trade promotion was not new by the last quarter of the nineteenth century, but the speed of the European 'scramble for Africa' and other colonial acquisition in the last two decades certainly was remarkable. The year after Stanley's discovery of the Congo basin in 1877, Leopold II of Belgium set up a Studies Committee for the Upper Congo to advance his plans for a free-trade colony in central Africa. What thoroughly embroiled Europe in Africa was a German general election that Chancellor Bismarck wished to manipulate. Foreign adventurues were a useful means of diverting German voters' attention from contentious domestic issues. As the attempts of the French to find a new way into the Chinese market had tied them down in Indo-China at the time, and the concern of the British to secure their communications with India was committing them in Egypt, Germany was left with almost a free

241

hand in Africa. Leopold achieved his objective at the Berlin Congo conference of 1885, with an international treaty guaranteeing free trade and navigation, and Bismarck gained a German empire in Africa five times the size of the Reich. The new territories were largely unproductive and supported few German economic interests. Not surprisingly, then, with his electoral problem solved, by 1886 Bismarck had lost interest in his colonial empire (Fieldhouse, 1973).

The larger French colonial empire of nearly 1·2 million square miles at the end of the century was also, with the exception of Algeria in the 1830s, conquered mainly after 1880. Italy belatedly tried to emulate its northern neighbours, despite being in a parlous financial condition, until defeated by the Abyssinians (Ethiopians) at Adowa in 1896.

British colonial activity followed a different pattern, most probably because British economic interests were already well established overseas, and because the liberal tradition of minimal government intervention was more firmly established. The administration of the British empire was a model of economy (Davis and Huttenback, 1986). When other countries were colonising in the 1880s British policy was still to hold back on grounds of expense. In 1883 the Queensland government's annexation of south-east New Guinea (to prevent further German and Dutch acquisitions) was not ratified by the imperial government until Queensland agreed the following year to guarantee a portion of the administrative expenses. Similarly, the British procrastinated in early 1883 when the German government indicated that it would be glad to see British protection extended to German settlers in South West Africa. British policy reversed only in the 1890s when British trading interests were apparently in danger of losing out through other countries' annexation of territory.

All these colonial acquisitions, and most of those of Russia in Asia, differed from the majority of temperate zone settlements in their substantial indigenous population and climate uncongenial to Europeans. The motives for colonisation, and the pattern of economic development imposed on the colonies, were therefore also quite different. Trade with the new colonies was relatively unimportant to the European powers. As Table 7.5 shows for the 1890s, Britain was the most reliant upon colonial trade, which accounted for one-third of her exports and over one-fifth of her imports. The only other power as closely dependent upon such trade was Spain, with almost a quarter of

Table 7.5 Total trade compared with colonial trade, selected countries, 1892–96 (annual average)

Imperial power	Colonial/ total imports (%)	Colonial/ total exports (%)	Colonial area (000 sq. miles)	Colonial population (million)
Britain	22·50	33·20	11,090	325·10
France	9·50	9·50	1,195	36·15
Holland	14·50	5·00	785	34·50
Portugal	15·80	9·20	834	7·90
Spain	9·70	24·00	323	8·50
Denmark	1·10	1·60	41	0·13
Germany	0·05	0·09	1,026	9·80

Source: Flux (1899).

its exports going to the colonies—and war with the United States was soon to change that. Germany, the most vigorous industrial state, was distinguished by the tiny colonial percentage of its trade. The new colonial empires were in fact even less important to the imperial powers than Table 7.5 suggests, because colonial trade was usually concentrated on one or two possessions. Nearly two-thirds of French colonial trade was with Algeria and Tunisia, India dominated British colonial trade, East India the Dutch, Angola was much the most important in the Portuguese colonial trade, and Cuba in the Spanish. All these colonies (except Tunisia) had been held long before the wave of colonisation of the last two decades of the century. That this new colonisation was economically necessary to the European capitalism of the time, as Lenin and others maintained, is hard to square with the small volume of trade involved.

As it ceased to be a technological leader in this period, Britain inevitably lost markets in advanced countries, but that did not trigger a new British drive to boost sales in the colonies. A larger share of colonial trade in total trade was an arithmetic consequence of lost markets elsewhere. British colonisation, unlike French or German, was defensive rather than offensive. Even granted this motivation, the effects of the new colonialism do not suggest that it was justified by the actual increases. Maizels's (1963) work shows that the pattern of products and of markets was not responsible for any increased sales of manufactured goods by the main colonial powers, Britain and France, during the period 1899–1913.

243

Not only was new colonial trade of little importance to the major imperial powers, there is little evidence of the exclusion of one European country's traders from another's colonies. German traders benefited from British power almost as much as the British in China and South Africa (Chapman, 1992). German exports to other West African colonies from 1889 to 1911 grew more rapidly than did German exports to German West Africa in the same period. British exports to German South West Africa increased by proportionately more than German exports from 1900 to 1911. French exports to British possessions in Africa rose by 60 per cent from 1889 to 1911, while French exports in total rose by almost the same proportion (Foreman-Peck, 1983: 116). The imperial powers staked their territorial claims where their nationals had already established trading interests, however small these were. This is further borne out by the close, but usually decreasing, dependence of colonies on trade with the imperial power. Trading patterns of colonial areas in these years were the cause, rather than the consequence of, colonisation.

Although colonisation did not in fact enhance the trade of the imperial powers, the administration of the colonies became for most of them a considerable financial drain. French colonial expenditure massively exceeded colonial receipts in 1898. Between 1894 and 1913 German expenditure on colonies, excluding defence, was greater than the entire value of German colonial trade. Similarly for the most recently arrived imperial power, Italy, which also directly spent more on colonial government than the value of its entire colonial trade in the years 1893 to 1932. The Dutch obtained a financial surplus from the Netherlands East Indies until 1874, but thereafter the surplus was eliminated by the rebellion in northern Sumatra. The other Dutch colonies of Surinam and Curaçao demanded subsidies. Great Britain, in contrast to most other powers, required its dependencies to be self-supporting. Loans were expected to be repaid eventually. Even Britain, though, could not invariably enforce financial self-sufficiency. In the 1890s the British West Indies were one of the few exceptions because the economy was so depressed. Some have seen the cost to Britain of empire as a whole in these years as entirely exceeding the benefits, although that must depend upon the alternative international economy that could be assumed to replace the empire (O'Brien, 1988, 1989). Certainly the new European colonies in the later nineteenth century were usually an expensive hobby that could not be justified by the trade they generated. Even the old colonies were not obviously a source of abnormally high returns on investment, broadly interpreted (O'Brien, 1982; Foreman-Peck, 1989).

European economic integration in 1910

Despite political friction over potential colonial territories, massive conscript armies deployed in expectation of, or to deter, a European war, and a tendency towards higher tariffs, the European and the world economies were quite open to the movement of goods and people by 1910. Relatively low rail and steamship transport costs and economic policies that, in historical perspective, were still liberal underlay these highly internationalised economic relations. By 1913 Europe's trade/ gross national product ratio, at a peak not achieved again until the 1960s and 1970s, indicated that the late nineteenth century nationalist/ liberal international order supported markets at least as free as those created by the post-1945 institutions of GATT and the IMF. Britain and Scandinavia returned to the 1913 level of integration with the world economy only around 1970 and Italy did so perhaps five years earlier (Grassman, 1980; Beenstock and Warburton, 1983).

In the half-century before the outbreak of the first world war European economic integration was advanced, although most statesmen had not planned it, and therefore the gains to Europeans from trade and specialisation were also increased. Increasing integration meant a tendency towards single European prices for all goods and services, for labour, capital and land. In practice, transport costs, state policies, adjustment costs and other influences prevented perfect integration between national economies but the proportion of internationally traded to non-traded goods increased. The second category is much less responsive to world market conditions, including as it does rents, wages, services and products with a high weight to value ratio. Nonetheless the prices of non-traded goods are ultimately affected by world conditions, most immediately in areas specialising in export products. So for centuries Bordeaux vineyard rents varied with the buoyancy of world wine demand. The rising ratio of traded to non-traded goods meant the European economies were more prone to fluctuate with each other and with the rest of the world economy. Booms and slumps spread more pervasively around Europe and the world, as was to be demonstrated devastatingly after 1929.

245

Conclusion

Did foreign trade matter as much as eighteenth-century mercantilists and nineteenth-century liberals thought? Three possible trade and economic growth patterns have been explored above. The first, where overseas demand expansion draws increasing volumes of resources into the foreign trade sector, corresponds fairly closely with the mercantilist interest in exporting and tied colonial markets. The second occurs when domestic supply expansion spills over into exports. The third, increasing market integration, also has some affinities with mercantilism. The acquisition of colonies in the eighteenth century was equivalent to a reduction of transport costs or tariffs, and declining transport costs drove both export and import prices down.

For Europe as a whole, as well as for the larger national economies within Europe, demand pull was probably not a persistent process. In the second case, trade allowed greater gains from specialisation than were available within national economies alone, but trade was a lagging, not a leading, sector here. The principal long-term source of the third configuration, falling transport costs, boosted domestic as well as foreign trade, though advances in ocean navigation were bound to influence the second more than the first. Railways and their improvements, by contrast, drove intra-European and domestic trade more than extra-European and foreign trade. Again with this pattern the only reason to give priority to overseas rather than domestic activity as a source of economic growth is that it is, and was, more visible, statistically and politically.

Trade mattered for strategic war materials, and for perhaps a few industrial inputs, the scarcity of which might have constrained economic growth. Small countries, like the United Provinces and Poland, excluded from non-imperial trade were unlikely to experience rapid growth in the eighteenth century. That was probably not true of larger countries like Britain and France, where the internal market for agriculture and industry supplied most wants. Colonial goods may have offered a work incentive but they are unlikely to have been decisive. The rewards of exploitation or theft are another potential route by which the foreign sector may have encouraged domestic economic growth. There is little evidence that the costs to European society as a whole were much less than the gains. The slave trade consumed European as well as African resources, albeit differentially. Later nineteenth-century colonies, especially those in Africa, were generally rather different from those of the eighteenth century in which Europeans later settled in considerable numbers. They were more expensive to run and the gains were fewer.

Within Europe trade spread new technology—most spectacularly with railways—as well as reflecting resource endowments, especially, by the mid-nineteenth century, of coal. Transport costs and human barriers limited trade but the first constraint was eased continuously throughout the period and the second pursued a more erratic path, reaching a trough in the later 1860s and early 1870s before rising again under the political impact of the depression that began in 1873. Higher tariff protection was associated with lower income. Some economies, notably those of southern and eastern Europe, were constrained by political difficulties which in turn limited the development of their infrastructure. Both their trade and their productivity remained low.

Even so, in the decade before the first world war Europe was highly integrated compared with what was achieved with more advanced technology, under the aegis of the Treaty of Rome, during the 1970s and 1980s. The intervening years underline the achievements of the framework of international economic relations after 1850, for they showed that neither the later nineteenth-century trend, nor that after 1957, was natural or inevitable. Hegemony does not seem to be the explanation; there was no dominant European or Western world player as the United States was in the generation after 1945. Rather the relatively benign international economic order of the later nineteenth century, by contrast with the 'jungle' of 1750, was achieved by general agreement or acquiescence among the major powers, because of their domestic economic and political transformation in the intervening years. Rapid economic growth without liberalisation in Germany proved an explosive mixture but even there political leaders' self-interest dictated commercial policies that were pacific by comparison with those of the eighteenth century. Within Europe the economic rise of Germany and, outside, the growth of the United States threatened to eclipse Britain and France. But how much the prosperity of each was intertwined by 1914 was demonstrated by the economic dislocation consequent upon Germany's effective isolation from the European economy in the early 1920s.

References

Allen, R. C. (1979), 'International competition in iron and steel, 1850–1913', *Journal of Economic History*, 39.

Ashley, P. (1904), *Modern Tariff History: Germany, United States, France*. London, John Murray.

Bairoch, P. (1974), 'Geographical structure and trade balance of European foreign trade, 1800–1970', *Journal of European Economic History*, 3.

Bairoch, P. (1976), 'Europe's gross national product, 1800–1975', *Journal of European Economic History*, 5.

Bairoch, P. (1982), 'International industrialisation levels', *Journal of European Economic History*, 11.

Beenstock, M. (1983), *The World Economy in Transition*, London, Allen and Unwin.

Beenstock, M., and Warburton, P. (1983), 'Long term trends in economic openness in the United Kingdom and the United States', *Oxford Economic Papers*, 35.

Capie, F. (1983), 'Tariff protection and economic performance in the nineteenth century', in J. Black and J. Winter, eds., *Policy and Performance in International Trade*, London, Macmillan.

Caron, F. (1979), *An Economic History of Modern France*, London, Methuen.

Chapman, S. (1992), *Merchant Enterprise in Britain: from the Industrial Revolution to World War I*, Cambridge, Cambridge University Press.

Coleman, D. C. (1969), *Revisions in Mercantilism*, London, Methuen.

Crafts, N. F. R. (1983), 'Gross national product in Europe, 1870–1910: some new estimates', *Explorations in Economic History*, 20.

Crafts, N. F. R. (1989), 'Revealed comparative advantage in manufactures, 1899–1950', *Journal of European Economic History*, 18.

Crafts, N. F. R., and Thomas, M. (1986), 'Comparative advantage in UK manufacturing trade, 1910–35', *Economic Journal*, 66.

Davies, K. G. (1957), *The Royal African Company*, London, Longmans.

Davis, L., and Huttenback, R. (1986), *Mammon and the Pursuit of Empire*. Cambridge, Cambridge University Press.

Fieldhouse, D. K. (1973), *Economics and Empire, 1830–1914*. London, Weidenfeld & Nicolson.

Flux, A. W. (1899), 'The flag and trade: a summary review of the trade of the chief colonial empires', *Journal of the Royal Statistical Society*, 62.

Foreman-Peck, J. S. (1983), *A History of the World Economy: International Economic Relations since 1850*. Brighton, Harvester Wheatsheaf.

Foreman-Peck, J. S. (1989), 'Foreign investment and imperial exploitation: balance of payments reconstruction for nineteenth-century Britain and India', *Economic History Review*, 2nd ser., 42.

Foreman-Peck, J. S. (1994), 'A model of nineteenth-century European economic growth', *Revista de Historia Economica* (forthcoming).

Goodman, J., and Honeyman, K. (1988), *Gainful Pursuits: the Making of Industrial Europe, 1600–1914*. London, Edward Arnold.

Grassman, S. (1980), 'Long-term trends in the openness of national economies', *Oxford Economic Papers*, 32.

Hatton, T. J., Lyons, J. S., and Satchell, S. E. (1983), 'Eighteenth-century British trade: homespun or Empire-made?' *Explorations in Economic History*, 20.

Hecksher, E. (1955), *Mercantilism*, London, Allen & Unwin.

Hertner, G., and Jones G., eds. (1986), *Multinationals: Theory and History*. Aldershot, Gower.

Imlah, A. H. (1954), *Economic Elements in the Pax Britannica*. Cambridge, Mass., Harvard University Press.

Israel, J. (1989), *Dutch Primacy in World Trade, 1585–1740*. Oxford, Clarendon Press.

Jevons, W. (1906), *The Coal Question: an Inquiry concerning the Progress of the Nation*. London, Macmillan.

Jones, C. A. (1987), *International Business in the Nineteenth Century: the Rise and Fall of a Cosmopolitan Bourgeoisie*. Brighton, Harvester Wheatsheaf.

Kennedy, P. (1988), *The Rise and Fall of the Great Powers: Economic Change and Military Conflict from 1500 to 2000*. New York, Random House.

Kindleberger, C. P. (1973), *The World in Depression, 1929–36*. London, Allen & Unwin.

Lévy-Leboyer, M., and Bourgignon, F. (1990), *The French Economy in the Nineteenth Century: an Essay in Econometric Analysis*. Cambridge, Cambridge University Press.

McCloskey, D. N. (1981), *Trade and Enterprise in Victorian Britain*. Cambridge, Cambridge University Press.

Maizels, A. (1963), *Industrial Growth and World Trade*. Cambridge, Cambridge University Press.

Milward, A. S., and Saul, S. B. (1973), *The Economic Development of Continental Europe, 1780–1870*. London, Allen & Unwin.

Milward, A. S., and Saul, S. B. (1977), *The Development of the Economies of Continental Europe, 1850–1914*, London, Allen & Unwin.

O'Brien, P. K. (1982), 'European economic development: the contribution of the periphery', *Economic History Review*, 35.

O'Brien, P. K. (1988), 'The costs and benefits of British imperialism, 1846–1914, *Past and Present*, 120.

O'Brien, P. K. (1989), 'Debate', *Past and Present*, 121.

O'Brien, P. K. (1991), 'Power with Profit: the State and the Economy, 1688–1815'. Inaugural lecture, University of London.

O'Brien, P. K., and Keyder, C. (1978), *Economic Growth in Britain and France, 1780–1914: Two Paths to the Twentieth Century*. London, Allen & Unwin.

O'Brien, P. K., and Pigman, G. A. (1992), 'Free trade, British hegemony and the international economic order in the nineteenth century', *Review of International Studies*, 18.

Shepherd, J. F., and Walton, G. M. (1972), *Shipping, Maritime Trade and the Economic Development of Colonial North America*. Cambridge, Cambridge University Press.

Smithsonian Institution (1927), *World Weather Records*. Washington, D.C., Smithsonian Institution.

Thomas, R. P. (1965), 'A quantitative approach to the study of the effects of British imperial policy upon colonial welfare: some preliminary findings', *Journal of Economic History*, 25.

Thomas, R. P., and McCloskey, D. N. (1981), 'Overseas trade and empire, 1700–1860', in R. Floud and D. N. McCloskey, eds., *The Economic History of Britain since 1700* I. Cambridge, Cambridge University Press.

Wolfe, E. R. (1982), *Europe and the People without History*. Berkeley, Cal., University of California Press.

Investment and finance

Investment—the accumulation of physical capital—grew with European industrialisation. It involved sacrificing current consumption to acquire a stock of increasingly specific assets for producing goods, hence investment is often regarded as amassing producer goods—machines to manufacture articles for subsequent consumption. However, investment is much broader, encompassing assets such as seed in agriculture, for the next harvest, and infrastructure, such as houses and railways, to provide services like shelter and transport. As discussed later, the growth of investment in agriculture and construction was often the greater extension of existing, pre-industrial activity. Moreover, during the inception of industrialisation, these were the most important areas of investment. Although the factory is frequently regarded as the most visible symbol of industrialisation, it was not to be commonplace in European manufacturing until the late nineteenth century.

The growth of physical assets, from seed and horseshoes to industrial equipment and houses, required financing. With the expansion in their volume—a feature of industrialisation—demands were generated for funds beyond individuals' reach, resulting in the further development of national, and international, financial systems. They linked savers with borrowers, so supporting the augmentation of the physical capital stock. However, many such networks during early industrialisation were private and informal, constituted by friends, co-religionists and business links, or were the greater development of customary relationships, as between tenant farmer and landlord. Such financial sources were ultimately constrained, which provoked the establishment of formal financial intermediaries, especially banks. The banks enlarged financial catchment areas and provided expertise in discriminating between competing outlets for investment funds. Yet the creation of banks was a response to many, varying demands arising with industrialisation—demands for economies to be monetised further as dealings expanded, for the transfer of funds between urban nodes of emerging markets, and for credit to support work in progress and trade. In all this, the financing of physical capital often proved to be a demand that arose only when industrialisation was well established.

The discussion here is in three parts. The first examines the pace of the onset of modern economic growth in terms of its implications for the expansion of investment, as both Gerschenkron and Rostow have seen the 'industrial revolution' as truly revolutionary—as being a 'spurt' of growth, or a 'take-off' period. They regarded its significant characteristic as being a sharp increase in physical investment, generating consequent pressure for mobilising financial capital. Such long-standing, influential views require re-examination in the light of subsequent research into the European economy's growth and its effects on investment and financing. The second major aspect is the expansion of investment in relation to the rise of income; accordingly, it looks at the burden that mounting physical investment placed upon income, in terms of consumption forgone. Some of the major components of investment are then considered in detail, beginning with the largest initial areas of investment—agriculture and house building—followed by railway construction during the mid-century, perhaps the most revolutionary aspect of Europe's accumulation of physical capital. Finally, the growing importance of industrial fixed capital in the late nineteenth century is reviewed. In some respects, these sections, by considering aspects of the expansion of physical capital, establish the financial demands generated by investment's rise. The concluding sections consider what effects this had upon intermediation, in terms of the founding of financial institutions, particularly specialist banks to facilitate railway construction and industrial investment. Lastly, patterns of investment and their financing are also considered in terms of international flows of funds, predominantly within Europe before 1870, but globally thereafter.

Investment and finance in models of industrialisation

Until recently, investment was stressed as a crucial force in industrialisation. This view arose largely from Rostow's generalised model (1960), based substantially on his interpretation of the British experience during the late eighteenth and early nineteenth centuries. Rostow

251

highlighted a rise, approaching a doubling, in the ratio of investment to national income as one of the key features of the 'take-off' period. Such a conceptualisation had its intellectual origins in the powerful impact of Keynesian theory upon economics. The increase of investment was also, following Schumpeter, seen as endowing the structurally changing economy with new, 'post-Newtonian' technologies, thereby greatly raising productivity. This interpretation of the onset of growth had substantial implications for its financing, especially when industrialisation took hold in relatively 'backward' economies, where savings were apparently at a low level and spread widely. These features have been held responsible for a shortage of financial capital, thereby constraining structural change; furthermore, with such disadvantageous backwardness, merchants, manufacturers and 'passive' investors would prefer risk-averse assets.

The generalities of the problems posed by achieving increased investment in less developed Europe were investigated by Gerschenkron (1952). Like Rostow somewhat later, he saw the initiation of industrialisation as a rapid 'spurt' of growth. Gerschenkron's particular interest lay in the consequences of the interaction between the onset of growth and what he termed degrees of economic backwardness. The latter can be demarcated by a gradient of economic and *social* development running from west to east across Europe. Britain, as the first industrial nation, occupied the highest point of material development and its society had been able to invest in the new technologies relatively easily. Early machines were comparatively simple devices and, therefore cheap to build and acquire. Consequently, the amount of income required for increased investment had been modest and the changes arising in financing methods relatively slight. Until the late nineteenth century British investment growth benefited from the substantial profits generated by the new technologies, which provided funds for reinvestment; therefore, there was little resort on the part of entrepreneurs to a formal capital market to aid the acquisition of fixed capital assets.

Gerschenkron believed that the 'follower' economies of continental Europe were confronted with higher initial thresholds of investment when their industrialisation got under way. They arose in part from the on-going development of technology, resulting in ever more complex and specific machines and the greater centralisation of production. Such a view implied that a 'follower' economy, handicapped

252

by impairments in the supply of savings, nonetheless had to embark upon substantial physical capital outlays. Gerschenkron divided the economies of continental Europe under two broad heads. North-western and central continental Europe, 'half-way down' the gradient of economic development, were categorised as relatively backward. Here the key problem was apparently the mobilisation of savings to provide sufficient investment funds to surmount the threshold. This required specific financing mechanisms—the creation of corporate investment banks—to act as substitutes, but with associated costs, for formal capital markets. These institutions swept together and chan-nelled savings, providing these funds to entrepreneurs on a medium and long-term basis for the acquisition of fixed capital. Consequently, the significant financial demands generated by the higher threshold of investment led to a special relationship between banks and industry—to the extent that the investment banks may not simply have facilitated industrialists' investment decisions but may also have become active partners in developing an economy's nascent industrial sector.

At the 'foot' of the gradient of development, in eastern Europe, especially Russia, Gerschenkron considered that the degree of back-wardness was almost absolute. Here the problem was not simply the development of particular financial institutions, but also the lack of entrepreneurship, so that private activity would not be sufficient to accomplish the task of industrialisation. Instead the state and its bureaucracy would have to take the leading role in both production and its financing.

These seminal ideas about the behaviour of investment and its financing provoked further discussion. Had the onset of European industrialisation involved revolutionary spurts of economic growth? If, instead, growth had been evolutionary, the consequences for invest-ment, and financial development, would have been very different from the stylisations of Rostow and Gerschenkron. Other more particular questions arose: namely, to what extent had investment grown during the early stages of industrialisation and in which sectors? Again, the more gradual the increase of capital assets, the less the arising 'burden' imposed upon current consumption and the smaller the arising pressure for consequent financial change. Thirdly, it was already clear that, from 1860, there were substantial emerging differences in banking structures between Britain and most other major European industrial economies. Did this imply that continental European banks had a different relationship with industry? These questions are explored in the following sections of this chapter.

The consequences of economic growth for investment

Trying to establish an economy's growth path from extant data sets is an extremely difficult exercise. International comparisons are even more perplexing, as, with their often very idiosyncratic natures, estimates of individual countries' historic national income are not on the same footing. Consequently, the historian is forced to put estimates and 'guesstimates' of varying reliability alongside one another. Nonetheless, taking proper care and applying caution, the task can be undertaken.

Bairoch's estimates (1976) suggest that Europe grew relatively slowly, with GNP *per capita* rising annually at about 0·9 per cent between 1830 and 1910. This is an average across the varying experiences of the continent's industrial, industrialising and non-industrial national economies. However, a relatively low rate of progress, especially in comparison with the post-1945 experience, was equally typical of Europe's industrial economies. The first—Britain, with Belgium, France and Switzerland—had annual growth rates of the order of 1·25 per cent *per capita* 1830–1910. The initial growth paths of later industrialisers, sometimes regarded as more 'explosive' in nature, were no more rapid; Germany, Austria–Hungary and the Netherlands grew at comparable rates of about 1·24 per cent per annum 1860–1910. The fastest growth was probably experienced by the Nordic countries—Denmark, Finland, Norway and Sweden—at an average of about 1·6 per cent per annum 1860–1910. These data suggest that industrialisation was a gradual rather than a 'revolutionary' process, albeit an acceleration, compared with previous experience of very gradual, or stagnant, material progress. Furthermore, nineteenth-century growth was sustained, with gains accumulating slowly but remorselessly over the medium and long term. This is in sharp contrast to the interpretation put forward by Rostow and accepted as a premise of his investigation by Gerschenkron.

Some historians still regard the German states as an example of a dramatic, initial 'spurt' of growth. The 'trigger' is frequently seen as the economic consequences either of the Zollverein or of the substantial wave of railway building over the mid-century. Other, parallel developments played, perhaps, an even greater role in stimulating the onset of sustained growth. They arose from trade linking Britain, the middle Rhineland and East Prussia. Rhenish manufacturers imported British semi-finished materials—pig iron and yarn—to make up, in rural workshops and cottages, into articles for consumption in markets to the east of the Elbe, where agricultural communities were enabled to make such purchases by income generated from grain exports to Britain. The Zollverein's tariff reductions may have assisted these dealings, but they also point to a '"proto-industrial" foreland' in 'Germany's' pattern of economic development. Consequently, this would emphasise evolution and gradualness, especially as Rhenish industry's origins lay in the sixteenth century (von Borries, 1970; Dumke, 1979; Kutz, 1974).

Deep historical roots may also have been characteristic of the industrialisation of other areas of continental Europe. Initial applications of Rostow's model to the experience of the western lands of Austria–Hungary provoked a debate over when a 'take-off' period may have occurred. Was it during the *Grunderzeit* (building years) of the mid-century or, rather during the acceleration of growth at the end of the nineteenth century—the *zweiter Grunderzeit*? Recently constructed indices of Austrian industrial production point to an earlier onset of growth—from the 1830s—and also indicate a pattern of low, but sustained, advance, albeit with some marked cyclical variations. Moreover, it seems that the foundations of post-1830 growth were laid by proto-industrialisation during the second half of the eighteenth century; an earlier onset of industrialisation within Austria having perhaps been stalled by the revolutionary and Napoleonic wars, and the ensuing fifteen years of dislocation and reconstruction (Good, 1984).

To generalise about 'European industrialisation' is dangerous, as there were substantial variations between countries and regions. Yet there was something approaching a common experience, in terms of gradual growth: 'revolutionary spurts' were the exception rather than the rule. Modest but sustained expansion had different consequences for investment than those arising from a more rapid 'take-off'. Nonetheless, 'follower' industrialisers may still have faced an investment threshold problem. It could have arisen from the time lag between the local inception of structural change—a shift from proto-industry to the factory—and the changing nature of manufacturing, in terms of technology and scale, generated by Britain's prior, and continuing, industrialisation. However, technological best practice, involving sizeable capital-intensive plants, was not necessarily best economic practice for creating profits. Within follower industrialisers, labour, given its numerical abundance, may have been cheaper to employ than capital, thereby putting some stress on maintaining hand rather than mechanised methods of production.

In contrast to Britain, manufacturing elsewhere in Europe remained geographically dispersed until at least the mid-century. Its largely rural context reflected not only continuing reliance upon water for power, and wood as fuel, but also the use of underemployed agricultural labour. Proto-industrial forms of organisation persisted, giving rise to regions in which industry predominated, rather than industrial regions, each having an urban centre as its kernel. Such manufacturing required relatively low levels of fixed capital but generated demand for credit to finance imports of semi-finished materials, work in progress and the export of goods to final markets, usually beyond the place of production. Consequently it placed emphasis upon the merchant as the industrial entrepreneur and his own financial resources, augmented by regional and intra-regional credit networks in which he participated. Furthermore, the growth of credit demand, with the significant expansion of production, and of trade both domestic and international, called for financial innovation—the emergence of formal banking. A further consequence of this pattern of change arose from its regional or local nature (Pollard, 1976). The process of investment was a challenge to communities, rather than national society, and it was often met initially by local financial developments and innovations. However, with the development of intra-European trade these industrialising districts were linked financially by emerging credit networks. Generally, formal banking began as a response to a growing demand for credit, with the financial servicing of rising fixed investment coming later.

Investment and its constituents

In reviewing the growth of investment, as with national income data, and for the same basic reasons, great care and caution have to be exercised when assessing the implications of the available estimates, and guesstimates, of the historical path of fixed capital formation. Here the growth of physical capital assets, primarily in the French and German economies, will be considered. Examining French investment data has advantages, on the one hand because France, along with Britain and

Germany, became one of the three major European industrial economies, and on the other because the territory of France remained almost
constant geographically, albeit suffering the loss of Alsace–Lorraine
after 1871. A review of the investment process in other European
countries is complicated by the unification of the nation state. Many of
the constituent states of 'Germany' before 1871 were also geographically segmented, and there were major differences, for example, in the
experience of Rhenish Prussia and of the Prussian lands east of the Elbe.

Unfortunately there is no major overview of the development
of investment within Europe during the nineteenth century. Consequently this chapter examines aspects of the rise of investment in
terms of national experiences, drawing upon available detailed case
studies. Although much attention has been directed to the growth of
manufacturing investment during early industrialisation, other sectors
accounted for significantly greater proportions of capital accumulation
until industrialisation was well established. Current results point to the
relative small scale of industrial plant and machinery within total capital
formation until almost the end of the nineteenth century. This has led
to the frequent repetition of remarks such as 'the manufacturing
investment costs arising from the initiation of industrialisation were
somewhat equivalent to the building of a single castle, chateau or a
prestigious town hall'. Physical capital investment was more substantial
in the building and agriculture sectors.

Construction improved as rising living standards, the product of
industrialisation, changed demands and tastes. Agriculture responded
to rising numbers, thereby avoiding a Malthusian crisis, and, with
increased productivity, enabled labour and other resources to be
transferred to the emerging industrial and service sectors. If agricultural
and property investment represented the further extension of existing
processes, revolutionary change in investment patterns came not with
industrial development but as a consequence of transport improvement,
particularly railway building. It was only from the last quarter of the
century that industrial fixed capital generally took on substantial
proportions.

In the case of France, the ratio of total domestic investment to
income rose from an annual average, by decade, of 7·2 per cent of GNP
immediately following Waterloo to 14·2 per cent prior to the Great
War (Lévy-Leboyer, 1978: 287) This represents a doubling, as posited
by Rostow, but over a century of change, rather than during a short

'take-off' period. Something approaching a doubling—a rise in the ratio to about 12.4 per cent—occurred during the half-century from the 1820s. However, this may be a misleading indicator, as the French economy (like the Habsburg economy) was markedly dislocated for some fifteen years following the collapse of the Napoleonic system, resulting in low rates of investment. The general impression derived from French data for the nineteenth century is of a gradual rise in total investment, paralleling a slow but sustained economic transformation of the country. Hence, this growth of investment does not imply a significant burden upon income; rather, its demands increased with the expansion of income. Rising income and rising investment, at a general level, moved together in an interactive way.

Europe's major economic activity during the first half of the nineteenth century was agriculture. It constituted the largest component of German annual net investment before 1850, accounting for some 30 per cent in the 1850s, but declining to about 15 per cent by 1914 (Tilly, 1978: 388). Agriculture during the second quarter of the century, particularly Prussian agriculture, tended to be a capital-intensive activity. Furthermore, many of the agrarian technical and organisational changes were adopted to alleviate the shortage of capital in the countryside. The growth of rural population provided almost costless labour to accomplish land improvement—a factor which was as important in parts of Scandanavia as in Germany. This approach to improvement and rising productivity was particularly crucial for small farmers, who lacked the support of landowners and were capable of making only small outlays. The major farmers could turn to the mortgage market, but smallholders—who, in Norway at least, made small but significant changes in methods and implements—were not to have the support of specialised credit unions, or savings banks, until the late century. Some assistance came in the mid-century with the rise in prices, which also encouraged investment, and from more liberal trade policies, which more readily allowed, as in Denmark, the import of British clay pipes for field drainage.

In Prussia agricultural investment largely took three forms—seed, the maintenance of livestock, and buildings. One early significant form of investment was the production of seed—a clear example of investment being forgone consumption. This burden decreased, as the general impression of all five main field cash crops—wheat, rye, barley, oats and potatoes—is of a declining proportion of annual output being reinvested as seed—from about 22·5 per cent in 1816 to about 18·4 per cent by 1840 (Tilly, 1978: 391). However, this trend of rising yields was sharply interrupted by the poor harvests of the mid-1840s. Some productivity gains were consumed by the expansion of livestock numbers, which resulted in rising feed costs. Livestock itself was an item of capital and its growing production generated further investment demands in terms of specialised buildings.

Tilly's best guesstimates suggest that during the 1830s net agricultural investment in Prussia was equivalent to 4·4 per cent of agricultural net value added (Tilly, 1978: 395). Livestock made up 64·3 per cent of agricultural net investment, buildings 32 per cent and seed 3·7 per cent. Agriculture comprised about 58 per cent of total Prussian net investment at the time, non-agricultural buildings 27·4 per cent and industry 3 per cent. A similar picture is given by somewhat comparable data for the Swedish distribution of gross investment in fixed assets. These place agriculture's share in the late 1860s at 28 per cent, lower than housing—31 per cent—but well in advance of either transport, 19 per cent, or manufacturing and mining, 14 per cent (Hildebrand, 1978: 604).

Within both French and Swedish total investment, the largest sector throughout the nineteenth century was 'construction'. It accounted for 61 per cent of French gross capital formation in the decade 1815–24, and 37·5 per cent in the decade before 1914 (Lévy-Leboyer, 1978: 287). This emphasises the importance of property development, arising from European urbanisation. 'Construction' is, of course, a broad category, including factories as well as residential buildings, together with roads and municipal services, such as water, gas, electricity, schools and hospitals. Factories could be regarded as a constituent of industrial manufacturing investment, but, in the French experience of economic structural change, large-scale manufacturing plants were uncommon before 1914. Whereas net investment in residential property increased annually at an average of 763 million francs between 1852 and 1888, the comparable figure for factories was only 50 million francs (Lévy-Leboyer, 1978: 285). By the close of the nineteenth century net annual residential investment was taking place at a rate of 640 million francs, as opposed to 126 million francs for factories.

Something approaching sudden, revolutionary change occurred during the mid-nineteenth century with the construction of the initial railway networks of Europe. In 1839 there was some 2,500 km of railway line in Europe, of which 1,600 km was in operation in Great Britain, while the only other countries each having more than 100 km of track were Belgium, France, Germany and the Habsburg empire. In 1870 the European railway system amounted to 98,000 km. Britain still had the most extensive network at 21,558 km, yet Germany now had 18,876 km of track opened for traffic and France 15,544 km and railways were to be found throughout the continent—from Scandinavia to Italy, and from Iberia to the Balkans and Russia. This important constituent of investment is discussed in Chapter 6.

European railway investment was not only a response to demands for improved communications, but, in turn, made possible what previously had been inconceivable. For many contemporaries the railway symbolised what was subsequently to be called the industrial revolution. Economic historians continue to debate, and try more precisely to delineate, the effects—short-term, medium-term and long—of the coming of the railway (O'Brien, 1983). Nonetheless, coupled with developments in oceanic carriage, the mid-century European railway construction boom constituted a pronounced change in transport and communications. The manifold effects were to be global, but, within Europe, one importance consequence was the coalescence of national markets, in turn leading to the emergence of a European market for practically every material product. This had great effects upon manufacturing, in terms of scale, organisation and technology. On the one hand, basic raw materials—above all, coal—could now be readily transported, whereas, on the other, machine-produced goods had access to wide hinterlands. As a result, the coming of the railway gave great advantages to urban factory production, sited at nodes in the new transport system, which was thereby able to undercut the economies of rural proto-industry. Workshop production continued, but now largely in an urban setting, for the manufacture of bespoke products aimed at the upper sections of the market which prized individuality and hand finishing.

There is a link between the outline railway networks of the mid-century and the subsequent growth of industrial fixed capital formation from the 1870s. Steam power may be taken as a convenient indicator of this development, as well as of centralised production. Even in Britain in 1870 steam power was used only across a restricted range of industries—substantially those which had experienced structural change from the late eighteenth century, namely textiles (and, above all, cotton), coal mining, iron smelting, founding and forging, and engineering. These industries had employed about 0·3 million nominal h.p. of industrial steam power in 1850, rising to 1·03 million h.p. in 1870. This growth is overshadowed by the wider adoption of power-driven machinery across most British manufacturing during the ensuing four decades, so that industrial steam power amounted to 9·65 million h.p. in 1907 (Musson, 1976: 436).

In 1869 French industry had some 0·32 million h.p. of steam power, as against approximately 0·625 million h.p. of water power. By 1907 steam power had grown to 2·47 million h.p., with a further 0·7 million supplied by other energy sources in an economy which suffered from inadequate domestic coal supplies (Lévy-Leboyer, 1978: 267). As in England, capital-intensive areas of manufacturing before 1870, although strategically significant, were nonetheless relatively small. A factory system had begun to develop from the 1820s, but even so it was often labour-intensive. In these nascent structural changes within industry before 1870, substantial capital investment was a feature only of iron production and textile spinning, subsequently joined by coal mining in the 1830s. Overall, productivity gains accrued from the better use of labour, the rural labour that moved into the major urban areas during the mid-century. 'Large' factories in many branches of industry became more common only from the late 1870s, although many were to experience excess capacity for a decade after the mid-1880s. Recovery came from the mid-1890s, marked by an acceleration in the growth of industrial investment in parallel with industrial production. Consequently, during the ten years before the Great War the annual increase in the amount of steam power installed, at 0·142 million h.p., was nearly twice the rate of the closing decades of the nineteenth century. This wider adoption of power for manufacturing was coupled with the development of new industries, such as motor car production, involving entirely new methods of manufacture.

Industry across the states that comprised the Zollverein in 1861 had possibly 0·1 million h.p. of steam power, placing it on a par with manufacturing in the much smaller country of Belgium. By 1875 industrial steam power in Germany amounted to 0·95 million h.p., thereafter increasing to 6·5 million h.p. in 1907, coupled then with a further 1·5 million h.p. from other energy sources (Landes, 1969: 292) This trend of growth in the use of steam power by industry follows that of Hoffmann's estimates of German business investment. These point to manufacturing investment rising from an annual rate of 120 million to 130 million marks per annum in the early 1850s to more than 2 billion marks by the 1900s, by when it accounted for more than 50 per cent of total net investment (Hoffmann *et al.*, 1965: 259–60) The relative unimportance of industrial fixed capital in Germany before the 1870s is borne out by Blomberg's estimates for the textile industries of the Zollverein, then the most important branch of manufacturing. The estimates show that in 1846 working capital comprised some 83 per cent of this industry's estimated capital stock of 156 million talers (468 million marks) (Tilly, 1978: 418–19).

There was substantial accumulation of capital assets in Europe during the nineteenth century. However, until the 1870s, even in the dominant industrial economies, it took place largely in agriculture, or as social overhead capital. With agricultural development and house building, although investment was significant, the financing requirements were largely met without substantial financial innovation. The state played an important role, although one that varied from country to country, in meeting the demands of transport development and, above all, in the mid-century creation of railway networks. But the investment demands of the mid-century revolution in transport also called for the creation of specialised banks—investment banks. The accumulation of industrial capital assets before the 1870s was relatively slight in comparison, as much of manufacturing production expanded without resort to steam power or the factory. Industrial fixed capital became of substantial importance only during the last quarter of the century, when steam power became much more widely adopted and the foundations of what has been termed by some the 'second industrial revolution' were laid.

Economic change and financial development

Until 1850 north-west continental Europe experienced structural change almost in the absence of substantial formal financial development. There were established monetary centres—Amsterdam, Frankfurt and Paris—which had emerged over past centuries as a result of trade and servicing the needs of the state. Yet the provision of credit and capital continued to be conducted privately, so that the initial financial demands of growth were met mainly by an increase in activity and in the numbers involved. This substantial continuity has led to the use of the term the 'old' bank in contrast to the rise of the 'new' corporate bank that primarily accompanied the onset of railway construction. However, continuity until the mid-century was not total. Further 'state' institutions were established, as with the Bank of France, while adventurous ideas for the further development of banking were conceived, although put into practice only in Belgium from the 1830s. This ability of the 'old' bank to finance the onset of modernisation in continental Europe was in sharp contrast to England, where formal banking services expanded from the mid-eighteenth century and joint-stock banking developed rapidly from the 1830s. The contrast was still evident in the early 1860s, leading *The Economist* to remark, 'The system of trade in France is a sound though incomplete one. Credit is very little diffused there; business is a ready-money business.'

The few specialist bankers in 1800 were largely located in the principal urban centres, but their ranks were substantially augmented by many others, especially merchants, providing financial services informally as an adjunct to their principal business activities. In Paris there was the *haute banque*, a group of financial houses largely of Swiss Huguenot origin. They gave the impression of substantial means, but probably more important were their personal influence and connections, compensating at times for the lack of liquid funds. Their composition changed substantially with the stresses of the revolutionary period and altered again thereafter, especially with the rise of Jewish firms such as Rothchilds. There were similar groups of bankers in other European capitals; in German-speaking areas they were known as *Hofbankiers* (court bankers), as in Vienna, where during the 1830s the leading firms were Baron Sina and Arnstein & Eskeles. Much of their business—the provision of trade credit across Europe and managing state debt—would come to be known in England as merchant banking. Evidence indicates that this banking, although of the *ancien régime*, could nonetheless mobilise finance abundantly and relatively cheaply—sometimes at lower cost than in London (Platt, 1984). Some of the bankers, as with the Parisian *haute banque*, had private industrial interests (Barker, 1973) and, from the 1820s, became involved in promoting insurance companies and then railway companies. At a much humbler level throughout Europe, as, for instance, in both Paris and the French provinces, there were smaller private banking firms, but again providing a personal service to relatively restricted groups of clients. Typical was Tardeaux Frères,

263

established in Limoges in 1809, which serviced firms in the local porcelain and shoe industries.

Before the 1830s the main private financial demand was for credit—to finance growing trade and inventories. Napoleon I had reconstituted a small Parisian note-issuing institution as the Bank of France to augment financial facilities, specifically to reduce interest rates. As a financial adjunct of the state, the Bank of France obtained a monopoly of the Parisian note issue from 1803 and was charged with discounting bills. However, it developed as a very cautious financial institution. Its shareholders and directors came largely from the *haute banque* and were only too conscious of the disastrous experience of John Law's experiments in the 1720s and, more recently, the *assignats*. This outlook was reinforced by the stipulations of the bank's charter and continuing close government supervision of its affairs; consequently, following the Restoration, the Bank of France closed its branches and was hostile to further development. Growing criticism developed of the financial facilities available in France. Jacques Laffitte pointed to a need for development capital for industry and, subsequently, the Pereires, influenced by the Saint-Simonians, argued for a marriage of banking and industry (Ratcliffe, 1973: 1975). These ideas were to have a profound influence upon the evolution of financial institutions during the mid-nineteenth century throughout Europe.

Although of humble origins, Laffitte rose to lead the *haute banque*, his house having a capital of 4 million francs in 1815 (Redlich, 1948). During his career he accumulated widespread business interests, which convinced him that the expansion of French commerce and manufacturing was constrained by a lack of readily available funds. Yet, despite many attempts, he failed to attain his goal of establishing an effective investment institution to support industrial growth. During his governorship of the Bank of France, 1814–20, he was unable to make it a commercial institution independent of the state. Similarly he made no headway in his private affairs during the early 1820s, being unable to finance officially approved canals, or to establish an industrial investment bank, his initiatives being rejected by a conservative state. The 1830 crisis ruined him financially, while his term as Louis Philippe's first Prime Minister ended in political disgrace. However, the 1830 crisis revealed a need for further financial development and, with some support from the *haute banque*, the Pereire brothers proposed a discount bank, backed by the state and private shareholders, as a source of liquidity to assuage the panic. But the Bank of France's opposition led to the resultant Comptoir d'Escompte of 1830–32 being only a temporary 'crisis' institution. Even so, it was the progenitor of the Comptoir d'Escompte, established in the 1848, and of the Crédit Foncier and Crédit Mobilier of the early 1850s. The ability to be more innovative was finally displayed by Laffitte in 1837, when he established the Caisse Générale du Commerce et de l'Industrie. The *caisse* accepted short-term interest-bearing deposits and invested some funds in industry in France and elsewhere. It made sufficient impact upon the Paris market to force the Bank of France to discount on a daily basis.

French financial development before 1850 can be interpreted in a number of ways. Slow institutional evolution was due to conservatism, most strongly expressed by the Bank of France, but it was also a product of the relative lack of demand for change, as development, largely at the local level, continued to be accommodated primarily through private informal networks. Nonetheless, visionaries such as Laffitte and the Pereires, who had considerable financial experience, sensed the direction ultimately to be taken. However, the change accomplished before 1850 arose substantially to allay the effects of political disruption and economic crisis, as with the Comptoir of 1830–32. Finally, despite French economic growth from the 1830s, Laffitte was unable to demonstrate completely the success of industrial investment banking. He, and others, were prevented from accumulating the necessary financial *masse de manoeuvre* by public share issues, as French company law, in part an expression of continuing conservatism, restricted the capital of his *caisse*, and of its emulators. Free incorporation was not available, and consequently the Paris and provincial proto-investment banks of the 1840s were forced, under the Code Napoléon, to be constituted as *sociétés en commandite*, in which only the sleeping partners enjoyed limited liability.

Before 1850 France was the seedbed of new ideas, but Belgium was the only national economy where experience was gained of corporate investment banking. Here the state took the lead through William I's foundation of the Société Générale pour favoriser l'Industrie Nationale des Pays-Bas in 1822. The aim was to invigorate his newly created country, arising from the Vienna peace settlement, which had combined the Netherlands and Belgium. Although William backed his bank substantially, it achieved little at first, as the public share issue was a failure, its directors were cautious, and its major asset—land—was illiquid. With the creation of Belgium in 1830 and its industrialisation, the Société Générale became an active investment bank. In 1835 it floated coal companies which it had acquired, nominating their directors and retaining a shareholding in them. During the next four years the Société Générale promoted thirty-one other new enterprises, involving an aggregate capital of 100 million francs (Cameron, 1961: 122). However, it also entered into a competitive struggle with the Banque de Belgique, created in 1835, which between 1835 and 1839 established twenty-four companies (Cameron, 1961: 123–4). The financial tussle between the two banks ended with the 1838 crisis, which revealed starkly the general underlying problem of the 'new' investment banking—the illiquidity of assets when the public clamoured to withdraw deposits. Consequently the Belgian experience of the mid-1830s pointed to both the advantages and the disadvantages of modernising banking techniques (Morrison, 1967). Under severe financial strain the new corporate investment banks themselves needed a lender of last resort, and this lesson was to be repeatedly pointed up in Europe, as in 1857 and 1873.

If new ideas about banking were formulated before 1850 and some experience was gained, the mid-century constituted a financial revolution. Largely it was provoked by the financing requirements of railway building. But its immediate origins lay partly in the financial consequences of further political and economic crisis, and partly in the modernising aspirations of a monarch. France was the crucible of the interaction between causes and consequences. As in 1830, the 1848 revolution caused a liquidity panic. Again Emile Pereire suggested establishing discount houses in the major cities; as before, they were intended to last only until the crisis was over, but some were long-lived. Emile founded the Comptoir Nationale d'Escompte de Paris, which in 1854 became a full corporate bank, thereafter developing into a leading commercial financial institution. During the early years of the Second Empire the Pereires put more of their innovative ideas into practice.

By 1850 the Pereires' main interest lay in establishing a railway investment bank, as indicated by their connection with the Sous-Comptoir des Chemins de Fer of 1848. They obtained the necessary charter for the Crédit Mobilier through the Foulds' financial support and the political influence of Fialin Persigny. This bank came to be very much a financial expression of the Second Empire, being formed three days before the plebiscite ratifying Napoleon III's reign, and subsequently underpining the emperor's railway policy financially. Although springing from railway finance, the Crédit Mobilier was designed as a 'universal' bank. It undertook short-term commercial banking, thereby enlarging its financial base so as to support government loan business, corporate finance and company promotion. The Mobilier's rise was rapid; by 1856 it was handling the finance of sixteen large industrial and financial enterprises, having an aggregate capital of a billion francs, a fifth of the volume of all securities quoted on the Paris Bourse (Cameron, 1961: 147–8).

The Crédit Mobilier lies at the core of Gerschenkron's interpretation of financial development in relatively backward economies. He stressed the 'great eruptive effect of the Pereires' and, in the personal antagonism between the Pereires and their former employers—the Paris Rothschilds—saw a social struggle between the 'old' wealth and the new. This personal rivalry was indicative to Gerschenkron of mounting social tension arising with industrialisation, which induced divisions between economic modernisers and conservatives. However, in reviewing the genesis of the corporate investment bank, Landes (1956) has shown that, generally, it was but a positive mutation of the 'old' bank. The inception of industrialisation—above all the coming of the railway—presented Europe's 'old bank' with profitable new opportunities; yet, as private family partnerships, they were often unable to take advantage of them. Members of the 'old bank' were accustomed to conducting their business in a restricted and confidential manner, arising from their capital being largely family wealth and the conscious selection of their clientele. Since 1800 these private banks, involved in 'high finance', had responded positively to economic growth; many had industrial interests, and in Paris they had, for example, backed to a degree Laffitte's new concepts. The *haute banque*, together with the Rothschilds, had moved into the developing field of corporate insurance, a new sphere but nonetheless complimentary to their main banking interests. They had further developed their techniques. The long established business of lending to governments was increasingly conducted through syndicates, constituted by the social fabric of the 'old bank'—filial and religious bonds as well as business ties. Moreover, acting in consortium was a ready vehicle by which to balance individual interest, spread risk and avoid offence/competition. However, the financing of railway construction could overstretch the ultimately limited resources of these 'family' banks and involved new business *mores*, disrupting bonds of confidentiality. The corporate investment bank, like the Crédit Mobilier, provided a way of combining the accumulated expertise of the 'old' bank with the possibilities of a greatly enlarged capital arising from public share issues. Furthermore, it could be regarded as a further complementary financial instrument, allowing a convenient division of private and more public affairs for members of the 'old' bank.

Seen in this light, the Crédit Mobilier, and its many emulators across mid-nineteenth-century Europe, was not a revolutionary discontinuity in financial development. Rather, it was an evolutionary step, a response to the changing nature of capital and capitalism. Indeed, many of the new corporate investment banks were founded by the 'old' private banking communities of Europe's financial centres, or at least by their more venturesome members. Nonetheless, there always seemed to be a glint of gilt rather than gold about the Crédit Mobilier itself, and it proved to be a financial mushroom, failing in 1867 and reconstituted by the Bank of France only on very onerous terms. Like the Crédit Foncier, the Mobilier had become heavily involved in financing Haussmann's creation of an imperial capital for Napoleon III. Consequently it came to have had an investment portfolio substantially composed of illiquid urban property assets. The Mobilier was only able to counterbalance this, for a time, by expansion—through the creation of affiliates across Europe. These had a *raison d'être* in railway building, especially the extension of some of the principal French companies' networks into Spain and Italy. But a slowing down or pause in the expansion had unfavourable repercussions upon the Mobilier and its directors' increasingly desperate measures to sustain it. As a result, a significant portion of mid-century financial development ultimately proved ephemeral, but the Mobilier left an enduring legacy. Within France, the Mobilier led to the counter-creation of the Société Générale in the mid-1860s, formed by Rothschild's associates within the 'old' bank to establish their own financial vehicle for railway building. In Germany the Darmstädter Bank (the Bank für Handel und Industrie in Darmstadt) of 1853 was a direct copy of the Crédit Mobilier; indeed, the Mobilier aided its creation (Cameron, 1956). Another of the so-called German 'D' banks, the Disconto-Gesellschaft, formed in Berlin in 1851, was modelled upon Emile Pereire's Comptoir d'Escompte of 1848. Similarly, the foundation of the Credit-Anstalt in Vienna by the Rothchilds was provoked by the Mobilier's attempt to establish an

Austrian affiliate. The effects of the Mobilier upon the structure of European finance can be also seen in the Rothschilds' formation, through Bleichröder, of the Berliner Handelsgesellchaft in 1856–57.

New financial institutions were coupled with a greater acceptance of innovative ideas in banking, assisted by the liberal commercial climate of the mid-century. Some of the many new corporate commercial banks, established alongside the *mobiliers*, also moved into investment banking, at least for a time. This was true of the Crédit Lyonnais, formed in 1863 by Henri Germain to meet the demand for credit among Lyons's metallurgical, silk and chemical industries. However, the Lyonnais became a national institution, opening a Paris branch in 1864—to be the bank's head office from 1878. By then it was the largest French bank, with deposits at 193 million francs and seventy branches, some overseas. Such maturity, and other factors bearing upon the bank, led its business to change, but until then investment banking had played a considerable role. Between 1867 and 1870 returns on the provision of substantial long-term lending and the flotation of securities accounted for between 40 per cent and 80 per cent of the Crédit Lyonnais's profits, then averaging 13·2 per cent per annum (Bouvier, 1970).

Europe's modern banking structure was largely established during the mid-nineteenth century. The new corporate banks provided many 'traditional' services, such as deposit taking, cash transmission and the provision of credit. This was commercial banking—the matching of short-term liabilities, consisting largely of the growing middle classes' deposits, with short-term assets arising from meeting the burgeoning demand for credit. Financing railway construction added a new, more risky dimension which called for innovative—corporate banking. When substantially dependent on mobilising short-term deposits, it endangered the banks' liquidity through a mismatch of the maturities of assets as against liabilities. Railway securities, even when issued on behalf of the state, or having a state guarantee, were less liquid and their value uncertain until the lines were built and carrying traffic. Furthermore, the creation of new banks and the promotion of railways tended to run into speculative excesses as expectations exceeded underlying reality. As a result, the mid-century financial revolution was an explosive metamorphosis, with crises in 1857, largely in Germany, in 1866 in Britain, following the third British railway-building boom, in 1873 in both Berlin and Vienna, and with an 'after-shock' in Paris during the early 1880s.

The connection between railway building and the emergence of the 'new' banks also led to another mismatch. Railway construction was a pan-European experience and outside north-western Europe it often preceded marked structural change by many decades. This was due to a number of reasons. First, some lines were extensions of the French system, as in Spain. Second, for example in Portugal, the railway itself was regarded as industrialisation—its construction being seen as an economic transformation. This had other consequences, because the 'new' bank tried to take root wherever iron rails were laid, so that some countries experienced financial development before industrial structural change. Consequently, Good (1973) found in some countries a lack of correlation in timing between the growth of the financial sector on one hand, and the onset of industrialisation on the other. Spain and Italy failed to experience sustained economic change with the advent of the railway, resulting in a precarious existence for their newly established banking structures, to the extent that they had to be re-established late in the century in response to new demands arising from industrial development.

Industrial banking

Much research stimulated by Gerschenkron has been concerned with bank–industry relations, particularly the supposed contrast in banking practices between Britain and Germany. It has been maintained that English banks concentrated on the provision of short-term self-liquidating accommodation, ultimately to the detriment of industrial capital formation, whereas the *Kreditbanken* supplied medium and long-term loans and undertook the promotion of industrial enterprises, so furthering Germany's rise to being the dominant European economy. Actually, 'industrial banking' was a subsidiary issue for Gerschenkron, his greater concern being how relatively backward economies met the financial demands of social infrastructure investment, particularly railway building. As indicated earlier, the substantial financing requirement of fixed industrial assets arose only during the last quarter of the century. Therefore, in development terms, it provided a further field of activity to which the corporate investment banks could turn after 1875. This might appear to be a logical step, but industrial finance was a different business, and the business climate of the late century was less optimistic than it had been at mid-century.

270

Throughout Europe the major form of industrial finance was the ploughing back of profits; profitability was the mainspring of business longevity. This source of funds was challenged during the last quarter of the century by many factors. One was the further development of international competition, which increased with the geographical spread of industrialisation and the fall in transport costs, which eroded local 'monopolies', in part the result of the coming of the railway. A perception of 'squeezed' profits depressed the business climate from the mid-1870s, leading to demands for tariff protection, and other means of regulating and securing markets. Furthermore, by inducing greater uncertainty, it made industrial investment more risky. This occurred as industrial investment was taking on an increasingly 'lumpy' form, as with the wider adoption of steam power. The greater development of industrial banking after 1873 took place in this climate of heightened business anxiety.

However, the roots of industrial banking had already been established by the mid-1870s. Belgian experience in the 1830s had shown its advantages and disadvantages, and it is now becoming clear, from research, that English banks during the late eighteenth and early nineteenth centuries had also financed the creation of industrial fixed assets, largely in iron and cotton, where the problems of fixed capital had first emerged. There are also indications that English banks continued this aspect of their businesses until the late nineteenth century, although primarily for established customers of proven credit-worthiness. If there was a contrast between continental European and English banking practices, it really developed only from the 1890s.

During the middle-years of the century the 'new' corporate investment banks had undertaken some industrial banking, often on behalf of the associated manufacturing interests of their 'old' bank founders. However, the German experience of the 1850s boom once more revealed that industrial banking *per se* was fraught with danger. Assisting railway construction was somewhat akin to a wholesaling activity, as it generally involved the flotation of large volumes of securities, issue by issue. This scale reduced costs, in terms of fixed charges, and, moreover, provided some guarantee of liquidity in the secondary market. Risk was also reduced if these issues were either floated on behalf of the state or, as in France and the Habsburg empire, carried a state guarantee of future dividends. Industrial loans, or promotions, were a very different matter, being much smaller in size, whilst their earning capacity was more subject to the vagaries of the trade cycle. Lastly, particularly in central Europe, mid-century financial euphoria was brought to an abrupt end by the 1873 *Krach*, when the collapse of the Berlin and Vienna stock exchanges severely shook investors' confidence in equities and induced greater prudence on the part of bankers.

With the deep cyclical slump of the mid and late 1870s, bankers' losses on industrial commitments mounted. In France, the spiritual home of the 'new' bank, the Crédit Lyonnais was led, for example, to disengage from industrial banking. Instead, it retained contact only with its largest industrial customers, as the bank's management saw size as offering some insurance against the risks of medium and long-term lending. The cutting of the Lyonnais's industrial ties went as far as the refusal of overdraft facilities. To sustain profitability, the Crédit Lyonnais turned elsewhere. In the mid-1870s it opened offices overseas to employ its relatively cheap domestic funds, coupling this move with lending to foreign governments. At home, during the muted cyclical upswing of the early 1880s, the Crédit Lyonnais became involved in land and the development of insurance. This shift in the business of the Crédit Lyonnais was not exceptional, either in France or elsewhere in continental Europe. During the so-called 'great depression' there was a retreat in industrial banking. However, with the restoration of business confidence from the mid-1890s, banks once more entered the field. Even so, some banks' managements had long memories. Louis Dorizon, of the French Société Générale, with Noetzlin of Paris-Bas, displayed a greater interest in industrial development but in 1913 was dismissed by his co-directors, apprehensive of the consequences.

Something akin to French late-century developments can also be found in Vienna and Budapest, where the 1873 *Krach* exerted the greatest impact upon bankers and private investors alike. Here the 'new' banks maintained themselves largely by floating railway securities for the Budapest government, anxious to modernise the Hungarian economy within the relative autonomy allowed by the *Ausgleich* (Compromise) of 1867. From the mid-1870s Austrian investors were prepared to acquire state guaranteed bonds, leading to a flow of developmental capital from west to east within the Dual Monarchy during the 'great depression'. For their part, Hungarian banks preferred to invest in relatively safe securities, such as mortgage bonds and public loans, so that even during the more confident 1900s securities constituted only about 11 per cent of Hungarian private banks' assets, whereas mortgage loans accounted for more than 40 per cent (Péteri, 1992: 33).

During the 1870s and 1880s the Viennese 'great' banks generally adopted a far more conservative attitude towards industrial banking. They supported only the largest, most prestigious industrial concerns, generally by supplying current account credit rather than longer-term accommodation. However, one particular feature of these reduced connections was the active role these banks played in cartelisation. Initially this was a response to the effects of the mid-1880s world sugar crisis upon refineries among their interests. It led to the banks becoming the sales offices for cartelised production arrangements, a relationship subsequently extended to petroleum, timber and other primary products. This involvement grew out of the banks' growing interests from the 1870s in raw material sales, in turn stemming from granting commodity credits, but it also provided added security, both through the cartels themselves, and through cash flows arising from sales passing immediately into the banks. Furthermore, the 'great depression' encouraged not only cartelisation but also horizontal combination. Ironically, the resultant medium-size and larger establishments enjoyed improved liquidity during the 1880s through funds generated from non-industrial activities, like extensive agricultural estates in the case of sugar and iron undertakings (Mosser, 1983). Consequently, even with restricted profits, these firms were not dependent upon banks for finance, either to sustain themselves or to further their development.

The 'great depression' had less effect upon the new Germany. Admittedly, there were the same responses by way of protection and cartelisation, but it seems that the business climate was only negatively affected during the deep slump of the mid and late 1870s. Buoyant growth resumed from the early 1880s, when the legal framework of the nascent German corporate economy was significantly changed. In 1884 company law was reformed as a response to the speculative excesses of the early 1870s boom, and the curbs and checks introduced strengthened the position of the banks as suppliers of capital in company promotions (Reich, 1979). The advantageous position of the major Berlin banks was heightened by the growing regulation of the major German *Börsen* (Tilly, 1986). The major German banks, increasingly national institutions, were able to undertake industrial banking

273

as a significant aspect of their business, so pursuing 'mixed' or universal banking, since they intermediated to a great extent upon the basis of their equity capital. By the 1910s UK banks' aggregate subscribed equity capital was equivalent to 9·7 per cent of their total assets, but for the German banks the ratio was as high as 23·5 per cent (Tilly, 1986: 236). Active industrial banking required this matching of long-term assets against long-term liabilities, but it involved costs, being more expensive than the mobilisation of deposits, and creating, through higher capital requirements, a barrier of entry into the banking system. Even this matching within balance sheets was not a total insurance against the increasingly known risks of industrial banking. As in Austria-Hungary, much of the German banks' relationships with manufacturing consisted of current account operations, and only when these were satisfactory were the *Kreditbanken* prepared to consider granting longer-term accommodation.

Furthermore, it seems that the Berlin-based German banks undertook the finance only of sizeable firms, so confining their industrial connections to particular areas of manufacturing—coal, iron, steel and heavy engineering (Neuburger and Stokes, 1974). This, again, was an attempt to reduce risk through financial size, perceived to ensure liquidity and greater creditworthiness, but it also involved costs. These arose because the German mixed banks, like all institutional variants of investment banking, were imperfect substitutes for a fully articulated capital market. Gerschenkron had specifically pointed to this impediment. However, Neuburger and Stokes maintain that the arising cost was substantial, since the size bias of the industrial business of the major German banks unbalanced the dynamic growth of the economy and thereby constrained it. Small and medium-size manufacturers failed to obtain the banking support they required, to the particular detriment of the development of light industrial sectors. It may have been due also to the disappearance of local and regional banks as a result of the amalgamation movement. Banking during the *Kaiserreich* became increasingly a Berlin-based business, with the resultant large nation-wide banks undertaking the custom only of national manufacturing concerns. The breaking of local ties between customer and banker, through the emergence of national managerial hierarchies as a consequence of bank amalgamations, could also explain the decline of industrial banking in England from the 1890s.

In Germany there was continuity in investment banking, from

274

servicing railway building in the mid-century to subsequently supporting major industrial concerns. Elsewhere, with the general resurgence of growth during the *fin-de-siècle* era, there was, to a degree, a resumption of industrial banking. This further change has already been noted in respect of some of the major French banks. But another characteristic of this period, when the term 'finance capitalism' was coined, was the beginnings of industrial banking on the periphery of Europe, where industrialisation became marked from the 1890s, as, for example, in Italy.

The northern Italian economy experienced significant change with the growth of hydro-electricity, and the expansion of iron, steel and chemical production. It arose from the activities of firms established in the 1880s and 1890s by scientists or technologists, beginning in a small way and consequently soon facing financial constraints. They were assisted by new banks formed from 1880 on, the largest of which by 1912 were the Banca Commerciale Italiana and the Credito Italiano, both having been established with the aid of German finance. These two institutions grew rapidly, coming to control over 60 per cent of the aggregate assets of all major Italian banks. BCI and CI were able to pick the prime industrial clients and co-operated by sharing underwriting, loans and comparable financial operations. Hence they proved more than a match for the other four newly formed industrial credit banks. Their only competition came from the two largest private railway companies, which, with the managerial reorganisation of the railway system in the early 1900s, diversified by investing in industrial securities.

The German Italian banks concentrated upon firms in hydro-electricity, chemicals, iron and steel, and engineering. The two banks, with BCI very much in the lead, supplied commercial banking facilities, but, as in Germany, combined them with providing loans of longer maturity and converting firms into joint-stock companies. These latter activities resulted in the two banks acquiring a significant voice in the management and entrepreneurial direction of their client industrial undertakings, once they had become public companies. BCI increasingly specialised in electrical power generation, beginning with the Societá Edison, and subsequently created a holding company—the Society for the Development of Electric Firms in Italy. BCI had a comparable relationship with the Unione Italiana Concimi, the largest producer of superphosphates. In the case of iron and steel, BCI and CI had a start in the heritage of assets arising from the defunct Credito Mobiliare and the Banca Generale. These connections, with others in shipbuilding and shipping, enabled BCI to establish a manufacturing complex—reflecting the scarcity of funds available at a time of rapid industrial growth (Cohen, 1967). The Italian experience from 1890 to 1914 demonstrates, perhaps, an extreme outcome in industrial–financial organisation arising from the interaction between the 'new' bank and the onset of growth.

Investment and finance abroad

European industrialisation was marked not only by the domestic accumulation of capital assets, but also by the rise of investment abroad. Until the late 1850s capital movements consisted primarily of transfers within Europe; increasingly thereafter such flows went beyond Europe, especially in the case of Britain. This is shown by Crafts's estimates of the European norm, which indicate capital inflows to the mid-century, followed by capital exports, rising in the British case to 11 per cent of national expenditure in the 1910s (Crafts *et al.*, 1991: 112–13).

Such flows, like all migration, arose from the interaction of pull and push forces, whilst they also grew out of international structures established long before 1800. However, that prior basis was disrupted by Britain's emergence as the first European industrial economy and by the dislocation of the revolutionary and Napoleonic wars, which augmented London's relative advantages. One prime pull factor was the marked expansion of international trade and the knowledge it brought of opportunities beyond the domestic economy. On the push side was the growth of income generated by industrialisation, especially its skewed distribution. Consequently the savings of the bourgeoisie rose significantly and they sought new profitable investment outlets. Before 1850 the main intermediaries were the 'old' bank and in London they retained this role until 1914 almost unchallenged. In continental Europe the 'new' banks became an ever increasing powerful force during the half-century before 1914 in directing this international flow of funds.

Until 1850 Britain was the world's most important exporter of financial capital. How much went abroad is difficult to establish; current estimates indicate that by 1870 Britain's capital exports totalled something in the range £0·5 billion to £0·7 billion (Platt, 1980).

Within this total, claims on American assets, especially railways, were already significant, as were Indian stocks, but the rest of the foreign securities held by British investors were predominantly European. London, as a financial centre, had substantial contacts with, and knowledge of, Europe. The City was a long-standing cosmopolitan community, with possibly 75 per cent of its merchants in the 1760s being 'of recent foreign extraction', namely Huguenots, Sephardi Jews and Dutch, who had their own churches and synagogues. This made London as much a European as a British city, perhaps even more so. From 1780 a wave of German and Jewish merchants and bankers settled in London, attracted by the new commerce in manufactured cottons, followed in the 1820s by Greeks, whose initial interest was the exchange of Black Sea grain for finished cottons (Chapman, 1992). These inflows further extended London's global commercial credit network, which now also encompassed the United States and was beginning to stretch out to Latin America.

British capital exports to Europe before 1850 have often been regarded as important in the spatial spread of industrialisation, compensating to a significant degree for inadequate local supplies of saving. However, many consisted of loans to governments, which in itself must have made any such compensation indirect, in terms of British holders replacing local holders of debt, allowing the latter to invest their savings elsewhere. The complexities of the mechanisms involved are shown by the restoration of French public debt following Waterloo, which involved substantial sales of *rentes*—security operations often regarded as the beginning of international lending in modern Europe.

As a result of a quarter of a century of political upheaval and economic disruption, the Parisian *haute banque* were hesitant about involvement in issues of long-term government debt. Consequently, in 1816 the securities were sold largely, and gradually, on the Amsterdam market, Europe's premier financial centre in the early eighteenth century. This was only possible through sequences of sales and at a heavy discount—43 per cent. The operations planned for 1817 involved 300 million francs, fifty times the volume of 1816, but it was raised by combining the resources of the major European mercantile houses with those of domestic savers. This twin approach was also employed with the French indemnity loans, totalling 700 million francs, required to lift the allied occupation. To gather the sum the Parisian *haute banque*, led by Laffitte, worked in harness with Baring's of London and their

277

Dutch associates Hope & Co. This combination created confidence, attracting subscriptions from investors in France and abroad. Thereafter Parisian bankers increasingly from their own resources, undertaking substantial flotations of *rentes* between 1820 and 1825. As a result the British share was probably no more than about 18 per cent and soon fell, owing to profit-taking (Platt, 1984: 7–11). With political stability apparently regained in France in the early 1820s, the bourgeoisie subscribed to *retes*, regarding them as a secure investment. Although rather unusual in type, the security issues rebuilding public credit after Waterloo constitute a pattern that was subsequently repeated. Foreign bankers and foreign capital were initially required to 'prime the pump' but thereafter raising funds was substantially a domestic operation.

British investment also played a comparable role in the finance of French railway construction during the 1840s. This interest began with the Paris–Rouen line, built by Brassey and, with its extension to Le Havre, an obvious attraction to the London & Southampton Railway as a London–Paris route. British involvement acted as one catalyst galvanising French domestic savings; another was James Rothschild's entry into French railway finance. However, during the mid-1840s British investors faced the competing attractions of domestic and French railway securities, and as home companies called up capital they tended to sell their French holdings. Other British activity was speculative rather than investment, being arbitrage to benefit from price differences between the London and Paris markets. This particular episode was largely brought to an end by the financial crisis of 1847 and the French revolution of 1848 (Platt, 1984: 18–27).

With railway building and the rise of the 'new' banks during the middle of the century, France became a major capital exporter alongside Britain. Yet again, though, historians may have exaggerated the role of French capital in Europe. Previously, for example, Spanish railways were regarded as almost entirely the product of French investment. The difference in income levels between France and Spain in the mid-century was much greater than that between Britain and France in the late 1810s, but domestic savings nevertheless played a significant role in the building of the Spanish railway system. Platt (1984: 114–17) concludes that, by 1870, foreign capital had an interest of only some 40 per cent in Spanish railways. Conceivably, this could have been to the detriment of Spanish economic growth, as Spanish society was relatively poor. Investing its limited resources in railways, along with government debt, may have left the economy unbalanced, with but limited development of industry and agriculture (Tortella, 1972). A possible contrast is with the extension of Hungarian railways later in the century, financed largely by Austrian capital, thus leaving local savings to support agricultural change and facilitate nascent industrialisation.

Foreign investment was part of a learning school for investors before 1870. They became more familiar with paper securities as assets, while the nature of these types of stocks and shares, backed by the security of the state or a large railway, with each issue large in scale, acted to wean the bourgeoisie away from land and houses. With the globalisation of economic opportunities, as a result of the world transport revolution, European foreign investment spread ever wider from the 1870s. This was particularly true of British investment; moreover, it developed in a way quite uncharacteristic of other European economies. During the half-century before 1914 the British and German economies exhibited comparable savings rates at about 11 per cent to 15 per cent of GNP, but in Britain's case only 5–7 per cent was invested at home, as opposed to 12 per cent with regard to Germany (Pollard, 1989: 58). Thus by 1914 British investors were responsible for about 42 per cent of total gross global foreign investment, against a share of 21 per cent and 14·4 per cent respectively for French and German investors. To establish the complete post-1870 European picture of foreign investment, it should be realised that three of the continent's smaller economies—Belgium, the Netherlands and Switzerland—were of some significance, with shares of 3·3 per cent, 4·4 per cent and 3·3 per cent respectively (Cameron, 1991: 13).

Predominantly British overseas investment remained concerned with the establishment of railway networks in the areas of European settlement overseas—temperate North and South America and Australasia. Other European investors sought wider horizons after 1870, although their savings for the greater part moved only across national boundaries rather than oceans. In the late nineteenth century Russia was the major European importer of capital, in 1914 accounting for about 10 per cent of gross global foreign investment, or in solely European terms some 41 per cent (Cameron, 1991: 13). This Russian experience illustrates a number of general features of international investment, so providing a useful case study. Post-1870 international investment within Europe consisted subtantially of funds flowing out from the north-western industrial core into Scandinavia, the Mediterranean world and the Slav lands of the east. Furthermore, this flow became increasingly concerned with the finance of industrial assets, while a growing connection came to be drawn between economic influence on the one hand and, on the other, political sway in international affairs.

Foreign capital had played a role in Russia throughout the nineteenth century, beginning with Dutch bankers before the Crimean war. As elsewhere in Europe, the main initial investments had been in state debt and then railway securities. Railway construction in Russia, with the support of foreign funds, continued until the end of the century, especially with the completion of the Trans-Siberian. However, from the 1890s, modern centres of heavy industry were established in European Russia, assisted by imported funds. French investors were the leading suppliers, motivated by political as well as economic factors, such as low domestic interest rates. French investors, holders of Russian state and railway bonds, turned to Russian company shares, attracted by the Russian tariff of 1891—which substantially closed the domestic market to imports—the stabilisation of the rouble and the demand for industrial equipment arising from military and railway orders. Foreign investment in Russian industry was initiated by Belgian investors, although some may have been French in disguise— taking advantage of the greater liberality of Belgian law and tax requirements. By 1900 French industrial investment totalled 792·4 million francs, largely in mining, iron and steel and engineering, and much of it took the form of Russian securities (rather than of French companies operating abroad) because of the financial penalties imposed by both French and Russian law. The largest geographical centre of this investment was in southern Russia—the Donetz basin, the Krivoy Rog and Nikopol–Maryupol. The inflow of French funds was interrupted by a Russian economic crisis and then by the Russo-Japanese war, to resume from 1909, when there was some diversification into oil extraction (along with British capital) and greater emphasis on metalworking and engineering.

French with other investments in Russia established industrial plants of considerable size, sometimes endowed with technology in advance of that used by the industry of the capital exporter. However, it was an almost pioneering activity, involving the building of social infrastructure, from roads to hospitals, and even the provision of policing. Such associated investments reduced overall profitability, with

Investment and finance

the highest returns arising on shares of companies which had either bought their land before the boom conditions of the mid-1890s, or obtained the right to import equipment duty-free. As a result the long-term rewards for many French holders of Russian industrial securities proved insubstantial (Crisp, 1960). If there was any major return, it was obtained by the French government through the build-up of its eastern political ally's military industrial complex and the securing of oil supplies, an increasingly important strategic asset.

Retrospective

One feature of European industrialisation was the growing role of investment, but until the late nineteenth century it was primarily a matter of agriculture, housing and transport. Industrial finance until the 1870s was largely a question of credit provision, with the support of fixed capital assets becoming of substantial significance only thereafter. A modern financial system evolved to meet the demands of industrialisation, but its nature and organisation changed significantly only as a consequence of the major investments that arose with the creation of railway systems. This provoked the establishment of the 'new' bank, an institutional structure which continued until the Great Slump of the inter-war period (Teichova, 1992). Even by 1900, however, large multinational companies were beginning to emerge, with the capacity to internalise the servicing of their credit and investment requirements. These corporate giants also marked another change in the pattern of European foreign investment, taking the now marked growth in industrial investment, both physical and financial, a stage further.

References

Bairoch, P. (1976), 'Europe's gross national product, 1800–1975', *Journal of European Economic History*, V.
Barker, R. J. (1973), 'The Perier bank during the Restoration, 1815–1830', *Journal of European History*, II.
Borchard, K. (1968), 'Staatsverbrauch und öffentliche Investitionen in Deutschland, 1780–1850', Doctoral dissertation, University of Göttingen, quoted by Tilly (1978).
Borries, B. von (1970), *Deutschlands Aussenhandel 1836–1856*. Stuttgart, Fischer.

Bouvier, J. (1970), 'The banking mechanism in France in the late nineteenth century', in R. E. Cameron, ed., *Essays in French Economic History*. Homewood, Ill., Irwin.

Cameron, R. E. (1956), 'Founding of the Bank of Darmstadt', *Explorations in Entrepreneurial History*, VIII.

Cameron, R. E. (1961), *France and the Economic Development of Europe, 1800–1914: Conquests of Peace and Seeds of War*. Princeton, N.J., Princeton University Press.

Cameron, R. (1991), 'Introduction', R. Cameron and V. I Bovykin, eds., *International Banking, 1870–1914*. Oxford, Oxford University Press.

Chapman, S. (1992), *Merchant Enterprise in Britain: from the Industrial Revolution to World War I*. Cambridge University Press.

Cohen, J. S. (1967), 'Financing industrialization in Italy. 1894–1914: the partial transformation of a latecomer', *Journal of Economic History*, XXVII; reprinted in R. Cameron, ed., *Financing Industrialization* II. Aldershot, Edward Elgar, 1992.

Crafts, N. F. R., Leybourne, S. J., and Mills, T. C. (1991), 'Britain', in R. Sylla and G. Toniolo, eds., *Patterns of European Industrialization: the Nineteenth Century*. London: Routledge.

Crisp, O. (1960), 'French investment in Russian joint-stock companies, 1894–1914', *Business History*, II.

Dumke, R. (1979), 'Anglo-deutscher Handel und Fruindustrialisierung in Deutschland, 1822–65', *Geschichte und Gesellschaft*, V.

Gerschenkron, A. (1952), 'Economic backwardness in historical perspective', reprinted in Gerschenkron' *Economic Backwardness in Historical Perspective*, 1965. Cambridge, Mass., Belknap Press.

Good, D. F. (1973), 'Backwardness and the role of banking in nineteenth-century European industrialization', *Journal of Economic History*, XXIX.

Good, D. F. (1984), *The Economic Rise if the Habsburg Empire, 1750–1914*. Berkeley, Cal., and London, University of California Press.

Hildebrand, K-G. (1978), 'Labour and capital in the Scandinavian countries in the nineteenth and twentieth centuries', in P. Mathias and M. M. Postan, eds., *The Cambridge Economic History of Europe* VII, *The Industrial Economies: Capital, Labour and Enterprise* 1, *Britain, France, Germany and Scandinavia*. Cambridge: Cambridge University Press.

Hoffmann, W., Grumbach, F., and Hesse, H. (1965), *Das Wachstum der deutschen Wirtschaft seit der Mitte des 19. Jahrhunderts*. Berlin and New York, Springer.

Kutz, M. (1974), *Deutschlands Aussenhandel 1789–1834*. Wiesbaden, Steiner.

Landes, D. S. (1956), 'The old bank and the new: the financial revolution of the nineteenth century', *Revue d'Histoire Contemporaine*, III; reprinted in translation in F. Crouzet *et al.*, eds., *Essays in European Economic History*. London, Edward Arnold.

Landes, D. S. (1969), *The Unbound Prometheus: Technological Change and Industrial Development in Western Europe from 1750 to the Present*. Cambridge: Cambridge University Press.

Lévy-Leboyer, M. (1978), 'Capital investment and economic growth in France, 1820–1930', in P. Mathias and M. M. Postan, eds., *The Cambridge Economic History of Europe* VII, *The Industrial Economies: Capital, Labour and Enterprise, Britain, France, Germany and Scandinavia*. Cambridge: Cambridge University Press.

Morrison, R. J. (1967), 'Financial intermediaries and economic development: the Belgian case', *Scandinavian Economic History Review*, XV.

Mosser, A. (1983), 'Concentration and the finance of Austrian industrial combines, 1880–1914', in A. Teichova and P. L. Cottrell, eds., *International Business and Central Europe, 1918–1939*. Leicester, Leicester University Press.

Musson, A. E. (1976),'Industrial motive power in the United Kingdom', 1800–70', *Economic History Review*, 2nd ser. XXIX.

Neuburger, H., and Stokes, H. H. (1974), 'German banks and German growth, 1883–1913: an empirical view', *Journal of Economic History*, XXXIV.

O'Brien, P. ed. (1983), *Railways and the Economic Development of Western Europe*. London, Macmillan.

Péteri, G. (1992), 'Financial change at a sectoral level: the interrelationships between banking and industry in Hungary during the 1920s', in P. L. Cottrell, H. Lindgren and A. Teichova, eds., *European Industry and Banking between the Wars*. Leicester, Leicester University Press.

Platt, D. C. M. (1980), 'British portfolio investment overseas before 1870: some doubts', *Economic History Review*, 2nd ser., XXXIII.

Platt, D. C. M. (1984), *Foreign Finance in Continental Europe and the United States, 1815–1870*. London, Allen & Unwin.

Pollard, S. (1976), 'Industrialization and the European Economy', *Economic History Review*, 2nd ser., XXVI.

Pollard, S. (1989), *Britain's Prime and Britain's Decline*. London, Edward Arnold.

Ratcliffe, B. M. (1973), 'Some banking ideas in France in the 1830s: the writings of Emile and Isaac Pereire, 1830–35', *International Review of the History of Banking*, VI.

Ratcliffe, B. M. (1975), 'Some Ideas on Public Finance in the 1830s. The Writings of Emile and Isaac Pereire, 1830–35', *International Review of the History of Banking*, X.

Redlich, F. (1948), 'Jacques Laffitte and the beginnings of investment banking in France', *Bulletin of the Business Historical Society*, XXII.

Reich, N. (1979), 'Auswirkungen der deutschen Aktienrechtsreform von 1884 auf die Konzentration der deutschen Wirtschaft', in J. Kocka and N. Horn, eds., *Recht und Entwicklung der Grossunternehmen im 19. und frühen 20. Jahrhundert*. Göttingen, Vandenhoeck & Ruprecht.

Rostow, W. W. (1960), *The Stages of Economic Growth*. Cambridge, Cambridge University Press.

Teichova, A. (1992), 'Rivals and partners: reflections on banking and industry in Europe, 1880–1938', in P. L. Cottrell, H. Lindgren and A. Teichova, eds., *European Industry and Banking between the Wars*. Leicester, Leicester University Press.

Tilly, R. H. (1978), 'Capital formation in Germany in the nineteenth century', in P. Mathias and M. M. Postan, eds., *The Cambridge Economic History of Europe* VII, *The Industrial Economies: Capital, Labour and Enterprise* 1, *Britain, France, Germany and Scandinavia*. Cambridge, Cambridge University Press.

Tilly, R. H. (1986), 'German banking' 1850–1914: development assistance for the strong', *Journal of European Economic History*, XV; reprinted in R. Cameron, ed., *Financing Industrialisation* I. Aldershot, Edward Elgar, 1992.

Tortella, G. (1972), 'Spain, 1829–74', in R. Cameron, ed., *Banking and Economic Development*. London, Oxford University Press.

Urban development

Of all the changes—indeed, the upheavals—that marked the European economy in the period between 1750 and 1914, few have made so visible an impact yet been so little examined by economic historians as mass urbanisation. A few numbers will show the scope of the phenomenon. As late as 1850 the urban population surpassed 30 per cent of the total only in England and Wales. By 1900 that country was 80 per cent urban, while Germany, Denmark and Belgium had more people living in towns than in the country and the proportion was rising everywhere (Hohenberg and Lees, 1985; Bairoch, 1988). From a slightly different angle, Europe's urban population in 1920 was just equal to the total, urban and rural, in 1800. Britain did more than lead the way in urbanisation, as it did in other aspects of economic transformation; its quantitative lead in urbanisation in fact proved greater and more lasting than its dominant role as 'workshop of the world' (van der Woude *et al.*, 1990). Yet, as we shall see, the patterns of urbanisation and the links with economic development—industrialisation in particular—would remain varied across Europe. Though a forerunner, Britain would not really serve as a model.

The focus on urbanisation is interesting in its own right, but it has a particular place in this survey for the light it sheds on other aspects of European economic development. The demographic story, for example, gains force and salience if one reflects that massive growth of population occurred despite the move of a great number of persons from areas of usual demographic surplus—farms, villages, small towns even—to urban locations with a tradition of natural deficit or to new but dense and ill served concentrations (Lawton and Lee, 1988). Moreover, the excess mortality typical of early towns, particularly larger ones, could only be aggravated by rapid growth, accompanied as it was by often severe crowding and pollution (Livi-Bacci, 1992). Housing construction, to say nothing of a sanitary infrastructure, systematically lagged far behind the movement of population, while industrial technologies in their early state were notoriously poor at controlling noisome or dangerous effluents.

Agricultural progress, including the development of ancillary activities from transport and marketing to processing and preservation, also appears more impressive if one reflects on the task of feeding growing millions of town dwellers. While imports from overseas came to play a significant role in supplying basic foods, notably grain, and in varying the diet, urban man and woman did not live by bread and coffee alone. From butter to beetroot, beer to bacon, growing the food and getting it to urban tables represented a formidable task, to say nothing of the fact that a rapidly increasing proportion of the total population came to play essentially no role in primary food production as such. Yet the causation did not run one way only. Urban demand and commercial organisation offered powerful incentive to increase farm output and tailor it to the market (Wrigley, 1987).

Finally, there is the matter of *capital*, since we cannot forget the factor of production that gave its name to Europe's transformed economic system. Here attention to urbanisation must sharpen one's appreciation of the burden that industrialisation placed on the limited supply of savings. There is the sheer volume of investment that the physical city represents: visible in the buildings, roadways, bridges and 'street furniture', from lamp posts to benches; less visible in the sewers, water pipes and gas lines. Beyond this we are led to focus attention on a neglected branch of economic activity that was by far the largest capital goods industry, namely construction. Apart from its size, what is most striking about this sector is that, with some important exceptions in the non-residential sector, it was among those least affected by the technological and organisational changes the term 'industrial revolution' naturally raises in our minds.

In gaining an overview of the urbanisation process, it will be important to draw appropriate distinctions, not only between countries and regions but also between different types of settlements. Many sorts of places grew, but one can, for example, distinguish the experience of established cities, some already sizeable before 1750, from that of new agglomerations of all sizes. Urban growth was in fact not universal. Even in Britain the impact of economic transformation on old market and cathedral towns was slight and tardy. Many towns in every part of Europe were largely untouched by the changes associated with industrialisation, while numerous small centres quite lost their urban character. In addition, it is at best reductionist and at worst simply inaccurate to equate rapid urban growth with industrial development, let alone with factories full of power-driven machinery. Trade, transport and politics played a major role; manufacturing as such could flourish in a low or moderate-density settlement pattern; much urban industry remained quite modest in both scale and technology.

We have briefly alluded to the demographic, economic and technical impediments to mass urbanisation. There was cultural resistance as well. From the Romantics who opened the nineteenth century to the Eugenicists and Arts and Crafts types who closed it, a never still chorus of voices clamoured against city life, warning of dangers to the health of the body and the salvation of the soul, of threats to morality, family, civil order and social stability (Lees, 1985). And they had plenty to rail against. From the Manchester slums that agitated Friedrich Engels to Gorky's 'lower depths' in Russia, the squalid conditions under which many, perhaps most, urban dwellers lived were difficult to exaggerate. The signature disease of the age was, after all, tuberculosis, which afflicted mainly those who lacked the air and light that the meanest country cottager could find outside the door for nothing.

Does this mean that the great urban migration must have been forced on those who moved? Certainly some had to flee the countryside when clearances or enclosures took their land and employment, or when the factory's goods elbowed those from the cottage aside in the market place. Plots of land could be divided only so many times when law and custom did not preserve the holding for a single heir and so force the other children out. War, dearth, revolution and persecution drove others, though most often beyond the seas. Yet it is clear that many, indeed most new urban dwellers who stayed did so out of choice, however mean the range of options open to them in the town (Moch, 1983). The diatribes against the evils of city life tended to come from the top rather than from the bottom—and, let it be said, from people themselves well and usually comfortably settled in the city!

Urbanisation begins in the countryside

Previous chapters in this book detail the transformations that conditioned and interacted with urban growth. But it is worth stressing just how much of what drove urbanisation had its origin in the countryside and in changes there that began centuries before but accelerated in the eighteenth century. This is certainly the case with population growth. One key factor was Europe's prevailing population regime, in which human reproduction responded to economic conditions while usually remaining a good deal less rapid than biological prospects alone would have permitted. The implication of the 'European marriage pattern'—marriage late enough and celibacy strong enough to hold crude birth rates down—is that eighteenth-century Europe harboured the potential for more rapid population growth by the simple expedient of younger and more nearly universal marriage (Livi-Bacci, 1992). When food supplies became more regular, and non-agricultural employment more available, fertility could and would increase. (A less understood factor is apparent climatic change and the reduced virulence of certain causes of epidemic mortality, such as bubonic plague.) Despite a rate of infant mortality that remained stubbornly high until 1900, and notwithstanding the negative effects of urban migration itself, Europe managed to sustain—indeed, to increase—its rural population throughout the period, while filling the towns and also settling vast regions overseas.

To feed so many more persons required great increases in the production and delivery of food. Again, the role of overseas agricultural areas, while important, is not the principal story. One can trace the technological and organisational roots of revolutionary agricultural change as far back in European history as fourteenth-century Flanders and the development of convertible husbandry, but certainly the growth of urban markets contributed to speeding the long process of diffusion of improvements. One noteworthy point, often misunderstood, is particularly relevant to our story. At least before the middle of the nineteenth century, and often later, the new agriculture was labour-*using* rather than labour-*saving*. With land worked every year rather than periodically lying fallow, and with farmers combining livestock and arable farming, the new techniques yielded more output while employing more hands on a given acreage. The consequence for the cities was that the exodus from the countryside was selective and drawn out, with big differences from place to place in the composition, pace and timing of rural out-migration. Indeed, much rural-to-urban migration involved persons who had already loosened if not severed their ties with the land: farm servants, landless labourers and, especially, those who depended for their livelihood on domestic manufactures.

The role of the countryside in the industrial transformation itself is perhaps not so well known. This too involved a centuries-long gestation period, during which manufacturing worked free of a medieval tradition of closed urban crafts (Berg, 1986; Gutmann, 1988). During and after the Middle Ages urban guilds strove to close out competition, technological change and organisational innovation. Despite their efforts, the range and scope of manufactures gradually expanded to include cheaper goods for a relative mass clientele, and new methods arose of organising and financing production through putting-out systems and other forms of commercial capitalism. One important way to break the hold of guild and other regulations was to transfer the activity in question from the town to unincorporated villages or rural cottages. The push for increasing output was in part driven by demand. Significantly, by 1700 the relevant market extended beyond Europe to settlements and trading posts beyond the seas. Though modest by later standards, early modern technological developments—for example, in metal smelting, glass and paper manufacture, and more effective waterwheels—also favoured rural locations.

Economic historians who have examined early manufacturing and its relationship with later, factory-based industry have come to use the term 'proto-industrialisation' to designate what some see as a distinct mode of production. The term 'proto-industry' is most commonly used to refer to rural domestic industry, principally textiles but also metalwares and the like. One driving force in its development was certainly the availability of cheap labour, originally in the form of agricultural by-employment—seasonal or from family members—and eventually from systematic underemployment in poor, densely populated areas. Rural proto-industry was very much a regional phenomenon; many farming areas lost rather than gained handicraft production as the division of labour progressed.

From the point of view of urbanisation, several consequences followed from the spread of cottage industry. First, rural domestic goods competed strongly with the products of long-established urban craft producers. Second, the availability of domestic work could have demographic consequences as well as causes. A strong argument has been put forward—though not universally accepted—that the more abundant manufacturing employment made it possible for young people to marry earlier and perhaps encouraged them to bear children, who could earn their keep from an early age. The upshot would be a level of dependence on industrial work going far beyond the original by-employment. The growing wage proletariat would then have no recourse but emigration if their cottage employment failed for any reason. Moreover, these potential recruits to the town and the factory had acquired at least some skills and the habit of industrial work. Third, the organisation of proto-industrial work involved much division of labour and so anticipated mechanisation (as well as increasing productivity along the lines famously set out by Adam Smith). Finally, the growing dependence of proto-industrial workers on purchased food stimulated commercial agriculture in other regions, a help in sustaining large urban populations later on.

The debate over proto-industrialisation has helped focus scholarly attention on manufacturing before the factory and the general use of inanimate power became dominant. It has also, even more usefully, encouraged economic historians who study the onset of modern economic growth to integrate the treatment of manufacturing, agriculture, population and social structure and to rethink the role of the countryside in industrialisation. Yet most commentators agree that the historical record presents a more complicated and nuanced picture than we have just sketched.

More is involved than the particulars of development in different regions. One important point is that the stress on rural domestic manufactures tends to diminish the importance and vitality of early urban manufacturing. The implied contrast between old-fashioned, guild-ridden urban crafts and free, capitalistic rural ones is grossly overdrawn. While all recognise that rural production required urban services, the proto-industrial model slights the directly productive role of towns, which always extended far beyond finance, trade and even finishing operations. Fine and luxury goods remained predominantly urban—for example, watches and instruments, fine textiles (printed cottons, silk) and clothing. So did much weaving and the manufacture of small metal goods, even in ordinary lines. Many regions developed close co-ordination between town and country, including such centres as Sheffield (cutlery), Geneva (watchmaking) and Rheims (woollens). Towns that strongly resisted change did lose out, but others, typically places free of strong guild traditions, took their place. In fact proto-industrialisation more often appears as a regional phenomenon involving towns, villages and farmsteads than as pitting country against town.

A second aspect that has received too little attention is the demand side. While proto-industrial goods were intended for wider markets, including those overseas, and thus did not depend on local demand, it remains true that general trends in economic conditions had equally wide-ranging effects. Until the middle of the nineteenth century the proto-industrial trade cycle was driven largely by the evolving balance between land and people (Hohenberg and Lees, 1985). As population grew, diminishing returns and the resulting competition for land caused labour incomes to fall. Overpopulation or crop failures—often related—would lead to high prices that snuffed out the discretionary incomes of ordinary folk, thus provoking a demand crisis in non-luxury manufactures. That industrial incomes should dry up just when bread or potato prices were highest was all the more poignant, and explains why hard times could quickly turn into a full-fledged crisis of subsistence. The 'hungry (18)40s', which devastated not only Ireland but many areas in the Low Countries, Scandinavia and Germany, were the last such crisis, and the best documented if not necessarily the most severe.

Cities were somewhat protected from crises of subsistence, in part owing to their permanent concern about secure sources of food. Yet they could also be caught in the squeeze, having to cope with floods of distressed migrants from the country at a time when provisioning and business conditions were already difficult. Moreover, the urban rich or landed magnates who bought their finery in town did not permanently escape rural distress. While the rents and taxes they collected initially rose with rural crowding, a collapse of the agrarian economy would eventually affect the urban economy and its manufactures as well.

Finally, it is necessary to look more closely at the way the proto-industrial process played itself out during the nineteenth century. In time, cottage production of ordinary manufactures would largely be displaced by mechanisation, at least in Europe. But the range of outcomes region by region is far richer than the dichotomy between a shift to factory industry in some places and total deindustrialisation elsewhere that some advocates (and critics) of the proto-industrial model have adduced. So, therefore, is the spectrum of effects on the growth of towns.

At one extreme, some regions integrated proto-industrial work with newer activities based on resource extraction, principally coal, and developed a strong manufacturing base implying intense urbanisation. Lancashire, the north of France and parts of Silesia are good examples. The vague nebulae of overgrown villages and thickly scattered cottages would spread and fill in like active bacterial cultures to form large and dense agglomerations. With time, centres of service and administration would rise to give some structure and genuine urban character to these new forms of settlement. At the other end of the spectrum, many regions witnessed the extinction of once active proto-industrial work which did not survive the competition from mechanised production. Linen weaving was hardest hit, perhaps, since cotton largely displaced it. Equally vulnerable was small-scale metallurgy based on charcoal smelting and local pockets of ore. Within a relatively short time these areas, many situated on the western fringe of Europe, had reverted to a fully agricultural status, the excess population having migrated.

Yet it would be a mistake to focus exclusively on the polar cases and so risk exaggerating the discontinuity between older and newer forms of industrial organisation and settlement. In many places the proto-industrial legacy showed considerable staying power, its flexibility and adaptability more than compensating for any technological backwardness. Mechanisation did make strides, of course. But the general pattern of small-to-medium firms and plants, rapid response to changing commercial conditions, and modest wage and overhead costs proved highly effective (Sabel and Zeitlin, 1985). In rural areas, scattered industrial settlements developed into 'rural towns' or remained as industrial villages. Here as in the coal-based conurbations the town grew up around the workshop or factory, rather than production seeking out a prior concentration of potential workers or an existing market centre. The differences between the two production-centred forms are those of scale and of the preponderance of light as against heavy industry. We shall also see that some urban forms of proto-industrial production and organisation proved equally long-lived and adaptable.

Varieties of urban settlement

The pattern of urban settlement growing out of the period of industrialisation is a complex one, difficult to describe in a few words even with a map before one. The process was, of course, well under way by 1750. Of the hundreds of substantial towns, sixteen had more than

100,000 inhabitants and another twenty-five or so harboured 50,000 to 100,000. Though most housed active crafts and manufactures, political capitals and ports dominated the 'top forty' list, save for Lyons and Leiden, which could fairly be called industrial. By 1900 it was rather *more* difficult to be precise about the list of urban leaders—we shall see why—despite enormous advances in statistical reporting. But one count would put Lisbon, with 363,000 inhabtants, in fortieth place, meaning a sevenfold rise in the threshold size since 1750 (Chandler and Fox, 1974). Ten industrial cities or agglomerations now figured in the leading group, still well behind the number of capitals and ports—note that London and Lisbon, the head and tail of the list, fulfilled both roles. How to sort out this urban explosion?

Most striking, of course, is the growth of the mega-cities, usually defined as those with a million or more inhabitants. No European city was as large as that in 1750, though London was closing in and Paris had over half a million. By 1914 nine cities officially qualified. Yet these data understate the large-city phenomenon in two ways. First, the twentieth-century city has become an *agglomeration* that invariably spills over its legal boundaries rather than ending neatly at a city wall or boundary. Today, for instance, Lyons qualifies as a middling city with about 450,000 inhabitants, yet the greater urban community officially numbers 1·4 million and is France's second largest. More important, by 1914 Europe had developed urban clusterings that might or might not include a large core city but in the aggregate housed well over a million people and in some cases several times that. These concentrations, closely associated with heavy industry and mining, sometimes with a proto-industrial heritage and sometimes not, we have already referred to as 'conurbations'. The Ruhr basin comes first to mind, perhaps, but they ranged from Lancashire and Tyneside in Britain to the Donets in southern Russia. The industrial conurbations were as dynamic in activity as their spatial arrangements were disorganised and were originally quite wanting in natural or produced amenities. In contrast, the largest stand-alone city, or 'metropolis', functioned as a political capital or as a financial and commercial centre—commonly both. While cursed with its full share of urban problems, the metropolis retained privileged access to private and public capital, benefiting from the fear of disorder and the thirst for prestige of social elites and national authorities alike (Sutcliffe, 1984).

While very large concentrations stir the imagination, tax society's ability to cope, and represent the more revolutionary aspect of urban development in the period, much of Europe's urbanisation took less spectacular forms. The old-versus-new-settlement dichotomy just noted, between the great capitals and the teeming industrial conurbations, recurs at more modest levels as well. Among established towns it was generally true that the larger ones grew more rapidly, though the rule was modified by other variables such as access to transport, and the area's resource and activity base. On the other hand, the amorphous concentration of population typical of industrial conurbations has its small-scale analogue in a large number of settlements that straggle along valleys and between hills in the uplands of Europe. As we have seen, these legacies of proto-industrial development have typically remained the domain of small and medium industrial firms, in textiles and a variety of other sectors, often exploiting cheap water power. Such settlements are widely distributed, from Catalonia in Spain to Thuringia in central Germany, with many in the foothills of larger mountain chains, from the Alps to the Appennines and Vosges. But, devoid of tourist attractions and wanting in administrative or other service functions, they attract little notice.

The types we have outlined do not exhaust the range of urban forms produced by the period of European industrialisation. Some towns grew up around particular ventures, a large plant or railway junction, for example. The suburbs around large cities also retained or developed individual social character, industrial or residential, bourgeois or popular. Finally, specialised towns became more prevalent with the development of improved transport, above all the railway: spas, seaside resorts, university towns, garrisons, even pilgrimage sites. Lesser ports, for example, tended to specialise in fishing or pleasure boating or served as naval bases.

At the other end of the urban spectrum from the metropolises, many small market centres gradually sank back to village status because they were too close to other towns or lacked a sufficient local base of activity. Above them in the urban hierarchy many more managed to hang on to basic urban functions but with no trend towards expansion and no apparent response to the monumental changes around them. Particular activities and services could be added or lost; the young tended to leave for larger places, while some newcomers came from the land; local rivalries were fitted to the political labels of the larger society; the same notables exercised local control and bargained with the state. This too was urban Europe.

Urban geographers have devised a number of approaches to explaining the spatial distribution of towns, the way the array of small and large places is apt to develop (Carter, 1976). One useful model builds from the services—marketing, administration and other—that towns provide for the surrounding rural area. *Central-place* functions motivate a regular scatter of towns, with one larger place serving a set of lesser ones and dependent in turn on a still more important centre. While central-place theory accounts nicely for the administrative and market hierarchies on the European plains, it leaves out a substantial share of urban development, notably that tied to large-scale industry and to networks of long-distance trade. Yet even before industrialisation and the dominance of the centralised nation state, and certainly since, urban development is intelligible only if one grasps the idea that cities function within systems, whose dynamics shape their activities, relationships and fortunes.

By 1914 the map of European towns looked quite different in certain ways from that of 1750, but most of the area was not unrecognisable. Least changed was southern Europe, which had been more highly urbanised than the north at the earlier time and also underwent the least economic change. To be sure, the principal cities were growing: Milan, Barcelona, Turin, Marseilles, as well as the political capitals. But even the major ports and commercial cities could not match the Glasgows, Hamburgs and Leipzigs of the industrialising heartland. After 1870, especially, overseas migration currents shifted their origins from northern Europe to southern (and eastern) regions, limiting the urban influx in the south. As for the eastern countries, also laggards or at best followers in economic growth, the pace of their urbanisation was stronger and more concentrated as a function of a later start. The capitals and other principal towns grew rapidly and modernised in part, while major industrial basins developed in Russia and in what would become Poland and Czechoslovakia.

Central Europe saw important urban development, with industry tending to gravitate to larger and older cities more than was the case farther west. Of course, the conurbations of the Ruhr and Saxony, based on coal deposits, stand out, as do the mushrooming of Berlin and Vienna, but they do not efface the balance that marked German urban development. The large provincial towns of Germany witnessed active industrial development, to a degree rarely found elsewhere in Europe in that type of town. It is worth reflecting on the contrast between German and British experience in the light of the state of the economy at the onset of rapid industrialisation. In Gerschenkron's (1962) terms, Germany was more 'backward' than Britain and industrialised correspondingly faster, yet the massive concentration of urban population in purely industrial cities and conurbations went further in Britain than in Germany. From the point of view of the urbanisation, the less 'backward' nation paradoxically developed the greater degree of imbalance.

On the other hand, balance is certainly the fitting term for urbanisation in the Low Countries and Switzerland. High-level urban functions tended to be distributed across several cities of moderate size rather than concentrated in one capital, as was the case, for example, in France. In the Netherlands three cities divided the high-order political (The Hague), financial/service (Amsterdam) and mercantile (Rotterdam) functions. The country also experienced slow urbanisation, finding itself, in the early nineteenth century, rather 'over-urbanised' in relation to economic needs. (Italy was in the same situation.) The Swiss pattern, also marked by gradual change, actually came to prefigure some characteristics of urban Europe in our own time. At least five cities in that small country carried on regular international exchanges and several others, such as Lugano, St Gallen and Lucerne, were much more than local market and service centres. This is true despite the fact that only three Swiss cities had more than 100,000 inhabitants in 1900, led by Zurich, with 150,000. Finally Scandinavia tended to concentrate much of its urban growth in a few cities, notably the capital and chief port(s) of each country. Industrial development, focused on resource extraction in its early stages, there engendered only limited urban development.

French urbanisation, like the country's economic development in general, offers a mixed picture. In absolute terms France did transform, and it was never far from the lead in measures of *per capita* income or total industrial production. But the uniquely slow rate of growth of population—easier to take as given than to account for in terms of other factors—profoundly influenced all other aspects, from agrarian transformation and population mobility to industrial structure. French urban development was equally distinctive, no doubt in part as a consequence of the unique demographic pattern. Paris grew greatly, to be sure. By the outbreak of the first world war some 3 million people lived within the modern boundaries established in 1860—today the number is fully a million less—while the suburbs expanded, massively if rather irregularly, as industry developed, giving a total population of 5 million for Greater Paris. The north and north-east regions developed along the lines of the Ruhr model of industrial sprawl near coal and iron mines or around Lille and other towns, some with very old industrial traditions (Arras) and others more recently sprouted (Roubaix, Lens). But with these and a few other exceptions—the Saint-Etienne basin and the port of Le Havre stand out—urban growth remained quite moderate. Just two of the provincial capitals and trading cities reached half a million in the 1911 census, and fewer than twenty cities in total struggled to the 100,000 mark. Yet one cannot say that France was less urban than other major countries in a qualitative sense. Paris almost defined what the world of the nineteenth century meant by bright city lights, while the French approach to town planning, inherited from the classic tradition via the baroque but implemented first and most fully by Baron Haussmann in the Paris of Napoleon III, influenced cities from Buenos Aires to Delhi (Sutcliffe, 1981).

As we have noted, Britain, the industrial and trading leader, also urbanised first and most completely. Nowhere else did so sharp a contrast emerge between the pre-industrial, market or cathedral town— Chester, Ely, Winchester, Lincoln and York come to mind—that remained almost untouched and the overwhelmingly industrial city with its explosive growth: Leeds and Bradford, Newcastle and Middlesbrough, Manchester and its ring of cotton towns, the five pottery towns that came to make up Stoke on Trent, Birmingham, Sheffield and a few others. The great ports did justice to Britain's seafaring role, to be sure: Glasgow and Liverpool, Cardiff and Bristol, Hull and Newcastle, Southampton and London itself. Yet the balanced provincial city, where industry flourished but did not dominate, was far less common in Britain than on the Continent. Only the East Midland county towns of Leicester and Nottingham comfortably embody this type.

Urban occupations and economic roles

Thus far we have focused on the industrial role of cities, though more will need to be said on the subject. But the growth of capitalism, or the modern market economy, was at least as distinctive for the development of exchange and finance as for that of production, and from the point of view of the city rather more so. Mills and factories might stand in the country; a bank belonged nowhere but in the centre of a larger town.

Distribution of goods, services and credit was the exclusive province of the urban economy, and the single largest source of urban employment in many places. The coming together of persons for exchange was equally important, which puts the spotlight on mobility and communication. Until the last few decades of the period, however, innovation and technological progress affected these sectors unequally. From the canals of the eighteenth century to the railway and telegraph, the first century of industrialisation saw great advances in inter-city transport and communication but little to change the way business was carried on *within* the city. By contrast, after 1850, and particularly by the end of the century, a true revolution was under way there, one centring on electricity. The telephone, the lift and electric light (following on gas) made extraordinary concentrations of market traders possible in every conceivable form of goods and services in what became known as a 'central business district'—in London, the city. These technological advances—the tram, the underground or metropolitan railway and refrigeration not least among them—also helped manage, if not resolve, the congestion generated by people and goods in the metropolis. In the first decade of the twentieth century the confident hope was that the internal combustion engine would overcome the limitations and nuisances of animal traction. *Hélas*, here the city obtained a servant that would in time very nearly devour its master, In the meantime, however, trams and other rail systems allowed the metropolis to spread out, and so relieved the almost unbearable settlement densities that had built up.

Markets employed many persons directly, from those who risked huge sums on the prices of shares to the humblest porter. The largest centres also attracted great concentrations of service businesses with armies of clerks, in banking, insurance, wholesaling, foreign trading, legal work, and many more. Whether for reasons of cost or insufficient *man*power, or because social values were changing, female labour gradually but massively moved into office and service occupations, though almost exclusively at subordinate levels. Increasingly, businesses specialised, so that each drew on more and more other businesses for everything from expert knowledge to repairs or the execution of sub-tasks. Paralleling the growth of services to business as well as to consumers—notable in the latter instance were shops and purveyors of food and drink—was the increase in public services. Despite a prevailing ideology that glorified *laissez faire*, individualism and private property, the complexities and propinquities of urban life in an industrialising world made increasing and insistent demands on government.

For all the importance of services, particularly in the principal towns, a surprising share of labour was employed in direct commodity production. Construction aside—and, as already alluded to, it was and remained a very large employer—industry could account for as much as 90 per cent of jobs in newer agglomerations, particularly in the early stages when commercial and other services were rudimentary at best. However, the manufacturing share was high even in the great capitals, and in many important provincial towns as well. The suburbs of some capitals, far from the pomp of state and the bright lights and smart shops, housed large-scale plants, particularly with the growth of industries in the second industrial wave—motor cars, electricity . . . Nonetheless, in the bigger cities certain kinds of small-scale production turn out to have been—and to remain today—especially important. The reasons tell us a lot about the working of urban economies. For a start, cities, particularly great ones, naturally specialise in new or unique products, those embodying innovation or fashion or made to the specifications of a particular client. The second factor favouring big-city locations for many small firms, despite higher costs, has been the availability of varied services and specialist labour, resources that large firms can accumulate in-house but small ones must find in the market. So important are these complementarities that small and specialised firms have long tended to cluster, even within cities, sharing auxiliary services and a client base with competitors. Economists point out that such *economies of agglomeration* outweigh the substantial disadvantages that small scale and more competition might impose.

Great factories and highly specialised firms making silk gowns or bespoke hunting rifles do not exhaust the range of big-city manufactures. Quite out of sight of the tourist and unknown even to most residents were—and are—hundreds of workshops, garrets and households where people assemble, sew, punch or paint. Proto-industry never left the town, and its scope—not always easy to gauge even in official statistics—has remained much larger than people recognise.

Cities house and readily attract large numbers of cheap, marginal labour, largely female and often migrated from a distance, and they also retain ancient but still lively traditions of craft skills.

Geographers work hard to find patterns in the diversity of settlements forms and the spatial distributions of activity among and within cities. In some cases the forces determining location are clear-cut and easy to identify. For example, the great ports of Europe developed industries that processed raw materials from far-flung points of origin. Where necessary, differential tariffs or colonial regulations ensured that it remain more profitable to ship the crude product despite its dead weight: raw versus refined sugar, grain rather than flour, and the like. Hamburg, Marseilles, Bristol, Bilbao and other cities boiled soap, cured tobacco and, of course, built and repaired ships. Yet with improving transport and more reliable, speedy communications the 'footloose' element in industrial location has tended to become stronger, the imperatives of bulk and weight weaker. Great firms can grow from tiny origins, often engaging in lines of production only remotely connected with their original activity, and yet remain where they began.

What has turned out to be far more difficult than to manage a business in an unlikely location is for regions or cities to renew their industrial base when a strongly established specialisation becomes obsolete. Large centres of mining, metallurgy, textiles, shipbuilding and other basic industries, especially those dominated by a few large firms in a handful of industries, have not proved attractive to new businesses or emerging lines. While this is principally a twentieth-century problem, it emerged even before 1900 and echoes the inability of many earlier cities to adapt their traditional crafts to new circumstances. For example, precociously mature industrial regions of Britain such as the north-east (Newcastle) proved unable to compete with towns quite bypassed by earlier industrialisation (Northampton) for such industries as boots and shoes or ready-made garments. Again, this phenomenon—new activities choosing 'greenfield' sites and workers, often female, new to industry in preference to redundant plants with experienced workers—played only a minor part in the period that concerns us. It has, however, emerged sufficiently strongly in our own time to be worth noting. Moreover, it applies today with equal force to the choice between transferring activities overseas or to depressed areas at home. In the nineteenth century the loss of momentum in some English regions and industries often profited the eager German (and American) challengers.

With these experiences in mind, we can use the historical record to draw out some generalisations about how urban economies function. First, the crucial work is not that carried on entirely within one town for its people or those immediately around, for all that many inhabitants live by 'taking in each others' laundry'. A town's *economic base* consists of those activities that serve outsiders, whose payments supply the town with its indispensable imports, whether of necessary food and energy or of goods and services that promise comforts, excitement, variety and novelty. And the second point, most true of large cities, is that the most urban 'commodity' or factor of production is in fact *information*. Ideas, innovations, new designs, fashions, arrangements, creations bubble up in cities or at least get their chance to conquer public favour there. Should they succeed too well—should, that is, a particular product (or service) develop into a regular staple of commerce—its production is almost fated to move to lower-cost locations. Cities simply tax producers too heavily, in terms of physical congestion costs and high prices for space and services, to support activities that do not profit from their privileged access to information. Nor did this comparative advantage diminish in the age of wire transmission, cheap newspapers, or with even more recent modes of communication that expand access to information. Quite the contrary happened, in that differential access to up-to-date, accurate information became harder to ensure yet no less important. In consequence, the information industries, from publishing to finance, advertising to research, absorbed an increasing share of skilled employment or human capital, and therefore greatly preferred urban locations. Indeed, by 1914 the concentration of activities and atractions in the capitals was particularly great, extending beyond business, finance and politics. Tourists, artists, *rentiers* and writers flocked to the centre, and their presence served only to heighten further the attraction of the place that drew them.

Urban society in the industrial age

In physical appearance the European town of 1914 is quite recognisable even today in many aspects, and it was destined to change comparatively little for the next forty years (save for wartime destruction and mostly conservative rebuilding). Yet in appearance, and as a place to live, the large city at least had come a long way since 1750.

For all its flaws and problems it was without question becoming a healthier and a safer place. More than that, urban life expectancy had recently overtaken that in rural places (Livi-Bacci, 1992). While medical science tended to save more lives than it cost by the time of the first world war, the balance there was only modestly favourable. Vaccination did make inroads into infant and child mortality, but fresh, unadulterated milk, pure water and the generalisation of sewers undoubtedly contributed more to the dramatic improvement in urban survival. Nor should one ignore the contribution of outdoor lighting and a professional police force in keeping violent crime in check. In fact, from the vantage point of the 1990s the first half of the twentieth century may represent a high-water mark in urban order and security for Western cities!

Despite improving prospects of survival, urban population growth remained almost as dependent on migration at the end of the nineteenth century as it had been earlier. This is true despite the fact that the age structure of towns, notably those that were growing fast, continued favourable to population growth. In-migration still contributed a disproportionate flow of young men and women. Also, town dwellers were now more likely to marry than in earlier times, when the proportion of apprentices, servants and clergy—to name a few categories with poor matrimonial prospects—had been higher. Nonetheless, the natural increase of urban populations typically remained or became low, though mining settlements offer an exception and there were surely others. The reason is that town dwellers—including many who were recent arrivals from areas of high human fertility—very quickly chose or learned to limit family size. The reasons are not simple to sort out, but economic incentives no doubt reinforced, and were reinforced by, changed social norms.

Urban populations were mobile in general, and not only because a high proportion of those counted as residing in this or that town had been born elsewhere. At least three other migratory streams complicate the basic story of village-to-town migration. Many persons moved from one town to another, perhaps several times in one lifetime and more often than not going from a smaller to a larger place. Some of these migrations involved long distances, and the capitals and major ports, as well as some industrial basins, gathered a rich mix of languages, dialects and nationalities. The *Gastarbeiter* and ex-colonial peoples of today's Europe are not nearly so novel as one might think, though the sheer numbers involved are unprecedented. Secondly, many people moved *out* of cities, even the largest. Some were temporary migrants to begin with, hired for a time for a particular job, or in town between agricultural seasons. They would return to the village unless marriage, a good employment opportunity or death converted their status to a permanent one. Others left because their hopes had not materialised, or to live out a quiet retirement. Finally. the mass of poor and near-poor or precariously respectable folk in cities frequently changed residence within the city. With limited belongings and a dwelling likely rented by the week, they could easily find a lodging to suit the needs and resources of the moment, as often as not only a few metres from the former abode.

The range of work and occupational statuses among town dwellers was as varied, and for many as insecure, as other aspects of life. It is easy to picture the city of the industrial age in terms only of the stereotypical proletarian, the semi-skilled worker going off to the factory twelve hours a day, six days a week, unless an economic crisis or a strike interrupted the routine. And in many areas that was indeed the life of adult males and of juveniles of both sexes. The infamous reliance on child labour, the blackest mark against industrial capitalism, had by 1850 pretty much ceased to involve children younger than thirteen or so, at least if they had a family. For all their monotony, danger and limited rewards, however, factory jobs by no means represented the worst in urban working conditions and pay, even though organised protest most often originated with these workers. Many in domestic work laboured longer hours for less, whether as servants, seamstresses or piece workers, and they had to furnish their own light, heat (if any) and space. Women, of course, were more numerous in the marginal categories than among mainstream factory workers. Other men and women, and young people, laboured out of doors as messengers, pedlars, carters, navvies, casual labourers and rag pickers, or in less legitimate pursuits. Yet almost any employment was preferred to enforced idleness in the absence of any reliable social safety net. Illness, infirmity, old age or economic crisis were the worst masters of all, and the workhouse—not by chance—was less agreeable even than job sites.

Distinctly above the mass of the poor and the destitute, yet far from free of material cares, were other armies of urban toilers who brought some skill or other capital to their work and exacted a corresponding return. The higher class of servants, craft workers—from chimney sweeps to joiners and tailors—clerks, shop assistants, artists and low-level supervisors made up the bulk of those whose economic lot was not easy depite their position above the rabble—or because of it. The city offered temptations and it also set standards. Respectability imposed costs, in clothes, the right lodging, the obligation to school one's children, and much else. It was easier to slide down owing to illness, discharge by an employer, bad luck or habits, or business failure, than it was to move upward. Yet of course some managed to better themselves.

Whether self-made or given a head start, a good many persons parlayed some property, enterprise or professional qualification into comfort or affluence. For all the stress that social scientists and the politics of industrial societies have placed on workers, on their sufferings and struggles, the group that defined nineteenth-century cities more than any other was the *bourgeoisie*. The true middle class can be defined as those wealthy enough to reckon in terms of property and wealth rather than just periodic income, yet not so affluent that they could quite forgo gainful employment. In terms of values, purchasing power, roles in the urban economy and, increasingly, political influence, the bourgeois made the city theirs. This was, after all, the era when the gold standard shored up the value of money and made financial projections truly meaningful. It is worth noting, too, that 'bourgeois', the term Marx used to characterise the architects and beneficiaries of capitalism, originally identified the citizen of a chartered town.

At the top, finally, were the truly wealthy, who added social privilege and what was left of *ancien régime* power and rank to the luxuries that large—and lightly taxed—incomes could bring them. But this elite continued the practice of dividing their residence between town and country, most likely adding frequent stays at fashionable resorts or in foreign cities to their annual round. Thus many of them were only in part true city dwellers.

The uses of urban space

Social distinctions remained strong in the cities of Europe. Though politically undermined by the unequal and fitful diffusion of suffrage, they were, rather, reinforced by the glaring differences in income and wealth generated by rampant capitalism. Still, the bourgeoisie—great and small—moved to shore up such distinctions, in effect if not necessarily in intention, with greater spatial separation in residential settlement. Rich and poor had tended to live close by one another in the pre-industrial or 'walking' city, if not indeed on different storeys— 'noble' and 'servile' in Italian parlance—of the same building. In contrast, those who built dwellings as a commercial venture in the nineteenth century would not take the risk that unsought propinquity might repel a desirable class of clients. More and more, uniform buildings lined up on similar streets in homogeneous neighbourhoods. Entire quarters of the compass were relegated to a limbo of fashion. Sometimes topography played a role, with workers forced to live near the factory while masters chose to reside above the smoke and noise. But historical accident or taste entered into it as well. It is difficult to know just why Britain's elites, like the rich in the United States, gravitated toward suburban or fringe locations while their counterparts on the Continent refused to relinquish control—except to commerce and finance—over the city's heart (Fishman, 1987). To be sure, London retained close-in concentrations of the affluent and fashionable, while elegant villas sprouted up on the outskirts of Paris or Vienna. But the contrast still holds. A similarly puzzling question is why some cities and countries stuck to low houses, even in large, dense urban areas, while others favoured the taller tenement.

In all large towns, however, the cost of housing posed problems for the less affluent (Daunton, 1990). Because land costs, in particular, outpaced any productivity improvement in construction or materials production, workers often spent more than was comfortable on their lodgings while still begrudging what social reformers and critics thought were suitable standards of decency and hygiene. At that, poor people often shared their dwelling with a paying lodger, further aggravating the crowding. Their meagre budgets simply contained too many higher priorities, from books to dancing, finery to drink. In a word, housing remained a perennial sore point, and by 1914 the demands for 'social' solutions, such as public housing, were growing more insistent.

Yet one should not forget the efforts made to improve the attractions of the bourgeois home. Standards of domestic comfort differed between countries, but the nineteenth century favoured the amalgam of excess and cosiness that acquired the label of Victorian far beyond the good Queen's realm. And mass production greatly increased the sheer volume of material possessions that ordinary folk brought into the dwelling, from textiles and furniture to cooking and eating utensils or books and knick-knacks.

Considerations beside space and furnishings were also important to the domestic standard of living: the location, the presence of servants—not merely for the rich—and, increasingly, utilities of all sorts. Some of these sources of amenity were purely market goods, but others had strong elements of what economists have come to call 'public good', and required collective provision. In closing our brief survey with a look at how Europeans coped with the challenges of mass urbanisation, we will look at both private and public capital. The aim is to make the reader appreciate that the European city of 1914, however imperfect, represented an enormous and hard-won achievement, a 'machine for living' as impressive as the engines and other inventions by which we usually distinguish the epoch.

Housing is the most basic durable good, and residences occupy the largest share of urban (and later suburban) land. We saw earlier that the construction of dwellings remained a largely pre-capitalistic enterprise, with small firms, traditional craft skills and modest technological change the rule. The same held true of those who supplied rented housing, the dominant arrangement even for reasonably prosperous European urban dwellers, at least in large cities. Property development remained generally piecemeal. Most landlords owned only a few dwellings, at most a few blocks. By contrast, the production and shipment of building materials, as well as the financing of construction, were more strongly influenced by the new forms of large-scale business organisation.

As for the internal design and layout of the individual dwelling, the market reigned here too, driven by tastes that revealed perhaps more than people realised of their aspirations and anxieties. Of course, enormous contrasts marked the range of accommodation, from luxurious villas and town houses to tiny rooms in the meanest tenement or 'rental barrack', yet space was carefully husbanded in all of them. The infamous courts and alleys of working-class Leeds or Roubaix squeezed as many units as possible out of an acre or a hundred metres of frontage, with little care for air and light. Back-to-back construction meant shared walls, few windows and small units. The large blocks typical of central Europe were built over 80–90 per cent of the plot, despite their relative height. But the same principle governed more costly dwellings as well, in that every additional bit of amenity, every extra square metre, had to earn its cost. Bourgeois flats in Paris skimped on private spaces (bed and bath) to maximise the display rooms, though most families in fact entertained little. English terraced housing preserved the illusion of the country cottage with postage-stamp green spaces front and back.

Rapid population growth, led by an influx of proletarianised rurals, brought appalling crowding and perennial complaints of housing shortage. However active, house building could not keep up with the need. In fact the demand for new housing outpaced even the swelling numbers of town dwellers, both because *some* improvement in standards (area per person, quality of construction, amenities) did occur and because existing dwellings were pulled down. Age could be a factor, but most dilapidated structures were rather recent, jerry-built tenements, often put up in the shadow of a factory to meet an immediate need. Much of the demolition, however, resulted from market-driven changes in land use. In the simplest terms, a potential occupier of the parcel in question would bid much more than the current user would or could pay. Or economic interests elsewhere would call for taking over the parcel to accommodate a railway line or other facility. Whether waged with market or extra-market means, the struggle for command of urban land was as unrelenting and fierce in the nineteenth century as the clashes of nations, of social classes, or of competing firms.

In an era of rapid technological change and economic transformation, mass urbanisation not only led to continual expansion of the physical city but also to far-reaching and repeated reworking of the land-use pattern. Considering the sway of *laissez-faire* and the prevailing faith in material progress, the wonder is not that market forces often proved stronger than tradition but that some of the medieval or baroque city remained. As it is, much of the old was swept away, and most of the rest almost swallowed up by the expanse of new development.

Nothing is inherently *less* plastic than the physical fabric of a town. The layout of streets, the sewers and conduits beneath them, the buildings themselves are utterly immobile. Yet we persist in using an organic metaphor—that of growth—to portray changes in urban land and space occupation. Geological analogies would probably be more suited to the rough, jerky processes of infilling, spread, vertical rise and categorical shifts in land use. (The time scale of change in urban space is probably closer to vegetable than to either animal or mineral, on balance.) Instead, geographers have coined terms such as 'morphogenesis' (form–origin), 'land-use succession' and the like (Vance, 1990).

In the competition for space, commerce made its needs felt most clearly and peremptorily. Rapid expansion in the wholesale and retail trades, and in other service sectors, from insurance and banking to entertainment, pushed most residences right out of the urban core. Moreover, as the numbers coming to work in the central business district multiplied, large-scale, land-consuming investments were required to carry them in and out, from wider streets to new railway lines. Since space was at so great a premium in the urban core, it is no wonder that underground railways were begun even before the advent of electricity solved the ventilation problem. In time, urban transport became efficient enough for workers to commute from almost anywhere and few practical limits on the spatial extent of the metropolis remained. In fact the issue of 'commutation' tickets, offering reduced railway fares to regular passengers, was a significant step in making transport cheap enough for the masses. Still, those who travelled farthest to work, for instance to the city of London, came from the verdant stockbroker belt or other upper middle class villa suburbs. Cost and the length of the working day kept commuting something of a luxury until more recently.

Changes in land use also affected urban residential areas, even though the principal expansion took place at the outer edge of the built-up area, displacing everything from market gardens and manorial estates to noxious pursuits once well out of sight and smell. A district could move up or down the social scale. While one thinks of the rich as able to outbid the poor, rents *per unit of area* could actually be higher in slums than in fine districts. So it took encouragement by the public authorities to get slums pulled down for redevelopment. The intention was to root out disease, crime and sedition; the effect, of course, was largely to shift the crowding to nearby working-class districts and so aggravate the very forces that generated blight. The opposite movement would seem to make rather more sense, namely for the rich to occupy new housing and leave their older houses to be subdivided for more modest tenants. However, on the Continent especially, this trickle-down pattern ran into resistance from elites. Furthermore, the

307

decision to relegate factories to the suburbs of large cities also forced workers to locate outside the core in a *faubourg* or *Vorstadt*.

In focusing on housing problems and other growing pains we should not forget that for those with means the city of the late nineteenth century became quite a pleasant place to live. Though old civic traditions weakened in many cities, and were absent in newer places, new ones could be created. Despite the market pressures on urban land, we shall see that some space *was* set aside for public squares and elaborately landscaped parks. However, capitalism also played a prominent part in constructing opportunities for pleasure. The leisure industries, including commercialised entertainment and recreation, to a considerable extent superseded civic and community rituals and public amenities as purveyors of urban sociability and *joie de vivre*. Shopping became a primary leisure activity, with an endless variety of goods appetisingly displayed behind plate glass in arcades and along busy streets. Space was also given over to numerous places of assembly, from clubs to taverns and cafés. Theatres and department stores joined the traditional churches and palaces as private civic monuments. And what was not established for profit—libraries, hospitals and schools of all levels—depended heavily on capitalist philanthropy.

The public sphere

The essence of urban life is interdependence. City dwellers congregate specifically to carry on activities that involve interaction; the density of settlement imposes close contact, desired or not; finally, the city is almost totally dependent for its sustenance, from food and fuel to wine and flowers. To organise, manage and contain this ceaseless flow of persons, goods, messages and sensory impulses requires a complex physical, social and institutional infrastructure. Networks of services, authority, information and energy must be designed and built, operated and maintained. While here too the market can play a role, externalities and public goods are so pervasive that no urban culture has come close to full privatisation even in the full flush of nineteenth-century enthusiasm. One example may help make the point. Public edifices such as royal palaces and property belonging to great aristocrats or religious institutions remained relatively immune from the market competition for space. A century later, residents and visitors alike are grateful that such open spaces and other islands of amenity have been preserved in the heart of great cities, and also that far-sighted persons insisted that some public parks should be carved out in the teeth of forgone profits.

We have already noted that a dwelling did not stand alone. Its inhabitants required a steady supply of water, a way to evacuate wastes, and access to sources of income and consumption goods, from food, drink and fuel to health and recreation. They also had to be policed, connected, administered, taxed, schooled and churched, willingly or not. Yet these collective goods were not easy to supply in the quantities and at the cost required. Many observers have seen behind the troubles of the urban ecology the dynamics of capitalism: its thirst for accumulation, its transformation of human ties into the impersonal nexus of the cash-driven market place, its antagonistic class relations, its ideological commitment to individualism, private property and the market. In addition, however, much can be accounted for simply in terms of the frenetic pace of change. Responsible urban elites, or town fathers, needed to be constituted in some places, renewed or rejuvenated in others. A new and professional system of administration had to be organised, trained, financed and supervised. The techniques of public health, water treatment, utilities and communication were evolving rapidly and typically experienced teething troubles (Tarr and Dupuy, 1988).

Yet conditions tended to get better with time, especially so when growth slowed. As indicated earlier, technology, including the sciences of administration, began to make a positive difference, as did wider political participation. Two political currents rate a mention even in a brief and mostly economic survey. One is municipal socialism, by which is meant the recognition that workers' representatives, once they moved beyond protest, needed to show themselves capable of exercising power responsibly as well as claiming it. While there was little opportunity for this on the national scale before 1914, it began to be seen at the local level. More significant was a recognition on the political right that the bourgeois order could be preserved from the threat of popular unrest and social revolution only if it improved living standards and offered some social protection to the masses. This may be dismissed as paternalism, even as a throwback to the Roman emperors' 'bread and circuses', but it made a considerable difference to urban conditions. The Christian Socialist political machine of Karl Lueger in Vienna and Chamberlain's mayoralty in Birmingham embodied these currents of authoritarian reform or democratic reaction on the local level. The new breed of urban politicians, in some ways not unlike American big-city machine bosses, did often prove fiscally responsible, energetic and adept.

To be sure, smaller towns developed no such complex and drastically modern institutions. Dealing mostly with simpler issues, their governance could remain with the old notables: squire, merchant, clergy, lawyer; where appropriate the newer factory masters added their economic weight to the balance. Once the firm was well established, say in the second or third generation, the capitalist dynasties would also furnish mayors or councillors and take a direct interest in the community's business.

For municipal leaders at all levels the strategic key was to secure a hearing in the seat of power, the national capital, where resources and power increasingly concentrated. Obtaining a branch line, a secondary school, or a budget appropriation for bridge repairs, these were becoming the real stakes of municipal politics, whatever party labels might be paraded and argued over. Of course, national styles differed here too, with more self-govenment in the Protestant north (as well as in the Catholic parts of Switzerland), greater centralisation elsewhere.

Conclusion

This survey has tried not to slight the positive aspects of urbanisation and the contribution of the urban economy to development. The object is not in any way to idealise the industrial city, let alone the living conditions it provided the poor and working classes, but rather to recognise both the magnitude of the challenges faced and the real accomplishments of the age. They stand up well against our own late twentieth-century urban litany of social pathology, congestion and sprawl, visual and economic blight, and environmental degradation. Nor, despite Mumford's strictures, has the capitalist city much to apologise for by comparison with the realities of the previous age, when baroque pomp often hid the worst squalor (Mumford, 1961).

It is nonetheless understandable that publicists, reformers, and other observers found the city's problems overwhelming and the piecemeal, gradual improvements discouragingly slow and pitifully inadequate. There was also a strong tendency to tie all sorts of issues, from family relations and income distribution to disease, crime and alienation, to defects in the built environment and the evil influence of city living generally. It was but a step to the argument that a good city would nurture a good society, a kind of collective version of *mens sana in corpore sano*. In practice this meant the design of ideal towns or portions of towns, an old art that flourished anew in an age given to social analysis and engineering.

This survey leaves the history of nineteenth-century urban planning to one side, only partly for reasons of space. From Fourier's Phalansteries to the linear city of Spain's Arturo Soria y Mata, utopian visions of cities had little real influence on the actual course of city building (Benevolo, 1980). There were however, a few major attempts to build or remodel on a truly large scale, as well as innumerable lesser realisations in urban planning and design. Garden cities have received much notice, though they amounted in practice to little more than pleasingly planned villa suburbs, hardly a solution to the massive problems of large industrial or commercial agglomerations. Barcelona's Example, or extension, came closest to embodying the vision of its designer, Ildefons Cerda, although the individual blocks as built failed to retain the open centre his plan called for. On the other hand, Baron Haussmann's herculean remodelling of Paris shied away from theory. What drove it? Considerations of security and fiscal advantage, for the most part, informed by a rough-and-ready neo-baroque aesthetic partial to grandeur and symmetry. In practice, wide new streets were driven *through* old blocks, which both eliminated slums—displacing their hapless inhabitants, of course—and yielded more rather than less of the valuable street frontage. Other large-scale projects resulted from opportunities such as the demolition of old fortifications. Vienna's Ring is the classic example.

Yet such ambitious undertakings remained the exception, which is why the same ones continually figure in historical surveys. Like its predecessors, the city of the Industrial Age embodied a mosaic of local initiatives and investments. Most of the pieces represented private capital—more often risk-averse than speculative—or utilitarian and conventional public infrastructure.

By the 1950s it was possible to score a satirical hit in French popular music by suggesting 'moonlight in Maubeuge' as a romantic holiday setting, yet Maubeuge and a hundred or more gritty manufacturing cities like it throughout Europe were the homes of more persons than the places that drew tourists and inspired poetic flights of romance

311

and nostalgia. All in all, Europe's industrial urbanisation will be seen as neither a triumph of civilisation nor a wholesale defeat of the human spirit by the forces of anomie and exploitation. But, however we may judge it, the magnitude of the enterprise dwarfs almost every other venture in human history.

References

Bairoch, P. (1988), Cities and Economic Development. Chicago, University of Chicago Press.

Benevolo, L. (1980), History of the City. Cambridge, Mass., MIT Press.

Berg, M. (1986), The Age of Manufactures, 1700–1820. Oxford, Oxford University Press.

Carter, H. (1976), The Study of Urban Geography, 2nd edition. London, Edward Arnold.

Chandler, T., and Fox, G. (1974), 3000 Years of Urban Growth. New York, Academic Press.

Daunton, M., ed. (1990), Housing the Workers, 1850–1914. Leicester, Leicester University Press.

Fishman, R. (1987), Bourgeois Utopias: the Rise and Fall of Suburbia. New York, Basic Books.

Gerschenkron, A. (1962), Economic Backwardness in Historical Perspective. Cambridge, Mass., Harvard University Press.

Gutmann, M. P. (1988), Toward the Modern Economy: Early Industry in Europe, 1500–1800. New York, Knopf.

Hohenberg, P. M., and Lees, L. H. (1985), The Making of Urban Europe, 1000–1950. Cambridge, Mass., Harvard University Press.

Lawton, R., and Lee, R., eds. (1988), Urban Population Development in Western Europe from the late Eighteenth to the early Twentieth Century. Liverpool, Liverpool University Press.

Lees, A. (1985), Cities Perceived: Urban Society in European and American Thought, 1820–1940. Manchester, Manchester University Press.

Livi-Bacci, M. (1992), A Concise History of World Population. Oxford, Blackwell.

Moch, L. P. (1983), Paths to the City. Beverly Hills, Cal., Sage.

Mumford, L. (1961), The City in History. New York, Harcourt Brace.

Sabel, C., and Zeitlin, J. (1985), 'Historical alternatives to mass production: politics, markets and technology in nineteenth-century industrialization', Past and Present, 108.

Sutcliffe, A. (1981), Towards the Planned City: Germany, Britain, the United States and France, 1780–1914. Oxford, Blackwell.

Sutcliffe, A., ed. (1984), Metropolis, 1890–1940. London, Mansell.

Tarr, J. A., and Dupuy, G., eds. (1988), Technology and the Rise of the Networked City in Europe and America. Philadelphia, Pa., Temple University Press.

Vance, J. E. (1990), The Continuing City: Urban Morphology in Western Civilization. Baltimore, Md, Johns Hopkins University Press.

Woude, A. van der, Vries, J. de and Hayami, A., eds. (1990), Urbanization in History. Oxford, Oxford University Press.

Wrigley, E. A. (1987), People, Cities and Wealth. Oxford, Blackwell.

Index

313